The Lees of Virginia

On 7 December 1865, Eugene Alonzo Poole, age twenty-eight and a Baltimore artist, arrived in Lexington, Virginia. He remained for a fortnight, painting a portrait and sculpting a bust of General Robert E. Lee. Poole's family was probably known to Lee, since he was well acquainted with the Baltimore community. The association apparently was close enough to coax the General from his well-known aversion to sitting for artists and photographers. At any rate, Lee was co-operative and, after young Poole had finished his task, the modest General permitted himself a word of cautious praise for the portrait by allowing as how the artist himself was pleased with it. The bust of General Lee has disappeared, but Eugene Poole and his family were so gratified to have one of the rare paintings done from life of Robert E. Lee that the canvas has remained with the artist's relatives to this day. By permitting its publication here, the owners allow the portrait to make its first public appearance. *Courtesy of Mr. and Mrs. Richard Poole Hankins.*

The Lees of Virginia

Seven Generations of an American Family

PAUL C. NAGEL

OXFORD
UNIVERSITY PRESS

OXFORD
UNIVERSITY PRESS

Oxford University Press, Inc., publishes works that
further Oxford University's objective of excellence
in research, scholarship, and education.

Oxford New York
Auckland Cape Town Dar es Salaam Hong Kong Karachi
Kuala Lumpur Madrid Melbourne Mexico City Nairobi
New Delhi Shanghai Taipei Toronto

With offices in
Argentina Austria Brazil Chile Czech Republic France Greece
Guatemala Hungary Italy Japan Poland Portugal Singapore
South Korea Switzerland Thailand Turkey Ukraine Vietnam

First published by Oxford University Press, Inc., 1990
198 Madison Avenue, New York, NY 10016
www.oup.com

First issued as an Oxford University Press paperback, 1992.
This paperback edition issued, 2007.
ISBN-13: 978-0-19-530560-9
ISBN-10: 0-19-530560-4

The Library of Congress has cataloged the previous edition as follows:

Nagel, Paul C
The Lees of Virginia : seven generations of an
American family / Paul C. Nagel.
p. cm. ISBN 0-19-505385-0
1. Lee family. 2. Lee, Robert E (Robert Edward,
1807–1870—Family. 3. Virginia—Biography.
4. Virginia—Genealogy. I. Title.
CT274.L44N34 1990
973.7'092'2—dc20 [B] 90-7195

ISBN 0-19-507478-5 (pbk.)

9 8 7 6 5 4 3 2 1
Printed in the United States of America
on acid-free paper

For Mary Tyler (Freeman) McLenahan
in grateful memory

Foreword

First, a word of reassurance to the many persons who, obviously in hope, have asked if Robert E. Lee figures in this family biography. Indeed so. The last four chapters are devoted to him, but more as a family member than as a soldier. I believe the authentic Robert E. Lee is found in the roles he cherished— as son, brother, cousin, husband, and father.

Many other fascinating Lees, both men and women, will greet the reader. They are Robert Lee's kinfolk across several generations. Their story during more than two centuries tells of tumultuous times for the Lees, their colony, and finally their nation. The family's public experiences, however, must serve mainly as a backdrop since my emphasis is on what the Lees meant to one another. An understanding of this family relationship, which was so important to them, is essential to reaching a fairer appreciation of the Lees.

Starting in 1640 with the arrival in Virginia of Richard Lee and Anne Constable, this book salutes, among others, such figures as Richard Lee II (known as The Scholar), Richard Henry Lee, Hannah Lee Corbin, Arthur Lee, Alice Lee Shippen, and Light-Horse Harry Lee, before it reaches the life and death of Robert E. Lee. Whether in opposing Nathaniel Bacon and his Rebels in 1676, or in condemning English colonial policy in 1776, or in turning back the Yankees at the Seven Days' battles of 1862, the Lees displayed valor of the highest order. Yet, while their chronicle has impressive political, economic, intellectual, and military attainment, it also contains more than its share of disappointments.

What is often overlooked across these exciting generations is that the Lees remained a force in Virginia and American history usually by being a well-knit family power bloc. In public affairs it was frequently their practice to maneuver as teams of parents and children, and especially as brothers, sisters, and cousins. The most notable example, of course, is the collaboration between the five Lee brothers, Arthur, Francis Lightfoot, Richard Henry, Thomas Ludwell, and William, during the American Revolution—when they had valuable assistance from such cousins as Richard "Squire" Lee.

Even when the Lees fell from grace, as in the unfortunate partnership of Light-Horse Harry and his brother Richard Bland Lee, they seemed usually to blunder ahead arm in arm. This comradeship, in fair weather and foul, doubles the importance of understanding how the Lees were bound as a family. Their rapport may explain why we have so few satisfactory biographies of the individual family members. The exceptions are Light-Horse Harry and Robert E. Lee; and in General Lee's case, many books about him are so enmeshed in military detail as to obscure the genuine R. E. Lee. I believe that his personality and career, like those of most of his kinsmen, can best be understood by seeing him at home—which is where this book takes the Lees.

Now, some advice to the readers. In stating all dates, I have used the modern English calendar which was established in 1752 when each year was made to begin with 1 January. Before 1752, England and America employed the so-called Old Style calendar wherein a year started on 25 March. As a result, for instance, Richard Henry Lee's Old Style birthday is 20 January 1732, even though a few weeks later the calendar showed 1733.

For today's readers, serious confusion comes from using the Old Style. Take the dates for the deaths of Hannah Ludwell Lee and her husband Thomas Lee, the builders of Stratford and the parents of the famous Revolutionary brothers. By the Old Style calendar, Hannah died on 25 January 1749 and Thomas on 14 November 1750. This left later generations of the family believing almost two years elapsed between the deaths of their forebears. Thomas actually survived Hannah by fewer than ten months.

For clarity's sake, therefore, I have Hannah Lee die in 1750 and Richard Henry Lee born in 1733. In like fashion, I silently apply the new year to all other dates before 1752 that fall between 1 January and 24 March. My doing so each time without calling attention to it should allow the story to be read comfortably within our present understanding of calendar years.

Another characteristic peculiar to these pages is my frequent use of first names in referring to Lee personalities. To call everyone by the surname which so many bore would be confusing and impractical. So I have relied on the given names or even nicknames by which the family knew each other. For example, Francis Lightfoot Lee was called Frank and Robert E. Lee was simply Robert. The effect should help the reader share the family's mood.

Letters and other papers written by the Lees constitute the source of what I have written. Since the family manuscripts are often scant, particularly in the seventeenth and the early eighteenth century, it means a number of the personalities must be sketched in vague outline. Someday, new caches of letters and journals may be uncovered, allowing the Lee family story to be told in greater detail and confidence. While I hope future biographers can bring the reader more evocative interpretations of the family than mine, I doubt that any will enjoy knowing this interesting family more than I have.

Finally, let me assure all readers that not even life-long Virginians can keep untangled the genealogical lines by which the Lees descended. Family members exhibited a fondness for marrying cousins. As a guide through the seven generations of Lees who are prominent in this book, the genealogical table shows their relationships. I hope no one will be abashed at having to refer even frequently to the chart. I'd be lost without it. And with it, getting to know the Lees becomes easy.

Richmond, Virginia   P.C.N
September 1989

Contents

Illustrations

Genealogical chart

Frontispiece Robert E. Lee in December 1865. This portrait by Eugene A. Poole was from life. Until now it has not been seen by the public.

Map Tidewater Virginia, showing places important in the Lee story

A word of caution is usually advisable when invoking the subjects and artists of Virginia portraits painted before 1750. After Independence, most families of the Old Dominion found themselves relying upon tradition to identify cherished likenesses handed down by earlier generations. This was because canvases tended not to have been signed or otherwise marked at the time they were painted in the seventeenth and much of the eighteenth century. The fact that many of these portraits often passed through the hands of various branches of a family, or even left a family's possession, has enlarged the uncertainty and confusion.

All of this is true of portraits from the first three generations of Lees. Since little of a scholarly nature can be established about these likenesses, and since this book re-creates the Lee family's outlook, it seems fitting that the illustrations of early Lees which appear hereafter should be ascribed according to family tradition. Where new insight seemed helpful, I relied upon the authoritative advice of Graham Hood, former vice president and Carlisle H. Humelsine Curator of the Colonial Williamsburg Foundation, to whom I am thus much indebted.

Following page 178
    Richard Lee the Founder around 1662

Commemorating the Bicentennial of General Robert E. Lee's Birth

There has been a welcome development in history publications during the twenty years since I began to write about General Lee and his ancestors. The result is an impressive array of family biographies from both sides of the Atlantic, bringing this book about the Lees of Virginia into a distinguished company. Whatever the reasons for such a publishing phenomenon, I believe these biographies could be particularly helpful in today's public discourse wherein the institution of the family has become central.

I'm writing this preface in the autumn of 2005 as a campaign gains momentum to make the refrain "family values" a rallying cry to oppose a rising moral relativism in American social, political, and religious thinking. "Family values" has thus become a call to arms for many who seek to reestablish American life and outlook upon their favorite beliefs, values that range from the sexual to the theological. In doing so, these campaigners—at least in my judgment—seriously misunderstand or misrepresent how families have generally developed across the generations.

While the family unit has served through centuries as a crucible from which the rules for human association have emerged, many conservatives appear not to realize that the resulting values have often been subject to change and are therefore a shaky platform for anyone seeking principles that are immutable. Consequently, it would be well, I believe, if those persons who use "family values" as ammunition against the supposed evils of our twenty-first-century culture would read about the fate of ideals as depicted in some of the recently published family biographies.

One of the most valuable of these is Barbara Caine's *Bombay to Bloomsbury: A Biography of the Strachey Family* (Oxford University Press, 2005). This family included the eminent literary figure and founder of modern biography, Lytton Strachey. In the late nineteenth and early twentieth centuries, he, along with other Stracheys, enjoyed participating in heated debate over the nature of social principles and values. The result was much altering of Strachey family belief and practice, a change that soon was taken up in English society outside the Strachey circle.

When I set out to write the story of the Lee family, I did not then realize how unusually instructive in the matter of family values it was. The best lesson begins in Chapter 2, which recounts the fate of a stern family value held tenaciously by Richard Lee II (1647–1715), leader of the second American generation. Known to Virginia history as "the scholar," this Richard, one of many Lees thus christened, had returned to England to spend his life in theology when deaths among his Virginia relatives obliged him to reappear in the colony as head of the family and to assume a commanding place in public affairs. He brought with him a belief popular in England at the time and even in parts of her colonies. It held that kings and governors were anointed by God, which therefore made established government a Divine instrument never to be challenged.

This value, cherished by Richard Lee II and so many others in Stuart England, nearly cost him his life. During the rebellion in Virginia incited by Nathaniel Bacon in 1676, Lee stood courageously for the power of king and governor. He never swerved from his faith in this principle as he endured two months of cruel treatment as a prisoner of the rebels. Nor did he ever flinch from continuing to believe that the colony should invariably bow to London, no matter that the passing years brought harsh treatment from the mother country.

Fortunately for this gentle and believing scholar, Richard Lee II did not live to see how his cherished doctrine of the divinity of established government was repudiated a century later by his beloved Virginia when it joined the colonial rebellion against England. That action would have caused him enough sorrow, but it would have been even more grievous had he beheld how three of his grandsons were among the leaders in this revolution that broke open in 1776. Richard probably would have condemned it as a revolt against God's appointed government, as did numerous of his grandsons' contemporaries. These rebellious grandsons were Richard Henry Lee (1733–94), William Lee (1739–95), and Arthur Lee (1740–92).

Of the three, Richard Henry was the most influential and prominent— William and Arthur served mainly in Europe, where they sought support for the Revolutionary cause. The trio had volatile temperaments that tended to handicap them as they campaigned for republican government in the colonies. Richard Henry was so stout a foe of monarchical authority that some considered him nearly as extreme in this cause as was Thomas Paine, author of the influential pamphlet *Common Sense*. Indeed, Richard Henry sounded so harshly critical against arbitrary rule when he arose to speak during the debates held by the Continental Congress in Philadelphia during 1775–76 that it led to his being denied a role he deserved, one that would have given him immortality. This was to serve as the author of the Declaration of Independence. His bluntness and impatience with the more cautious members of Congress led to fears that his pen would produce a document so fierce against English governance that it would do more harm than good. Also, Richard Henry's impolitic manner was eroding his political support back in Virginia, obliging him to hasten back to Williamsburg to mend fences. His absence made it easier for Congress to assign a more intellectually agile and diplomatic Virginian, Thomas Jefferson, the task of drafting a declaration for independence based on values that would have appalled Richard Lee II and his family only a hundred years earlier.

(Since this book first appeared, a new biography of Richard Henry Lee has been published: J. Kent McGaughy, *Richard Henry Lee of Virginia* [Lanham, MD, 2004].)

Richard Henry and his two brothers were by no means alone among Richard II's progeny to repudiate what had been one of their family's cherished values. Among other descendants was one who seemed to topple every principle in sight. This was Henry Lee III (1756–1818), known both in his day and to history as "Light-Horse Harry." His misbehavior as a Revolutionary War officer, governor of Virginia, and congressman led him into the bad grace of George Washington and then a time in jail before he fled into exile abroad. During the era of Richard Lee II and his son Thomas Lee (1690–1750), sometime governor of the colony of Virginia and great-uncle of "Light-Horse Harry," the family was renowned for observing honor in all dealings, public and private. Harry, on the other hand, spent a lifetime turning these family values upside down, all the while never acknowledging that he was in error.

Today, it seems clear who had the right on their side in the clashes during colonial days over values between generations of the Lee family. After the American Revolution, however, it becomes more difficult to choose sides in what proved to be a deepening conflict amongst Lee family values. By then, the story had reached the era of Richard II's most famous descendant, his great-great-grandson Robert E. Lee (1807–70). It would prove to be one of the instructive ironies of Lee family history—and America's, for that matter—that "Light-Horse Harry," the notable scoundrel in the family's story, should be the father of General Robert E. Lee, today the most revered member of the family—a son, I should hasten to point out, who had almost no contact personally with his father.

Robert E. Lee's greatness, of course, evolved from his career in the American Civil War. The nature of that struggle brought mayhem to Lee family values, just as it fractured the American Union. The Lees were affected to such an extent that one son, General Robert E. Lee, led the army of the rebellious Confederate States of America while a kinsman, Admiral Samuel Phillips Lee, commanded much of the naval forces of the United States of America. Admiral Lee was the grandson of Richard Henry Lee.

It remains one of the most intriguing events of the Civil War when, just before hostilities began in earnest, President Lincoln and his military advisors decided that command of the federal forces should be given to Robert E. Lee. Had he accepted the post, the course of the war would surely have been very different. For Lee, a Virginian who loved the Union and who deplored the presence of slavery, the decision which the federal government demanded of him was agonizing. Pulled toward the Union by one set of values, he was tugged in the opposite direction by loyalty to "his country," Virginia, and the impulse to defend her. It was a close call between one set of family values and another. Lee's selection of rebellion—which meant he agreed that the sovereignty of the states were supreme in the federal Union— had a devastating effect on the history of America.

This struggle over principle within the family distressed both the South's General Lee and the North's Admiral Lee, as well as other kinsmen. On the strictly personal side, however, the differing allegiances brought one conflict that especially grieved R. E. Lee. It was when a favorite nephew, Louis Marshall, chose to enter the United States Army. General Lee was very fond of his sister, Anne Kinloch Lee (1800–64), who had married William L. Marshall of Baltimore, a kinsman of Chief Justice John Marshall. It was their son Louis who eventually was decorated for bravery in battles against the very army that his Uncle Robert commanded. Ultimately, the breach caused by differing beliefs parted these branches of the family forever. The Marshalls removed to California from where they ignored their Southern relatives. Each side of the family had found moral absolutes from which they would not waver.

Public opinion today generally reveres the name of General Robert E. Lee. For instance, it is in celebration of his birth in 1807 that a bicentennial version of this book is being published by a distinguished press based in England and New York City. But 140 years ago, numerous Americans north of the Mason-Dixon line, if polled, would doubtless have urged that Lee, the leader of the rebellious army which had slain many Yankee sons, should be hanged as a traitor. On the Confederacy's side, however, the prevailing sentiment felt mostly disgust that an admiral from the family of Lee should have led the Federal navy. For the South, it meant that one who bore the name of Lee had rejected a cherished Southern political principle that placed the Union's member states superior to a central authority in Washington.

And here, indeed, was the challenge to the Lee family's values, and to those of many other families, North and South. In the days of such Founders of the nation as Richard Henry Lee, the grandfather of Admiral Samuel Lee, the new Federal Union was deemed an experiment among participating states. But by the time the generation of Robert and Samuel Lee came to maturity, the once-experimental Union was acclaimed by many, including Abraham Lincoln, to have become an Absolute, a permanent and unbreakable moral value. The tumultuous career of the Federal Union in our national ideology during the nineteenth century should be a painful reminder that putting a belief under the shelter of "family values" does not assure that it will remain unchanged or unchallenged.

Returning for a moment to Robert E. Lee, in one respect he shared a value with his ancestor, Richard Lee II. Both men were deeply religious. The similarity stopped there, however, for General Lee would never have seen God's Almighty Hand working out of the office of the President of the Confederate States of America. Ultimately, Lee openly disobeyed Jefferson Davis when, after the surrender of Confederate forces at Appomattox Courthouse, Lee ordered his troops to put down their arms and return to their homes. Davis had insisted that the soldiers take to the hills and valleys, where he directed that they become a guerrilla force and continue the struggle for Southern independence. Instead, General Lee's religious faith was of such a personal nature that he preferred to accept the South's defeat as God's punishment upon his own sinful self. The same moral certitude entered the explanation Robert E. Lee gave his wife for why the war had brought the loss of their beloved home, Arlington, which had come down to them from George Washington. The reason offered by Robert was that the family had sinned by not cherishing this blessing enough—so that God was obliged to punish them for their offence.

(A fine biography of General Lee was published after my book about his family appeared: Emory M. Thomas, *Robert E. Lee, A Biography* [New York, 1995].)

There are, of course, many other fascinating shadows and lights that the reader will glimpse in this biographical portrait of the Lee family—as there would be in treatments of other families. I'll take a moment to mention only one more—how the Lees measured the status of women. Here we return to a scene which was much more subdued than the political realm of the family. In his generation, General Lee deemed the female to be such a frail creature (it seems likely that his attitude was due mostly to the childlike character of Mrs. Lee) that he was loath to see any of his daughters leave the family circle. He bound the girls to himself so closely that none of them—and there were four—ever married.

What a contrast this was with the experience of Robert's first cousin twice removed, Hannah Lee Corbin (1729–82), whose colorful career is recounted in Chapter 4. Hannah was the daughter of Thomas Lee, sometime royal governor of Virginia, and his wife, Hannah Ludwell, both strong personalities who deliberately trained their daughter to stand on her own. The young woman did not fail them. In fact, she may have startled her parents by traits that their neighbors generally called Hannah's independence of spirit and force of character. A more vivid contrast with General Lee's suppressed daughters is difficult to imagine.

It was not that Hannah's career was so startlingly different from that of most women in eighteenth-century Virginia. What is significant is that the closely knit Tidewater society retained at least a grudging respect and tolerance for the defiant behavior of Hannah. Even in her youth she was an ardent reader of English literature, becoming one of the colony's most impatient patrons of London booksellers. These merchants did not mind her spirit, but they deplored her tardiness in paying their charges. They could not have known of her financial problems after she became a young widow. Hannah found her husband's will had decreed that she would lose her inheritance if she remarried. She saved her ownership of a landed estate—one that was impressive in size but of little profitable yield—by defying the established church and society and entering what proved a life-long liaison outside of marriage. This was with a physician by whom she bore two children.

Although a religious enthusiast, Hannah seemed more than willing to live in the sinful state denounced by the Church of England. This was because she found blessed assurance through having her errant union sanctified by the Baptist faith, deemed by Virginia to be a denomination of heretics. Yet, despite her extraordinary values and behavior, Hannah retained the affection of her family—although her brothers Richard Henry, William, and Arthur Lee admitted they had misgivings about their sister's behavior, despite their love for her. The same must also be said of her neighbors in the counties where she lived and where she oversaw her extensive plantation properties.

While I have here offered these glimpses of Robert E. Lee and his ancestors to illustrate how values and principles tend to change from generation to generation, I hasten to assure readers that they will find much more of interest in this great family's story than simply this lesson for our day. In doing the research for this book I read letters and journals that brought me sometimes to laughter and occasionally near to tears. The history of the Lees is a succession of triumphs and failures, happiness and sorrow, all often nothing short of poignant. I predict that every reader will find both enjoyment and benefit from this account of the endlessly colorful and intriguing Lee family.

* * *

In closing, I wish especially to thank Sheldon Meyer of New York City, who, before his retirement, was for many years senior editor at Oxford University Press. During that time he was much more to me than editor of the five books I had the privilege of publishing with Oxford. As my friend and counselor for more than thirty years, Sheldon came to know well my weaknesses and strengths as an author and historian. Consequently, it was he who persuaded me to make family biography my main interest. As I look back across the books I have published, I draw the greatest satisfaction from the five biographies of families that are part of that group. I believe they represent the best of my writing. If I am correct in this appraisal, then much of the credit is due to Sheldon Meyer.

Sheldon must share that credit, however, with my wife, Joan Peterson Nagel. During our six decades together, she has been critic, genealogist, and comforter while we worked as one to finish a dozen books. They are her achievement as well as mine. Now we hope for a quiet time together that will allow us to read while leaving the writing to others.

P.C.N.

The Lees of Virginia: A Selective Genealogy

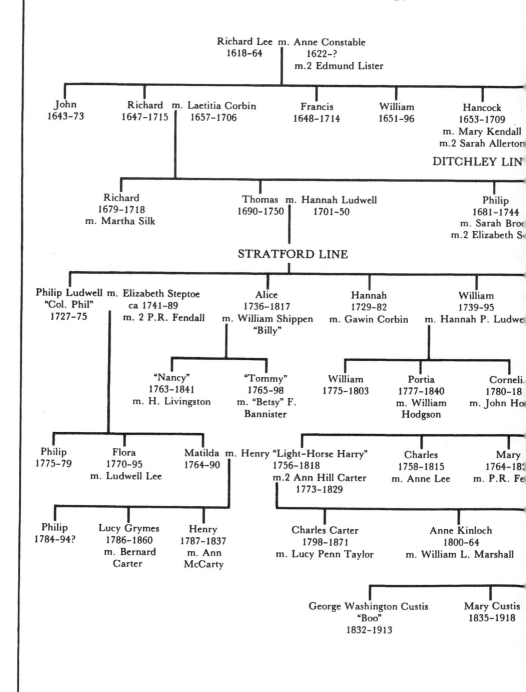

Richard Lee m. Anne Constable
1618–64   1622–?
m.2 Edmund Lister

John   Richard m. Laetitia Corbin   Francis   William   Hancock
1643–73   1647–1715   1657–1706   1648–1714   1651–96   1653–1709
m. Mary Kendall
m.2 Sarah Allerton

DITCHLEY LIN

Richard   Thomas m. Hannah Ludwell   Philip
1679–1718   1690–1750   1701–50   1681–1744
m. Martha Silk   m. Sarah Broc
m.2 Elizabeth S

STRATFORD LINE

Philip Ludwell m. Elizabeth Steptoe   Alice   Hannah   William
"Col. Phil"   ca 1741–89   1736–1817   1729–82   1739–95
1727–75   m. 2 P.R. Fendall   m. William Shippen   m. Gawin Corbin   m. Hannah P. Ludwe
"Billy"

"Nancy"   "Tommy"   William   Portia   Corneli
1763–1841   1765–98   1775–1803   1777–1840   1780–18
m. H. Livingston   m. "Betsy" F.   m. William   m. John Ho
Bannister   Hodgson

Philip   Flora   Matilda m. Henry "Light-Horse Harry"   Charles   Mary
1775–79   1770–95   1764–90   1756–1818   1758–1815   1764–18
m. Ludwell Lee   m.2 Ann Hill Carter   m. Anne Lee   m. P.R. Fe
1773–1829

Philip   Lucy Grymes   Henry   Charles Carter   Anne Kinloch
1784–94?   1786–1860   1787–1837   1798–1871   1800–64
m. Bernard   m. Ann   m. Lucy Penn Taylor   m. William L. Marshall
Carter   McCarty

George Washington Custis   Mary Custis
"Boo"   1835–1918
1832–1913

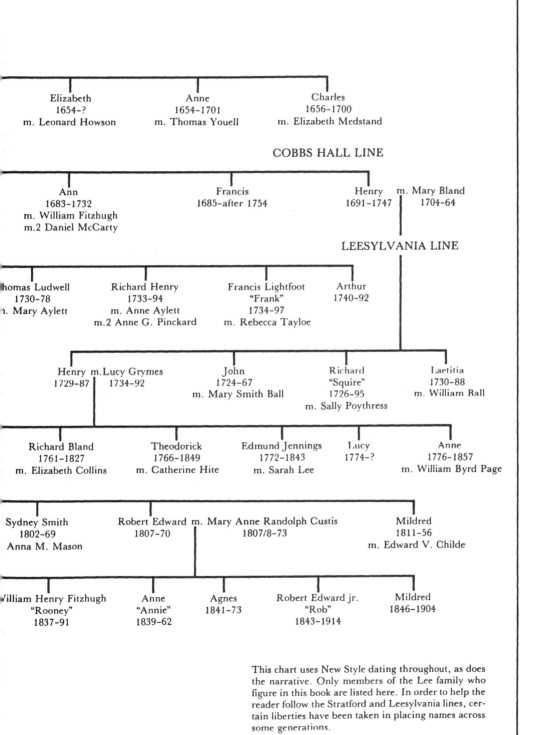

Elizabeth
1654-?
m. Leonard Howson

Anne
1654-1701
m. Thomas Youell

Charles
1656-1700
m. Elizabeth Medstand

COBBS HALL LINE

Ann
1683-1732
m. William Fitzhugh
m.2 Daniel McCarty

Francis
1685-after 1754

Henry m. Mary Bland
1691-1747   1704-64

LEESYLVANIA LINE

Thomas Ludwell
1730-78
m. Mary Aylett

Richard Henry
1733-94
m. Anne Aylett
m.2 Anne G. Pinckard

Francis Lightfoot
"Frank"
1734-97
m. Rebecca Tayloe

Arthur
1740-92

Henry m. Lucy Grymes
1729-87   1734-92

John
1724-67
m. Mary Smith Ball

Richard
"Squire"
1726-95
m. Sally Poythress

Laetitia
1730-88
m. William Ball

Richard Bland
1761-1827
m. Elizabeth Collins

Theodorick
1766-1849
m. Catherine Hite

Edmund Jennings
1772-1843
m. Sarah Lee

Lucy
1774-?

Anne
1776-1857
m. William Byrd Page

Sydney Smith
1802-69
Anna M. Mason

Robert Edward m. Mary Anne Randolph Custis
1807-70   1807/8-73

Mildred
1811-56
m. Edward V. Childe

William Henry Fitzhugh
"Rooney"
1837-91

Anne
"Annie"
1839-62

Agnes
1841-73

Robert Edward jr.
"Rob"
1843-1914

Mildred
1846-1904

This chart uses New Style dating throughout, as does
the narrative. Only members of the Lee family who
figure in this book are listed here. In order to help the
reader follow the Stratford and Leesylvania lines, certain liberties have been taken in placing names across
some generations.

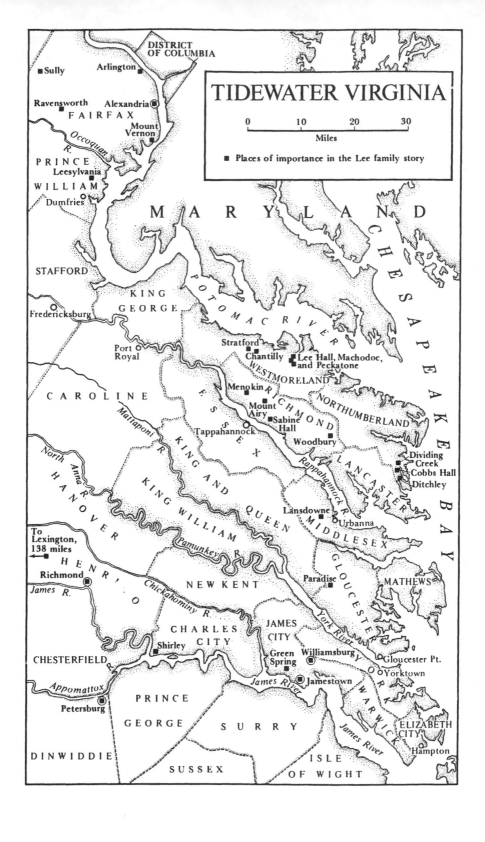

TIDEWATER VIRGINIA

| 0 | 10 | 20 | 30 |

Miles

■ Places of importance in the Lee family story

At Mrs. Shippen's

Late in August 1774, strangers began rolling into Philadelphia. They arrived from all along the Atlantic coast for an extraordinary meeting. History knows it as the Continental Congress, called because citizens of the American colonies objected to their treatment by England. While most of these newcomers had to learn their way around the city, one of them knew exactly where to go.

Richard Henry Lee of Virginia went directly to the residence of his sister, Alice Lee Shippen. Her husband, Dr. William Shippen, was one of Pennsylvania's leading physicians and medical educators. He and Alice relished the arrival of her brother. Since Richard Henry had been important in summoning the Congress, there was sure to be good talk where he stayed.

Alice was not disappointed. The gathering at her house included the first conversations between representatives of what became the two most famous families in American history, the Lees of Virginia and the Adamses of Massachusetts. But none of this was apparent when the Congress assembled. Only the Lee family had earned a measure of prominence, beginning in 1640 when their founder arrived to become a leader in Virginia. Meanwhile, since 1633 the Adamses had toiled unobtrusively as small farmers in Massachusetts.

It took the quarrel with England to summon an Adams from obscurity. This was John Adams, who arrived ahead of Richard Henry Lee. On Monday, 29 August 1774, the thirty-eight-year-old farmer and lawyer from the small town of Braintree appeared in Philadelphia. He was much dazzled by what he saw, noting with astonishment how the streets "are all equally wide, straight, and parallel to each other." The following

Friday, Virginia's delegates came to town, and a delighted Alice Lee Shippen made her brother Richard Henry comfortable.

The next morning, Saturday, 3 September, John Adams found himself invited to breakfast at Mrs. Shippen's. He was charmed by her, as well he might be, for his hostess was no ordinary resident of Philadelphia. A year younger than Adams, Alice Shippen had been educated with her brothers at Stratford, a plantation on the Potomac River. She then lived for a time in London, where she caught the eye of Billy Shippen, whom his prominent Pennsylvania family had sent abroad to finish medical studies. Their romance ended Alice's intention to spend the rest of her life in England.

After her marriage, Alice returned to America and became mistress of one of Philadelphia's finest houses, where the admiring John Adams discovered her to be "a religious and reasoning Lady." Alice knew how to make a friend of Adams. She assured him that the people of Boston "could not have behaved through their trials with so much prudence and firmness" without the influence of "a Superior Power." Even after John had met the men in Alice's family, he carefully included her when he praised the Lees: "They are all sensible, and deep thinkers."

When Alice's brother Richard Henry joined them for breakfast, John immediately found himself favorably impressed with another member of the Lee clan. "He is a masterly man," John informed his diary. Forty-two years old, R. H. Lee was "a tall, spare man" over six feet in height, with reddish hair. His commanding presence carried a touch of drama, for he covered a maimed left hand with black silk to conceal damage left when a gun exploded in a hunting accident. After he had completed his education in England he entered Virginia politics at age twenty-six. In the House of Burgesses and elsewhere R. H. Lee had been one of the earliest to talk against English misrule, even though his family had thrived for more than a century under the empire. Lee's graceful manner of speaking, both in public and private, was enhanced by an air of assurance, which some who watched mistook as arrogance.

The style did not seem to trouble John Adams. He had arrived at Alice Shippen's house wondering whether he had the courage and wisdom to serve in the Congress. Upon finding that Richard Henry's stouthearted views were much like his own, John grew more confident—and even more admiring of his new friend. They quickly agreed that colonial opposition to English policy had been "feeble and incompetent." It was time, said Richard Henry, "to make vigorous exertions." Adams soon called Lee "the most spirited and consistent of any [delegate]."

After breakfast was finished and Richard Henry's eloquence had subsided, he and John departed, unaware that they had formed a partnership which would be instrumental in bringing about America's independence. Not that the two men were personally much alike. Adams went off to eat "dryed smoaked sprats" and read letters and papers from home. Lee spent the afternoon drinking burgundy with John Dickinson, the Pennsylvania farmer whose influential writings he much admired.

When John and Richard Henry were reunited that evening at dinner, the Virginian was "very high," a condition which a compassionate Adams noted did not keep his new friend from continued imbibing until nearly midnight. Then it was Sunday morning and the duty-bound Adams managed to attend the Presbyterian service, where he observed the congregation was small and not very "polite." It seems unlikely that Alice Shippen got her brother up for church, for he needed time to recover from celebrating his arrival in town. He could not even appear on Monday morning, 5 September, when the Continental Congress assembled in Carpenters' Hall.

But if he lost any momentum, Lee soon caught up. John Adams' diary often referred to the contributions Richard Henry made to the debate. Adams was particularly struck by the Virginian's stern assertion that liberty, so essential to life, could not be given up "when we enter into society." A few weeks later, John served as a member of Richard Henry's committee to prepare an address to the King. It was a glimpse of events to come when Lee's draft, designed for royal eyes, was rejected by the Congress as immoderate and disrespectful.

Soon more cautious delegates became alarmed by the Lee-Adams alliance, obliging the pair to assure careful colleagues such as George Washington that they were not aiming for separation from England. Yet, when the Continental Congress reconvened a year later, in November 1775, worsening relations with England led Richard Henry and John to consider what form of government each colony should establish when it broke from the empire. Presently the Philadelphia collaboration between Lee and Adams had its finest moment. On 7 June 1776, Richard Henry Lee arose in Congress to offer the motion for American independence. Immediately it was seconded by John Adams, who then made a powerful address.

Almost at once, affairs began turning sour for the Lee family. Fearing Richard Henry's sharp temper and belligerent pen, the Congress excluded him from the committee created to prepare an announcement of the separation from England. It was a quieter Virginian, Thomas Jefferson, who earned fame for penning the Declaration of Independence. His motion forgotten, Richard Henry went back to Virginia in disgust. There would be more disappointments and difficulties for the Lees—in Virginia, in Philadelphia, and abroad. Besides R.H. these would embroil his famed brothers and cousins—Thomas Ludwell Lee, Francis Light-foot Lee, William Lee, Arthur Lee, Light-Horse Harry Lee, and Richard Bland Lee.

Forty years later, long after R.H.'s death, a family member sought to coax John Adams into agreeing that Richard Henry was actually the author of the Declaration. While the aged Adams could not give such credit to the Virginian, he spoke of his sympathy for the Lees, asserting that the family had produced more persons "of merit" during the Revolution than any other family. Even so, Adams conceded that temperament and events had led the Lees into much private anguish. That family's reward, predicted Adams, "cannot be in this world."

Alice Shippen had recognized the Lees' plight much earlier. At the end of the Revolution, she told Abigail Adams: "I have learnt to mourn for injured worth and merit" as she saw how her brothers had "sacrificed every other prospect for the sole one of serving their country, and how are they rewarded!" As a proud Lee, Alice added: "the wounds we receive are deeper because they wound our country."

Her family's future was more dismal than even Alice anticipated. Affairs worsened after 1790, so that by 1833, well after Alice died, one Lee had consoled another with the prediction: "However prostrate and o'er clouded may be the fortunes of our house, it may yet boast an aristocracy of talent and patriotism, which poverty or slander can never tarnish or take away." The hope was soon fulfilled to an astounding degree when Robert E. Lee mustered such magnitude of character that the name of Lee joined those of Washington and Lincoln in the world's regard.

The joys and sorrows, triumphs and tragedies, experienced by seven generations of these Lees from Virginia are depicted in the chapters ahead. Arrogant, imprudent, and impetuous they frequently were, yet they cherished the American republic and foresaw its perils sooner than most citizens. Surely a courageous group, this family deserves a larger measure of their nation's understanding and appreciation.

∿ 1

The Founders
1640–1670

The story of Richard Lee, the family's founder in Virginia, glows with success. His achievement was the sort many residents of seventeenth-century England yearned to duplicate. They peered across the Atlantic, drawn by hopes for wealth and eminence said to be found along the James River. Of course, there were other colonists whose careers are too easily ignored. For some, Virginia was a last hope, an outlet for desperation, while many had not even a choice in the matter. They often arrived in chains with no future except to toil for their betters. But of those who came freely, carrying ambition, talent, and industry, few who survived the New World's rigors had the good luck that transformed Richard Lee from a Britisher of modest beginnings into a Virginian of highest standing.

Not until recently has the extent of Richard's triumph been uncovered. Lee family tradition had long insisted that Richard could claim an illustrious background. But the story arose from myth rather than genealogy, since the emigrant himself left no information about who his parents were. Furthermore, generations of Lees did not know even the name of Richard's spouse, Anne Constable, let alone anything about her.

According to a legend Richard helped to foster, he was from Shropshire, a county bordering Wales and located about one hundred miles northwest of London. In the seventeenth century the area had several Lee families, two of whom used the arms of Reyner de Lega or de Le', a Norman prominent around 1200. From these lines Richard was alleged to have descended and his birthplace to have been Coton Hall in the manor of Nordley Regis, although those who wove the story could never offer a convincing date for Richard's birth.

Family tradition goes on to tell of a Gilbert Lee, said to be Richard's uncle, who left Shropshire for London, where he prospered as a sea captain and then as a merchant. This Gilbert Lee died childless sometime after 1621, leaving his considerable estate to a nephew, John Lee, who carried on the business. John is supposed to have brought his cousin Richard down from Shropshire to learn the ways of London. With this experience, Richard presumably sailed for Virginia.

While it may have gratified early Lees thus to believe that the family founder grew up in genteel surroundings on a manor in Shropshire, there is no evidence to authenticate this tradition. Instead, the recent identification of Richard's parents shows that he was from Worcestershire. His father was John Lee (sometimes spelled Lies or Lyes), a clothier whose business was in Worcester, along the road running through the West Midlands. Coton Hall was located twenty miles northward. Richard Lee's mother was Jane Hancock from Twining, a town twelve miles south of Worcester. Her family was also in the cloth trade. The couple probably was married before 1616.

For centuries these facts slumbered in English probate and parish records until an American genealogist, William Thorndale, recognized where the dusty trail might lead. In December 1988 the *National Genealogical Society Quarterly* published the results of his sleuthing. Although Thorndale found no connection between Richard's father, John Lee, and the Lee gentry from Nordley Regis and Coton Hall in Shropshire, he says that such a link may someday be discovered. Certainly Lees across the generations have believed in this line of descent.

John Lee and Jane Hancock's first child, born in September 1616, was called John. The second son and future emigrant to Virginia, Richard, was probably named after an uncle and christened on 22 March 1618. One other offspring, Thomas, survived to maturity. John Lee, the father, died in February 1630, and his widow Jane soon remarried. Her second husband survived only a few months. Jane Hancock Lee died in 1639, leaving a will which favored sons John and Thomas to the apparent disadvantage of Richard.

Little is known of Richard Lee and his brothers before 1639, except that John, the eldest, was apprenticed in 1633 to a Hancock kinsman who had moved to London and become a wine merchant. Richard's whereabouts and intentions are a mystery until, soon after his mother's death, he set sail for Virginia, having recently passed his twenty-first birthday. The date of Richard's arrival in Jamestown is unclear, but it was probably late in 1639 or early 1640. What happened thereafter must be construed from fragmentary records.

These reveal a Richard Lee whose ability and good fortune made him one of the wealthiest and most influential citizens of Virginia by the time he died at age forty-six. His promising nature evidently worked to his advantage even before he appeared in Jamestown. Circumstantial evidence implies that Richard's Hancock relatives may have brought him to the attention of Sir Francis Wyatt, whom King Charles I had appointed governor of Virginia in 1639.

The young Lee is said to have come along when Governor Wyatt sailed for Virginia. Wyatt was not new to the colony, having served as the first royal governor nearly twenty years earlier. Thanks to his tie with Sir Francis, Richard Lee began life in the colony as clerk of the quarter court, within the secretary of state's office. That we know he held this post is our only proof Richard was in Virginia during 1640. His presence can be found nowhere but in the colony's records.*

After his start as a protégé of the governor, Richard Lee moved from one triumph to another, taking care that his early land patents designated him as "gentleman." At the end of his life, he held high office and owned about 15,000 productive acres in Virginia and Maryland. He also had many slaves and much livestock. Shortly before his death, Richard also purchased an impressive English estate in an area near London called Stratford-Langton.

Of incalculable importance to his progress was Richard's fortunate marriage. When the young man accompanied Governor Wyatt to Jamestown, the official household also included a young woman, Anne Constable, whose identity later became lost to the family record. Even her name was unknown for two hundred years. Now, thanks particularly to the work of David Halle, genealogist for the Society of the Lees of Virginia, we know that Anne was baptized in London during 1622 and that she was one of many daughters born to Francis Constable.

Perhaps because of her father's connections, Anne became a ward of Sir John Thorowgood, a personal attendant upon King Charles I. This affiliation would have made it easy for her to know the family of Sir Francis Wyatt and to accompany them to North America. Anne's background and early associations meant that Richard Lee moved socially upward when she took him as husband.

There is a legend which speaks of Richard and Anne being wed in the new brick church at Jamestown during 1641 or 1642, with Governor Wyatt giving the bride away. Anne's decision to marry may have owed something to King Charles' impatience with Governor Wyatt for being

*One such document, however, has misled some historians into insisting Richard came to Jamestown as early as 1637. They claim Lee's official signature was affixed to a land patent of 22 May 1638. To the contrary, study of the manuscript shows Richard wrote only a clerical postscript, dated 25 May 1640, saying that the patent of 1638 had been surrendered and reassigned.

unable to reduce long-standing political bickering in Virginia. In 1641 the Crown summoned Sir Francis home, appointing in his stead Sir William Berkeley, who arrived at Jamestown during February 1642. Instead of returning to England with the Wyatt entourage, Miss Constable evidently preferred life in the colony as young Richard Lee's wife.

She gambled that the new governor would not penalize the groom for being an official in the Wyatt administration. It proved a sound bet. During much of his long career in Virginia, Governor Berkeley was an astute and amiable politician. He was careful not to deal harshly with Wyatt's supporters, so that Richard continued as clerk of the quarter court while he settled into married life.

Mrs. Richard Lee possessed what must have been a magnificent physique. She bore at least ten children, including two sets of twins. She survived great Indian dangers with her husband and accepted several uprootings and moves to new residences. These included a return to England, where Anne set up a new home in which she handled family affairs when Richard sailed back to Virginia on business. He died there in 1664. Obedient to her spouse's will, Anne returned to the colony, remarried, and finished raising the family her late husband had left.

All of that was twenty years after the new governor, William Berkeley, had opened a broad future for Anne's husband by naming him attorney general of the colony in October 1643. Thereafter, a close affiliation with Sir William helps explain Richard Lee's astonishing progress as a public figure. He was to be a member of the House of Burgesses, high sheriff, colonel in the militia, secretary of state, and was named in 1651 to the Council of State, an appointment second in importance only to that of the governorship itself.

Richard's talents included an adaptive nature. No matter what political principles were in vogue at the moment, Lee appeared to thrive. His career survived such upheavals as the beheading of Charles I, the establishment of parliamentary rule, the rise of Oliver Cromwell's Protectorate, and finally the call to the throne of Charles II during 1660. Unfortunately, there is no record of Richard's thoughts as he deftly switched from royalism to the Protectorate and back to the Crown.

Clearly, the Founder was dogmatic only in matters of worldly success. He made survival and prosperity his concerns. But then, how else could Richard and Anne Lee have bequeathed comfort, power, and wealth to children and grandchildren? One achievement of these emigrant Lees is evident in the contrast between the primitive world they found at Jamestown and the kingdoms of comparative ease their sons and grandsons inherited.

The first Lees' triumph in Virginia perfectly fulfilled the hopes of many other newcomers, though few of the estimated 75,000 English men and women who reached Virginia between 1625 and 1675 would be as fortunate as Richard. Many of them simply failed to survive attacks by disease and Indians. The colony's population in 1664, when Richard died, was still under 40,000. For this adventurous community, land was the source of prestige as well as sustenance.

Means used by Virginians to acquire land included purchase, judicious marriages, and appointment to remunerative local and colonial offices. Also, land patents were granted to those who brought indentured servants into Virginia, which meant that for paying the passage of such persons, Richard Lee received not only their services for several years, but also fifty acres per individual. He used this circumstance skillfully.

No matter where they dwelt in the colony, like that of other early Virginians, Richard and Anne's existence was inseparable from the magnificent rivers that still give the Tidewater its character. As mercantilists, the first four generations of Lees depended upon the majestic Chesapeake Bay and the streams that fed it. These were highways for commerce both local and with Europe. In 1640, the colony clung to the lower of three peninsulas or "necks," formed by Virginia's four major rivers; the Potomac, the Rappahannock, the York, and the James. The colony's first capital, Jamestown, and its successor, Williamsburg, were located on the neck between the James and York rivers.

The first Lees lived for nearly ten years on this lower neck. There, and elsewhere, Richard and Anne would occupy rude wooden cabins set in clearings, and as near the water as possible. Brick dwellings were uncommon until the eighteenth century, and in Richard's day tree stumps testified how recently the region had been unspoiled. For a time, however, Richard was less interested in clearing land for planting than in what commerce would bring him.

Immediately after his arrival in Jamestown, Richard began to profit not only from the income brought by his public offices but also by trading with the Indians for fur and skins. He had the advantage of association with a John Lee, probably his brother, who was a merchant in London. Such a business needed a Virginia location well situated for Indian commerce. Consequently, Richard and Anne settled first by Tindall's Creek on the north side of the York River.

Within a year, they had to flee. The Powhatan Indians undertook to drive out all white invaders, whom they called trespassers on land claimed by the venerable chief Opechancanough and his predecessors. More English settlers were slain in this uprising of 1644 than during a similar butchery in 1622. To escape the Indian wrath, the Lees removed with their infant son John to land south of the York, where they remained for nine years on ninety acres, situated a comfortable ride from James-town, making it easy for Richard to handle his official duties in the capital.

From this spot on the York River, Richard sailed in the spring of 1650 for the Netherlands. He was then secretary of state for Virginia, a post making him the appropriate person to be errandsman for Governor Berkeley. The latter wished to receive a renewed appointment as governor from the son of the beheaded Charles I. The Prince was an exile in Holland, calling himself Charles II.

As the family told it, Richard was such a passionate royalist that he undertook the trip in order to kneel at the foot of the fugitive sovereign and implore him to take refuge in Virginia. It is a charming tale, but the reality is that Richard's official status obliged him to represent Governor Berkeley in Europe. Thoroughly practical, Lee saw the advantage in such a journey and chartered a Dutch vessel, filled it with goods, and traded them to great profit in Holland.

When Richard returned to Virginia, he brought not only Sir William's commission (which proved worthless) but also much personal financial gain. This he presently used when he found himself with time to become a planter. Oliver Cromwell had forced Governor Berkeley into a pouting retirement, which meant that the governor's associates also were removed from their official posts. Richard Lee turned at once to establish a plantation away from Jamestown. He was in a position to do so, since, along with the cargo he had carried back from Holland, he brought thirty-eight indentured servants. The acreage he was awarded for them helped Richard during 1651 to secure land grants on the peninsula between the York and the Rappahannock rivers, where a fragile peace had been established with the Indians.

For three years, 1653 to 1656, Richard and Anne lived on a plantation beside the Poropotank River in the newly created county of Gloucester. It was wilderness, but their advantageous location bestrode routes of Indian commerce. Richard built a warehouse and made his property a center for trade as well as agriculture. Perhaps to denote their relief at being away from the confusion which had overtaken Jamestown, the Lees called their new home Paradise.

By another of his astute moves, Richard became at least part owner of a trading ship, whose cargoes regularly brought more indentured servants with headrights, which Richard used to enlarge his Virginia property. With successes like these, Richard never saw himself mainly as a planter. Relying on Anne and his business associates to manage affairs at Paradise, he began frequent travels abroad, formally designating himself as an Englishman who was a merchant and trader to Virginia. In the years between 1652 and 1659, he spent thirty-six months in England compared with forty-six in Virginia.

During one such trip, from February 1654 to September 1655, Anne accompanied Richard, leaving the children at Paradise to be supervised by John Woodward, who shared in the Lees' affairs. This journey witnessed one of the few episodes in the life of the early Lees about which we have any detail. Anne and Richard brought their table silver with them to England, perhaps to have it properly marked with some family insignia. It was a step they regretted. When they sailed for Virginia in the summer of 1655, they were compelled to leave the silver—two hundred ounces of it—in the hands of authorities who detained it under a law which forbade the export of precious metals.

Eventually, Richard's agents persuaded the English government that the silver had been used in Virginia before being brought to England for private purposes. Retrieving the silver required that Cromwell's government be assured Richard Lee was "faithful and useful to this Commonwealth," and that he had ventured to Virginia well before civil war broke out in England. The silver was released to the Lees, and it graced the family dining room until 1729, when it apparently was stolen during a robbery at the home of Richard's grandson, Thomas Lee.

Soon after returning from England, Richard and Anne moved their family to Virginia's Northern Neck, the peninsula formed by the Rappahannock and the Potomac rivers. Leaving Paradise in the care of overseers, late in 1655 or early 1656 they crossed the Rappahannock and resettled on a spot acquired from the Indians. It sat where Dividing Creek entered Chesapeake Bay, near what is today the town of Kilmarnock. Here they owned 1900 acres.

Richard brought with him two associates, Miles Dixon, another merchant, and Hugh Wilson, a mariner. Probably these men had shared in the Lee business for many years. Their presence meant Richard could feel easy that affairs were in trustworthy hands on occasions when he left Dividing Creek, which Richard often did, for he clearly had no intention of settling quietly on Chesapeake Bay.

He pushed on to purchase an additional 2600 acres at Machodoc Creek, which emptied into the Potomac River a short distance above the Bay. Like the Dividing Creek site, it was an ideal port for ships traveling between Virginia and Europe. An even more farsighted acquisition was 4000 more acres farther up the Potomac, near where the city of Washington would rise. One of these tracts, containing 1000 acres, was to be the site of Mount Vernon. Richard also owned property in Maryland.

Richard's Virginia seat at Dividing Creek was in Northumberland County, where he became at once a powerful figure, receiving rank as colonel of militia. In time, he was restored to his place on the Council of State when Sir William Berkeley was re-established as governor after Charles II took the throne in 1660. The date marked two decades since Richard began his adventure in North America, twenty years that had brought him dazzling economic and political rewards. William Lee, Richard's great-grandson, was justified in calling his forebear "a vigorous spirit" and "an enterprising genius."

Yet, in spite of all this success, it appears that, even at Dividing Creek, Richard remained restless and began planning a permanent return to England. We are left to speculate whether this decision was made by Richard or whether Anne Lee may have pressed to take her family to a more civilized setting. Anne had given birth to her tenth and last child, Charles Lee, on 21 May 1656. Eight of her offspring, six sons and two daughters, survived.

Looking out across Chesapeake Bay from their home on Dividing Creek, Anne and Richard both must have mused over what their children's education and future would be in the Northern Neck. Both parents were well aware that Virginia lacked a genteel setting for raising children. Guests at Dividing Creek were often chiefs of neighboring Indian tribes known as the Wicomico and the Chicacoan. Lee youngsters had as companions mostly indentured servants or what their parents would have considered even less edifying company, that of black slaves who had recently begun arriving to do the hard work at Dividing Creek. Richard Lee was among the planters who led in importing Africans as chattel. In 1660, he claimed 4000 acres and the headrights due him for importing eighty blacks.

Such primitive surroundings afforded few resources to prepare Lee offspring for a proper life and outlook. If they remained in Virginia, their education had to be brought from England in the person of tutors, who were usually impecunious young males aiming for the Anglican priesthood. So, with better days seemingly ahead for England, Richard evidently decided it made good sense, financially and culturally, to conclude his stay in Virginia.

The first step in this direction was taken as early as 1658 when Richard sailed for England with his eldest son John, who was to be trained as a physician. After enrolling the boy at Oxford, Richard dutifully lobbied the English government on behalf of himself and other Virginia tobacco planters. Then he steered himself and his family in their new direction by choosing a location near London where he, Anne, and the children would make their home.

He purchased an estate at the village of Stratford-Langton. Signing himself "Richard Lee of London," he acquired one of the largest properties in that neighborhood, a choice reputed to earn an annual income of 850 pounds, so even here Richard kept an eye on gain. Stratford-Langton was described as the place where wealthy London citizens built country houses. It must have seemed a good place for Anne and Richard to complete the rearing of their family.

Despite the purchase, Richard had no intention of turning his back on his New World wealth. Though a resident of England, he could continue as a Virginia planter and merchant. Whenever necessary, he planned to make the voyage—usually requiring less than a month—to Virginia for business and for the duties of his seat on the Council.

Having made this decision and bought a home in England, Richard set out for Virginia in 1659 to turn his affairs over to a capable manager before he and his family began life in suburban London. Richard brought with him to Dividing Creek his choice as the person to be left as chief steward over the Lee plantations. This was John Gibbon, who appeared ideally prepared for the responsibilities Richard intended for him. At age thirty Gibbon had notable military, business, and other worldly experience. He was a graduate of Cambridge and had served in one of England's wealthiest households, that of Thomas, Lord Coventry. Gibbon's relatives were to include the historian Edward Gibbon, author of *The Decline and Fall of the Roman Empire.*

According to Gibbon's later testimony, Richard promised him 1000 acres of land and eventual marriage to one of the Lee twin daughters (then six years old). The prospect was insufficient, however, to prevent the new steward from a serious case of homesickness after he learned in 1660 that the royal family had been returned to the throne. So, after Richard took time to find another steward, Gibbon and all the Lees sailed for England in February 1661.

After Richard and Anne established the family at Stratford-Langton, they presented their youngest son Charles for christening, much more easily done in England than on the banks of Dividing Creek. A next step was to find a school for their second son, Richard, apparently a precocious fourteen-year-old. At some point, Anne and Richard had their portraits painted, after which Richard heard the call of business at Dividing Creek. Accompanied by his son John, Lee was back in the Old Dominion by 1662.

Although he had reached age forty-four and the rank of country gentleman in England, Richard Lee gave no indication of relenting in his search for wealth. Nor did he disregard the responsibilities that accompanied his standing as perhaps the leading private citizen in Virginia. During 1663, the last year of his life, Richard kept busy, not only as the pre-eminent member of the Council of State, but by improving life in Northumberland County. He also bought additional property, choosing well-located acreage in Maryland.

The purchase was among his last acts. Richard never saw Anne and his children again. Death found him at Dividing Creek on 1 March 1664, He must have been ill for a time, since the record shows an erratic participation in county management. He prepared a new will on 6 February 1664 in which he identified himself as a sometime resident of Virginia, "but lately of Stratford Langton, in the County of Essex."

In his last hours, Richard changed his mind about wishing his children to mature in England. Without his guiding hand upon the family's complicated international commercial and financial affairs, he believed that Anne must bring her brood back to Virginia so that the Lee kingdom could be divided among the heirs. Toward this end, Richard directed that the Stratford-Langton estate be sold and the proceeds spent in completing the education of the eldest sons John and Richard. Any remainder was to be paid to the twin daughters, Elizabeth and Anne.

At Richard's death, Anne Constable Lee was forty-two. Lamentably, no shred of paper survives to impart a sense of what she was like as a person. Her portrait shows a woman of poise and beauty, with the mark of amiableness. She returned to live at Dividing Creek, which Richard bequeathed to her for life, along with another nearby plantation. She had received a third of the contents brought from the house at Stratford-Langton, as well as ten white servants, five black slaves, twenty sows, and an abundance of corn.

When Anne married again, this time to Edmund Lister, Richard's will obliged her to give up only the blacks, who reverted to the property of the younger children. But for reasons unknown, Lister brought suit against his step-son, John Lee, who was executor of Richard's will. Unfortunately, the outcome of the litigation is lost, and Anne Constable Lee Lister disappears from the record. The date of her death is unknown, although legend has it she was buried beside Richard near the house at Dividing Creek.

Except for sons Francis and Richard, the Founder's children accompanied the Widow Lee back to Dividing Creek. Seventeen-year-old Richard remained to complete his studies, probably at Oxford. Evidently he was a very successful student, who may not have thought much about worldly matters since his older brother John, as principal heir, would see to carrying out their parent's will. Dutifully, John had surrendered his hopes for medical study to take up the family's leadership.

John had inherited the property called Machodoc on the Potomac in what had become Westmoreland County. He also received three islands in Chesapeake Bay, slaves, servants, livestock, grain, and what his father called "the great new bed." He soon was a major figure in Westmoreland County, serving as leader in the militia, justice of the peace, high sheriff, and as a member of the House of Burgesses.

At John's death in 1673, unmarried at age thirty, the contents found in his small house suggest the disarray of a busy and lonely frontiersman. His bedroom held a saddle and other equine furnishings, as well as a pistol, six quarts of hominy, and six containers of some unspecified oil. As befitted an Oxford alumnus, John owned books estimated to be worth 4000 pounds of tobacco. However, his living room was more notable for being furnished with sixteen shovels and two frying pans.

John Lee may not have spent as much time at home as one would expect. Nearby was America's first country club, of which John was a founder. At the spot where their four estates cornered, John and three associates built a banqueting house "for the better preservation of that friendship which ought to be between neighbors." The partners included Henry Corbin, whose descendants would be of prime importance in the Lee family story. At least once a year, each of the four owners formally agreed to be host for a lavish party—"an honorable treatment"—fit for all their friends. John Lee paid for the second entertainment after Henry Corbin led off.

There was even a serious feature to the festive association. Every four years, the property owners pledged to join in "a procession to every man's land" in order to re-mark the boundaries. This enlightened relationship did not survive the four neighbors who designed it. Three of them died soon after creating the club.

In addition to his Machodoc plantation, John had other property matters on his mind. As principal executor for his father's will, he looked after the legacies of the other heirs, a task he did not live to complete. When John died, these remaining legal chores fell to Richard, as the next eldest son. While he originally had inherited only the Paradise plantation in Gloucester County, at John's death Richard became owner of the Machodoc property on the Potomac.

Before taking up the story of the second Richard Lee, whose descendants are the principal characters in this book, we should see what happened to the rest of the Founders' children. Two of them established Lee family lines that come down into our time. This was not to be true, however, for Francis, Richard and Anne's third son. His career illustrates the trans-Atlantic scope necessary at the time for most of Virginia's upper class. Following his father's final wish, Francis became the Lee representative in London.

Citing permission given in his father's will, Francis had remained in England until 1670, probably as an apprentice with business associates of his parent. He then came to Virginia to look over his inheritance, his father having bequeathed him properties on the York River, along with five black slaves, ten white indentured servants, and a quantity of cattle, hogs, corn, and tools.

More important for Francis, as it turned out, was that he now owned his father's shares in two trading vessels, the *Susan* and the *Elizabeth and Mary*. He soon sold his legacy of land and returned permanently to London in 1677, where he prospered as a merchant. He died in November 1714 and was buried in the great vault in the chancel of St. Dionis Backchurch. His will left loving acknowledgments of his elder brother Richard Lee, head of the family back in Virginia, as well as of Richard's son Richard, who had come to London to join Uncle Francis as a family businessman.

Listed in the Founder's will after Francis had been three others sons: William, Hancock, and Charles Lee. The Dividing Creek estate was apportioned among them after their mother died. William had the smallest share since he had received his father's land in Maryland. So far as we know, William Lee never married. He died in Northumberland County in 1696 at age forty-five, after following what had become a family habit of public service. At various times, he was a justice, captain of the militia, member of the House of Burgesses, and local agent for London merchants.

But William certainly broke new ground when he bequeathed his considerable acreage in Virginia and Maryland to a young widow, Mary Heath. A merry debate has continued over just who Mrs. Heath was. Lee family members long insisted that she must have been William's daughter or even his wife. But she was neither. Mary was a close friend or companion of William, who named her executrix of his estate as well as principal heir. After William's death, the now prosperous Mary Heath married Bartholomew Schreever, who, judging by utterances in his will of 1727, remained on good terms with those Lees who were still living along Dividing Creek.

On the other hand, Mr. and Mrs. Schreever were not cordial toward Richard Lee, who was now leader of the family's second generation. A strait-laced fellow, Richard was disgusted by seeing William's generous portion of their father's Virginia kingdom leave the family in a manner causing speculation and gossip. In 1707, Richard found a way to retrieve the property. Re-reading his father's will, he discovered a flaw. In stipulating bequests for his three younger sons, the elder Richard omitted in each case the legally vital term: "and his heirs forever." In effect, this left the three beneficiaries title to their property only for life. Afterwards, their estates would revert to the heir-at-law, which Richard had become when John died.'

Convinced that his father had not intended to limit these legacies, Richard sought in September 1707 to make them perpetual, doing so, he said, "out of natural affection." He renounced any right and title to Hancock and Charles' legacies, but he displayed no such generosity toward Mary Heath Schreever, William's heir. Richard brought suit against her and her husband to recover the legacy. Eventually, courts in both Virginia and Maryland found in Richard's favor, and the late William Lee's patrimony was restored to the family. The Maryland acreage became home for a later branch of the family, the Lees of Blenheim.

The two remaining sons of Anne and Richard, Hancock and Charles Lee, had male issue. Hancock's inheritance at Dividing Creek eventually was known as the Ditchley estate, and today his descendants are known as the Ditchley Lees. Hancock must have received the largest portion of his father's vigor, for he strove to make his property grow, particularly on the Virginia frontier. His heirs eventually became pioneers in Kentucky, producing a President of the United States, Zachary Taylor, and a Chief Justice of the Supreme Court, Edward Douglas White.

Thanks to Hancock, a remarkable bloodline entered the Lee genealogy. After the death of his first wife, Hancock took as his second spouse Sarah Allerton, the daughter of Isaac Allerton, who was one of John Lee's associates in creating the neighborly club. Sarah's grandfather Isaac Allerton had arrived in New England on the *Mayflower* and married Fear Brewster, daughter of the venerated Elder William Brewster. Sarah Allerton Lee bore five children, including twins born after the death of their father. So confident of Sarah's integrity was Hancock that his will imposed none of the cautionary restrictions husbands in those days usually placed upon young widows lest they remarry in a fashion harmful to the estate.

The Ditchley property, which Hancock willed to his son (yet another Richard), included just under 1000 acres. It can be visited today, lying as it does near Kilmarnock between the north and south branches of Dividing Creek. Still owned by Lee descendants, it has a fine house built around 1762 by Kendall Lee, Hancock's grandson. The descendants followed Hancock's example of being active in Northumberland County affairs.

Charles Lee, the youngest son of Richard and Anne, lived longest with his mother and eventually inherited the middle third of the Dividing Creek estate. His share has come to be known as the Cobbs Hall plantation, after the house erected on the site where Anne and Richard had first lived. The building standing there today is the third such dwelling, for Richard and Anne's home apparently was replaced in 1720. The present structure was put up in 1853. Six generations of Lee males named Charles have lived on this portion of the Founder's property.

Admirable as these Ditchley and Cobbs Hall lines of Lees may have been, their careers continued mostly in the private realm while the public renown for the family grew from descendants of the second Richard Lee. Appropriately, the life of this Richard was itself extraordinary. Although the surviving manuscripts reveal all too little about him, enough is known to disclose how different he was from his father, the Founder. The contrast is evident in the fact that this leader of the second generation of Lees is known as Richard the Scholar.

~ 2

The Scholar
1664–1715

When his father, the Founder, died in 1664, young Richard Lee was a student in England, presumably at Oxford. Although he was only seventeen at the time, we are told his talents had already profoundly impressed the faculty. According to Richard's grandson, William Lee, some of England's "great men" guaranteed if the youth was allowed to remain at Oxford, they would see that he rose "to the highest dignities" in the Church of England.

As the senior Richard was dying, he asked that all his children but Francis return to Virginia, a request his bookish son Richard obeyed after graduating from Oxford. Family lore says young Lee, in a woebegone mood, reluctantly exchanged the libraries and erudite talk of a great university community for residence on the remote Poropotank River in Gloucester County, Virginia. He had inherited the old family place, which was still called Paradise, a name that would have seemed ironical to Richard—if there is any truth to what we are told about his return.

Like most legends, the one concerning young Richard Lee contains mostly romance and assumes that the Founder was an imperious father determined to banish to the wilderness a son whose talents shaped him for an elegant place amidst Europe's learned men. Instead, the elder Richard was disposed to be considerate of his offspring. While his will encouraged the family's re-establishment in Virginia, Francis Lee, the rising merchant son, was told to remain in London, but only if he chose. The father also spoke of his eldest son John's need to travel in Europe, and he recommended that the youthful Richard continue to study in England. The father apparently hoped that his namesake would pursue the law.

Probably, Richard Lee's will simply intended that his eldest sons be in Virginia long enough to oversee the disposition of the estate, leaving the future in their hands. Only the remote properties were bequeathed to these educated lads. Richard assigned the family headquarters, strategically located at Dividing Creek, to the widow Anne and thereafter to younger offspring. What seems most likely, then, is that the Founder, himself preferring to live in England, expected his three eldest children, John, Richard, and Francis, might share that view.

Young Richard may indeed have planned only a short stay in Gloucester County before sailing back to England and, given his tastes, a career in Anglicanism. At least he remained a bachelor and was still footloose when a melancholy event took away his choice. In 1673, the childless John Lee died, so that Richard suddenly found himself head of the Lee clan and owner of John's Machodoc Creek property in Westmoreland County. Dutifully, Richard left Paradise in the hands of overseers and removed to Machodoc. He never went from there to England.

As if to demonstrate he would remain in Virginia, Richard quickly found a wife. She was a daughter of one of his Machodoc neighbors, Henry Corbin, who ranked among the most powerful persons in the colony and had also been a participant in the "country club" which John Lee had helped establish. An immigrant with a lineage traceable to the Norman conquest of England in 1066, Corbin had prospered in Virginia and now owned a sprawling plantation called Peckatone, situated next door to Richard's new property.

Henry Corbin had married Alice Eltonhead, who produced three sons and five daughters. Of these, the eldest was Laetitia (called Lettice by her family), born in 1657, and thus ten years Richard Lee's junior. The pair were wed in 1674. Henry Corbin died a few months later. Although his widow Alice married again, it seems that she ended her days with her daughter Lettice at Machodoc, rather than with her son Gawin (pronounced Go-win), who had inherited Peckatone.

Immediately after his marriage, Richard was elected by his neighbors to the House of Burgesses. Then, in 1676 and at age twenty-seven, he was named to the highest governing body in Virginia, the Council of State. Richard's father's old friend, the aging Sir William Berkeley, was still governor and must have been pleased to recommend another Lee to the King for this high appointment. From Machodoc, Richard had a several days' ride to reach Jamestown, where the Council met. He traveled at a time when colonists were growing fearful and angry, more so than at any point since Virginia's earliest days.

The Old Dominion's woes had been apparent even before the first Richard died. The Founder had joined Governor Berkeley in a vain attempt to persuade Charles II's government to discard parliamentary enactments called the Navigation Laws. This was legislation Virginians deemed a menace to their main source of prosperity, the shipment abroad of tobacco. These statutes stipulated that colonists send their produce only to England, doing so entirely in English ships. The Lees and numerous planters were thus cut off from other customers, and England was soon glutted by tobacco.

Tobacco prices had fallen so low as to make the crop a losing proposition. To worsen matters, England's war with The Netherlands brought Dutch ships on raiding parties to Virginia. These vessels had moved up the James River, burning merchant ships loaded with tobacco. It seemed that neither Governor Berkeley nor the ministry in London could agree on how to defend Virginia, which only increased the population's anxiety.

There were other causes for general uneasiness, including a spate of severe weather, giving Virginia more than a taste of the damage hurricanes ("gusts") left. But more disquieting was a growing sense that Governor Berkeley was losing his once remarkable capacity to unify the colony. To a large part of the worried community, Sir William appeared increasingly arbitrary. Public restlessness arose from the perception that Berkeley relied only upon a circle of cohorts whose personal profit from such intimacy angered the outsiders. Furthermore, no general election for the House of Burgesses had been called in fifteen years. It meant that the same old faces kept showing up in Jamestown.

This simmering trouble boiled over in 1676 because of a rumor. The Indians were said to be planning another attempt to eradicate the white invaders. Faith in Governor Berkeley's long-standing policy of conciliation with the tribes was shaken by outbreaks of violence along the frontier. Many Virginians believed that Sir William was more interested in saving his lucrative stake in Indian trade than in safeguarding the lives of colonists. At the same time, the Governor proved quite willing to increase taxes imposed on the economically depressed populace, and for purposes which many considered foolish or selfish.

Fears of Indian massacres were at their height when Richard Lee took a seat on the Council of State. It seemed as if the colony's social discipline was dissolving. The Old Dominion's populace was comprised of many more elements than merely fortunate heirs like Richard. Virginians now included such groups as freed indentured servants, poor immigrants, and less successful planters, most of whom were prone to believe the worst rumors, particularly after legislation in 1670 had excluded the landless citizens from voting. These persons often believed in signs, and thus were much dismayed by ominous occurrences during 1675, including large comets that appeared nightly, pigeons in flocks so huge as to blot out sunshine, and an infestation of vicious flies.

It was easy for many citizens to blame these troubles on the Governor and the Council, whose members were now being called a corrupt and incompetent palace guard. As one of them, Richard Lee found himself sorely tested only a few weeks after arriving in Jamestown. Nothing less than civil war broke out, an uproar led by Nathaniel Bacon. Not until a century later, in 1776, did Virginians experience excitement comparable to that which seized the colony in the summer of 1676. The parts played by Lees in these revolutions of 1676 and 1776 were entirely different.

Nathaniel Bacon had only recently arrived in Virginia to make his fortune. He was well connected, being a cousin-by-marriage to Governor Berkeley, who arranged a place in the Council for Bacon at about the same time Richard Lee took a seat. The two men were the same age. But whereas Richard proved at once a fiercely loyal supporter of the Governor, Bacon swiftly placed himself in violent opposition to Sir William. Claiming to lead "the people," Bacon defied the government at Jamestown and demanded reform.

Capitalizing on the dissatisfaction in Virginia, Bacon assembled an army against Governor Berkeley. While calling attention to specific grievances, particularly the feeble Indian defense, Bacon's wish was to empower the people. Toward that end, he announced the names of those persons who he said had usurped the rights of "the commons of Virginia." Among them was Richard Lee, who, along with nineteen others, was cited by Bacon as a "wicked and pernicious" partner with Governor Berkeley. The rebels demanded that these twenty men be tried and judged, and warned that citizens who sheltered the accused would themselves be charged as traitors to the people and would see their property confiscated.

For governor Berkeley and those who sided with him, this upheaval smashed the dream of a Virginia filled by an obedient, peaceable folk. Sir William had stoutly opposed general literacy, believing that when the underclasses learned to read only trouble ensued. But in the crisis, the Governor wavered. Facing united and angry opposition, he tried first to accommodate and then to suppress his foes.

Endangered by their leader's vacillation, Berkeley's supporters chose to scatter. Richard Lee returned to Machodoc, but not for long. A contingent of Bacon's men was sent to bring him to justice. In dispatching search parties for Lee and other Berkeley sympathizers, Bacon relented slightly. He announced that if the twenty malefactors would recant and stay out of the rebellion's way, they would be unmolested. Many took this reprieve, but not Richard.

He had the courage of his convictions. Richard believed all social order, including Virginia's, was imposed by God and should be maintained, no matter the "zealous inclination of the multitude." It was the public's "hopes of levelling" which drew it to Bacon, Richard contended. Otherwise, he insisted, "all his [Bacon's] specious pretences would not have persuaded them." Were it not, Lee said, for the evil in the hearts of the populace, Bacon's rebellion would never have occurred.

Since he refused to keep his views to himself, Richard was carried off in chains by those who paid no heed to his insistence that the lawfulness imposed by the King and his representatives came from Heaven. Anyone acquainted with Richard's library knew his choice of books preached that Englishmen, whether they lived along the Thames or along the Potomac, owed absolute fidelity to the Crown and to the structure of society endorsed by God and Sovereign.

Richard became a prisoner and was forced on a grueling four-day ride to Bacon's headquarters at the village of Middle Plantation, about five miles from Jamestown. There he was held for nearly two months, suffering hardships which impaired his health. Somehow he survived, while Bacon was less fortunate. After burning Jamestown and taking other drastic steps which raised doubt and confusion among his followers, Bacon fell ill and died suddenly in late October 1676. The agitation ended soon afterwards.

At what point Bacon's prisoners were released is uncertain, but Richard was quick to return to his post as Councillor. His good friend Sir William Berkeley, however, was recalled to London and scolded by the King for being needlessly harsh in prosecuting many who had supported the revolution. Now out of office and disgraced, Berkeley promptly died, while as his successor in Virginia the Crown sent a series of governors who were instructed to re-emphasize that Virginia was a dependency of England.

Except for the continued restrictions on commerce, which most residents opposed, Richard probably agreed with this campaign to make the colony defer to London. Many of his neighbors dissented, however, and a difference of political philosophy came to divide Virginia's powerful men. Richard Lee aligned himself with the conservative camp, a group often called the Trimmers. Its members wished above all to preserve order.

What is known of Richard Lee after 1677 indicates his views were no secret. As a member of the Council of State, he sided with governors Thomas Culpeper and Francis Howard as they bolstered Britain's imperial policies. When a citizen uprising again seemed brewing, this time in 1689, Richard was one of those who moved at once to see that fomenters of revolution were captured. Unfortunately for Richard, Parliament itself became rebellious in 1688, when it removed James II as king and substituted Mary of Orange and her husband William.

Now it was Richard Lee who found himself in the awkward role of rebel. In 1691, members of Virginia's Council of State were required to swear loyalty to Parliament's design of a limited monarchy. For Richard, this was heresy. If he took the oath, he believed he would be conceding that man rather than God created kings. Consequently, he refused to swear. The stand cost him heavily, for in addition to being a colonel in the Westmoreland County militia and a local justice, he held the valuable appointment of collector of the Crown's revenues for the Virginia side of the Potomac River.

Because of his devotion to principle (or his stubbornness), Richard was removed from the Council and as Potomac revenue collector. He was not in disgrace very long, however. Perhaps Jamestown and London felt Richard should be allowed to make his point, for he was soon restored to the Council and the collector's post. More likely, Lee's return to favor was because the Crown had reason to be grateful to him for easing a tense situation in the vicinity of his Machodoc plantation.

This came to pass after 1690 when the monarchy showed it was serious about keeping the Northern Neck a private domain of certain faithful royalists. Thanks to a grateful crown, the Fairfax family was now the Proprietor of at least a million acres between the Potomac and Rappahannock rivers, extending from the Chesapeake Bay to the headwaters of those rivers. Here, of course, was where the major part of Richard Lee's lands lay, making him, along with many others, tenants of the Proprietor. They were each liable to an annual quitrent, a nominal amount of tobacco paid to the Proprietor's agents.

Great was the furor among Richard's neighbors when the Fairfax agents, one of whom was Lee's close friend William Fitzhugh, made a determined effort to collect these payments. If they consented to the "rent," most landholders argued, they would endanger their rights as owners. The result was a dangerous standoff, until Richard Lee stepped forward and agreed to pay the Proprietor the annual amount. Others then followed suit, and the crisis subsided.

While little is known about Richard's brave stand, one can assume he may have taken some grim satisfaction in surrendering self-interest to the higher demands of royal authority. Since the divinely appointed Stuart kings had been inspired to create the Proprietorship, how could puny man defy the arrangement? At least this probably was Richard's learned reasoning.

The act of allegiance to the Proprietor may have been Richard's last major public deed. By now past fifty and beyond the age when his father had died, Richard evidently was in poor health. Perhaps, too, he was weary of seeming always to be the one who opposed changes that he deemed threats to Virginia. His final appearance as a member of the Council was in 1698. Thereafter, for fifteen years he stayed close to his home at Machodoc.

Richard withdrew from public life possessing a sterling reputation. In 1712, Governor Alexander Spotswood wrote a description of Lee to his superiors in London, calling him "a gentleman of as fair character as any in the country for his exact justice, honesty, and unexceptionable loyalty in all the stations wherein he has served in this government."

A more intimate assessment was made by Richard's friend William Fitzhugh, who lived up the Potomac in Stafford County. Born and reared in England, Fitzhugh was a brilliant lawyer, planter, and man of affairs. Writing in January 1688 to "the honourable Colonel Richard Lee," Fitzhugh thanked him for some "free and full advice," and added: "I know you are too well practised in the topics and [in] honour and generosity, to render advice other than fair and candid."

Then came a charming eulogy. Richard Lee, according to his friend Fitzhugh, was "not Yorkshire enough to set the course of your advice by the compass of your interest." Fitzhugh was recalling that Yorkshiremen were sometimes known for a sharp and cunning style. But even Richard had his practical moments, and not only when Fitzhugh acted as an agent for the Northern Neck Proprietor. It was a great coup for the Lee family when Richard's only daughter Ann entered a brilliant marriage with William Fitzhugh's son and namesake.

Richard's vigorous days were past when his youngest sons Thomas and Henry knew him. It was through them that family recollections of Richard came down. These lads, who were only seven and eight when Richard retired, would remember a frail and aged parent who, after 1698, worked among his books, scribbling notes in Greek and Latin. Of all the volumes on his library shelves, none was more appropriate for the last years of Richard's life than one by George Webb, the Bishop of Limerick, entitled *The Practice of Quietness, Directing a Christian How to Live Quietly in This Troublesome World.*

Family tradition implies that Richard and Laetitia Lee spent their days living quietly on the Potomac. This view leaves the Scholar's years of courageous behavior almost forgotten. Consequently, the second

Richard Lee is the most misunderstood and underappreciated member of the clan. Sad to say, even a sort of disgrace was imposed on him by his grandson, William Lee, who drew up a brief family history which pictured Richard sitting on his hands and doing nothing to improve his patrimony. Richard Lee "spent almost his whole life in study" was William's complaint.

Although he conceded that Richard held offices of "honor and profit," the grandson contended such rank "yielded little to him." William mourned how his forebear "might with ease have acquired what would produce at this day a most princely revenue." As it happened, a number of Richard's descendants, including William himself, nearly ruined their lives by pursuing money. It would have spared the family considerable mortification if certain later Lees had emulated the honesty for which their grandsire Richard was remembered.

Instead, Richard's descendants patronizingly assigned him into seclusion with his books while they claimed opportunity knocked unheard. But this assessment ignored his character and what happened in Virginia during his life when tribulations, including economic reversals, afflicted the colony. In hardship, the second Richard's behavior shows he was at least as courageous as his father. In the 1670s, Virginia began a transformation which persons like Richard the Scholar feared would corrupt society. His gallant fight against "progress" may explain why Richard disappointed his descendants.

The contents of Richard's library are a guide to his character. He owned more than a fine classical collection. Among the three hundred titles housed at Machodoc were volumes rare even in England, as well as some of the popular writings of the day. Richard and his family could read about astronomy and grammar, ethics and philosophy, conduct and heraldry, history and biography, as well as law and government. Even so, the preponderance was of religious topics. Fifty-seven theological books suggest that here was where Richard himself may have turned most often, along with his three volumes defending the beloved martyr, King Charles I.

The library at Machodoc lacked frivolous books, which presumably made it the more dependable as a foundation for educating Richard and Lettice Lee's children. While Erasmus' mildly satiric *The Praise of Folly* was present, it could be offset by several tomes dedicated to assailing the Jesuits and the Puritans. Generally, the library contained a comforting assortment for one of Richard's outlook, books drawn mostly from titles published earlier in the seventeenth century. Still, no one can be certain if Richard's mind was closed. While the inventory of his estate showed an absence of books printed after 1680, the depression in tobacco prices may have kept Richard so short of cash that he could not afford to buy recent publications.

Richard had been retired to his study for only a few years when Laetitia Corbin Lee, his spouse of three decades, died on 6 October 1706 in her forty-ninth year. She and Richard had produced at least seven children, six of whom lived to become adults. Nothing survives about Lettice Lee except a portrait, probably painted by an itinerant and unknown artist. Fortunately, as with many such crude efforts, the canvas left a glimpse of Lettice's disposition. Unlike Richard's portrait with its grumpy demeanor, his mate looks out with a tranquil, pleasant gaze.

When a stone was placed over Lettice's tomb in the garden at Machodoc, someone—presumably her husband—had engraved upon it that she was "a faithful wife" who could claim the distinction of being a child of Henry Corbin, "Gentleman." The epitaph went on: "A most affectionate mother, she was also distinguished by piety toward God, charity toward the poor, and kindness to all."

Richard lived another eight years, long enough to see his sons and daughter well begun in life. Their later success, of course, was indebted to the care with which Richard prepared his will, obviously seeking a fair distribution of his property among the six offspring. Nine days before his death, Richard completed his final testament, a document notable for the meticulousness with which it described the many legacies. Richard surely remembered the trouble caused by the loose wording of his father's bequests.

Richard's will began with an unusually ardent thanksgiving: "I, Richard Lee of Cople Parish in Westmoreland County [am] of sound and perfect sense and memory (blessed be God for it)." He took pains in bequeathing "my soul unto God that gave it me, hoping by his infinite mercy and by my dear Savior Jesus Christ, his intercession and the merits of his passion, it shall at the last day be reunited with my body and glorified." Until that final trumpet sounded, Richard asked that his mortal remains should lie next to those of "my dear wife."

Only after addressing these crucial topics did Richard turn to his earthly goods "which it hath pleased my good God to bless me beyond any desert of mine." Lettice and Richard's eldest son, named John, had died in infancy. His place was taken by Richard, now third of the name, who was born in 1679. He inherited the family's main residence at Machodoc with its 2600 acres and a supply of livestock. It was a patrimony he never occupied.

This Richard had departed Virginia several years before his father's death to become a tobacco merchant in London. He joined the firm of his uncle Thomas Corbin, Lettice Lee's brother. Young Richard apparently prospered and married well, his wife being Martha Silk, who was something of an heiress. When her husband died, outliving his father by only three years, Martha Silk Lee and their three children were left in comfortable circumstances. Martha sold the Machodoc property to her brother-in-law Thomas Lee.

When Martha died, around 1734, her three youngsters, George, Lettice, and Martha, came to Virginia. George eventually retrieved the ancestral Machodoc property from his Uncle Thomas Lee and renamed it Mount Pleasant. On that land, near the town of Hague, visitors today may visit the graves of Richard and Lettice Corbin Lee, along with those of several descendants. In time, it was George Lee's turn to be buried there, but before that occurred he made a charming contribution to the Lee family story.

In 1752, George married Anne Fairfax Washington, six months the widow of Lawrence Washington, half-brother of George Washington. Lawrence had been owner of Mount Vernon, an estate comprised of land once claimed by the first Richard Lee. Eventually, a protracted and bitter controversy between the Lee and Washington families saw the land awarded to the Washingtons. When Lawrence died he gave Mount Vernon to his widow for her lifetime, after which it was to pass to George Washington.

Since George and Anne Lee apparently were unwilling to remove from Mount Pleasant to Mount Vernon, they made George Washington their tenant. Annually thereafter, George Lee collected 15,000 pounds of tobacco or its monetary equivalent (something over 80 pounds sterling) as rent from George Washington. The arrangement lasted until 1761, when both George and Anne Washington Lee died and Mount Vernon finally became Colonel Washington's possession.

The Machodoc property (or Mount Pleasant) had been the extent of Richard the Scholar's bequest to his business-minded son in London. After disposing of Machodoc in his will, Richard turned to the rest of his children. The second son, Philip Lee, received most of the property across the Potomac (near where U.S. highway 301 today enters Maryland). By the time his father died, Philip had lived in Maryland for a dozen years. He built a famous mansion called Blenheim and sired eighteen children. His grandson, Thomas Sim Lee, was a member of the Continental Congress and an early governor of Maryland.

Much less is known about Richard's third son, Francis Lee, born probably in 1685. As with all the children, there are no facts about Francis' education. Alongside his brothers and sister, Francis was probably trained at Machodoc, surrounded by his father's fine library and tutored by young men brought over from England. Francis took medicine as his interest. In one of the few letters to survive from the period, Francis' sister, Ann Lee Fitzhugh, complained in 1722 of a violent pain in the neck and announced her intention of consulting "Brother Francis" about it.

Evidently Francis spent his life—he died after 1754—on the property bequeathed to him by the Scholar. This was the Paradise estate of 1350 acres in Gloucester County, which had been Richard's original inheritance from the Founder. Along with it came an assortment of slaves and livestock. However, as Francis left no male issue, Richard's will decreed that Paradise should revert to the heirs of Philip Lee in Maryland—who eventually allowed it to slip away from the Lee family.

The only daughter at Machodoc was Ann Lee, born in 1683. Except for two slaves, she received from her father's will what proved to be nothing—the family's faltering claim to the vast acreage surrounding Mount Vernon. By her first husband, William Fitzhugh, she had a son, Henry, through whom Ann became the great-grandmother of Mrs. Robert E. Lee. After her Fitzhugh spouse's death in 1715, Ann wed Daniel McCarty, a powerful figure in Westmoreland County who was then serving as speaker of the House of Burgesses. She had several children by McCarty and survived him until 1732, when she was buried on the Fitzhugh estate, Eagle's Nest, in King George County.

Remaining to be considered in Richard the Scholar's will were Thomas and Henry, the youngest sons of the Scholar. They acquired more than the modest bequests usually left to children born last. Thomas, whose birthday was in 1690, received the land at Dividing Creek and in Maryland which his father had reclaimed by legal action from William Lee's heiress, Mrs. Schreever. He also had a share of slaves, livestock, and household furnishings. But the most important gift was Richard's realization that Thomas had great ability. The father placed him in positions which made Thomas prosper even while Richard himself still lived.

Tradition contends that Thomas was bequeathed only a few crumbs by his father, encouraging some to say that Thomas' brilliant career was an American rags-to-riches triumph. Actually, Richard had arranged that Thomas succeed him as the Crown's Potomac collector of shipping duties, a lucrative office. As if this were not sufficient, the father lived to see his talented son hold the even more rewarding post of agent for the Northern Neck Proprietary. No wonder, then, that the fair-minded Richard should decree in his will that in the event costs should be levied against his estate, Thomas must pay a portion larger than that of any other heir.

The Scholar's youngest son Henry was not left so advantageously. Born in 1691, Henry Lee received from his father some acreage adjoining the main family property at Machodoc. He also was given a number of slaves and horses. Richard made a special point of entrusting the slave "old Peg" to Henry, just as he carefully bestowed "my chest of drawers in my hall" jointly upon Henry and Thomas. The Scholar's great collection of books was not mentioned in the will, which implies it was left to accompany the Machodoc house and land.

In closing his will, the Scholar insisted that he did not wish his estate tied up by the tedious process of appraisal and valuation. Confident that his heirs would amicably divide the property, he named as executors his sons Thomas and Henry, along with their brother Richard in England. Then the old man put down his pen. A few days later, he was dead at sixty-eight, a great age for the time as well as one of the longest spans in seven generations of male Lees. He was buried at Machodoc, next to Lettice.

The epitaph carved for Richard was appropriately understated. It noted first that whenever Richard Lee had served in office, "he was a zealous promoter of the public good." Next, visitors to the grave were reminded that the deceased was "very skillful in the Greek and Latin languages and other parts of polite learning." Finally, there was the assurance that Richard had "quietly resigned his soul to God, whom he always devoutly worshiped."

Such a tribute was probably composed by Thomas and Henry Lee. These young sons had lived with their father in his last days. The two were much more than brothers. They would always remain friends and associates in a partnership that powerfully shaped the Lee family's commanding role in Virginia and American history. From them descended the famous Lees of Stratford and Leesylvania.

ᦞ 3

The Partners
1700–1750

As he died, Richard the Scholar may have feared his male line faced extinction in Virginia. His eldest son Richard lived in England, while Philip, the second in line, had settled in Maryland. Daughter Ann was busy continuing the name of another Virginia family, the Fitzhughs. Son Francis, the physician, gave no promise of male offspring. This left only Thomas and Henry, whom their father must have looked upon as settled bachelors when they cared for him in his last days.

After burying their parent, the pair continued with brother Richard's consent to reside at Machodoc. Since the house had at least ten rooms, the two need not get in each other's way. The younger, Henry, was more like his father, quiet and mostly devoted to home. The elder, Thomas, by the manner in which he combined materialist and political zeal, would be a reincarnation of his grandfather, Richard the Founder.

Barely past twenty-one, Thomas Lee already held two lucrative posts, positions awarded to him through help from his father and his uncles. In 1712, when the elderly Richard wearied of responsibility as naval officer for the South Potomac district, one of six such offices in the colony, Governor Alexander Spotswood informed London: "I thought I could not better reward his [Richard's] merit than by bestowing that employment upon his son."

A noble reward it was, for it kept money and influence in Lee hands. Since the British government wished careful records kept of goods shipped into and out from Virginia under the restrictive terms of the Navigation Acts, the six naval officers were to be imperial watchdogs, and well paid for their trouble. Besides a salary, they received 10 percent of all duties collected on enumerated products such as tobacco, furs, skins, wool, rice, and many others coming through their offices. All revenues were sent to London with a detailed accounting. The job was a demanding one, requiring much certifying, record-keeping, and visiting of vessels passing on the Potomac.

Thomas Lee kept this post until his rise to the peak of Virginia politics after 1730 made him ineligible for it, whereupon he took care that brother Henry succeeded him. And when Henry died, his son Richard, barely twenty-one at the time, received his powerful Uncle Thomas' endorsement, thereby continuing the naval office in Lee family hands, where it remained until the Revolution made the post obsolete.

As if the custom job were insufficient to keep him busy, young Thomas Lee had undertaken another office, a great piece of luck brought by his helpful father and uncles. He was agent for the Northern Neck Proprietary, the Fairfax and Culpeper families. The assignment was even more influential and enriching than collecting naval revenues.

Thanks to royal generosity, the Proprietor was nominally owner of the huge area between the Potomac and Rappahannock rivers. This meant that Virginians could purchase land in the region only through the Proprietor's agent in the colony. Grants were approved on a kind of leasehold basis, requiring that the claimant annually pay to the Proprietor a sum, usually in tobacco, known as a quitrent. This was collected by the agent. It was work needing detailed knowledge of the roughly five million acres in the Proprietary.

As Thomas discovered, the endless horseback rides through the region brought an invaluable acquaintanceship with many enticing locations, not to mention leaving him in the ideal position to secure some of the best acreage for himself. There was no better proof that this could be done than the acquisitive success of Thomas' predecessor as agent, Robert Carter, who had served in the post for the preceding ten years.

Carter's vast estate and lordly style brought him the title of "King," for ultimately he came to own something like 300,000 acres. By comparison the best efforts of Thomas Lee were puny. He drew together a mere 30,000 acres to divide among his heirs. How Thomas Lee replaced King Carter as agent for the Proprietor is one of the more colorful stories in colonial history.

In 1710 there died in England the aged Margaret, Lady Culpeper. The event left the Northern Neck in the hands of her widowed daughter, Catherine, Lady Fairfax. Being short of cash, Catherine listened closely when told that her enormous Virginia estate should be yielding more income than Robert Carter's management was producing. It happened that Lady Fairfax's adviser was Thomas Lee's uncle, Thomas Corbin, the London merchant.

What followed is an instructive example of how extended families in colonial Virginia were themselves well-knit empires. Thomas Corbin suggested that Lady Fairfax replace Carter with Edmund Jenings (later, some family lines altered the spelling to Jennings), who happened to be another uncle of Thomas Lee. After marrying Frances Corbin, Lettice Lee's sister, Jenings had gone on to a notable career in Virginia, including service as attorney general, Council member, acting governor, and secretary. He was residing in London when Thomas Corbin brought him to Lady Fairfax's attention. She promptly named Jenings as her agent.

Being himself heavily in debt, Jenings must have seen this appointment as a heaven-sent path out of his troubles. But since he preferred for the moment to remain in England, Jenings assured Lady Fairfax that his nephew Thomas Lee would make an aggressive resident agent. This may have been particularly agreeable to Lady Fairfax, for Thomas was the son of the venerable Richard Lee, who had been the first Virginian to acknowledge the justness of the Culpeper-Fairfax demands upon Northern Neck landholders.

In December 1711, Thomas was officially designated Lady Fairfax's "true and lawful attorney," empowered to make all collections for her. At the same time, this action formally revoked the power previously given to Robert Carter, so that, as resident agent, young Thomas Lee, barely twenty-one, had to knock at the door of the great King Carter and ask for the accounts and other documents belonging to the Proprietary. Thomas proceeded carefully.

Hearing of his appointment only from his Uncle Jenings, Thomas prudently asked Lady Fairfax herself to give him authority. Without being armed with word from her, he predicted Robert Carter would be stubborn. The young man assured his employer that he would not move "until I have more particular instructions from your Ladyship."

Although King Carter finally bowed to Lady Fairfax's action, he and some of his descendants held a grudge against the Lees, deepening a family rivalry long after anyone could recall what caused it. "King" Carter and his allies considered the Lees to be pushy upstarts, a feeling going back to the heyday of Richard the Scholar, where trouble between the Lees and Carters arose over policy matters after Bacon's Rebellion. Nor had the relationship warmed when "King" Carter was named successor to Richard Lee at the time the latter retired from the Council of State.

As he awaited credentials, Thomas was not idle. He signed a land grant of 100 acres to his cousin, Charles Lee. Even after he was undoubtedly in office, Thomas was methodical in his dealings with Lady Fairfax. Among his few surviving letters are several to her in which he sought to assure Her Ladyship that she was receiving all due income.

The contract called for Lady Fairfax to be paid 425 pounds sterling annually from the rents Thomas collected. The remainder, if any, went to Thomas and Uncle Edmund.

Delay in compensating Lady Fairfax often occurred because Virginians met their debts with tobacco, which the agent then had to ship to England for conversion into cash. Here, again, blood proved thicker than water. Who, of course, was chosen to sell the tobacco for the Proprietor but Thomas' brother Richard Lee, who was a London merchant.

Thomas must have been a busy official, handling both the Fairfax agency and the naval office. Brother Henry evidently was Thomas' invaluable associate, an essential presence since Thomas was often absent traveling for the Proprietor. Between the brothers, a much-needed orderliness and efficiency came to characterize the award of land patents, ending what had been chaos under previous agents.

Leaving Henry in charge of affairs at Machodoc, Thomas explored the far reaches of the colony. From these travels, he grew fascinated by the "upcountry" above the falls of the Potomac, as well as the region beyond the Appalachian Mountains. In his view, the Potomac should become a rich trade route into these western settlements.

Bringing Henry in with him, Thomas put his money behind this vision, and the pair began buying commercial sites upriver. In time, Thomas owned 16,000 acres in that area, much of it resting between the Great and the Little Falls of the Potomac. This gave him portions of what became Fairfax County, as well as parts of nearby Loudoun and Fauquier counties, purchases possible since Thomas had a purse larger than that of most young Virginians of his social status. While many families suffered from a continuing depression in tobacco prices, Thomas was not limited to the modest agricultural revenue from lands his father bequeathed him, but drew a measure of wealth through the naval office and the Proprietary.

After Edmund Jenings returned to Virginia in 1716, Thomas officially handed the agency to him, although retaining administrative management at Machodoc until 1719, when Lady Fairfax died. Thomas was now twenty-nine, an age then reckoned the prime of life. It was time he should think about what great estate he might create. Since his inheritance had not included an impressive piece of property, Thomas eyed a site of 1,443 acres, perched twenty miles up the Potomac from Machodoc. It offered one of the most imposing presences in Virginia, since its water frontage displayed white-tinted, towering palisades, which gave the land its name, The Clifts. The place sat on an extraordinary geological formation. Only in three other locations—Los Angeles, Austria,

Belgium—can one see a similar compaction of sea matter from the Miocene era.

Perhaps because of its grandeur, The Clifts was one of the earliest locations purchased along the Potomac. In 1651, Nathaniel Pope, ancestor of George Washington, acquired it, after which it descended through Pope's widow, who returned to England, to another Nathaniel Pope. It was with him that Thomas Lee had to deal. So off to England he went in November 1716, leaving Henry to manage affairs at Machodoc. Thomas returned to claim The Clifts in August 1718, paying 375 pounds sterling, including all slaves, livestock, and other contents. Eventually, it became the site of Stratford, the Lees' most famous plantation.

Thomas had other errands abroad. The most charming of his surviving letters was one written to "Dear Harry" back at Machodoc, assuring him that Thomas' tailor would fashion clothes to Henry's order. The letter also reported to "Harry" on Thomas' meeting with Martha Silk Lee, their sister-in-law, whom he called "certainly the best woman in the world." As for her husband (and Thomas and Henry's brother) Richard, who had inherited Machodoc, Thomas reported: "I have had all the kindness from brother I could have wished." The letter also contained a touch of homesickness, Thomas confessing: "I long to see you, dear Harry." He also sent his love to brother Francis and sister Ann.

The bond between Thomas and Henry apparently was not weakened when they finally got around to marrying. In fact, Thomas' keen interest in The Clifts may have been spurred by a romance which, from what little is known about it, began before he sailed for England. The young woman was Jenny Willson of a prominent family, who had inherited, it was said, 3500 pounds sterling. Evidently Jenny and Thomas became engaged before he went abroad. Thomas' eagerness to buy The Clifts may have been stirred by thoughts of how Jenny's wealth could improve that estate.

But going to England ruined "Tom" Lee's hopes. While he was away, Jenny's mother died of the measles, obliging Thomas' fiancée to move in with her aunt, a Mrs. Roscoe. The latter's son James, who was thus Jenny's cousin, evidently was undeterred by Jenny's betrothal to Thomas Lee, nor apparently was she. Soon after Jenny agreed that James should become her guardian, the two were married. Onlookers predicted that "Poor Tom Lee will be disappointed."

Indeed he was. Virginia could boast few marriageable women with anything like Jenny's wealth, and Thomas Lee seems to have been as practical about matrimony as he was about real estate. Lees of the next generation would recall as one of the few observations by Thomas Lee to survive, his saying "that the first fall and ruin of families and estates was mostly occasioned by imprudent matches to embeggar families and to beget a race of beggars."

Thomas obviously kept this rule in mind. After losing Jenny, he delayed his search for another well-to-do mate until he had strengthened his credentials by advancing in politics. It did not suffice that he had been a justice and a colonel of militia before he reached thirty, so Thomas sought election to the House of Burgesses (today called House of Delegates) in the General Assembly, which no longer met in swampy Jamestown, but in Williamsburg, situated amidst estates belonging to the oldest and wealthiest families in Virginia.

Going to Williamsburg for the General Assembly thus brought Thomas into a more promising locale for finding a rich wife. Unfortunately for him, securing a seat in the legislature was to be as difficult as finding a proper spouse. In fact, Thomas' first political campaign bore few marks of the shrewdness which seems to have been his prime quality. In his political debut during 1720, Thomas' ambition appears to have clouded his judgment. He challenged no less than his brother-in-law, Daniel McCarty, for his seat as a burgess.

It promised to be an exercise in futility. McCarty was not only politically well-established, but he had held one of the colony's mightiest posts, Speaker of the House of Burgesses, in the previous session. Nevertheless, at the polls Thomas appeared the victor and in November went to Williamsburg to claim his seat. Meantime, McCarty had appealed to the General Assembly, charging irregularities in the election. After a legislative hearing, which divulged that Thomas' supporters included many who were not entitled to vote, Thomas was denied his seat on 8 December 1720.

Since he had seemed supremely confident, the outcome must have surprised him. During the hearings, Thomas wrote frequently and confidently to "dear Harry," assuring his brother that even McCarty's "closest friends say I have justice on my side." Thomas dispatched the trusty Harry to locate election records needed—he would find them, Thomas said, "by the window." Meanwhile, the foe "looks indeed dismally, and like what he is." It did not daunt Thomas that McCarty's appeal was being managed by "King" Carter. No matter, said Thomas: "The people are finding Colonel Carter has bossed the Northern Neck for some years and I believe has paid for it."

When Thomas was ordered to stand down from his seat, having occupied it for thirty-nine days, he had the consolation of not departing empty-handed. He received 4,905 pounds of tobacco for this abbreviated service. Apparently Thomas proved a good loser, for he and his victorious brother-in-law remained on amiable terms, and when McCarty died in 1724, Thomas was elected his successor as a burgess. He continued thus until 1733, when the death of "King" Carter created a vacancy in the Council of State, the upper house in the General Assembly. Being appointed Carter's successor as a councillor must have been sweet indeed to Thomas Lee. He could feel he had retrieved the seat that once belonged to his father and grandfather.

While Thomas' trip to Williamsburg in 1720 may have brought a temporary political reversal, it revived his marital aspirations. That autumn he was observed frequently visiting at Green Spring, the legendary estate a few miles from the capital. Once the home of that great friend of the Lee family, Governor William Berkeley, Green Spring had become the seat of one of Virginia's most powerful families, the Ludwells, themselves allies of Thomas' forebears.

After Sir William's death, his childless widow had married Philip Ludwell, who had children from a previous marriage. By 1720, Green Spring had descended to the second Philip Ludwell, whose wife Hannah represented the Harrisons, another distinguished Virginia clan. Among the children of Philip and Hannah Ludwell was a daughter, Hannah Harrison Ludwell, born in 1701. Although she was eleven years Thomas Lee's junior, Hannah was one of the colony's great heiresses. It promised to be a perfect match by Thomas' exacting standards.

Setting out to win Hannah Ludwell, Thomas spent a considerable sum to entertain the Williamsburg and Green Spring neighborhood with a fine ball in December 1720. Such a gesture must have been necessary to impress the barons along the James River, who had to be shown that a frontiersman from up in the Northern Neck could cope with polite society. In this respect, Thomas did his best to comply. Embarrassed by knowing little of Latin and Greek, according to family tradition he laboriously taught himself a smattering of these refinements.

Nothing further is known of Thomas' wooing of Hannah Ludwell. Both were past the customary age of a first marriage when they were wed at Green Spring in May 1722. The groom had reached age thirty-two, and the bride was twenty-one. She brought to the union the impressive sum of 600 pounds sterling. This was Hannah's inheritance from her grandfathers Harrison and Ludwell. According to a solemn agreement signed by Thomas, the money was to be returned to Hannah if she became a widow.

The successful union of Hannah and Thomas could be a tribute to the power of love. Evidently neither was easy to live with. Thomas was spurred by a restless drive, a relentless ambition, and a proud nature. These attributes were also found in Hannah Ludwell, which was scarcely surprising. In her blood she had acquired something of the tempestuous nature of her grandfather, the first Philip Ludwell. He had been renowned for his arrogance, for his impatience with the pompous and trivial, and for his unbridled ways. Twice he was expelled from membership on the Council for uproarious behavior.

And of course Hannah Ludwell also had Harrison blood, which, when combined with the Ludwell strain, promised exciting, even alarming genetic results. The Harrisons were as famous for strong natures as the Ludwells. Hannah's Aunt Sarah Harrison had earned a kind of fame for refusing at her wedding ceremony to promise obedience to her husband (her father pledged she would!). From this background, Thomas' bride acquired a strong personality, only slightly softened by her musical talent.

Hannah's descendants recalled her being an imperious woman preoccupied with conforming to the standards of the "high-toned aristocracy" which she wished to establish on the banks of the Potomac. The fact that Thomas Lee was not known for modesty and humility may also have fostered Hannah's prideful nature, if only for self-defense. A disgruntled contemporary called Hannah's husband "a haughtily overbearing Virginian." Later, one Lee called Hannah "shrewish."

Marriage obliged that Hannah move to a less pretentious residence at Machodoc, where she would have to put up with her husband's bachelor brother Henry. But this would not be for long. It required about a year for Henry to take heart from Thomas' example. A second bride came to Machodoc. Henry, like Thomas, went to the old settlements along the James to find a wife, possibly someone he met while attending the parties surrounding Thomas and Hannah's wedding.

Henry courted and won Mary Bland, who had recently passed her eighteenth birthday. It was another astute matrimonial choice, for Mary had descended from some of Virginia's greatest family names, including Randolph and Bennett. As with Hannah Ludwell, marriage meant that Mary Bland traded a more stylish life along the James for the rural pleasures of the Northern Neck. There Mary and Henry briefly joined Thomas and Hannah in the Scholar's rambling house. Soon, however, Henry transferred his share in the lease of Machodoc to Thomas and moved to the adjacent acreage he had received in his father's will. Here Mary and Henry built their own house, which they named Lee Hall.

Though Hannah and Thomas were often pulled apart by his increasing political duties, their separation seemed actually to strengthen a loving relationship. Near by, at Lee Hall, Mary rarely lacked the companionship of her husband. Henry remained as concerned with Westmoreland County affairs as Thomas was devoted to life beyond the

Northern Neck. Every local office was held by Henry at some point, except that of burgess, which would have taken him away from Mary and their children. It would also have meant leaving the Lee brothers' complicated interests to the care of underlings, particularly after Thomas and Hannah moved upstream around 1740.

Precisely why Hannah and Thomas Lee decided to leave Machodoc is uncertain. One reason probably came out of trouble caused when Thomas sternly fulfilled his duties as a justice of Westmoreland County. He took pains particularly to punish unruly behavior by immigrant convicts often dumped into Virginia by an English government eager to be rid of them. Had Thomas been lenient with these rootless newcomers, he might never have left Machodoc.

Rumors had abounded around the county concerning grudges held by vagrant newcomers whom Thomas had treated severely. But nothing more serious than talk came of them until late in the evening of 29 January 1729, when Thomas, Hannah, and other occupants of Machodoc were asleep. Thieves crept into the building and, after grabbing what they could of the silver and other family treasures, set fire to the place before fleeing. They also torched an office building, as well as the barns and other structures.

The old wooden house was quickly aflame, leaving barely time for all but one sleeper to escape. A young servant girl died in her bed. Thomas, Hannah, and their children leaped from upper windows into the cold night with only "their shifts and shirts on their backs," as Governor William Gooch indignantly described the event to the Lords of Trade in London. Since a pregnant Hannah had to drop from the second story, the fall caused her to miscarry. A search for the culprits began at once, but they were never caught.

The loss for the Lees was staggering, one claim estimating the cost to be at least 50,000 pounds, including 10,000 pounds in cash. Given Thomas' role as naval officer, as a commercial agent, and as a slave trader, it is conceivable that such an amount of money was on the property. Looking back, the most distressing aspect of the tragedy, aside from personal harm, surely was the burning of Richard the Scholar's library, which, as Governor Gooch pointed out, was "a very good collection of books."

Writing of Thomas and Hannah's plight, a Maryland journalist summed it up: "everthing entirely lost." The misfortune outraged and frightened most Virginians, beginning with Governor Gooch. Such an event was a form of lawlessness peculiarly threatening to the society on the Potomac where an aristocratic few lived upon the toil of a servile class, both black and white. Thus, when Thomas petitioned for compensation from the government, claiming his loss resulted from a faithful performance of judicial duty, Governor Gooch was more than sympathetic.

He used the "villainous" treatment of Lee to illustrate for authorities in London why Virginia was justifiably angered by the arrival of "pernicious" felons. As for the dutiful Thomas, according to Gooch he surely deserved 300 pounds from the royal coffers. This amount, said the governor, would help to lessen Lee's loss, "which he is not well able to bear." The money was granted accordingly.

What Thomas and Hannah thought about the disaster went unrecorded. It must have been clear to them that even with Hannah's wealth, the fire left them in no position to undertake a move. Until they could recover some of their assets, income from the customs and commercial business at Machodoc was essential. Nor could this be relied upon as before, since the revenue was faltering while another depression plagued the colony. So, having to remain at Machodoc until better days, Thomas and Hannah probably moved into Lee Hall with Henry and Mary until a replacement could be built not far from the ruins of the Scholar's house. They put up a smaller structure, again made of wood.

From this temporary headquarters, Thomas and Hannah set out in search of new fortune. It appeared almost at once, owing to the death of Thomas' enemy, Robert "King" Carter. In 1733 Thomas was given Carter's seat in the Council of State, where the profitable administrative and judicial work called members frequently and at length to Williamsburg. As a councillor, Thomas was obliged to give up being custom officer for the Potomac, but he arranged that this rewarding post was turned over to brother Henry. For such a good turn, Henry agreed to pay Thomas a cut of the revenue.

Meanwhile, Thomas' elevation left the resourceful Hannah with the business of running Machodoc. A bill of exchange survives from 1734 which is drawn to the order of Mrs. Lee. While both Hannah's and Thomas' names were recorded separately on the bill, hers was clearly the principal part in the transaction. It was a status rarely accorded a Virginia woman whose husband was alive.

As their prospects improved, either Thomas or Hannah, or perhaps both, took a long look at their surroundings. Machodoc was the ancestral family seat, but the manor house had been destroyed. Now that Thomas had a lifetime and profitable appointment as councillor, there was no longer any need to live near Machodoc. Brother Henry could handle the naval office nicely, having done most of its work all along. A sense of release led Thomas and Hannah to consider moving upstream to The Clifts, that beautiful property Thomas had purchased nearly twenty years before.

In 1734, Thomas finally took the legal steps needed to record his ownership of the Clifts. Why he had postponed doing this for so long is unknown. Later generations of Lees remembered Hannah as instigating the move. It was said that she also designed the dwelling to be built at the new location. Meanwhile, Thomas made up for lost time by enlarging the property with purchases of adjacent acreage.

Construction of a house did not begin until after 1738, and may not have been completed in Thomas' lifetime. The property and the new residence were renamed Stratford, perhaps to honor the estate in England which the first Richard Lee had established shortly before he died. No one can say for certain who designed the mansion. The best clue, however, came from Thomas and Hannah's eldest son, Philip Ludwell Lee. After inheriting the place, Phil deplored to guests that Hannah's architectural preference rather than Thomas' had been followed.

He showed visitors the conventional sketches his father had chosen for the house's design, and then Phil directed the onlooker's attention to the unique mansion actually erected, saying it was done because of his mother's demands. Wifely pressure, Phil insisted, made Thomas Lee " 'put up this very inferior dwelling now over my head.' " One look at Stratford was all that was needed, Phil claimed, to display " 'what it is to be ruled by a woman.' " While Hannah's son may or may not have spoken in earnest, the fact remains that Stratford's great house is an extraordinary building, one that might well have been the idea of a person with Hannah Ludwell Lee's vigor.

By the time Thomas and Hannah died, Stratford had grown from the original 1443 acres to approximately 4800 acres. Their heir, Philip Ludwell Lee, would enlarge the property to its zenith of nearly 6600 acres. The land had several purposes. First, there were the surroundings which supported the great house itself. The area below the house and on the river contained a mill, a landing, a warehouse, a ships' store for the receipt and dispatch of cargoes, and even a shipyard for construction. The rest of the acreage was alloted to satellite and tenant farms.

On such an estate, the term "family" indicated more than the owners and their children. It included the slaves, skilled artisans, servants, and even the tenant farmers with their own dependents. All shared in producing essentials for existence as well as commodities to be exchanged for those things which the Lees wanted but could not create. From sixty to a hundred humans were involved when the premises hummed at full operation. If at times many of Thomas' numerous slaves and servants could not be kept busy at Stratford, they were assigned to more distant properties, including Machodoc.

Weavers, carpenters, coopers, blacksmiths, shipwrights, millers, brewers, herdsmen, and shoemakers were some of the trades practised by members of the Lee community. Hard physical labor was necessary everywhere, from the gardens, vineyards, and orchards which raised foodstuffs and decorative items for residents, to the toilers in the fields, where tobacco, corn, wheat, oats, and barley were harvested. Special pleasure was brought by the fruits, including grapes, apricots, apples, pears, peaches, and cherries. In a good season, all this effort produced such a comfortable lifestyle at Stratford, and at similar Virginia estates, as to be envied by visitors from English country dwellings.

The commander over the kingdom of Stratford was most often Hannah Ludwell Lee. If Thomas did not rule at home, it may have been only that he was weary from governing elsewhere. Then, too, he may have so admired Hannah's capacity for management that he preferred to have her in charge. She lived on the plantation much more than he did, for by the time Stratford was built, Thomas' presence was increasingly needed in Williamsburg, requiring four days to reach. There he spent much of each year until his death in 1750.

In 1749, Thomas became president of the Council of State. As such he had to serve as acting governor and commander of Virginia's forces when Sir William Gooch retired to England. His formal commission as governor arrived after Thomas was dead. Brief though his service as Virginia's chief executive was, Thomas earned the commendation of Lords Halifax and Pitt for his prudence and sagacity in striving for peace with the Indians, and for seeking amity with those who dissented from the established Anglican church.

Actually, Thomas Lee's greatest attainment as a public figure had a continental scope. His early experience as agent for the Northern Neck Proprietary trained him to look beyond the Virginia tidewater and piedmont regions. Always hopeful that the Potomac River would become a commercial avenue into much of North America, Thomas tried to assure that this river, which passed before much of his property, would someday be filled with profitable traffic.

Once he had invested all his available resources in the land around the falls of the Potomac, Thomas devoted much of his private and public energy to making the frontier safe and prosperous. The first necessity, safety, required eliminating the threat of Indian uprising. The second, which would follow the first, called for encouraging settlement on both sides of the Appalachian Mountains. Consequently, Thomas sought to be a skilled negotiator with the Indians.

A monument to Thomas' diplomacy was the Treaty of Lancaster in 1744. Through it, an important agreement was reached with the Iroquois, as the Six Nations confederacy of Native Americans was called.

This was the most powerful Indian coalition on the continent. Taking along William Beverley, Thomas traveled in style as Virginia's commissioner to the Lancaster pow-wow. He made the excursion something of a family outing by including his son Philip.

The trip was hardly an ordeal for the party, particularly in Annapolis and Philadelphia, where the diplomats were treated handsomely. The women of Annapolis not only introduced their guests to ice cream but also danced them to exhaustion. Hosts in Philadelphia provided a bowl of punch "big enough to have swimmed half a dozen of young geese."

In the frontier hamlet of Lancaster, money, gifts, and much rum reinforced Thomas' eloquent addresses to the Iroquois sachems and warriors. The upshot was tribal surrender of virtually the vast Ohio basin. The treaty ceded to the white invaders portions of western Maryland and Pennsylvania, as well as the region that would eventually be known as the Northwest Territory. This achievement was so gratifying to the colonies that Benjamin Franklin printed a pamphlet containing Thomas Lee's appeals to the Indians.

All of this, however, did not leave Thomas content. In 1750 he wrote to the Privy Council in London that Virginia extended "to the South Sea to the West including California." For Thomas, this was not idle talk. The advantages to be won in the continent's huge interior were clearer to him than to most colonists. Thus, it was his leadership which created the Ohio Land Company, to which the English government in 1749 granted 500,000 acres. These embraced the vital region where the Ohio River originated.

Thomas was the Company's first president, succeeded at his death by Lawrence Washington. The Ohio Company became something of a Lee family enterprise, since among major participants were several of Thomas' and Henry's sons. Another active figure was the Lees' cousin Gawin Corbin, who was also Thomas' son-in-law. All were inspired by Thomas' assertion that in the Ohio country "more people may conveniently settle than at this time inhabit Pennsylvania, the Jerseys, and New York."

France's intentions for North America did not foresee having Lees or any other Englishmen settling west of the Appalachians. Consequently, international rivalries ruined Governor Thomas Lee's courageous plan to have the Lee family accrue wealth and power for themselves and Virginia through a land development scheme. Even in his ailing last days, Thomas kept on horseback, stubbornly inspecting Virginia's backcountry. Few figures in the colonies recognized so clearly as he what a westward course of the white man's empire would mean, but he died long before events bore out his vision of the West.

Even so, the first of the Lee partners to depart was not the hard-driving Thomas, but the gentler Henry at Lee Hall. He died in the summer of 1747. The place where Henry was interred is uncertain, but the likely spot was the family cemetery where his parents rested. This plot was in the garden next to the ruins of the house destroyed in the famous fire of 1729. Appropriately, this Lee graveyard became known as the Burnt House Field burying ground. While it eventually was crowded with the remains of Lees, only a few graves at the site can be identified today.

Henry's widow, Mary Bland Lee, lived on at Lee Hall until May 1764. Her husband's will asserted that she would have the house for life. This turned out to be longer than anyone expected, as Mary survived for seventeen years. She lived with her son Richard until her death at age sixty. Among her pleasures was to receive annually "three casks of the best cider" produced at Lee Hall, a token of Henry Lee's thoughtfulness.

Unlike her long-lived sister-in-law Mary, the mistress of Stratford, Hannah Ludwell Lee, was relatively young at her death. When Hannah died at age forty-nine on 25 January 1750, Thomas demonstrated how the family capital was not Stratford, but downriver at Machodoc. Hannah's corpse was carried to a grave in Burnt House Field. A month later, on 22 February, Thomas wrote into his will a request to "be buried between my late, dearest wife and my honoured mother." But Thomas did not stop here. He went on to direct "that the bricks on the side next my wife, may be moved, and my coffin placed as near hers as is possible, without moving it or disturbing the remains of my Mother."

On 14 November 1750, Thomas Lee died at age sixty. He had been declining for most of the year, spending some of the summer at the mineral springs in Virginia's western hills, a remedy of which many later Lees would partake copiously. Much of the business from the governor's office in Williamsburg had to be carried to Stratford for disposition, and Thomas was able to sign documents virtually to the day he died.

Thomas' body was removed downriver to Machodoc Creek and the Burnt House Field cemetery. Recently, investigation has shown that his coffin was installed exactly beside Hannah's. One assumes that another of Thomas' last wishes was also followed. In his will, he said that "having observed much indecent mirth at funerals, I desire that last piece of human vanity be omitted." Instead, he asked that only his relatives and a few friends near Machodoc stand in silent witness as he was interred. Nothing was to be said but the words of the Anglican order for the burial of the dead. However, Thomas recommended that a funeral sermon "for instruction to the living" should be preached at the parish church near Stratford.

The sermon was by no means the last word spoken about Thomas Lee. Posthumously, more was divulged for the historical record about Thomas' style and character than is contained in any manuscript from his lifetime. Only when Thomas was safely in the Burnt House Field cemetery did many of his enemies deem it prudent to show themselves.

The most interesting revelation about Thomas came from the Machodoc community, on which, even after moving to Stratford, Thomas kept an iron grip. Evidently, he considered his former neighborhood a fiefdom. When Henry Lee died, his son Richard had taken over management of Uncle Thomas' affairs. To his personal embarrassment, Richard found there was a limit to local tolerance for the often heedless and tyrannical ways of Thomas Lee.

What particularly angered the populace was that, after establishing himself at Stratford in 1740, Thomas had refused to comply with the law and resign as a vestryman in Cople Parish, of which Machodoc and Lee Hall were part. Since Stratford was located at the other end of the county, it was in a different Anglican Church parish. But there was dissent about more than Thomas' staying on as vestryman.

According to his opponents, Thomas packed the Cople Parish vestry with his relatives, who could be counted upon to do the great man's bidding. He did this because in colonial Virginia the laymen who made up the vestry were important in governing the community. Consequently, if Thomas were supported on the vestry by the votes of compliant kinsmen, he could—and did—control much of what went on in the area.

It left the inhabitants of Cople Parish fuming. After Thomas' death, they set out to clean house in the vestry. It mortified the Lee family when, in October 1754, Cople Parish worshippers officially implored the House of Burgesses to dissolve their vestry and allow them to choose a new group. Everyone knew that the petition's purpose, while not naming the late Thomas Lee, was to create a body free of his lingering influence. Informally, the legislature was assured that Thomas Lee had "caused many of his own relations to be elected who [were] actuated solely by his directions."

Quite willing to believe this, the majority of the burgesses held that the petition to elect a new vestry was deemed "reasonable." A hearing was arranged for May 1755, when the burgesses, the councillors, and the governor all lent an ear to those who recounted for the public the powerful ways of the late Thomas Lee. It was a scene which pained

Thomas' good friend Landon Carter of Sabine Hall, who was one of the Carters who chose to forget his family's feud with the Lees. Since he was a burgess at the time, Carter could record in his diary the goings-on over Thomas at the capitol. These led him to lament how the people of Cople Parish had acted from "malice and venom."

Mainly, as Carter pointed out, the intent of the petition was to let a suppressed popular animosity toward Thomas Lee spill out. So great, wrote Carter, was "the general aversion to Colonel Lee that the most trifling act perhaps of his life should extend . . . to many years after his death." As a result, said Carter, persons like Speaker John Robinson, who had long been at odds with Thomas Lee over land policy and other matters, at last had a chance to drink "very large drafts of rancour and revenge against Colonel Lee." Pondering this unhappy scene, Landon Carter called it "a good lesson for those who fancy power."

The rancor over Thomas Lee eventually subsided. Today, his grave, along with those of his wife and other relatives, is tucked away in one of the quietest spots in Virginia, the family's Burnt House Field cemetery. Richard Henry Lee and his two wives are among those buried there. Today, the place seems remote and peaceful, surrounded by a brick wall in the center of a treeless acreage near the Potomac's bank, well away from a rural highway. Often, the only stirring is that of bald eagles, the symbol of the American Republic. To the sentimental, these can be seen circling in tribute above this, the Lee family's principal burying ground.

∼4

The Squire and the Widow
1750–1795

The deaths of Thomas and Henry Lee, masters of Stratford and Lee Hall, opened a new era in the family's story. Thanks to another generation, the Lees' world would soon extend beyond Potomac plantation society and Williamsburg politics, reaching to faraway places like Philadelphia, Edinburgh, London, Paris, and even Berlin.

Four youngsters were born to Henry and Mary Bland Lee at Lee Hall. The first, John Lee, arrived in 1724, making him senior among the fourth generation of Lees along the Potomac. Next was Richard Lee, born in 1726. In 1729, Henry and Mary named a third infant Henry, whose greatest fame would be as grandfather of Robert E. Lee. In 1730, while she was yet only twenty-six, Mary Bland Lee produced her last child, a daughter Laetitia, named after her grandmother Lee.

Hannah and Thomas' first child, a son born a year after her marriage, died in infancy. The baby lived long enough to be christened Richard. Not until 1727 did Hannah have a baby that survived. Born in February and given the name of Hannah's adored parent, young Philip Ludwell Lee remained the favorite of his mother. The mother then gave her own name to the next child, Hannah Ludwell Lee, who was born in February 1729. Then, according to family lore, the mother showed little interest in the six children that followed: Thomas Ludwell (1730); Richard Henry (1733); Francis Lightfoot (1734); Alice (1736); William (1739); and Arthur (1740).

All these children were probably born at Machodoc, thereafter moving with their parents to Stratford, where Hannah Lee had both the role of parent and estate manager. Thomas left her largely to fend for herself as superintendent of offspring, servants, and slaves, a complex role that apparently strengthened her attributes of stern will and self-centeredness.

Hannah's younger sons remembered her as so preoccupied that she preferred they run with the children of plantation workers, thereby learning that life for most Americans was rough and tumble. As a matron, Hannah concentrated her regard upon Phil and Hannah, her eldest children. Of the two, Hannah became one of the memorable personalities in Virginia, sharing this role with her cousin Richard of Lee Hall. The pair provides a colorful beginning to the story of this famed fourth generation of Lees.

Although he was the second son, Richard Lee took over Lee Hall in 1747 through his father Henry Lee's will. No explanation was offered why John Lee, the oldest son, received less land and fewer slaves than Henry bequeathed to the others. John's age was twenty-three, while Richard was then twenty-one. The youngest son, Henry, was eighteen and a student at the College of William and Mary. Lettice, the only daughter, was seventeen. While John remained at Lee Hall long enough to join Richard in listing their father's possessions, he departed the Northern Neck soon thereafter to resume a career he had begun in Essex County. Soon, Henry and Lettice also went their separate ways.

Lee Hall must have been a handsome place by the time Richard inherited it, if the 1747 inventory of its contents is any guide. The house was commodious and well-furnished, situated among impressive surroundings which included magnificent walnut trees envied even by the owners of Green Spring. There may have been no better quarters in Virginia than Lee Hall to live as a "country gentleman," which was how Richard Lee styled himself. Others would describe him differently. His cousin, Francis Lightfoot Lee, tactfully described Richard as "the oddest man in the world." Nevertheless, the voters of Westmoreland County respected him. Richard represented them in the legislature from 1757 to 1793.

Most of Richard's relatives called him "the Squire," in part, perhaps, to distinguish him from his Stratford cousin, Richard Henry Lee. The two had more than a name in common, for they shared a fondness for lavish entertainment, which may have been a more substantial explanation for Richard's nickname. His zeal as a host created one of the most famous parties in Virginia's social history.

A "housefull" gathered at Lee Hall in January 1774 for what came to be known as "the Squire's anniversary feast." The crowd was invited to celebrate Lee Hall's fiftieth birthday, as well as Richard's having presided over the place for half that time. He bid his numerous guests to arrive on Monday and to remain at least until Friday. Seventy persons, an equal number of men and women, descended upon Lee Hall.

One of these was Philip Fithian, a recent Princeton graduate who was employed as tutor for Robert Carter's children at Nomini Hall, a famous plantation in the neighborhood of Lee Hall. Perhaps because Fithian was a stranger to Virginia, he found he had less stomach than most for the uproarious frolic which the Squire's "anniversary feast" soon became.

Fithian recorded in his journal how guests amused themselves in various chambers by "drinking for pleasure," by card playing, by singing " 'Liberty Songs,' " and by talking politics. When dinner was announced, the gentlemen restrained themselves, in some cases with difficulty, while the ladies partook first. Then the men made such a rush for the table that only the "nimblest" could get at the tasty items supplied by the Squire. Fithian was particularly startled by the variety of beverages available— "several sorts of wine, good lemon punch, toddy, cider, porter, etc."

At seven the dancing began, accompanied by a French horn and two violins. There were minuets, gigs, reels, marches, "and last of all, country dances." Young Fithian found the sight of the ladies particularly pleasing—they were "dressed gay and splendid, and when dancing, their silks and brocades rustled and trailed behind them!" The tutor was relieved to record that, while the wives of the two Anglican parsons were often seen on the dance floor, neither husband participated nor did they enter the gambling rooms.

Those who chose not to dance returned to gaming, drinking, and singing, amusements renewed with fresh fervor after dinner. Ten or more guests would "put their heads near together and roar," although the good-natured Fithian had to chuckle at the "unharmonious" results. Philip remained for merely part of the week's revelry. But even the hardier fell by the wayside sooner than planned. Finally, on Thursday night those with the greatest endurance gave up, being "quite wearied out." Although the Squire followed after them, imploring one and all "to stay the proposed time," the party was over. Some of the less sturdy guests managed only to reach neighboring plantations before collapsing.

Unfortunately, the reputation of Lee Hall's master was more than that of a spectacular host. Perhaps the Squire hoped his great celebration would encourage his friends to tolerate his rough edges. If so, it succeeded. Richard was no social outcast. Doors in the best houses of Westmoreland and adjacent counties were open to him. Landon Carter at Sabine Hall and Robert Carter at Nomini Hall each received him, although at the latter residence, Philip Fithian recorded with amazement an occasion when the Squire remained after dinner and led his young cousin Lancelot Lee in consuming three bottles of madeira and "two bowls of toddy!"

One of the Squire's female cousins visited Lee Hall in 1772 and came away calling the forty-six-year-old Richard a barbarian by nature. Should he ever marry, said Grace Lee, who hailed from the Maryland side of the family, "if his wife civilizes him, she deserves to be canonized." Grace did not mention one of the Squire's assets—he was famous for being a person of few words. Richard's friend Landon Carter was astonished that anyone could convey so much so briefly. Meanwhile, even those allied with the Squire by blood found it best to watch him carefully, cautioning each other to be wary of Richard's "evasive and cunning nature."

The Squire might take pride in holding his financial cards close to his vest, but his astuteness evidently was lacking when he put aside business and politics to address affairs of the heart. Until late in life he could not find a woman who would marry him. The failure was assuredly not because the Squire was an old bachelor too shy for romance. Nor could he blame his family for hindering him. Even his older brother John encouraged him from his own happy marriage to a widow. Speaking in 1750 of the "transport of joy" brought by "an affectionate spouse," John urged Richard to accept a woman's initial rebuffs "as entices of further pressing on."

It may have been good advice, but there were no happy results. By 1755 John was once more endeavoring to help the Squire. "I have sincerely your welfare at heart," the older brother insisted, as he produced a widow lady, one Mrs. Chickeston, who "I think is suited to your temper." She was "a very good, prudent, and virtuous woman." Her appeal also included a "considerable" income. John predicted that the widow would probably accept the Squire, who, his blunt relatives liked to remind him, was passing his prime.

They did not know their man. No aging widow would do for the Squire, who kept a preference for younger women. When brother John learned that Richard fancied a lassie at Green Spring, he rushed to warn him. "Drop the thought," John urged. It was not merely that the Ludwell prospect (another female to bear the name Hannah) was eleven years younger than the Squire and that her temper and the Squire's would be "no way agreeable." Rather, John feared the Squire's "labour would be in vain," since the Ludwell fortune "would be a long time a-coming, and perhaps not in your life. And besides, a person of great expectations is suited to a large purse, and not for yours or mine."

Accordingly, the Squire turned his search elsewhere, but still with no success. His campaigns were becoming something of a sensation in the Northern Neck, causing brother John to send further advice. "You know very well you have spent a great deal of precious time, money, and wore your constitution much in amours, and at last hustled [roughened] your character thereby." Take a good widow, urged John, "and give your enemies no further opportunity to laugh at your expense."

Three years later, in 1758, the Squire once more had been "discarded," this time by a woman with no property. The catastrophe was so grave that the victim turned for encouragement to his younger brother Henry, who sent him comfort in the form of fish and ducks. Henry's words must have been less solacing than the gift, for he conceded to Richard that it was humiliating to be rejected by a poor lady. "To be thus treated by my inferiors in point of fortune would give me a gorge of courtships," said Henry.

But there was a brighter side, Henry observed, reminding the Squire that had he won the impecunious young woman, he would have found "happiness can't well subsist on poverty." But what was a man to do? Taking a wife from glamorous circumstances also had its perils. Henry admitted such a woman expected "as a matter of right" to keep "maids in waiting" at her husband's expense. He urged Richard to bear in mind what a "very weighty burden on your estate" such a spouse would prove to be.

By now, the Squire's personal life may have grown so notorious as to hinder his forays toward matrimony—perhaps his habits had been a handicap all along. In 1773, when Richard was well past forty, a close friend sent a confidential report to the Squire's cousins: "He looks fresh and hearty; and is, I am afraid, as lewdly indulgent as ever, from the appearance of his waiting maids, Bab and Henny." The sight of the Squire's black concubines brought a lascivious prediction: "If ever he marries, you may depend on it (as I told him the other day), it will be with some mop-squeezer who can satiate his filthy amours in his own way."

At this point, perhaps in part because no legitimate heirs were in sight, the Squire began treating a nephew as his own son. This was the lad soon to gain fame as Light-Horse Harry Lee during the Revolution. After his graduation from Princeton and before war broke out, Harry often visited Lee Hall. The uncle took the young man about the neighborhood, where Harry made a pleasing impression. It soon was taken for granted that the dashing cavalry officer would be heir to Lee Hall and to the Squire's estate, which had come to total nearly 10,000 acres, 1,694 of which surrounded Lee Hall.

It was not to be. At the close of the Revolution, the Squire found a wife, making a match no family member might have foreseen. Beyond age sixty, Richard brought as a bride to Lee Hall a sixteen-year-old first cousin known for her beauty. Her name was Sally Poythress. She was a granddaughter and he a grandson of Richard Bland. Before the Squire died in 1795, just short of seventy, he had fathered four lawful children.

Richard Lee outlived his cousin Hannah Lee, whose own career caused nearly as much talk as Richard's doings. Hannah Lee was the sort of person about whom people tended to exclaim. They spoke of her astonishing "independence of spirit and force of character" and her "practical sagacity and success." She bore more than the name of her mother, the mighty ruler of Stratford.

Growing up at Stratford gave young Hannah a better preparation for life than many Virginia women received. Her mother exemplified power of will and aggressiveness as she managed a complicated home and plantation during the long absences of her husband Thomas. Furthermore, daughter Hannah had benefited alongside her brothers and sister from excellent tutors, so that she came away with an enthusiasm for literature which never diminished.

In the autumn of 1747, Hannah married Gawin Corbin at Stratford. The bride was eighteen and the groom twenty-three. The event illustrated what was supposed to happen in Virginia's best society, for it bound even closer two of the colony's leading families who were already allied. The nuptial pair were first cousins once removed, Gawin's father and Hannah's grandmother had been brother and sister.

As Mrs. Gawin Corbin, Hannah moved twenty miles downstream and became mistress of Peckatone, one of the most beautiful houses on the Potomac. The property had been named for an Indian chief and had been owned by the Corbin family for nearly a century. The house looked across a lovely garden to the river. With its two floors and broad porches at front and rear, Peckatone was an impressive sight, especially as it was one of the earliest brick structures thereabouts. It was a landmark, visible from the Lee family cemetery at Burnt House Field. One of Hannah's closest neighbors was the Squire at Lee Hall.

Virtually nothing survives to tell what sort of marriage Hannah and Gawin experienced in their twelve years together. Evidently Hannah quickly became pregnant, for their daughter Martha was born in the spring of 1748. There were no more children, although Hannah later bore a son and daughter by a different partner. We know that Hannah and Gawin made Peckatone a social center for that quarter of the Northern Neck, while he played his part as a country gentleman by being a county justice.

Only one personal glimpse of the couple remains. A relative who knew them well emphasized how Hannah was a constant reader who filled shelves along the wide halls of Peckatone with fine books. Gawin, on the other hand, would have nothing to do with literature. When purchases were ordered from London, it was Hannah who selected which of the latest publications should be shipped to Peckatone. Since the quick-tempered Hannah had little time for those whose interests differed from hers, overflowing bookcases at Peckatone might speak of an incompatible marriage.

At age thirty-five, Gawin Corbin died, probably in December 1759. He departed life sounding like a suspicious and unhappy husband who hoped that from the grave he could prevent Hannah's future happiness. Gawin's will remains notorious in the Northern Neck for what it did to Hannah. It installed her as one of the executors of a document which she viewed with undisguised disgust. While the will left Gawin's sizable estate to Hannah (she would have to surrender half to her daughter at the latter's majority), it stipulated that should Hannah remarry (as most young widows would soon have done) or leave Westmoreland County, she must surrender the bulk of her inheritance.

Clearly displeased with her late husband's prohibitions, Hannah proved singularly uncooperative. The chief executor, Hannah's brother Richard Henry Lee, found himself exasperated by his "dear Sister," as he tried to settle Gawin Corbin's estate. She skillfully postponed meeting the last obligations in Gawin's accounts, until, finally, her brother complained that her delaying tactics must end. It was only necessary, he told her, that she sell "one middling slave." Dealing with Hannah and the estate was, said Richard Henry, "the most troublesome business I have ever been concerned with."

Debt, it turned out, was the lesser vexation created by Gawin's will. The greater hindrance for Hannah was the cost she would face if she remarried—and the Widow Corbin was unwilling to live apart from her husband's physician, Richard Lingan Hall. He was a widower with few possessions other than his medical practice, which included the families of Richard Henry Lee and George Lee. Hall had signed as a witness when, "weak of body," Gawin Corbin made his notorious will in October 1759.

After Corbin's death, Dr. Hall was installed as a permanent resident of Peckatone, and Hannah soon became pregnant. Even so, she remained the Widow Corbin and retained her legacy. In 1761, when news of this liason reached Hannah's youngest brother Arthur, a medical student in Edinburgh University, he sent an indignant letter to Richard Henry. "Is she irrevocably lost? Angels would weep at it!" He begged his brother to try "to recall her," and not to be easily repulsed—"persevere." The family crisis made young Arthur poetic: "Sooner in me might every faculty be changed than I would cease to love her. Even now compassion steals upon me and melts me into tears for her perversion."

Actually, Arthur may have been just as appalled by another aspect of Hannah's taking Dr. Hall into Peckatone. The physician was one of the Northern Neck's early converts to the rising Baptist movement, and in time Mrs. Corbin joined the sect. The Baptists outraged most Virginians, all of whom by law were to entrust their souls to the Church of England. News of his sister's rejection of Anglicanism may have outraged the orthodox Arthur Lee as much as reports of her association with Richard Hall.

Mrs. Corbin and Dr. Hall continued living together at Peckatone without benefit of the Anglican Church's sacrament of marriage. And when a son was born in 1763, the mother formally recorded herself as Hannah Corbin, widow. The infant was named Elisha Hall Corbin. Presumably, an undisguised event of this nature would be unacceptable to such leaders of Virginia society as the Lees. And yet Hannah's relations with her family remained cordial—she was still "dear sister." Even brother Arthur wrote from England: "I cannot help offering my love to our sister Corbin. . . ."

The larger community also seemed to accept the bond between Widow Corbin and Dr. Hall. It appears unlikely that the public and the Lee family considered themselves to be condoning a sinning couple. Instead, Hannah and Richard's defiance was more likely that of living together by the sanctification of a dissenting religious sect. While there is no record to prove it, Hannah Corbin and Richard Hall most likely had a Baptist wedding.

As members of the sect, it would not trouble them that such a marriage had no legal validity in Virginia. Widow Corbin was exceedingly pious and equally stubborn, as was Dr. Hall, who had borne the abuse inflicted on the first Baptists in Virginia. Furthermore, in the case of Hannah and Richard, a Baptist-confirmed union actually brought an advantage.

It worked greatly to Hannah's benefit that hers was technically an illicit liaison. She remained the Widow Corbin and in compliance with the terms of her late husband's stringent will. In the eyes of the law, she was unmarried. Thus, having embraced both the person of Richard Hall and the Baptist faith, the Widow Corbin dextrously served God without mortifying the flesh.

While the arrangement displeased some relatives, the reason was less Hannah's association with Richard Hall than her mingling with the Baptists. Hannah's reply to these criticisms bristled with confidence. She wrote to sister Alice: "I am not surprised that you seem to have a mean opinion of the Baptist religion. I believe most people that are not of that profession are persuaded we are either Enthusiasts or Hypocrites. But my dear Sister, the followers of the Lamb have been ever esteemed so. This is our comfort!"

Hannah knew what it was to be pressed to conform. In 1764 a zealous Westmoreland County official presented her name and that of Dr. Hall to a grand jury for indictment as failing to attend Anglican services. However, such action was mostly a token and the Corbin-Hall duo paid no heed, continuing to live together and worship as usual.

Of the two, Hannah appears to have been dominant. In addition to managing her plantation and personal accounts, she looked after Dr. Hall's charges and receipts as a physician. It was not that Richard Hall was oblivious to all but his call as a healer. He tried occasionally to be aggressive, even renting land from Hannah to raise tobacco. At one time, he served as sheriff in Fauquier County, where he briefly owned some property which eventually he sold to Hannah.

Aside from winning the affection of Widow Corbin, Hall's was hardly a successful life. Many patients were dissatisfied with him as a physician. Two malcontents were members of the Lee family, one of whom died with a grudge against Hall. This was George Lee, who, at his death in November 1761, left Hannah's brother, Richard Henry Lee, as principal executor of his estate. When Dr. Hall presented a bill for attending the late George, Richard Henry's reply was blunt. He advised Hall to expect nothing. "I have this to promise—that Col. Lee imposed a dying injunction on me not to pay your account."

While he had the doctor's ear, Richard Henry had more to say. He brought up his own bill from Dr. Hall, a fee which he admitted he had put aside "because I found it in many respects extremely exorbitant. Among other things, the charge for Elixir Asthmatick with you is 7/6 [seven shillings, six pence] an ounce when I have the account of several apothecarys in Williamsburg where for that medicine the charge [was] only 7 pence an ounce." But another fee particularly irritated Richard Henry, who reminded his physician of what happened recently when Hall had accompanied Hannah to Richard Henry's residence.

During the visit, Richard Henry suffered "an Epileptic fit," prompting Dr. Hall to administer a few drops of medication Richard Henry had on hand. For doing so, Hall sent a bill in the amount of more than a pound. This was merely the most outrageous of the charges which Hannah's brother warned he could challenge. In short, Richard Henry was disappointed in Hall, who once promised "to practice on the most moderate terms." Should he revise Richard Henry's account "on reasonable terms," the patient pledged: "I will not delay to pay you one minute."

There were different complaints from England. One merchant who had waited nearly four years to be paid for money he had advanced Dr. Hall was outraged when he learned that the physician had switched his modest tobacco business to another company. Even worse, Hall sent his former agent much less than was owed, causing the latter to complain that Hannah's companion was "using me very ill." Hall had moved his account to William Molleson, whose firm also served as agent for Hannah Corbin.

This business arrangement became confusing, despite the care with which Hannah tried to keep her accounts apart from Dr. Hall's. Aware of who held the upper hand in the Corbin-Hall combine, William Molleson himself took pains to notify Hannah in 1773 that he had received a letter from Dr. Hall "which puzzles me very much." Indeed it might, for the doctor had sent instructions that all money due to Hannah's account was to be deposited in his. Hall insisted he had the "legal right" to issue such an order. Furthermore, he demanded to know every debt Mrs. Corbin might incur.

While Molleson could sympathize with this last request, for Hannah was usually heavily in arrears in paying for her many purchases from London, the merchant still considered it wise to notify her of Dr. Hall's strategy, although he could not resist using the occasion to implore Hannah to reduce her obligation to his firm. Evidently such payment remained painfully slow, nor could Hannah and the doctor agree on their finances. Finally, in some exasperation Molleson informed Richard Hall: "I should be glad to have the account with Mrs. Corbin and you settled. She says one thing and you another. I am at a loss how to act between you without giving offense."

At this point, Molleson threw up his hands. "Pray settle the matter amicably," he urged. This may not have been easy. Every glimpse of Hannah shows her to have traits of self-reliance, impatience, and wilfulness. Without qualities like these, she could hardly have endured a career at odds with society. The male population of Westmoreland County, including Dr. Hall, often was the victim of her temper as she competed in a man's world. One luckless person who condescended to Hannah was mightily rebuked, making him reply: "Your extraordinary angry letter did at first surprise me, but I impute it to your passion that has hurried you to give so dreadful a description."

The Squire at Lee Hall seemed to get on well with Widow Corbin. He saw that she received the latest political intelligence, while her letters to him were cordial and direct. In one, Hannah said: "I shall send tomorrow for the hogs you so kindly promise me. And as Adam is not engaged now, you are extremely welcome to him for whatever time you wish him." Nor did the Squire hesitate to press Mrs. Corbin for payment as he reminded her of "the pork and books I bought at Williamsburg for you."

Even so, being a family member did not guarantee protection if one stood in Hannah's way. Her son-in-law would be especially unlucky, for he represented the unhappy occasion when Hannah was compelled to surrender Peckatone after her daughter Martha (known as Patty) was married and became its new mistress, having passed her twenty-first birthday in 1769. Until then, Patty had lived under the strange arrangement at Peckatone—with her mother, Dr. Hall, and the two children born to their union. When she was free to marry, Patty was ready and her guardians agreed on a mate—George Turberville, the son of Martha Lee Turberville, first cousin of Hannah Lee Corbin. George was six years older than Patty.

For Hannah Corbin, a day of reckoning had now arrived. The nuptials meant that her late husband's estate must be divided equally between his widow and his daughter. It was a painful moment for Hannah, whose rule at Peckatone must end. As blood descendant, Patty Corbin Turberville would be mistress of Peckatone.

On 28 September 1769 the split was made, with none other than the Squire presiding. From the division, along with slaves, stock, and much realty, Hannah also emerged with a new home in Richmond County. It was called Woodberry, situated near the Rappahannock River. She took her family there, but for legal purposes retained a residence in Westmoreland County, where the division of the estate had left her other properties. These she turned over to James Pressley, an overseer.

To that point, it seemed the reallocation was reached in good humor. But the mood soon changed. Patty's husband, George Turberville, began dropping hints that his mother-in-law had been dishonest in the dealings. George believed that Hannah had walked off with real estate and slaves that should have been part of Patty's share. Since the sketchy record does not show where the truth rests, Turberville's version may be unfair to Hannah.

Although he waited until 1782 when Hannah was dead, her son-in-law then demanded the division of the Corbin property be reconsidered. The Squire, still very much alive, was obliged to give a deposition about how the slaves had been apportioned between Hannah and Patty. His version, combined with other testimony, indicated that, without putting a fine point on it, Hannah had "borrowed" some of Patty's slaves and had not returned them.

It was also divulged that when Hannah was desperate for cash to pay her taxes, she sold one of her daughter's slaves. Apparently she transgressed further by claiming the sale was only for her lifetime, a detail she failed to disclose to the purchaser, who was later understandably indignant. Other revelations made after Hannah was dead and unable to defend herself suggested that, in George Turberville's words, she had shown "no love or regard for her daughter." He also complained that "she used me so ungenteel."

As the story ran, Hannah had been "mean" with Patty as the daughter was growing up, refusing to comply with Gawin Corbin's instruction that, after his death, money be spent for his daughter's "education and maintenance." According to Turberville, Patty received only "trifling" benefits, and that Hannah had kept Patty in clothing unacceptable for public wear and not warm enough for winter. In short, according to her son-in-law, Hannah "did everything in her power" to injure Patty.

While the Widow Corbin undoubtedly drove a hard bargain and was not easily trifled with, Turberville's picture of her appears unduly harsh. Evidently he always resented having a strong person as a mother-in-law, so his accusations must be weighed against the few surviving letters Hannah wrote to the Turbervilles at Peckatone. Brimming with affection and candor, these messages seem those of a loving mother.

After being obliged to surrender Peckatone in exchange for Woodberry, Hannah's life was not easy. The folks at Peckatone heard all about troubles on Hannah's property. "Somehow, I am always engaged in the most difficult enterprises without my desiring it," Hannah once lamented. She openly wished to be rid of a tenant. "I really would give a hundred pound he was gone of the plantation, for he is a general disturber of the peace."

Beside her own problems, Hannah had to help Richard Hall in his medical practice. Enough of Hall's professional correspondence remains to show something of how an eighteenth-century physician proceeded. One distressed patient was a person of few words. He informed the doctor: "I took the Purge but never work't." Many of Hall's summonses were from planters worried over stricken slaves. Some owners were so impatient for the physician's attention to their valuable "property" that they sent their own horses to assure Hall's prompt arrival. In some urgent cases where her husband was unavailable, Hannah herself made the call.

Judging by Richard Hall's career, men of medicine did not become wealthy. In his case, at least, little was left after his death but debt. He died in the spring of 1774 while in Fauquier County, where he was supervising one of Hannah's properties. In his will he spoke of "my son

Elisha Hall Corbin, born of Mrs. Hannah Corbin" and "my daughter Martha Corbin, born of Mrs. Hannah Corbin." As his executor, the financially pinched Hannah wasted no time before pressing those patients whose accounts were in arrears. Hall's demise occurred just as the Revolutionary era imposed new economic handicaps on Virginia planters like Hannah. Now, she had Dr. Hall's debts as well as her own.

Hannah was warned that existence would become more difficult in Virginia. As the crisis between England and America deepened, her brother William, writing from London, advised her to change her style of living. Watching a collapsing market for Virginia's tobacco and other products, William used gallows humor to cheer Hannah: "With common industry you cannot want meat and raiment, tho it may be coarse." He knew his sister's stylish tastes.

The Widow Corbin had never denied herself luxuries and preferred not to begin late in life. Her accounts suggest that even in the darkest season of the Revolution she continued to live far above the level recommended by William. In 1777, packages from Europe arrived for Hannah containing Irish linen, much clothing, china, cutlery, draperies, medicines, and books. Also a great quantity of rum was delivered. Over the years, Hannah's debts were often for items such as silks, a "very good" second-hand carriage, great quantities of coffee, much kitchen equipment and foodstuffs, as well as the services of a London seamstress. Once, Hannah ordered six pair of morocco slippers ("pumps") for a daughter.

Nor did she lose her enthusiasm for reading. Her favorite London merchant was Nathaniel Young, Bookseller. Among the titles she ordered were *Rival Mother, History of a Lady of Distinction*, and *True Merit, True Happiness*. She purchased a three-volume edition of *Lady Montagne's Letters*. While many practical titles were represented, ranging from midwifery to cooking, Hannah's preference was literature. One order included *History of Miss Somerville* and *Vicar of Bray Street*, each in two volumes, as well as a copy of *The Curate of Coventry*.

Hannah also relied upon her sister Alice, now Mrs. William Shippen in Philadelphia, to shop for merchandise not available in the Northern Neck. Once, after receiving a consignment from Alice, Hannah sent a worried acknowledgment. The shipment of apparel had arrived, "but the most valuable part, the books, I never have got." Alice was asked to locate medicines for Hannah's "sickly family." Needed were camphor, spirit of lavender, salt wormwood, emetic tartar, salt petre, and a large quantity of Peruvian bark, indispensable for battling malarial fevers.

It was not upon commerce but upon religious faith that Hannah tended to dwell in letters to Alice. She asked Alice to pray "that the

Grace I daily sue for may be granted me." These sisterly supplications were evidently crucial to Hannah, who told Alice "when I consider what an unprofitable servant I have been, I am on the brink of despair and give myself up. It is a dreadful thing to have both temporal and eternal happiness to fear the loss of."

Painfully, Hannah recalled once trying to live without heavenly aid—presumably before she converted to the Baptist faith and met Dr. Hall. How she dreaded the memory of those days, a time when she had wished "to be left to myself." Said Hannah: "I have woefully experienced what a mangled situation when I desired to be in my own hands. And surely never poor mortal had so much reason to sing Free Grace as your poor sister." Had not an "exalted Redeemer" brought pardon and "mercifully snatch[ed] me from the Fire when so many thousands infinitely better by nature have been permitted to sin on till they have sunk to endless misery[?]"

When the public outcry against the Baptists became loudest in Virginia, late in the 1770s, Hannah stood fast. Meetings of the sect were violently interrupted by some who genuinely feared the rising success of the movement and by others who simply enjoyed a fight. For them, Hannah's home became a target since she made it a haven for Baptist worship. In 1778 a large congregation from around the Northern Neck assembled on Hannah's property to hear sermons by a famed but fugitive Baptist preacher. "Widow Corbin" is said to have defied and driven off armed intruders.

The one occasion Hannah chose to leave the Northern Neck was in order to visit Philadelphia in 1780. It proved an instructive excursion for the Widow. Meeting the prosperous citizens of that city reminded her of her struggle to coax some profit from the near-exhausted land in Virginia. Even so, Hannah claimed not to envy the burghers of Pennsylvania, explaining to Alice: "I am thankful that my lot is not among the high and great. I know that the rich and great are not the favorites of Heaven."

While Hannah called down blessings upon the "poor in spirit" and admired those who thought little "of worldly grandeur," she remained something of a paradox, never giving up her fight for a place in the scheme of things. Today, some historians praise the Widow Corbin as the first female in America to advocate a woman's right to vote. This acclaim is based on statements she supposedly made during 1778 to Richard Henry Lee.

Hannah's letter has never been found, but we can infer from her brother's reply that Hannah wrote not for female enfranchisement, but that widows who owned property might have a voice in choosing legislative and revenue officials. It was for this class of women, left to struggle with property in which they usually held only a temporary or life interest, that Hannah campaigned. Despite the legend about her, Hannah did not fight for larger rights or for all women.

On 17 March 1778, Richard Henry sent Hannah encouragement and enlightenment. Casual readers of this letter have contended Richard Henry agreed that women should have voting rights with men. Actually, like Hannah, he referred only to widows and unmarried females who owned property. He did not object, he assured his sister, if such women should appear at the polls. But, Richard Henry added, Hannah must remember that votes were cast aloud and before a multitude, making it (according to males) "rather out of character for women to press into those tumultuous assemblages of men where the business of choosing representatives is conducted."

What Hannah thought of her brother's tactful reply is unknown. Certainly she had surrendered none of her pugnaciousness when she penned her will in 1781. The document began with a tart announcement: Hannah wanted the world to know that she was in her "perfect senses, as I hope this writing drawn up with my own hand will testify." Facing death, Hannah indicated no wish to be buried beside either Gawin Corbin or Dr. Richard Hall. Instead, she said simply that she could be interred anywhere. It merely depended on "where my Lord shall separate my nobler part."

Hannah lived another eleven months and probably died at her Woodberry estate in Richmond County. Tradition says her remains were deposited with those of Dr. Hall at some spot near the town of Farnham. To her son and two daughters she bequeathed properties in Richmond, Westmoreland, Fauquier, and King George counties. Skeptical of her son Elisha, Hannah included a warning that if he in any way interfered with what was coming to his younger sister, who was still a minor, Elisha would forfeit his entire inheritance. As executor, the Squire was entrusted to carry out his cousin Hannah's wishes.

The Widow Corbin was fifty-seven when she died. At first, the Squire hoped her debts would amount to no more than twice the value of her estate—minus her slaves. This prediction was painfully short of the mark, for appraisers found the furniture at Hannah's Woodberry home "very indifferent" and the stock "very poor." Meanwhile, her creditors clamored for payment, leaving the Squire determined to glean more than he anticipated from an auction of Hannah's slaves, as well as from such unpromising items as a broken harpsichord, an English dictionary with its binding missing, a history of Scotland written in Italian, a treatise on venereal diseases printed in French, and "a very old blanket."

Among the appealing commodities to be auctioned were twenty-four gallons of apple brandy, 180 barrels of corn, and a complete set of the works of Alexander Pope. These items and the slaves notwithstanding, the sale produced far less than Hannah owed. How her executors met this problem is uncertain.

The two great houses where the Squire and the Widow once presided outlasted their colorful owners, but only for a time. Early in the nineteenth century, Lee Hall burned to the ground. Peckatone stood longer, but one family member who visited it was moved to lament: "Oh! it filled my heart with sadness to wander through the deserted halls of Peckatone and view the desolation that a few short years have made." The building was destroyed by fire around 1886. Then the Potomac widened, which meant that Peckatone's ruins became submerged. And so they remain.

Hannah claimed to recognize the fleeting nature of earthly treasure, so the fate of her once princely home would have been no surprise. Unfortunately, she left no opinion about what happened to Stratford, the other great house in her life. Nor did she comment concerning the careers of her Stratford brothers, who became as famous for contentiousness as the Widow Corbin had been. Indeed, these brothers emerged from home in a feisty mood.

5

"Dear Brother . . ." 1750–1774

Both the Squire and the Widow had sought a cordial relationship with their kinfolk at Stratford, whose occupants tried to reciprocate in the spirit of a letter which the eldest among them, Philip Ludwell Lee, wrote to the Squire: "When one person was tied by blood to another, as I am to you, nothing shall be wanting on my part to make us enjoy a constant and harmonious friendship."

Though his nature was very different from those of the Squire and the Widow, Phil Lee, whom his relatives always called Colonel Phil, was an extraordinary personality in his own right. While the Squire was described as a "rough diamond," Colonel Phil earned the characterization once applied to his parents, being considered haughty, condescending, and even rude to persons of lesser station.

Much of Phil's early life was spent being educated in England, a process that included Eton. At some point, he returned to Virginia, tried being a planter, but apparently so enjoyed the cultural riches of London that he went back for what he must have expected would be an extended stay. Phil was studying law at the Inner Temple when his father died in 1750, an event which summoned the son to Stratford and the role of executor of Thomas Lee's estate. Even so, Phil always thereafter called England "home."

A description of Phil survives from 1752, soon after he had returned from England to take up his patrimony. It pictures him as a young snob determined to have his way among the common folk of Williamsburg. The account was written by Daniel Fisher, a merchant new to Virginia, who had reason to be angry with Lee, and thus may not have been entirely fair with the young man, who at the time was seeking a place to stay in Williamsburg.

Coveting Fisher's accommodations, Colonel Phil evidently was very demanding in urging that the merchant break his lease and turn the place over to Lee. Refusing to do so, Fisher not only castigated Phil's "arrogant, hauty carriage," but used him to generalize about Virginians of the Lee class. They "are utterly void of all sensations unconnected with their mean pleasures, interests, or revenge." In 1757, after Phil was appointed to the Council of State and was given the distinction of "honourable," Fisher still growled: "I hope never to have any more to do with him."

After inheriting Stratford, Colonel Phil took the place to its zenith in beauty and prosperity. It was he who made the plantation more than highly successful. He turned the great house into a center for music and lively conversation, a development aided by a judicious marriage. Phil eventually came to realize a great Virginia house required a hostess, as even the Squire testified through his energetic, if bumbling, search for a lady to install at Lee Hall.

Near Stratford was another fine residence, Homony Hall, the property of James Steptoe. With his second wife, Elizabeth Eskridge Aylett, Steptoe had a daughter Elizabeth who became heiress to the estate at the death of her father. In his will, Steptoe had named his neighbor and friend, the master of Stratford, as her guardian. Phil promptly married his ward in 1763. He was thirty-six when he gave up being a bachelor.

Thanks to Elizabeth Steptoe's arrival as mistress of Stratford, Phil became a genial host who delighted in entertaining neighbors and strangers. As a kinsman later asserted: "[Stratford] was a very grand place in Col. Phil's time." While he seems never to have rivaled the Squire's famous party at Lee Hall, Phil's relatives heard about a particularly "jovial" two-day entertainment Colonel and Mrs. Philip Ludwell Lee gave at Stratford in 1773. Most of their worthy neighbors attended.

The memorable feature of Phil's hospitality was its music. His musicians seemed to be everywhere. In the summer, they performed on the roof, perched on flooring laid between the clusters of chimneys. While most Virginia hosts announced dinner by ringing a bell, guests knew it was mealtime at Stratford when the musicians began a melody in the great hall. And when Phil went visiting, he took along a troupe of horn players drawn from the musicians retained at Stratford.

These trumpeters were seated atop the lumbering Stratford coach, making triumphal noises to announce Phil's arrival. He badgered contacts in London for sheet music his musicians could use. Once, he set out to locate the complete works for harpsichord by Tartini and by Scarlatti. These were especially needed when Phil and Elizabeth's daughters

Matilda and Flora began learning to sing and play. Their instructor was a resident music master named Leonard.

Phil did not neglect Stratford's place as an agricultural, milling, mercantile, and nautical center. He even assembled a fine group of horses for racing and breeding. In 1766, he acquired Dotterell, said at the time to be the second fastest horse in England. Amazingly, he did all this as the Virginia economy grew increasingly depressed. Prices dropped, while costs and debts mounted. These were circumstances which toughened the outlook of an already tight-fisted and rigorously business-like Colonel Phil.

There was another reason why Colonel Phil may have been diligent in advancing Stratford's well-being. In mid-eighteenth-century Virginia, the colony buzzed with gossip about elder sons of other families whose behavior was a sad contrast to Phil's. Some citizens spoke of an alarming degradation of the colony's rising generation. The talk claimed William Byrd III was squandering everything within his reach, falling 100,000 pounds in debt. Another subject was Landon Carter's eldest son, Robert Wormeley Carter, known as "Wild Bob" because of stories about his gambling and other dissipation. Armistead Lightfoot was said to have drunk himself to death, and Robert Burwell's career was allegedly brought down by alcohol and gaming.

How much these stories affected Phil is unclear. What is certain is that he became unpopular among the rest of his family—his brothers Thomas, Richard Henry, Francis Lightfoot, William, and Arthur, and his sister Alice shared a camaraderie wrought by mutual chagrin at what they considered to be the snail's pace at which Phil served as their parent's executor. This unhappiness prevailed among the Lees until Phil's untimely death in 1775.

Phil's brother Thomas Ludwell Lee was the other executor, but Tom had not returned to Virginia to help with the assignment, choosing to remain in London and complete his legal studies at the Inner Temple. Since this took five years, it meant that Tom, the brother most capable of giving Phil good advice, was unavailable when the older brother reappeared alone at Stratford to face the challenge there.

Among his burdens was Phil's responsibility to be both father and mother to the four young Lees still living at Stratford. These were youngsters Phil hardly knew, since he had been abroad most of the time they were growing up. The eldest was Frank, who was sixteen. Next to him was Alice, age fourteen. Then came William at eleven and, finally, Arthur at ten. As guardian, Phil could rely upon the help of the children's tutor, a clergyman from Scotland named Craig, about whom virtually nothing is known, not even his first name.

Mainly, Phil's task as guardian appeared simple. He was to carry out the terms of his father's will. Thomas Lee's final testament may have been lengthy and complicated, but it made clear that the eldest son, Philip himself, was to receive the bulk of the estate, upwards of 12,000 acres, which included the 4800 at Stratford. Besides all the land in Westmoreland County, Phil inherited everything his father owned in Northumberland County, as well as much of that in Stafford County. He also received acreage on Maryland's Eastern Shore as well as two islands. In addition, there was a large tract of land along the falls of the Potomac. With this legacy came an army of slaves, well over one hundred of whom toiled at Stratford, not to mention the many blacks who were assigned elsewhere.

In their turn, the next three sons were to own the comparatively modest balance of their father's realty, all located upriver from Stratford. To Tom went some of the Stafford County land, along with fifty slaves and his father's gold watch and seal. Richard Henry became owner of land in Prince William County, where there were forty slaves. Frank was given land in the part of Fairfax County that soon became Loudoun County. He received thirty slaves.

William and Arthur, the youngest sons, were each to be given 1000 pounds sterling at age twenty-one, along with the yearly proceeds paid by the Squire from his income as naval officer. The two brothers were also promised training in a trade or profession so, as their father put it, "they may learn to get their living honestly." In one regard, William and Arthur were treated like their elder three brothers, being awarded 200 pounds each to be used in building houses for themselves.

Alice Lee, the only child Thomas actually mentioned by name in his will, was also to receive 1000 pounds when she married or arrived at age twenty-one. Until then, Thomas decreed she would be given board and an education "out of my estate." Impatient with conditions at Stratford, in 1760 Alice sold her prospective legacy to brother William and emigrated to England.

Thomas Lee stated in his will that he had taken the greatest care in dividing his earthly goods among his children. "I hope I have expressed [this] so plainly that a lawyer will not find room to make constructions prejudicial to my family." Alas for these good intentions—they were undone by Thomas' stipulation that the legacies not be distributed until all debts were paid.

As chief executor, Colonel Phil took this admonition literally, to the disgust of the others. In March 1754 the brothers and Alice brought suit in chancery to compel Phil to show cause why the estate was not being settled promptly. Also at that time, Frank, Alice, William, and Arthur, all still minors, successfully petitioned to escape the guardianship of Colonel Phil. They asked that their cousin Henry Lee, the Squire's younger brother, replace him.

Although the chancery suit continued until 1764 when the court finally dismissed it, before then Phil went so far as to allocate the realty due his brothers, thereby allowing probate proceedings to be completed in 1758. But the legacies of money and other effects went unfulfilled. Phil defended this policy by pointing to the many lingering claims made by businessmen and others against the estate. These, Phil insisted, must first be settled. Since this did not occur during the brothers' lifetime, they were never quite reconciled with Colonel Phil. Not even the other executor, the astute Thomas Ludwell Lee, could relieve the family's unhappiness.

After finishing his legal education in London, Tom returned to Virginia around 1756. His presence may have prompted Phil finally to turn over the legacies in realty coming to his brothers. Tom promptly removed to his farm in Stafford County. There he became a leader in Virginia politics and eventually joined in the struggle for colonial rights. Since Tom preferred no larger sphere than his county and state, his contribution has fallen into obscurity, even though John Adams reported hearing that Thomas Ludwell Lee was "the most popular man in Virginia, and the delight of the eyes of every Virginian."

Like Tom, Richard Henry had been studying in England when their father died. Since age twelve, he had been enrolled at Wakefield Academy in Yorkshire. At news of his parent's death, Richard Henry did not hasten back to Virginia, but went to the Continent. He probably reappeared at Stratford in 1753 when he was twenty.

Being a frail person physically, Richard Henry then devoted the next five years to reflection and to reading in Stratford's library. In 1757, he joined brother Tom in marrying sisters. These were Anne and Mary Aylett, the step-daughters of Colonel James Steptoe, owner of Homony Hall, the plantation near Stratford. It was the Aylett women's half-sister, Elizabeth Steptoe, who married Colonel Phil.

Unlike Tom, Richard Henry chose not to take his bride upriver to the property he had inherited. Instead, he and Anne remained in Westmoreland County, probably for mixed reasons. Colonel Phil had consented to lease Richard Henry a handsome riverfront portion of the Stratford estate. It came with a stunning view of the Potomac. There, around 1760, the younger brother and his bride built their home and called it Chantilly. While it was named after a chateau near Paris, its style was more utilitarian than handsome, made of wood with two stories.

But it was neither the vista nor a wish to keep Colonel Phil company that held Richard Henry near Stratford. His own inherited plantation, in what was still remote Prince William County, had nothing of sophisticated society as found in Westmoreland County. Richard Henry's tastes ran more to books and politics than to managing an isolated farm. Also, he had come across a timely bit of good luck. A few months after his marriage, his kinsman Augustine Washington decided against seeking re-election to the House of Burgesses, giving Richard Henry a chance to win the seat. His success made removal to Prince William County out of the question.

On the other hand, Francis Lightfoot Lee, Richard Henry's next younger brother, showed that exile to the frontier did not necessarily mean estrangement from politics and society. Frank's inheritance was even more distant from established life in Virginia. He was a bachelor when he went up to the newly created Loudoun County, located on the Potomac above where the city of Washington would be established. While remote, the county had seats in the House of Burgesses and Frank was quickly elected to one.

The family gave Frank Lee the nickname of Loudoun or Colonel Loudoun. It was good-natured teasing, which the genial Frank accepted, knowing that while he might live afar, he was free from Colonel Phil's dominance. For a dozen years, Frank remained single on his lonely plantation, an isolation relieved by trips to Williamsburg and visits in Westmoreland County. When Frank did marry in 1769, he chose a distant cousin from near Stratford. This was Rebecca Plater Tayloe, whose family seat was Mount Airy in Richmond County. At seventeen, she was half Frank's age.

Becky Tayloe's father, the wealthy Colonel John Tayloe, could not endure the thought of banishing his daughter to Loudoun County. So he made the pair an irresistible gift, a thousand acres of his own estate. It entailed that the bride and groom agree to reside near Mount Airy. They accepted and called their place Menokin, an Indian word for the surrounding creeks and hillocks. Their house was of Palladian design, its thick walls made of brown sandstone which were stuccoed with white lime mortar. With it, Frank became part of the Tayloe family circle. Yet he and Becky were not far from Chantilly and Stratford.

William Lee, the brother next in line after Frank, had inherited no land. He did get some attention from Colonel Phil, who decided to capitalize on William's talent for numbers and business by bringing him into Stratford's office to learn to be a merchant.

Among the brothers, this left Arthur Lee as Phil's main problem. Arthur was the baby of the family and seemed the most precocious of the siblings. Evidently Richard Henry valued Arthur's talents and helped persuade Phil that the youngster deserved a better education than Virginia afforded. So, painful though the prospective expenses were, Phil agreed in 1754 that Arthur should study in England at Eton, Phil's own school. Arthur was to aim for a career in medicine. (He became an M.D. but shrank from practice.)

Late that year, the lad left Virginia, carrying letters of introduction Phil had written to a prominent London family, Mr. and Mrs. James Russell, into whose care he consigned Arthur. Ann Russell was a cousin, being the daughter of Uncle Philip Lee who had settled in Maryland.

Phil wrote in detail to the Russells and also to officials at Eton about Arthur's well-being. In fact, he left little to the judgment of these English custodians. James and Ann were even told who should provide Arthur's medical attention. Further, "I desire my brother may have a suit of plain cloth clothes made as soon as he gets to you of such as is fit for a boy of his age [14] and other things for his dress proper to wear with it." There should be a suit for winter and one for summer, no more. "He will have occasion for little or no pocket money as he is to get his living by his head."

Repeatedly, Phil stressed Arthur's modest expectations, the older brother pointing out that the boy "has not an estate to support him as a gentleman without a profession. So the more he minds his studies, the less time he will have to spend money." Phil begged cousin Ann not to send Arthur additional money "out of kindness" for such would really be "of great disservice to him."

When Arthur reached Eton, he brought another round of directions from his guardian. Writing to a faculty member and distant relative, the Rev. Thomas Dampier, Colonel Phil gave the hardly needed admonition that since Arthur had been brought up in the Church of England, "I would have him strictly and regularly adhere to it."

Once his soul was assured, Arthur was to "learn everything that is taught at the school. I intend him to be a physician which is what he now chooses." However, after the school had gotten to know Arthur, Colonel Phil suggested to Dampier that "I shall be greatly obliged to you to inform me what profession you shall think him fittest for." As to the matter of money, no more than the basic tuition of sixty pounds was to be lavished upon Arthur. Further, "I hope you will let him have as little pocket money as ever any boy had at your school and rather less."

Finally, Phil wrote to the young student himself. "I desire you will take care and behave yourself soberly, virtuously, and religiously." Arthur was sternly ordered to obey the Russells and the Reverend Mr. Dampier. If he had any leisure hours, the young brother had Phil's permission to learn "such necessary and innocent accomplishments" as "musick, dancing, and fencing." Since these were not available at Eton, Arthur was told he must pay for them out of his pocket money, which Colonel Phil took pains to stress was Arthur's purely from the kindness of the older brother's heart.

Arthur's guardian did not overlook his own interest while superintending Arthur's. Phil carefully explained Arthur's status to the influential mercantile firm of John Hanbury, the company that had a large claim against Thomas Lee's estate. Thus, Phil thought it well to explain why Arthur was being placed with Russell, Hanbury's competitor. It was because "his lady is a near relative of mine. If I was to send him to anybody else, Mrs. Russell (who is daughter to our father's brother) would take it amiss." Had it been otherwise, Phil carefully assured Hanbury, Arthur "would have come to you."

While Phil continued to curry favor in London, hoping to enhance both his purse and his political career, Arthur spent the next four years at Eton. There is no record of how he fared. By the time he returned to Stratford around 1759, he saw how his brothers had scattered to their marriages and properties.

Though often separated by distance, the brothers remained knitted by affection. The salutation beginning all letters exchanged among them was "Dear Brother . . . ," and it genuinely bespoke the love and respect these five men felt toward each other. They were also linked by impatience with Phil's continued balking at paying the monetary bequests, an intransigence particularly hard on William and Arthur. While the brothers pressed Phil, he stuck to his defense: he must postpone closing the estate until suits against it were concluded and money owed to or by Stratford had been collected or paid.

Despite Phil's cultivation of the English merchant, John Hanbury, the latter persisted in suing the Lee estate and won the case in May 1770 before the General Court in Virginia. Colonel Phil was ordered to pay 600 pounds sterling at once. Resisting, Phil bought time—and further trouble with his brothers—by appealing to the Privy Council in London which sustained the Virginia judgment in 1772. Even so, Phil prolonged the controversy and it was not finally disposed of until after his death in 1775.

More dismaying to the family was Phil's tendency to take refuge in issues much simpler than the Hanbury litigation. There was the time, for example, when Phil admitted a debtor who owed Stratford 3000 pounds had surrendered his property in payment. Unfortunately for Arthur and William, Phil deemed it imprudent at the moment to sell the land, so he rented it for three years. After that, he predicted it might be sold and the money used to begin paying the younger brothers' bequests.

Phil claimed it was not he, but the poor loans and unwise investments made by Thomas Lee that kept legacies from being fulfilled. "My best endeavors were not wanting. I have done all I can." None of this convinced William and Arthur, who departed Stratford in 1769 to settle in England, the former as a fledgling merchant and the latter as a law student. From that distance, they kept clamoring for their bequests, on which interest had accumulated to a considerable sum. The latter Colonel Phil consented occasionally to pay.

At times the comical side of the impasse struck even Arthur, a refreshing change in one who regularly announced the world was persecuting him. With a chuckle, Arthur summarized for Richard Henry a message received from Colonel Phil in 1769—"a long and serious Jobation [a reference to the style of Job in the Bible] for being so ungrateful as to squeeze anything from him."

Phil preferred to rebuke Arthur for having left Stratford, where he could have roomed indefinitely for nothing, arguing that Arthur's move to costly London was foolish. "I cannot forbear laughing at the extravagance of his conceptions," Arthur conceded to Richard Henry, adding "but it is laughing too much at my own expense." Arthur admitted he was rankled when, as he put it, Phil "prays God to forgive me for making so unjust a demand upon him and to turn my heart."

Arthur's cheerful moments were rare. He was more comfortable fulminating against Phil's "ill faith." Typically, Arthur growled: "Good God, what trouble does not the having been born to a fortune give me—how much has the reverse fatigued the possessor of Stratford." There was loud assent from the brothers in Virginia. The usually mild Frank Lee advised Arthur and William to bring a new suit against Phil to force payment of their patrimony.

The step made William hesitate, for his situation was quite different from Arthur's. While William tended to be the more impatient of the two, as a new London merchant he hoped for Phil's tobacco business as well as that of Phil's friends among Northern Neck planters. Consequently, William sought to be tactful, while Phil tirelessly used every advantage he had over the young merchant.

Colonel Phil knew that in beginning a London business, William needed good references in Virginia. Counting on this, Phil tried to pressure William into helping secure a favorable settlement of the Hanbury suit, "it being against our Father's estate," Colonel Phil reminded him. The implication was clear, William's eventual payment depended on what he might be able to do in influencing the Privy Council to find in Stratford's favor.

This suggestion was the last straw for William. Late in 1770 he agreed with Frank and Richard Henry that only the courts could induce payment of his inheritance. "As to Col. Phil, I give him up and shall certainly order suit to be commenced immediately against him." William asked that Richard Henry undertake a delicate mission to Stratford and inform Phil of the decision to sue. Also, Phil should be notified "that he must apply to someone else to take care of his appeal against Hanbury." It was a move brother Frank applauded. "The behavior of Col. Phil gives me a good deal of concern. I really fear he has lost sight of all good principles."

Momentarily forgetting his self-control upon learning William intended suing (which never occurred), Phil called his younger brother "impertinent." He informed William: "I value your threats as little as I do yourself. Such a step would bring all out and would do for you forever." Phil warned that he would no longer speak well of William as a merchant, adding: "You would never hear from me again."

The faster Phil's pen raced across the pages of this indignant letter, the angrier he became. "You say I am living in affluence and on your industry, and you by the sweat of your brow." Scoffing at this, Phil taunted the younger brother for resorting to intimidation. "I wonder, when you know my temper so well, that I may easily be led, but will not drive, that you should threaten so much as you do." Did William not realize that only "my great brotherly love" had kept the former's business in Virginia from failing?

In the eyes of Arthur and William, the most devastating witness against Colonel Phil was Phil himself. He was involved in other misdealings which the younger brothers saw as proof of malfeasance. Was Phil not once rebuked by the Westmoreland County Court, of which he himself was a member, for holding an indentured servant past the contracted time? Was it not Phil's practice to say in one part of a letter how broke he was, and then blithely go on to ask help in locating servants or luxuries for Stratford? These latter requests kept William and Arthur mindful of the glamorous style of living practiced by Colonel Phil.

At times, the exchange between William and Phil became hilarious. Phil would request that William purchase for him "the latest minuets, songs, and country dances, both music notes and words of each." Then, if space in the shipment allowed, William was told to include magazines and newspapers. Phil hinted that he knew Frank and Richard Henry each received the latest London reading material by the "basketfulls" from William, and at no cost. William mischievously obliged Phil by enclosing a bill for the periodicals he sent with the next shipment. An outraged Phil replied: "Don't send me any [magazines], for I only wanted those you had read for yourself, when you had done with them."

Not only did Colonel Phil use money to enhance the social and cultural life at Stratford, but his brothers knew he was spending heavily to improve the house, its outbuildings, and the land. Here was another reason he cited to justify delay in paying the legacies. Phil was convinced that every child of Thomas and Hannah Lee would approve the dutiful care of the family mansion. "As you know, the repairs of my great house are large every year," Phil regularly reminded William.

Toward that end, Phil asked William to locate a good carpenter who would emigrate to Virginia and accept the modest wage Phil lamented was all he could afford at Stratford. When William insisted that competent help was difficult to recruit for Westmoreland County, Phil snorted in disbelief. Shiploads of eager workers were arriving in Virginia "every day, which makes it strange that you should say I could not get [even] a clerk." Perhaps to teach the master of Stratford a lesson, late in 1773 William located a person represented to be a carpenter. The result pained Phil. "The servant you sent me for a joiner has no trade at all. Says he was a sailor." To make matters worse, "he is an immense eater."

Why were only servants of good quality selected for Richard Henry, Phil pointedly asked. "Brother R.H. has an excellent ship joiner and gardener from you. For all of this I thank you." The injudicious Phil made a bad situation worse by telling William that the non-carpenter sent to Stratford was simply more proof that William was a poor businessman. Phil was always ready to scold and advise a younger brother, tactics he must have known would anger the sensitive William. "When I was in London and got a servant for a friend," Phil reminisced, "I always had him try'd by my tradesman that there might not be an imposition."

Perhaps most exasperating to his brothers was Phil's readiness to spend large sums in England with the hope of bribing his way into high office. He was particularly interested in becoming chief secretary of Virginia, a profitable appointment coming from those who had the ear of the King. Phil began his campaign in 1770, while the aged incumbent, William Adair, was still living.

At this moment, said Phil, "it may be got cheap," and he commissioned William to rummage about London to see how large a bribe would be needed. "Whatever money is necessary, if they don't ask more than I like, I will get to pay on your letting me know the sum." Then, as if remembering his excuses for not providing Arthur and William's inheritance, Colonel Phil pointed out that if the brothers helped him land this office, with its emoluments, "I shall then be able to assist you all beyond your wishes."

And if the Secretary's post was out of reach, William was to investigate at the "Lords of the Treasury" office what it would cost to make Phil the comptroller for the district including Westmoreland. It would be especially advantageous, Phil asserted, for then the captains of merchant vessels would have to come to Stratford, sparing him "the risk, trouble, and expense of boarding them in a boat." Phil anticipated that the sum of 150 pounds sterling ought to buy the post. William, by the way, felt obliged to agree such tactics were needed. "Venality is so predominant that no place can be obtained without purchase."

Within the family, William appears the one who eventually came closest to understanding Phil. The erratic, stubborn, and self-seeking character of the eldest brother was, in William's view, quite simply attributable to self-delusion. In 1774, William sent a gentle reproof to brother Frank. He must never take Phil at his word. This was said after Frank had accepted Phil's claim that he was authorized by William to name a local agent for the latter's business, which was untrue. Surely, William chided Frank, by now "you must know him [Phil] well enough." The record was clear. "Whatever he has settled in his own crazy head, he gives out to the world as being absolutely fixed."

William's succinct words form a reasonable definition of Philip Ludwell Lee's character. But the other "dear brothers" are less easily understood, and remain as baffling personalities even today. Although all five were among the leading figures of the American Revolution, there is no wholly satisfactory biography of any of them. And within this quintet, surely the most bewildering individual was their leader, Richard Henry Lee.

⌇6

Politics in Virginia 1758–1774

While he could be as self-centered as Colonel Phil, Richard Henry's nature was far more complex. Even his imposing presence was misleading, for he was actually frail. He suffered from epilepsy and he sometimes drank to excess. The fingers from his left hand were missing, blown off when a gun exploded during a mishap while hunting swans in 1767. He kept the deformity covered with black silk, leaving only the thumb exposed. Such delicacy, however, did not preclude Richard Henry's being a fierce hater. A brutal political foe, yet he was just as strenuously affectionate and loyal toward his friends.

Particularly, Richard Henry was devoted to his brothers, who often called him R.H. They appeared willing to follow his every command—of which he uttered many, usually beginning: "You will. . . ." Because of animosity in the family toward Colonel Phil and because of the comradeship Richard Henry offered his brothers, his residence at Chantilly replaced Stratford as capital for the Lee family. Chantilly became the brothers' rallying point. Even so, a walk of three miles was all that separated the two dwellings, and relations between Stratford and Chantilly were never broken.

Unfortunately, Chantilly was often an unhappy place. Personal difficulties dogged its occupants. In 1769, Richard Henry confided to Arthur: "I have been so covered with affliction this past winter that I have thought but little of any thing except my own unhappiness." He begged forgiveness for his behavior: "Continue my dear brother to love me, and to believe that I am and ever shall be your most affectionate brother."

As a physician, Arthur Lee worried about Richard Henry, particularly when the latter suffered attacks of epilepsy, "this subtle and strong enemy of life," which was so "terrible." Admitting the cause of epilepsy was mysterious, Arthur offered opinions hardly reassuring to R.H. According to Arthur, epilepsy could be the result of immoderate exercise, drunkenness, a diseased brain, an over-active mind, or even from "too frequent enjoyment of women."

Richard Henry was also accident-prone. He had numerous mishaps, especially while riding and hunting, of which the maiming of his left hand was only the most severe result. Here again, brother Arthur was ready to advise. He pointed out how carelessness seemed to cause R.H.'s accidents, citing particularly the occasion when Richard Henry went hunting accompanied only by slaves. He had been incapacitated by a fall, leaving him, according to the horrified Arthur, "at the mercy [of] the dastardly temper of the Negroes."

Highly strung, quick to take offense, and anxious by nature, Richard Henry seemed always worried, often upsetting his digestion. He fretted about many topics, ranging from his health, the morals of his sons, his constant need for money, and ultimately to Britain's treatment of the colonies. With so much to irritate him, it was no wonder that one of R.H.'s favorite medications was the expensive Harlem Oil. Thirty drops taken on a lump of sugar was an "infallible" treatment for "the flatulant colick."

Often, of course, Richard Henry's mental and physical distress was justified. In December 1768 he reported being utterly "worn out" from anxiety and fatigue as he watched pneumonia threaten his spouse. His "good little wife" Anne died four days later, on 12 December. She was thirty years old and left two sons and two daughters. Frank Lee stood by Anne's death-bed and soon described what took place to brother William.

"I sustained the most affecting scene of a most tender hearted husband parting forever from a loving and beloved wife." Frank went on to marvel how "nature has most kindly ordered that the most violent passions . . . smooth themselves." Already R.H. "talks of another wife." In the early summer of 1769, Richard Henry married a "pretty little widow." Anne Gaskins Pinckard was noted more for her charming person than for any wealth. Even so, the brothers approved the match. Arthur Lee begged the new husband to allow his bride to make him happy. "I most ardently pray that her goodness may prevent you . . . from feeling the loss of the tender and amicable wife and mother that is gone."

The comfort of the second Mrs. Richard Henry Lee proved considerable, but it meant new problems. Anne began producing babies at an alarming rate, further imperiling their father's purse. "Five children already, another far advanced in the stocks, with a teeming little wife are circumstances sufficiently alarming," grumbled Richard Henry. There would be nine youngsters from his two wives.

Affairs at home readily put R.H. in poor spirits. Why should he expect any good luck, he complained, "Having never hitherto been favored by fortune, I incline to doubt her future benevolence." Actually, it was as much his luxurious manner of living as it was a numerous progeny that kept Richard Henry always looking for money. His income derived mostly from the "up country" land and slaves left him by his father. But the tenants and managers in Prince William County rarely sent enough, and the difference could not be made up from the poor land around Chantilly leased from Colonel Phil.

Financial necessity often led—and sometimes misled—R.H. Lee to conclude that his remedy rested in a lucrative political office. By 1772 he had completed fourteen years in public life, most of the time as a legislative leader. While he had become a person to be reckoned with, his labors brought few of the monetary rewards that came to those who held such posts as speaker, treasurer, auditor, or councillor. Even a county clerkship had more significant rewards than being a burgess.

Mainly, the barrier between Richard Henry and financial ease was the wide dislike for him, so that enemies usually blocked any lucrative appointment. It was certainly not that R.H. lacked talent in dealing with people. He was a brilliant debater, a hard worker, and he could be charming when he tried. In approaching others, he said, one must use "a little well applied flattery." "Ply them up," was another favorite expression. "Take much pains" with those whose support you require, Richard Henry advised William. If need be, one must even show "contrition."

R.H. often disregarded his own advice. By nature aggressive, he was frequently influenced by anger and envy. These emotions tended to shape his relations with a powerful political bloc in Virginia, many of whose members had been enemies of his father. Richard Henry considered them oligarchs from the James River region who selfishly controlled the colony. As it happened, all of them seemed to have far more wealth than came R.H.'s way. Against this group, Richard Henry mustered an alliance.

This tactic was apparent the moment he first entered the House of Burgesses in 1758. When R.H. arrived he brought with him more than the name of a famous family. It seemed he had the entire Lee clan in tow. He had rounded up a team of relatives, whose members looked to him for guidance. In the election which chose Richard Henry for the legislature, Westmoreland County voters also elected the Squire from Lee Hall as their other representative. Meantime, the Squire's brother Henry Lee of Leesylvania was named burgess from Prince William County.

A trio of Lees alone would have been impressive as newcomers, but two of R.H.'s brothers also took their seats for the first time that same autumn: Frank from Loudoun County, and Tom from Stafford County. This marshalling of relatives was more than coincidence. Only careful planning could have brought all of them election simultaneously. Three years later, Cousin John Lee from Essex County took a seat. It was a heady display of Lee family power, which also included Colonel Phil's place on the Council of State.

Obviously, more was on Richard Henry's mind than the satisfaction of electing so many relatives. He wasted no time after reaching the capital in demonstrating his purpose, that of avenging the family's honor. His target was John Robinson, the long-time Speaker of the House of Burgesses and head of the colony's old guard. The Lees knew that Robinson had led in 1755 when the legislature besmirched the name of Thomas Lee by endorsing claims that the late Lee had abused his power in Cople Parish administration.

Robinson's machinations against the Lees were hardly a surprise. He had close connections with the family of Robert "King" Carter, Thomas Lee's enemy. Carter's death had put Robinson in charge of a faction that bore no friendship for the Lees. The animosity stemmed in part from disputes over exploiting the continent beyond the mountains. Robinson's group was behind the Loyal Land Company, the chief rival of the Ohio Company, founded by the Lees. Consequently, Richard Henry's brothers, his Ludwell and Corbin relatives, and other allies expected him to confront Robinson.

How he did so may have surprised them. As if to demonstrate that Robinson might be guilty of far graver misdeeds than were ascribed to Thomas Lee, Richard Henry exposed a dubious practice that Robinson carried on while everyone seemingly looked the other way. It arose from the fact that the Speaker also held the office of treasurer, disobeying wishes of the King's ministers in London. Robinson's friends comfortably defeated Richard Henry's motion that the offices be separated. But Lee did not let the issue die. He had simply made his first move, knowing that more was at stake than Robinson's greed for office.

The next step earned Richard Henry the enmity of numerous Virginians, who thereafter blamed him for their considerable embarrassment. Through R.H.'s maneuvering, it came to light that John Robinson, in his role as treasurer, had illegally aided many friends by loaning them paper money for which his office was responsible. These loans were made in expired Virginia currency, bills that the treasurer was legally obliged to destroy.

Robinson did not burn the money, but instead secretly turned it over to financially embarrassed allies. They were expected eventually to repay Robinson whose accounts as treasurer still showed the money in circulation. But Virginia's hard times persisted and most of Robinson's loans could not be repaid. As outsiders, of course, the Lees had never benefited from this cosy relationship with the Speaker-Treasurer. Led by Richard Henry, the family and its allies kept pressing to elect a new treasurer and to audit the colony's books.

Amid the controversy, John Robinson died, making it inevitable that a thorough investigation of his official accounts would be made. It was the sort of analysis the Lee party had been demanding. The result displayed before all the world how many notable families were heavily in debt to the late treasurer. Indeed, the audit showed that at least 100,000 pounds were still out in illicit loans, and that another 10,000 pounds of technically invalid currency had been invested by Robinson in his father-in-law's lead mines.

While Robinson's friends claimed that this monetary malfeasance had been beneficial in stimulating the economy, the uproar came to be called the Robinson Scandal. It soiled the names of many prominent Virginia families, some of whom had differences with the Lees going back many years. Their animosity was now redoubled and pitched at Richard Henry, the person who first clamored to have the squalid Robinson story brought to light. But this was not the only reason R.H. was disliked.

His foes could remember another tacit insult. It, too, had been issued at the start of Richard Henry's career as a burgess, leaving numerous Virginians happy whenever Lee himself fell into trouble. After beginning the protest against John Robinson's power, Richard Henry then rose in the House to denounce Negro bondage and the trade that fostered it. His indignant remarks, uttered in 1759, have been called the most extreme anti-slavery statement made before the nineteenth century.

Stressing that blacks were "equally entitled to liberty and freedom by the great law of nature," Richard Henry looked about the House chamber and challenged the great planters there to show themselves Christians and "pay a proper regard to the dictates of justice and humanity." It was a statement not easily forgotten—or forgiven. Soon, when Richard Henry made a spectacular blunder, he found his earlier tactics left him little sympathy across Virginia.

In 1764, just as R.H. was seeking to topple John Robinson, his own ambition and greed betrayed him. It happened after he heard reports that England might be creating a new political office in Virginia, one to be responsible for collecting revenue from a tax to be imposed upon documents and publications used in the colonies. Although he hastened to apply for the position under the Stamp Act, Richard Henry lost it to George Mercer, whose family was allied with Speaker Robinson.

Naturally, when news of Richard Henry's willingness to be a tax collector leaked out, many of his contemporaries wondered if his hunger for almost any appointment had led him to throw principle aside in seeking the stamp agency. R.H. had been among the earliest in the House of Burgesses to deplore England's increasing repression of her colonies. Thus, the intent of the Stamp Act should have been as clear to Lee as it was to most others. Much bad feeling had already passed between London and America before 1764, caused by the Ordinance of 1763, the Sugar Act, and restrictive currency legislation.

In lamely defending himself, Richard Henry claimed he had not at first recognized the grave meaning of the Stamp Act. Few Virginians could accept this excuse from a man who had all along been pleading with London not to infringe upon Virginia's rights. Greatly embarrassed, Richard Henry promptly proceeded to worsen matters by behaving as if stricken by a guilty conscience—or by outrage at being denied the lucrative collectorship.

The most that can be said for R.H. Lee in 1765 is that he believed the only way to atone for his mistake over the collectorship was to lead in harassing those who proposed to obey the controversial revenue law. If this was his strategy, it did him little credit and encouraged observers to question both his emotional stability and his wisdom. Richard Henry's behavior seemed to threaten the very liberty he professed to champion. "My mind has been warmed," he admitted, "and I hardly know where to stop."

In late September 1765, as enforcement of the Stamp Act began, Richard Henry initiated a startling public protest. It took place in Westmoreland County and aimed to desecrate an effigy of George Mercer, the person who had won the post of stamp agent. Bearing placards saying "Money is my God" and "Slavery I love," Mercer's effigy was placed in a hangman's cart and accompanied by costumed black men, who were actually Richard Henry's slaves. Lee himself, dressed as a chaplain, followed solemnly behind, prepared to hear "Mercer's" dying words.

To the crowd, Richard Henry read his own satirical composition while pretending it was Mercer's plea. Ironically, the "confession" may have spoken more about himself than Richard Henry intended, for he had Mercer acknowledge: "It was the inordinate love of gold which led me astray from honor, virtue, and patriotism." After making the effigy plead guilty for seeking to put his own country in chains, Richard Henry saw

"Mercer" hanged not once but twice during two days. The effigy was then burned.

George Mercer and his family were soon avenged. They quickly arranged wide publicity for the story that Richard Henry himself had sought to be stamp agent. In turn, this move drove Richard Henry to rally his family in even more ardent opposition to England's tax policy. The next step, under Lee's auspices, was the signing of the memorable Westmoreland Resolves on 27 February 1766.

Citizens who affixed their names pledged to fight the Stamp Act "at every hazard and paying no attention to danger or death." Originated by Richard Henry, the resolves aimed to crush "every abandoned wretch who shall be so lost to virtue and public good" as to comply with the new tax law. Obedience to the King was permissible only "if consistent with the preservation of our rights and liberties."

The Westmoreland Resolves had a pugnacity and bluntness not heard thereafter among the various colonies for some time. It had a sharper tone even than the Declaration of Independence. The Westmoreland signers included, beside Richard Henry, three of the Lee brothers—Frank, Tom, and William—as well as the Squire. They and their fellow "Associates" intended to bring "danger and disgrace" to anyone honoring the stamp law. They also pledged, "at the risk of our lives and fortunes," to defend any person threatened by stamp agents.

In short, Richard Henry and his cohorts intended to disobey His Majesty's law, while punishing those who complied with it. They wasted no time. When Archibald Ritchie, a merchant in the neighborhood, proposed to attach the required stamps to documents accompanying a shipment he was sending to England, Richard Henry published a call to arms. "Everyone should look on Ritchie as the greatest enemy of his country," said Lee, who then urged that Ritchie be punished if he carried out his intention. The unfortunate merchant was warned to expect "that *fear may haunt him in his dreams.*"

Richard Henry and his group were true to their word. With many of them brandishing arms, a crowd was assembled to seek out Ritchie, force him to remove his hat, and then to read aloud an apology written for him (apparently by Richard Henry). He was told to agree not to buy the stamps, and if he refused, the mob threatened to strip him to the waist, hitch him to a cart, and lead him to a pillory where he would be exhibited. What would happen thereafter was left to his imagination. A protesting Ritchie finally submitted and read the apology.

Soon Parliament rescinded the Stamp Act, and the reign of terror in Westmoreland County subsided. The Lees, however, remained suspicious of England. R.H. urged Arthur to put aside his travels in Europe and come home, where he was needed. "Liberty can never be supported without arts and learning," so that "when the best of her sons" left America, danger ensued. "America, then, has a parent's claim to her descendants." They dare not reside amid tyranny. Given the uproar he had caused over the Stamp Act, small wonder that Richard Henry complained to Arthur of nervous digestion. The young physician sent back a prescription calling for paper to be dipped in liquefied opium and then placed on the pit of Richard Henry's stomach.

Despite his abdominal problems, Richard Henry began a campaign to succeed his deceased enemy, John Robinson, as speaker in the House of Burgesses. He went so far as to admit he had erred in seeking to be Virginia's stamp tax collector, and urged Virginians to allow his recent strenuous leadership against the tax to blot out his blunder. While even under better circumstances, Lee's hopes to become speaker would probably have been futile, he had no chance now. The speaker's chair went to a foe of the Lees, Peyton Randolph, and for several years the Lee coalition was largely ineffectual.

Meanwhile, Richard Henry continued to be injudicious. In 1774, he again laid principle aside and this time allowed a financial pinch to turn him into a salesman of slaves. He proposed to be deliberate about what he was undertaking. Unless one were careful as a slave trader, R.H. said, "the risks, the expenses of attending sales, advertising" would leave barely "porter's wages." Such income apparently was enough to make the effort worthwhile for Richard Henry. His surviving memorandum book shows him selling slaves.

He did so despite a rare scolding from brother Arthur Lee. Learning that a consignment of blacks was being sent to Richard Henry for distribution, Arthur warned that should the public see R.H. Lee in this role, it would "certainly wear an awkward appearance, that a strenuous opposer of this trade should be an agent in it." Arthur begged his brother to "consider this circumstance, and act accordingly."

Arthur's advice arrived at a point when Richard Henry may not have much cared what the public thought. Bruised financially and politically, he talked seriously of leaving public life. Had the worsening quarrel between the colonies and England not opened a new theater for his talents, he might well have dropped out of sight, leaving a dubious reputation mostly for erratic and disgruntled behavior. As it happened, however, fresh political opportunities left Richard Henry little time to sell slaves.

Later in 1774 his correspondence grew more spirited, as he recognized another forum in which to display his penchant for opposition. Ironically, it was Lee's decision to campaign for the liberties of white colonists that reduced his plans for a slave agency. By moving his energies to the floor of the Continental Congress, Richard Henry found the arena in which his personality and tactics would make him famous. His success, however, owed much to the presence with him in Philadelphia of his brother Frank.

It is difficult to recognize Francis Lightfoot Lee as a member of a family that had become known for pride and aggressive behavior. After Arthur admonished Richard Henry against becoming a slave trader, he turned with obvious relief to praise Frank for being *"calmness* and *philosophy* itself." It was an apt description, so that Frank Lee always entered political struggle reluctantly, and was kept in the fray by pressure from his brothers. He much preferred a quiet, bookish existence and to peer at life from afar.

But whenever Frank became involved he had a mind of his own. In his kindly style he often challenged Richard Henry's views. Dr. Benjamin Rush contended that Frank had "a more acute and correct mind" than R.H.'s. This talent made a different impression on Landon Carter at Sabine Hall, across the road from Frank's Menokin: "Poor Frank, he is really a very good fellow, but he is now and then a little too absurd in argument."

Had Richard Henry and Frank Lee been able to concentrate upon national issues in Philadelphia, the repute and achievement of their family would probably have risen much higher than it did. Unfortunately, the statesmanship of R.H. and Frank in the Continental Congress was hampered and finally overcome by the international troubles of Arthur and William Lee, who were abroad. Ironically, the careers of these "dear brothers" in London at first had promised to outshine those of their kinsmen in Virginia.

~ 7

Ambition in London
1768–1774

After William Lee helped his sister Alice escape Colonel Phil and go to London in 1760, the two of them lived with Philip Ludwell, their mother's widower brother. He had recently emigrated from Virginia with his three daughters. There were no sons. When William returned to Stratford in 1763, he doubtless carried memories of cousin Hannah Ludwell. As Uncle Philip's eldest child, she would someday be mistress of Green Spring, once Sir William Berkeley's vast estate on the James River.

Between 1763 and 1768, William worked at Stratford as business aide to Colonel Phil, an experience William believed taught him how to succeed were he to reappear in London as a merchant for Virginia planters. Having no land of his own and approaching age thirty, William thought a try at international business was worth the gamble. He chose to leave the banks of the Potomac and go abroad, turning his possessions over to the care of brother Frank.

Originally, William intended to put as much distance between himself and Stratford as possible, planning to settle in India and join a business there. But then came news of Uncle Ludwell's death in March 1767, which meant that Cousin Hannah was now a wealthy orphan. Marriage may not have been in William's plans before departing Virginia in 1768, but it entered his mind soon after he reached London. His brother Arthur, who had given up his brief practice of medicine and was now in England studying law, reported to Frank: "[William] has changed his voyage to India in the Prince of Wales into one to the land of matrimony in the Miss Ludwell. As a warm climate suits not with him, I hope he will find a temperate one in the place of his destination."

On 7 March 1769, his wedding day, William could hardly be blamed if he marveled at how he seemed to have met his financial needs so soon.

He was not exactly gentlemanly in describing his success. Fate, he said, had "completed the full measure of my felicity by putting me in unrivalled possession of the dear and amiable Miss Ludwell."

Hannah Philippa Ludwell, the new Mrs. William Lee, was approaching her thirty-second birthday. The couple began what seems to have been a happy union, although William fell ill early in the marriage, as did Frank soon after being wed to Becky Tayloe at about that same time. On recovering, William observed to Frank: "One would have thought that two old stagers like you and myself would not have been discomfited by matrimony, but none of us knows our strength till we are tried. I was very near kicking the bucket, but thank God I have now weathered the cape, and am rather stouter than when in Virginia."

Hannah had more serious physical problems. For a time, she proved unable to carry pregnancies to term. There was at least one still-born child before her first living infant, a son, arrived in 1775. But even so, the baby's twin brother died. By then, Hannah was thirty-eight. She evidently had expected trouble bearing children. What she could not anticipate were the difficulties from another quarter, the wealth she inherited.

Philip Ludwell's will divided his estate among three daughters. When one of them, Frances, died in 1768, her share was split between Hannah and Lucy, the remaining sister, who was half Hannah's age. Lucy was sixteen, and already displayed the notorious Ludwell trait of aggressive pride. Her behavior after Hannah and William's wedding more than hinted at the trouble ahead.

Lucy announced she had no intention of becoming a ward in the Lee household, nor of having William manage her wealth. Two months later, she married John Paradise, a London dilettante of bookish tastes who was eight years her senior. Lucy's unexpected nuptials prompted William to write to Virginia, urging trustees to be in haste about dividing the Ludwell inheritance between the two heirs.

Under the best circumstances, closing the complicated Ludwell estate would have been difficult. The procedure became exasperating since Hannah and Lucy were abroad. William turned to Richard Henry and Frank for help, explaining why he begged them to "exert yourselves." They must remember "how extremely irksome it is to have any connection with [Mr. and Mrs. Paradise], which must unavoidably be the case as long as the estate continues as it is."

Frank and Richard Henry did not need to be told how high the stakes were. Philip Ludwell's legacy was eventually valued at nearly 13,000 pounds sterling. It included real estate on both sides of the James River, as well as residential property in Williamsburg. There were many slaves, livestock, and crops. The part most prized, of course, was Green Spring, the magnificent plantation with its ancient Jacobean house, located near Williamsburg.

As the eldest heir and with first choice, nearly all of Green Spring would come to Hannah, which she sought to enlarge by asking that she be awarded her late sister's portion of land at Green Spring. William encouraged this strategy, but Hannah needed no help. Even before marriage, her motto was: "I would ever wish to avoid the reality or appearance of an unsteady disposition." Therefore, claiming her "birth right," Hannah told her father's trustees exactly what she wanted.

Nor did Hannah mince words. With her eye on Green Spring, she said: "I will by no means have anything to do with the houses in Williamsburg." Her tactic backfired. When the division was completed, Lucy Paradise came out better than anticipated. The appraisers found the land Hannah demanded was so much more valuable than Lucy's share that fairness required Lucy be awarded the rest of their deceased sister Frances' allotment. Indeed, Hannah had to give Lucy many slaves to get all the property she craved that pertained to Green Spring.

To William and Hannah, it seemed an eternity passed before the executors concluded their demanding task. Even the often impatient Richard Henry, who kept watch on the proceedings, recognized there was good reason why it took so long. Not so William, who kept urging action, all the while suspecting foul play. He now rarely referred to "my wife's property," choosing instead to be blunt about it. "As immediately as my marriage, I had an absolute right to a half the estate."

Eager to be installed as master of Green Spring, and to receive its profits, William began threatening legal action against any parties who would prevent this outcome. He told Richard Henry and Frank in February 1770: "Should the estate not be divided, I must entreat you to insist on its being done immediately, and if refused, to take such methods as you shall think proper to compel them to do it." To this, Richard Henry replied by cautioning patience. There was no cause "for force, nor would any undue pressing have been proper."

Finally, late in 1771, William and Hannah could feel assured that Green Spring and its more than 7000 acres was safely theirs. With it came sage counsel from various Lees. Richard Henry advised the couple to return to Virginia at once and live on the estate. If the owners were personally at Green Spring, he predicted their presence would double the property's yield, which R.H. estimated should amount annually to 1500 pounds. "No manager can be got who will by any means equal an intelligent and diligent master." William was warned that to sell the estate at current prices would be foolish.

Knowing of William's hankering to be a merchant and foreseeing that this might keep him from settling at Green Spring, Richard Henry decided to speak candidly. "Why should you venture into the uncertain ocean of commerce for that which you already possess, a genteel independent fortune?" The same view was heard from other relatives. Cousin Richard Corbin, who had been a trustee of the Ludwell property sent word that "the old beaten path of . . . the planter's way will not suit with the present modern improvement in husbandry." Success would require William's full attention.

Naturally, Colonel Phil had something to say, but on a more delicate aspect. He reminded the lucky William not to overlook Hannah's mortality: "As you will not have the land by your wife after her unless you have a child by her born alive, and then only for life, you should get it made over to you by her, at least enough for you to live well on . . . and do it without delay."

William evidently took Phil's advice, but not that of Richard Henry. If he had two profitable years as a London merchant, these he said would bring as much income as "all my estate is worth." Should he stay four years, William gleefully predicted that he could then keep a carriage and an English country house and live "like a prince." Filled with optimism and considering his wife beyond the age for successful child-bearing, William talked of taking "much pleasure in providing something for the children of my brothers."

Only to Richard Henry did William confide a more important reason why he and Hannah did not remove to Green Spring: "Mrs. Lee appears determined upon staying here." It was a costly decision. Nothing but unhappiness came from being absentee owners of Green Spring. Mainly this was due to William's increasingly suspicious nature and his unduly high opinion of his own ability. From afar, he sought to direct even the smallest details of life at Green Spring.

To make matters worse, William told Cary Wilkinson, the Green Spring overseer who had served the Ludwells long and well, that he had no confidence in him. As a result, Wilkinson soon went to work for Lucy Paradise and her husband. Leaving the skilled Wilkinson to his own methods in running their Virginia property, the Paradises earned considerable income, while a frustrated William and Hannah heard mostly about losses.

A disappointed William began to mistrust more than overseers. He doubted the motives even of Robert Carter Nicholas, a widely respected Virginia leader who had succeeded John Robinson as treasurer of the colony. Nicholas was the principal trustee in carrying out Philip Ludwell's will. William's suspicious behavior became too much for Nicholas, who withdrew from further association with the Ludwell estate, saying to William, "it is not in my power to attend to your business in the manner you, perhaps, may expect."

The often obtuse William professed to be amazed at Nicholas' action, assuring Richard Henry and Frank: "I know not the least cause of offence I have ever given." Soon, even the patience of these long-suffering brothers was taxed by William's belief that only he was competent to manage each aspect of Green Spring, including that of his slaves' religious life. When William heard that Baptist and other "new light" clergymen were seen along the James River, he ordered "my people" kept from "these vagabond preachers" who, he contended "encourage more wickedness than any other kind of men."

In the days when it was well managed, Hannah and William's plantation was largely self-sufficient, producing tobacco, indigo, wheat, corn, cotton, and flax. Its orchards were famous, as were its stables. Descending from the house to the James were beautiful gardens, and the residence was, like Stratford, unlike any other mansion in Virginia. However, as Richard Henry kept reminding William, money and attention were now required to keep the place up. The grand porch alone was a worry. "It will absolutely tumble down presently if 'tis not thoroughly and speedily repaired."

Unfortunately, William wanted to take money from Green Spring, not pay for the privilege of owning it. Deluded by anticipations of wealth flowing in from Hannah's legacy, William found his determination to be a tobacco merchant in London at first brought more expense than profit. After a brief and abortive association with an established firm, he decided to be independent. He named his ship *Liberty,* and promised reliable and patriotic service to Virginians he sought to make his clients.

William campaigned strenuously for business, seeking that of George Washington by assuring him: "Mrs. Lee will particularly attend to the choosing any thing her good cousins Mrs. Washington and Miss Custis may want for their own use." But competition was keen, costs were high, and William's business was handicapped by the miserable earnings at Green Spring. Nor were tobacco prices co-operating. Instead, they remained in a state of collapse, so that the value of tobacco cargoes shipped to William for sale fell below the costs of goods ordered by plantation households.

Faced by these grim facts, William admitted he needed aid from Colonel Phil and the Squire, who were among the most influential planters on the Potomac. By now in a state of panic, the insecure William's pleas to Phil sounded pitiful: "Let me intreat you to stand firmly by me at this most critical time." He begged for more business.

Both Colonel Phil and the Squire were quick to see William's predicament and tried to convert it to their advantage. Each demanded to have the profit in acting as William's agent. Recognizing that he faced a problem he was ill-equipped to solve, William turned to brother Frank, whose sweet nature evidently could cope with the sensitive personalities at Stratford and at Lee Hall. Taking pains to be quiet about it, Frank became as much of a manager as William was willing to accept in Virginia.

He was also judicious, finding it prudent to let William deal with the Widow Corbin when she became outraged by the young merchant's blundering during his early inexperience. William could be remarkably contrite toward Hannah, sending word that "my sister's objection . . . will at all times have great weight with me." He informed Frank that he, William, had learned a lesson. Now, he said, "[I] consider it my business to avoid giving offense." This was especially a necessary approach, he admitted, when "[I] think of Stratford and Lee Hall."

The delicate strategy he and brother Frank agreed on was to keep both the Squire and Colonel Phil believing that each had the lion's share of William's business, while actually the real agent was Frank. This obviously meant, as William put it, "care must be taken lest Col. Phil suspect." Phil, of course, did suspect and probably felt justified in a counter-dissimulation. He pretended to offer William all the influence Stratford commanded, while he actually sent much business to William Molleson, another kinsman-merchant in London. Phil also urged William to trust Molleson. "As I love you both, I shall take care your interests here shall not hurt one another."

This advice must have made the dour William smile a bit. He confided to Richard Henry that Molleson "hates me more than, I hope, all the rest of the world does, and has taken every measure in his power to injure me." William Molleson had married Eleanor Russell, who was descended from the Lees of Maryland, making the Mollesons part of the Lee family in Colonel Phil's eyes, if not William's. The latter suspected Molleson's patriotism, and rightly so. As ill-feeling deepened between England and her colonies, Molleson stuck with the Crown, while William became an outspoken critic of the ministry and Parliament.

When the outbreak of the Revolution put an end to commerce, William's company had established a good record, despite a shaky start. He and Hannah had fixed their home and business at 33 Tower Hill. Their success was due in significant measure to Hannah, whom William called "my good rib." Her refined taste was invaluable in locating personal items ordered by Virginia wives and daughters. For example, only Hannah could be trusted when Becky Lee, Frank's wife at Menokin, decided that she and her mate needed a new bed. No male advice was sought. William admitted to Frank that the brothers "dare not speak" on the subject, "as our *Mistresses* have had all the direction of this business." Even so, William could not resist confiding: "I *will* whisper that I am of opinion I cou'd have managed it somewhat cheaper; however, if they are pleased, we must be contented."

William needed an able business partner like Hannah as he often gave his time to running errands in London for his brothers, particularly Richard Henry, who opened his financial woes to William. The latter was eager to help, saying to Richard Henry: "Nothing in life would give me more pleasure than to aid in placing you in that state of independence which no man on earth deserves more."

Indeed, whenever William heard one of R.H.'s frequent threats to withdraw from public life, he became uneasy. As a merchant doing business in Virginia, William needed the vigilant Richard Henry looking after his interests in the House of Burgesses. Thus, he must have winced when the older brother wrote: "I find the attendance on Assemblies so expensive and the power of doing good so rarely occurring, that I am determined to quit that employment."

It took more than merely William's good intentions if Richard Henry's requirements were to be supplied. Although R.H. grabbed at almost any chance for larger income, he yearned especially for a lucrative seat on the Council of State in Virginia. "If therefore I am to continue in the public service, it must be in the Council," he announced. When someone pointed out that this would be unseemly with Colonel Phil already a councillor, Richard Henry offered what he claimed was an irrefutable reply: if the brothers were honest, then "no leagues of vice will ever be entered on, and a union in virtue can never be improper." William agreed with this reasoning and willingly tried bribery to bring Richard Henry the coveted appointment.

Securing such a post even for a popular colonist required dropping silver in many palms in order to prod the English government into making an appointment. It would be doubly expensive in Richard Henry's case because of the troubles he had caused over issues like the stamp tax. Even R.H. conceded that for the moment no Lee could expect a "favor." Still, the family must fight so that "virtue [meaning the Lees and their allies] must shortly drive vice and folly off the ground." These were words William loved to hear. He began a purusit of the Council post for Richard Henry, even though brother Arthur predicted it "would be in vain."

William graphically described his tactics. "Being determined to be as good as my word," he reported to R.H., "away I went to a member of parliament." Getting nowhere there, William turned to an elderly lady who knew a duke's brother who in turn was intimate with Lord North. "To her I promised fifty pounds down or five pounds per annum during her life if the Duke and Lord North would get you appointed."

Arthur Lee was correct. None of these schemes worked, leaving a discouraged Richard Henry confiding to William that he would accept even a county clerkship, adding: "I would wish this to be secret." Among R.H.'s latest expenses was the cost of educating his oldest sons, Thomas and Ludwell. One would aim for the law, the other for the church. R.H. proposed that the lads come to England and attend St. Bee's in Lancashire. There, instead of the hundred pounds charged annually by an American school, Richard Henry foresaw the cost being a third of that amount.

Once more, William was pressed into service. Dutifully, he dipped into his own purse as well as his scant reserve of patience as he followed Richard Henry's instructions, which were largely exhortations for youthful frugality. The investment paid off. The youths were good students, while William found himself becoming quite fond of them. In 1774 he could gladden Richard Henry's heart by reporting of the nephews: "They are really most excellent children that I feel a particular pleasure in having the care of them."

It was fortunate that Richard Henry's sons made few worries in London, for enough anxiety was created there by the behavior of Arthur, William and R.H.'s youngest brother. Most of Arthur Lee's adult life had been spent in the British Isles, first enrolled at Eton, then studying medicine at the University of Edinburgh, and now reading law in London's Middle Temple. As a medical doctor, a member of the Royal Society, and soon called to the English bar, Arthur was surely one of America's most learned men. Some might say he was America's wisest fool.

The family worried over Arthur because he had difficulty making use of what he knew. He shuddered at practicing medicine. Legal matters bored him. And when he entered public service, his great courage and book-wisdom were not compensation enough for the weaknesses in his personality. Alice Lee's husband Billy Shippen, who had been a medical student with Arthur, admired his intellectual prowess. After all, Arthur had graduated first in his class at the University of Edinburgh. Dr. Shippen neatly diagnosed his brother-in-law's plight: "Dr. Lee's conduct is singular and whimsical." Even so, said Shippen, "I love him."

The baby of the Stratford family, Arthur Lee never attained a mature personality and judgment. Orphaned at a young age, shamefully treated by his eldest brother, long apart from relatives he cherished, Arthur hesitated to yield himself to others. He shrank from the surrender marriage would entail and remained an eccentric bachelor who seized travel or any other excuse to justify his unsettled state.

To William's dismay, Arthur's wilfulness made him one day enthusiastic about studying law, while on the next he sought some new pursuit. He liked to roam the British Isles and Europe, often talking as if he held Virginia in low esteem. In those moods he would call England "the Eden of the world and the land of liberty," but in the next breath he spoke of yearnng to be at home and of a fondness for his family.

Arthur's letters often displayed his confused sentiments. His reports on a visit to Holland were eloquent in praise of Amsterdam, until suddenly he switched to describe how "the place abounds with the lowest obscenity." He had been horrified at what he felt was female immodesty, and was appalled that the Dutch should allow vice to contribute to the public good by obliging "every lady of pleasure" to pay a tax. Only feebly did he occasionally reproach himself for "the ambiguity of my expression."

During a moment in 1769 when Arthur recognized his plight, he confessed to Frank: "I am now the only unhappy or single person of the family, nor have I any prospect of being otherwise. . . . I often feel so homesick that I cannot bear the thought of living forever from you." Try though he might to praise marital love, Arthur usually ended with a sardonic quip about the female. Again to Frank, he said: "Three whole days was Eve satisfied with Paradise, and without flattery I believe her daughters are equally constant."

Nevertheless, despite his handicaps, Arthur, like William, managed to find friends among Londoners who must have been fascinated by these "colonials" who claimed that Americans had the same rights and liberties as Englishmen. Further, the amazing London Lees were clearly willing to fight for their rights, although they professed to hope that the struggle would not permanently estrange mother country and colonies. Rather, the Lees wished to awaken Great Britain to the injustice being heaped upon Englishmen who lived in places like Boston, Philadelphia, and along the Potomac.

For a time their work in London made William and Arthur the more famous of the six Lee brothers. Soon after he returned to England in 1769, Arthur was named assistant agent for Massachusetts to aid Benjamin Franklin, serving in this capacity from 1770 to 1774. This came about because, before reappearing in London, Arthur had traveled through the Middle Colonies and New England in 1768, where he made a favorable impression on Sam Adams and other early leaders of resistance. They named him sole agent after Franklin angered the Crown and was sent packing to America in 1774.

As an agent, Arthur corresponded with leaders in New England. He also became a pamphleteer in London, and was widely reprinted in Massachusetts, Virginia, and elsewhere. Arthur's experience in writing tracts began during his brief Virginia visit in the late 1760s, when he thought of establishing a medical practice. He soon realized this was not his calling, so he turned to political agitation, and in 1768, while still in America, published an imitation of the Pennsylvania essayist John Dickinson's *Letters from a Farmer*. Arthur called his tracts the *Monitor* letters. Their tone placed a premium on exhortation: "Shall we not sink into slaves? O liberty! O virtue! O my country!"

As soon as he could get back to London in 1769, Arthur eagerly began a series of essays which ran to 1774. Most of them were entitled the *Junius Americanus* letters, all marked by the clamorous tone of his earlier publications. They were meant primarily to encourage the Sons of Liberty movement in Massachusetts. In this work as in other matters, Arthur's style was a startling contrast to that of his agent-colleague in London, Benjamin Franklin. The latter was soft-spoken, shrewd, realistic, and quite willing to compromise. Lee was mistrustful, angry, and always eager to confront and challenge. Later, when this pair of envoys was assigned to work together as American representatives in Paris, nothing but trouble ensued.

When not agitating, Arthur moved in England's literary circles, where he had the useful friendship of James Boswell, a onetime schoolmate. With such good contacts, Arthur was soon conversing with Dr. Samuel Johnson, Richard Price, Catherine Macaulay, Joseph Priestley, and other extreme Whigs. In these circles, Arthur proudly referred to his election to the American Philosophical Society in 1768, made possible by his good record as a medical student in Edinburgh. His new associates in London soon saw that Arthur was chosen for the Royal Society, although its calm precinct was less attractive to Arthur than the company of persons who enjoyed opposing the ruling faction in England. Here, William's special friends were the notorious John Wilkes and William Petty, the Earl of Shelburne.

Just as Arthur robbed time from his legal studies in the Middle Temple to mingle with English radicals and anyone else who might sympathize with colonial complaints, so William Lee tended increasingly to leave his mercantile business to consort with those who preferred amity (and prosperous trade relations) between mother country and colonies.

There were many influential Londoners of this persuasion. They made it possible in July 1773 that William Lee and Stephen Sayre, an even more vocal American, were elected as London's two sheriffs. William's acceptance speech had the florid quality of Richard Henry's assertions back in Virginia: "It shall not be my fault if we do not transmit to our posterity undiminished, and even untainted, those glorious privileges and immunities which our ancestors have so nobly handed down to us."

William's astonishing election came about because a male resident of Virginia could come to England and claim the same political pedigree as a resident of London. This meant William could contest for any office—and he conceded privately that his goal was a seat in Parliament. The sheriff's job was the first step, and the next was that of an alderman, which post became William's in May 1775. It was a position he could keep for life, if he wished.

As alderman, William issued official expressions of alarm at England's treatment of the colonies. His constituents were largely sympathetic, being mostly those Londoners whose financial connections made them concerned at the breakdown of good will and commerce between England and America. Arthur in particular had high hopes this sentiment would be contagious, and that larger numbers of Englishmen would demand that mistreatment of the colonies be stopped.

More realistic than Arthur, William advised his brothers in America that a united front among the colonists was the tactic most likely to impress the English ministry and Parliament. He was therefore outraged when he heard that Virginia planters who did business with him feared that his increasing political involvement would prevent him from getting the best price for their products. "Tell these cavaliers they do not know me," William advised Frank, adding: "the greater difficulties I have to encounter, the *greater* I am." Let Virginia look to its own vigor, William cautioned. "There appears too much canting and milkiness in some, who I am afraid will prevail."

With the tie between the colonies and England loosening, William called for more courage among his relatives. He recommended to the Squire that he "prepare for the worst." To sister Alice and her husband, he sent the alarming, if colorful, suggestion that they make ready "to browse with the goats on the mountain shrubs or meet death with intrepidity." In May 1775 he informed brother Tom that the English government was "wicked and bloodthirsty." If these alarums were taken less seriously than William intended, it was because in the same mail he usually enclosed pleas for more tobacco shipments.

While William and Arthur campaigned in London for colonial rights, the same issues were bringing new political opportunities for their brothers in Virginia. In fact, Richard Henry's role as dissenter had begun to pay dividends. Events proved to be on his side. Most of the calls by Virginians for patience toward English policies and for reconciliation came from the Lees' enemies. The Crown's harsh replies, however, seemed to hand Richard Henry and his brothers the robes of prophets. The more repressive England became, the more Virginia politicians seemed to side with R. H. Lee.

Using this advantage, the Virginia-based Lees, encouraged by their London kinsmen, led in creating committees of correspondence among the colonies and in forming associations to halt the importation of English commodities. The Townshend Acts, the Tea Act, and the Quebec Act were cited as proof by Richard Henry and his allies when they denounced England's attitude toward America's rights. They pointed out how London was making it painfully clear that, while Englishman at home might be taxed only with their consent, those in the New World had no such defense.

The contacts first made by Arthur in Massachusetts were handy for Richard Henry. From Arthur's friends, R.H. received prompt reports on the most severe oppression in the colonies. These bulletins were skillfully employed by Richard Henry and the Squire to keep the House of Burgesses in step with the anti-English agitation in the Boston area. When that city's port was closed in 1774 and other indignities were suffered, Richard Henry assured Sam Adams that Virginia considered the plight of Massachusetts to be "the common cause of British America." The colonies "will owe their political salvation, in great measure, to the present virtue of Massachusetts Bay."

After the crisis drew blood at Lexington and Concord in 1775, the Lees could be found battling for American liberties on three fronts. In Philadelphia, Richard Henry and Frank were the radical contingent in Virginia's delegation to the Continental Congress. In Williamsburg, the Squire and Tom Lee pushed the House of Burgesses to accept independence as the price of preserving liberty. In London, William and Arthur continued calling for a change of Crown policy that might avert a break between mother country and colonies.

Looking back to these exciting days from his old age, John Adams eulogized the Lees as "that band of brothers, intrepid and unchangeable, who, like the Greeks at Thermopylae, stood in the gap, in the defense of their country, from the first glimmering of the Revolution in the horizon, through all its rising light, to its perfect day."

While the Lees probably would have accepted such praise, they might dissent from Adams' talk of how the Revolution had been perfected. Richard Henry Lee particularly never forgot how, once the rebellion had begun, men and events appeared to turn against him and his family.

❧ 8

A Test of Courage
1775–1779

In 1775, the Anglo-American empire collapsed, smashing a relationship cherished by four generations of Lees. The courage of the family's earlier personalities had been tested amid circumstances very different from those that tried Richard Henry and his brothers. They would be even more sternly challenged. Having to break with England grieved them, as it did most Americans.

Among those who still referred to the mother country as "home" was Colonel Phil. By dying in 1775, he was spared seeing others in the Lee family defend the move for independence. Although at the time of his death Phil was a senior statesman in Virginia, his papers contain no comment on the increasing tension between the Old Dominion and England. One wonders if he tried to ignore the fact that much of the imperial agitation came from his brothers and their cohorts.

At the end of his life, Phil still preferred to concentrate upon himself and Stratford. He and Elizabeth Steptoe, his wife, had noticeably improved the plantation and its manor house. Their two daughters flourished. And Elizabeth was pregnant with what the couple hoped would be a son through whom the estate, now more than 6500 acres, might safely descend. It must have been Phil's intent to wait until he was sure of a male heir before making a will.

No last testament had been drawn when a "nervous pleurisy" overcame Phil soon after New Year's Day 1775. He suffered much before he died on 21 February, but with ample time to call for pen and paper and prepare a will. Evidently he chose not to, perhaps refusing to believe he was near death. On 24 February, his forty-eighth birthday, he was laid beside his forebears in the Burnt House Field cemetery at Machodoc.

The future of Stratford, and the rest of Phil's kingdom, now reverted to the guidelines in Thomas Lee's will of 1750.

Elizabeth, Phil's widow, could not be present for her husband's burial service as she was at that very moment giving birth to the much desired son. Now, by law and Grandfather Thomas' decree, the infant became the master of Stratford. Given the name of his deceased father, little Phil did not live long, dying in a fall down the stairs at Stratford. The accident meant that the plantation then would go to Colonel Phil's daughters.

Anticipating the child's death seemed a special worry for Henry Lee, the Squire's brother, who said that Colonel Phil's demise left proud Stratford depending on the life of a frail infant. This troubled Henry mainly because, as he reminded William Lee, "the honour of the family [must] be fixed at Stratford." A female heiress would likely marry and the estate would disappear as a Lee asset. Henry Lee, by the way, offered the only words of praise for Phil recorded by any family member. "In him Virginia has lost an able judge and America a truly great patriot."

Such were not Richard Henry's thoughts when, on the evening after Phil was interred, he notified William and Arthur of their brother's death. In no hurry about breaking the news, R.H. began the letter by fuming against England's "foolish and wicked" ministry. Only after these fulminations did he mention that "the honorable Colonel Lee of Stratford was buried this day." While he called the event "a public loss," Richard Henry explained he simply meant Phil's vacancy on the Council would likely be filled by a "raw" boy. This device, R.H. claimed, was London's way of putting royal sympathizers in power, instead of "grave, sensible Men."

A few weeks after Phil's demise, a catastrophe completed the break between England and her colonies. British troops and Massachusetts citizens fought at Lexington and Concord on 19 April 1775, confirming the worst fears of the Lee brothers and causing Richard Henry another bout of severe digestive disorder. His condition must have inspired his startling language: "The dirty Ministerial Stomach is daily ejecting its foul contents upon us."

During the next year Richard Henry and Frank were leaders as the Continental Congress sought to make America what the Lee brothers called "the Asylum-elect of Liberty." The two served on countless committees and attended most of the debates in Philadelphia. In Virginia, their partners were brother Tom and cousin Squire, who worked to keep politics at Williamsburg in step with the Continental Congress.

From this collaboration among various Lees came astonishing results. Virginia's act empowering Congress to declare for separation arrived in Philadelphia at the very moment Richard Henry needed it before making his famous motion for an independent America. This timing greatly amused an appreciative John Adams, who wrote to the Squire: "Is it not a little remarkable that this Congress and your Convention should come to Resolutions so nearly similar . . . ?"

Brother Tom had not only transmitted Virginia's resolves for independence to R.H., but his was the most important hand in preparing them. Imperfect though he considered them, Virginia's declarations should be useful, Tom claimed. His chief regret was that in drafting them he found that he had to desist from giving Virginia's call for action "a preemptory and decided air," and he warned R.H. that timidity and hesitation threatened the Old Dominion's stand.

On 7 June 1776, after Congress heard Richard Henry's courageous motion and speech in behalf of colonial freedom, it chose to delay the final vote on breaking with England until a committee had drafted a declaration of independence. R.H. was not named to that committee, as custom decreed he should for having moved the subject. Instead, he was publicly humiliated.

This came about because congressional leaders for independence were fearful to the last moment that their path would be blocked. Not until the spring of 1776 had the Middle and Southern colonies finally become willing to face the drastic propositon of breaking from England. Thereafter, the Northeastern delegates, the most ardent for independence, wanted no misstep to cause them to drop the prize. Such a disaster appeared likely when part of the Virginia delegation demanded as its price for continued co-operation that Benjamin Harrison, instead of R. H. Lee, be on the committee to pen any declaration of independence.

Harrison, and his ally, Carter Braxton, were not only powerful members of Congress from the Old Dominion, they also represented Richard Henry's implacable Virginia enemies. The ghosts of King Carter and John Robinson whispered not only in Williamsburg, but they had followed R. H. Lee to Philadelphia. Confronted by the need to hold Virginia in line, the friends of independence had to keep Lee from the committee assigned to draft the declaration.

However, it was asking too much of the New England representatives to put the ponderous and arch-conservative Benjamin Harrison on the committee. In exchange for agreeing to pass over Richard Henry, the managers for independence got the Virginians to accept a quiet colleague, Thomas Jefferson, as one of the drafters. Harrison was safely discarded, and the committee, made up of John Adams, Benjamin Franklin (back from London), Roger Sherman, and Robert Livingston went to work with Jefferson. Instead of Lee from Stratford and Chantilly, it was Jefferson from Monticello who earned immortality by drafting the Declaration.

The strategy was anguishing for Richard Henry as he realized he would have no hand in the triumphant writing and adoption of a Declaration of Independence. No one had contributed more to making possible such a moment. It was to soothe R.H., as well as to assure the preparation of a good constitution for Virginia, that brother Tom Lee sent word to R.H. in Philadelphia: "Let us have the satisfaction to see you [here] assisting in the great work of this convention." According to Tom, Richard Henry's presence was required to hush those impetuous members who would mar the document "with a thousand impertinencies; from being in the end a jumble of unintelligible parts." Establishing sound governance in Virginia, said Tom, demanded "the protecting hand of a master."

These words were balm for Richard Henry after his humiliation by the Continental Congress. He announced an immediate departure from Philadelphia, explaining he hastened home to comfort a sick wife and to aid in writing Virginia's constitution. Nevertheless, from that day R.H.'s optimism about America's future was never restored. Having been denied what would be the high point of any career, Richard Henry thereafter usually talked discouragingly and in melancholy terms. He forecast rough sailing for the new American republic.

He was not the only worried Lee. Amid the exultation after adoption of the Declaration, Frank admitted he was uneasy. He urged that R.H. return to Congress, assuring him that those unspeakable enemies Braxton and Harrison were heading back to Virginia. Frank claimed Richard Henry's strength would now have a new usefulness in Philadelphia. He was required to bolster many weak-kneed delegates, whom Frank predicted would allow military disappointments to produce a submission to England on less than desirable terms. "The evil is coming which I always dreaded," Frank reported. While "every effort should be to oppose the enemy, we are disputing about government and independence."

Frank stuck to his post, doing what he could to keep Congress steadfast. His assignment was eased by the presence of his wife, Becky Tayloe, who had no children to worry about at Menokin. She remained in Philadelphia with her husband most of the time, while Frank was perpetually dealing with military, domestic, and foreign issues. Without intelligent labor on the part of at least a few delegates, he predicted to his confidants, "what a fine fund of ridicule will our fine systems afford to our victorious adversaries."

Frank worked tirelessly, taking a moment late one wintry night in

Philadelphia to pen a few lines to Landon Carter: "I have little time I can call my own, and that irregular and uncertain. It is now past twelve at night and Mrs. Lee calls to bed." Ironically, it was not a crisis in Philadelphia which overcame Frank, but one in Virginia. In mid-1777, R.H.'s tribulations in Williamsburg brought Frank to resign his seat in the Congress as a gesture of brotherly loyalty.

One of the reasons many persons "detested" (Landon Carter's word) Richard Henry Lee was that he kept an air about him which implied that he and his allies had a monopoly on righteousness. A second reason was that R.H.'s enemies could claim that his impatience with Virginia conservatives reflected an admiration for New England. Numerous Virginians believed Richard Henry's vanity had made him the captive of clever Massachusetts politicians. And, of course, many in the Old Dominion still bristled when reminded of Richard Henry's attacks on Speaker Robinson and on the Mercer family.

Consequently, Williamsburg housed many politicians who pointed gleefully to any misstep Richard Henry might make. Once again, the victim gave them much to cackle over. As 1777 began, R.H. was obliged to report to friends that "very malignant and very scandalous hints and innuendoes concerning me have been uttered in the house." These reports grew from stories about how Richard Henry had treated tenants on his land in Fauquier County (formerly part of Prince William County).

It seemed that during the pinched times on the eve of the Revolution when cash was scarce, Richard Henry had advised his tenants to pay him in produce. Then, when war began, Congress met the shortage of hard money by issuing Continental currency, the value of which was soon debased. With the paper money worth little, Richard Henry's enemies were elated to learn that he had refused to accept this Continental currency as payment from his renters.

The story allowed Lee's foes to charge that he was destroying the value of a form of money which he, as a delegate to Congress, had the dubious wisdom to help create. It was another predicament in which Richard Henry found himself accused of duplicity, of hypocrisy, and of greed. So powerful did the sentiment against him become that his opponents in the Virginia legislature had no trouble defeating him when, in May 1777, it was time to re-elect delegates to the Continental Congress.

Quickly, the news reached Philadelphia that Richard Henry had been unseated. Frank Lee did not hesitate to respond. Along with Mann Page, Jr., a Lee ally, he resigned from Congress, even though the two themselves had been re-elected. They informed George Wythe, Speaker of the House of Delegates, (as the House of Burgesses had been renamed in Virginia's constitution of 1776), that they could not continue serving Virginia when, behind their backs, their valued reputations might at any moment be destroyed. Frank said he preferred to return home and take "a more humble station, less exposed to envy, hatred, and malice."

Meanwhile, the outraged Richard Henry notified the governor of Virginia, Patrick Henry, that, while "I look with indifference on the malice of my enemies," he wanted "virtuous men" to know the truth. "I ought at least to be heard in my defense." He also took care to claim that actually he did not regret failing at re-election, "for I have long panted for retirement from the most distressing pressure of business that I ever had conception of."

The power of Richard Henry's oratory soon restored him, if somewhat battered, to his congressional seat. He traveled to Williamsburg in June 1777 and explained his side of the story to the legislature. It was high drama on 20 June when R.H. took his seat in the House of Delegates and, while the secretary recorded it, requested an inquiry "into certain matters injurious to his reputation and public character which . . . had been alleged against him."

Members of the Senate were summoned to listen as witnesses testified and then as Richard Henry "was heard in his place." Unfortunately, the proceedings were only summarized, but Lee's address was said to have been powerful. His argument probably reiterated what he had told Governor Henry—that as an impecunious public servant with a large family he needed income, and that he had acted to benefit his tenants by giving them permission to pay him in tobacco, something in their power, instead of demanding cash, which most of them did not have.

After Richard Henry concluded and the senators withdrew, the Lee family enjoyed one of its finest hours. So impressive had Richard Henry's self-justification been that the House of Delegates, which so recently had disgraced him, now voted that the Speaker thank Lee for the "faithful service" he had rendered Virginia. As R.H. listened, "standing up in his place," George Wythe proceeded "with peculiar pleasure" to attest "as far as I could judge" of Richard Henry's "zeal truly patriotic" which had been employed for the good "of your country in particular and of the United States in general."

It was said that the Speaker (who was Lee's close friend) had tears in his eyes when he made the statement. Clearly relishing his triumph, Richard Henry replied by giving thanks for this expression "of candor and justice . . . not undeserved." Then he added that Virginia's approbation was the highest reward he could wish to receive for serving the public. A few days later, R.H. was once again elected a delegate to Congress, replacing George Mason, who offered a well-timed resignation.

In August 1777, Richard Henry and Frank were back in Philadelphia, Frank agreeing to withdraw his resignation once his brother was vindicated. But soon after they took their seats, they suffered a personal sorrow. The family and Virginia lost the steadying influence of Thomas Ludwell Lee who would die in 1778. Although he had preferred not to join his brothers in the national arena, Tom's public service was nonetheless distinguished. He, along with the Squire, was trusted by more Virginians than was Richard Henry. Without Tom Lee's work the cautious majority of Virginia politicians might not have been held in line to support American independence, or to back a new constitution for Virginia and a declaration of human rights.

After he and R.H. had seen to a suitable new government for the Old Dominion, Tom next joined George Mason, George Wythe, and Edmund Pendleton in revising Virginia's laws. Their committee redesigned the statutes for the state's newly independent status. Then Tom was elected one of the five judges who would sit as Virginia's supreme court. At this critical point, Thomas Ludwell Lee died on 13 April 1778. He had suffered from rheumatic fever for six weeks at his home, called Belleview, in Stafford County.

It was a measure of Richard Henry's great affection for "my ever dear brother" that he left his political entanglements in Philadelphia in 1778 and sat with Tom until the latter's death. Surviving were seven children and "a very disconsolate widow," as R.H. reported to Arthur. The scene, he said, brought him "infinite pain." He told George Washington that the melancholy event "removed every other consideration from my mind."

For a time, these private as well as public considerations kept R.H. in Virginia. He was nearly broken in health by the strain of duty in Philadelphia, where he had continued to be disappointed by Congress. The months had left him lethargic and convinced that "virtue" in the new American republic was endangered. The only way to assure the nation's happiness, Richard Henry admonished Sam Adams, was for it to remain pure. "When we cease to be virtuous, we shall not deserve to be happy."

Once back in Congress, Richard Henry thought he and his family now had proof of the danger to American virtue. Unsurprisingly, the threat emanated from an attack on the Lee clan, although this time it came not from long-standing animosities in Virginia. This latest assault upon the Lees had both national and international origins. During the summer of 1778, the family's name became a more divisive element in Continental politics than it had been in Virginia.

The controversy had festered for over a year in Europe when angry charges began to be exchanged between Arthur and William Lee on one side, and Benjamin Franklin and Silas Deane on the other. What ensued has fascinated and baffled generations of historians who have sought to trace the quarrel's descent into intrigue, spying, deceit, envy, greed, towering rage, and ultimately a partisanship that caused much damage to Congress during and after 1778. While the Lees' valor did not desert them, it could not avert the so-called Lee-Deane affair or a taint upon the family.

Probably, the conflict was inevitable once Congress had sent Arthur and William on diplomatic assignments to Europe. By early 1777, the brothers had left London and were on the Continent, Arthur preparing to serve as one of the three commissioners to the French government, whose support for the American cause was vital. William was named Congress' commercial agent at Nantes, the French port from whence most of the materials desperately needed in America were shipped. The brothers arrived believing they had enlisted in a glorious fight for freedom.

Visibly shocked by what they found in France, Arthur and William soon concluded they had been thrust into a nest of vipers. They claimed their American associates in Europe were using the Revolution to enrich themselves. The Lees' response made a shambles of America's first excursion into world diplomacy. Strong tempers and suspicious natures disqualified both Arthur and William as skillful combatants in the rough and tumble of Parisian politics.

Arthur's colleagues on the American commission were Silas Deane and Benjamin Franklin. A Connecticut merchant and former delegate to the Continental Congress, Deane allowed personal profit to shape his supervision of large sums of money given or lent by European powers to the rebellious colonies. Franklin was willing that Deane be left to expend these funds, allowing the world-famous Pennsylvania writer and scientist time to do that which he preferred and did so well—charming the French people and their officials on behalf on the American cause.

Immediately, Arthur suspected that Edward Bancroft, Deane's selection as secretary for the commissioners, was a spy for England, and that Deane was co-operating with him. (A century later, when British archives for this period were opened, Arthur Lee's indictment of Deane and Bancroft as spies was corroborated.) Not only did Arthur advertise his doubts about his associates, but he also was openly hostile to the French government, allowing his critics to say he was at heart an Englishman.

Deane and Franklin soon were sick of Arthur Lee, whose superior manner immediately made life miserable for the commission and French officials. Meanwhile, at Nantes, William discoverd that he was at the mercy of the commissioners in Paris and that his commercial agency was largely powerless. Primarily this was because Silas Deane wanted William out of the way so that a company (in which Deane had a personal stake) led by the powerful Pennsylvania financier Robert Morris could reap huge commissions. These could readily be harvested by those in Nantes who bought and sold goods for America, including the ships brought into port as prizes of war.

A merchant by profession, William was naturally eager for profit. As an agent, he was unsalaried and obliged to live by commission. He was also honest, however, which he found put him at a disadvantage in Nantes. He soon was convinced that other agents sent by Deane and Franklin, including the latter's nephew, were corrupt. At the very least, they proved skilled at confusing public money with their own. It was the same charge Arthur leveled against Silas Deane.

Nor were the Lee brothers mollified when they were sent on brief assignments as emissaries to Austria, Prussia, and Spain. These excursions, hopeless from the start and meant to get them out from underfoot in France, were embarrassing failures. For this, Arthur and William readily blamed Deane and Franklin, so that animosity between them and the Lees soon was out of control.

Arthur and William were further handicapped because they could know little of what was happening in Philadelphia. English seizure of vessels carrying mail from America to Europe doubled the ordinary hazards of getting messages safely across the Atlantic by sailing ship. With mail rarely arriving, the Lees had a sinking feeling that not even their brothers cared to write to them. The resulting unhappiness made the two react even more violently in their controversy with Franklin and Deane.

As early as the summer of 1777, Arthur was speaking of his "cunning" colleagues who "have endeavored to ruin me here," and who, he warned Richard Henry, "will attempt the same with you." Soon he was even more blunt, saying of Franklin: "I am satisfied he is criminal towards the public." Perhaps Arthur's most extreme charge was that Franklin could "breed mischief enough for twenty worlds," and that the old man wished to be "solon and the Dictator of America."

When John Adams arrived in Paris in April 1778 to join the commission, he was aghast at the confusion and rancor he found splitting the American delegation. Hearing Arthur and William talk of little but "plunderers who have grown fat on the public spoil," Adams warned Richard Henry that the American emissaries seemed to do little but "run down characters," "paint in odious colours," and "excite or propagate suspicions."

No one admired the Lee family more than John Adams, but even he came quickly to concede that Arthur was a handicap. Adams never took seriously the baseless rumors about Arthur's wartime connivance with England. Nor did he think the ill-will among the Paris commissioners was entirely due to Lee family pride. Mainly, Adams found, the key to the tragic quarreling was Arthur's "unhappy disposition."

Adams endorsed Arthur's integrity and patriotism, "but I know his prejudices and passions," and these, said John, were fatal. He found Arthur's usefulness diminished by several characteristics: "His countenance is disgusting, his air is not pleasing, his manners are not engaging, his temper is harsh, sour, and fierce, and his judgment of men and things is often wrong." Later, Adams wrote that by nature Arthur Lee "went on through life quarrelling with one person or another."

Benjamin Franklin, the target of much invective thrown by Arthur, was even more explicit in judging his enemy. Franklin gave his opinion to the unhappy man himself in April 1778. It was a moment when the elderly diplomat was exhausted by Arthur's endless letters of reproach and accusation, as well as the Virginian's habit of insulting the French people and their government. "I do not like to answer angry letters," Franklin replied to Arthur, and then went on with devastating candor.

Franklin said he had put up with Arthur because of "my concern for the honour and success of our mission, which would be hurt by our quarrelling," and also because of "my respect for your good qualities." But it was no longer possible to be silent about Lee's most serious problem, by which Franklin meant a "sick mind, which is forever tormenting itself with its jealousies, suspicions, and fancies that others mean you ill, wrong you, or fail in respect for you." The old man warned "Dr. Lee" that "If you do not cure yourself of this temper, it will end in insanity, of which it is the symptomatic forerunner."

In Arthur Lee, Benjamin Franklin had been dealing with one of the most exasperating personalities in American history, one who was convinced that he knew better than anyone how to crusade for liberty and virtue. Thus, Arthur was disgusted by Franklin's wily style, his patient compromises with the French government, and his clever method of ingratiating himself with the French people. Also, Franklin was quite prepared to look the other way if bribery, espionage, and other dubious practices were necessary to secure an alliance between America and France and to arrange for munitions and other desperately needed supplies to reach the rebellious states.

Consequently, Franklin embodied everything Arthur claimed to despise, while actually the Pennsylvanian was an astute diplomat and experienced in the ways of the world. But the means Franklin tolerated for national advancement horrified Arthur, and William as well. They believed that the sins of Franklin, Silas Deane, and Edward Bancroft struck at the heart of liberty and the new republic. Ironically, thanks to the connivance of Deane and Bancroft, the unedifying rancor among the American commissioners became known in all its pitiful detail to His Majesty's secret service in London.

Eventually, Arthur and William's description of the mess in Paris reached Frank and Richard Henry in Philadelphia. They reacted in a fury which brought the antagonisms in France to dominate the debates in Congress. The delegates from New England and the Southern colonies, all tending to share agrarian sympathies, mostly supported the Lees. The Middle colonies, with their mercantile bias, inclined toward Deane and Franklin. It was a close division, but when Richard Henry moved in November 1777 that Silas Deane be recalled to explain what he had been up to, the resolution passed.

Meanwhile, Deane's allies were spreading the word in Virginia and elsewhere that William and Arthur Lee were handicapping the Revolutionary cause. The charges were familiar: the brothers' arrogant dealings with the French, their sympathies for England, their incompetence as negotiators, and even hints that they were stealing public money. For a time, Richard Henry expected that the family's repute would deflect these rumors. "It is happy for mankind that depraved hearts are commonly joined with weak heads," he told Frank.

But Frank was less sanguine, observing that Deane's friends, "by their lies and intrigues, have so far carried their point as to throw some little discredit upon us." By then, it was June 1778, with Richard Henry so unhappy over the waywardness of Congress that he took a long vacation at Chantilly. Once more, Frank was left in Philadelphia to guard Lee family interests against Silas Deane, who reached Pennsylvania in July 1778.

Deane brought a trump card with him. He claimed credit for the fact that the French recently had signed a treaty assuring aid for America. No one doubted that French support was crucial for sustaining independence, and most delegates were impressed when Deane disembarked in the company of Conrad Gerard, the first French envoy to the

American confederation. Gerard gave quiet support to Deane's charges that Arthur Lee was so disliked and mistrusted by the French government that his presence menaced the still delicate relations between the two nations.

Debate over Deane's assertions and what to do with him deepened the rift in Congress and spilled into newspapers, where articles revealed congressional debates supposed to be secret, as well as selections from confidential correspondence. The publicity served to make Deane uneasy, for he knew the Lees were dangerously close to the evidence about his traitorous activities. Consequently, he created a diversion by attacking the Lee family in a newspaper letter printed on 5 December 1778.

The brothers agreed Deane's barrage was more than "a charge against the Lee family." Frank called it the first attack by a "very dangerous party" whose aim was to topple "all the old friends of liberty and Independence." He believed that the group would stop at nothing. As the controversy worsened in the winter of 1778–79, it produced the gravest hour in the Lee clan's history since Nathaniel Bacon had imprisoned Richard the Scholar a century before.

Amid the family's crisis, the stout heart was Frank's. He fought in Philadelphia while Richard Henry licked his wounds in Virginia and sent his brothers gloomy messages, such as: "I am really tired with the folly and the wickedness of Mankind, and wish most heartily to be retired absolutely." His attitude compelled Frank to suppress his own disgust at national poltics in order to bolster the spirits of Richard Henry. While Frank did not deny that he, too, was "tired of the knavery and stupidity of the generality of mankind," he kept reminding R.H. that "it is our duty to stem the current as much as we can, and so do all the service in our power to our country and our friends. The consciousness of having done so will be the greatest of all rewards."

Privately, Frank Lee feared that the worst of all mishaps was overtaking the new Republic. Virtuous men—and he had particularly in mind brother R.H.—were coming to feel that "there can be no condition in life more unhappy than to be engaged in the management of public affairs with honest tendencies." Trying to keep from scolding, Frank reminded the hibernating Richard Henry that "hard as the lot is it must be borne at least till things have got into a tolerable way." Finally, he succeeded in stirring Richard Henry into a public defense of the Lee family by having him publish a newspaper reply to Deane. It did little to calm the storm.

Unrelentingly, the faction supporting Deane kept at its aim, which was as Frank put it, "to blacken the Lees and make Deane the greatest man in the world." Even though Congress seemed inclined to disown

Deane, William and Arthur's mistakes made them equally vulnerable. "If our brothers are not disgraced now, they will be ere long," Frank informed R.H., "for they will always land in the way of bad men and no villainy will be left unpracticed to ruin them."

To heap insult upon injury, Deane and his friends announced that the inept William and Arthur Lee had received their positions abroad only because Richard Henry had insisted they be appointed by Congress. Incensed by this, R.H. further bestirred himself. He answered charges about the Lee family's "inordinate ambition and undue influence" by stressing that the Lees came from "an ancient and honorable family in Virginia," and that its critics were in fact the real betrayers of public welfare.

The fight seemed to restore Richard Henry, so that in February 1779 he set out for Philadelphia to help the valorous Frank defend the family. It was too late. The pair could not save their brothers. Congress was finally weary of the shrill "suspicions and animosities" generated by both sides. It was decided that America's representation in Europe needed overhauling. Silas Deane was not reappointed, and Arthur and William Lee were dropped from their posts.

While this upshot made the Lee family feel more alienated than ever, much worse was the fate of Silas Deane. After Congress removed him, he was abandoned by the powerful mercantile faction. He returned in a private capacity to Europe, but found no welcome among his onetime cohorts in treachery. He lost himself in drink and futile appeals for help. While fresh rumors about his work as a spy were circulating, Deane died mysteriously in September 1789 as he was about to sail from England for America. Quite possibly the cause was poison administered by his former accomplice, Edward Bancroft, who feared Silas knew too much.

All this was in the future. Back in 1779, with his brothers dismissed from office, Richard Henry summed up the family's predicament by asserting to his old friend George Mason: "Look around you, do you anywhere see wisdom and integrity and industry prevail either in council or execution? The demon of avarice, extortion, and fortune-making seizes all ranks." In a loud display of his notorious self-righteousness, Richard Henry spoke of "villains," "miscreants," and the "corrupt hotbed of vice." As for Franklin himself, R.H. pointed out: "It is the curse of man, that the vicious part of his nature outlives his reason."

Glumly, Richard Henry and Frank returned to Virginia in July 1779, both having resigned their seats. They departed Philadelphia with R.H. lamenting: "I see nothing but disgrace, contempt, and ruin." Meanwhile, the city had become more divided by their name than Williamsburg had ever been. Some observers in Philadelphia found it difficult to believe that one family could cause such turmoil. "Gracious Heavens!" exclaimed Robert Treat Paine from Massachusetts, "is it possible that in the infancy of our rising Republic, two brothers of one family should represent . . . these United States at four of the principal Courts of Europe; and that two others of the same family should exercise the greatest acts of sovereignty in our great Council[?]"

In Virginia, Richard Henry announced that he was "quite tired of the wickedness and folly" now ruling public life. Frank, on the other hand, tried as usual to be philosophical. He was simply elated to be back at Menokin. "The post of honour is a private station," he announced, and he hoped the Lees would find quiet pursuits where "honour and fortune will be less dependent on the villainy and folly of mankind."

Such advice proved hard for Richard Henry to swallow. As one whose life had been devoted to politics, the success of his opponents in chasing four Lees from office was a particularly bitter dose. His chagrin was such that, late in 1779, he spoke of abandoning Virginia. How serious he was remains uncertain. But there is no doubt R.H. felt forlorn at Chantilly. At age forty-six, living on land rented from Colonel Phil's heirs, facing the costs of a family to which babies seemed always arriving, and cut off for the moment from a place of power in the Old Dominion, Richard Henry considered starting over.

For a new home, he looked to Massachusetts, confiding to John Adams: "I feel myself much interested in the establishment of a wise and free republic in Massachusetts Bay, where yet I hope to finish the remainder of my days." Knowing that some explanation of this astounding announcement was required, Lee admitted he and Virginia had become incompatible. "The hasty, unpersevering, aristocratic genius of the south suits not my disposition and is inconsistent with my ideas of what must constitute social happiness and security." More important for R.H.'s mood, perhaps, was knowing that he and Frank had, in their last days in Philadelphia, been pushed into the minority in Virginia's delegation to the Continental Congress.

Gradually, however, the gloom lifted at Chantilly and the magnetic power of public life drew Richard Henry back. Not so for Frank. Confident he had taken more than his turn in championing liberty and a virtuous republic, he was content. After 1779, Frank remained mostly in seclusion, serving only briefly in the Virginia senate. At that time his charming letters to his wife Becky show how his heart remained at Menokin. Frank soon retreated to Becky and stirred no more from home.

Neither R.H. nor Frank was in Philadelphia late in 1780 when Arthur returned from Europe, while William remained behind. Going to the Austrian Netherlands, William had settled in Brussels where, with his wife and children, he awaited the war's end. Meanwhile, Arthur arrived in Philadelphia eager to clear his name and that of all Lees. However, nothing the family could do made personal relationships any easier for him to handle in America than in Europe. Even the comfort of a reunion with his sister Alice was not enough to calm Arthur. But then, Alice had challenges of her own to face.

9

Romance in Philadelphia 1760–1788

Alice Lee Shippen happily received her youngest brother Arthur upon his arrival in America late in 1780. It seemed natural that he should seek her for consolation. Alice was the nearest to a mother Arthur could remember after the death of his parent, Hannah, in 1750. Even at age forty, a little boy peeped from Arthur's correspondence with Alice. He would implore "dearest sister" to choose a wife for him, so long as the selection was "young, beautiful, and good."

On his return from Paris, Arthur took from his sister what he most needed: words of praise. Alice liked to say how much she admired her youngest brother "as the citizen and the patriot." She spoke scathingly of the sinister "villains," led by the despised Benjamin Franklin, who, she charged, had so cruelly mistreated Arthur. Another appeal of Alice's household for Arthur was the comfort of hearing her husband Dr. William Shippen repeat a favorite refrain: "It matters not what the world will say."

Characteristically, Arthur had not been certain what he should say when, in October 1779, Congress had notified him that he was "at liberty to return to America." As he prepared to sail home in 1780, one part of Arthur boasted that Congress "cannot disgrace a man who is shielded by innocence and evidence against every accusation." He directed Richard Henry to begin a libel suit against Silas Deane, the damages to be 200,000 pounds. (The defendant fled out of reach to Europe.)

Such bravado, however, could not silence that omnipresent other part of Arthur's nature, his anxious and insecure side. Even before reaching Philadelphia, Arthur began talking of how "delicate" and "difficult" it would be to vindicate himself "without adding to the flames." Ought he to demand "a public trial," he asked Richard Henry? Or should he "appeal to the people at large?" Neatly, Arthur summarized his problem: "I shall be very much at loss how to act."

Finally, with most of his Parisian bluster drained away, Arthur timidly suggested that perhaps Congress had done enough to shame itself when it repudiated him. Who can "conceive what can condemn my adversaries, if their own actions have not[?]" Instead of fighting, he would take asylum in Virginia and "repose myself."

Arthur remained with the Shippens for several months, setting out for the banks of the Potomac in January 1781. He did not go empty-handed. Congress had promised to reimburse his expenses incurred while serving abroad. Friends among the Massachusetts radicals had arranged that Arthur receive an honorary doctorate from Harvard and be elected to the American Academy of Arts and Sciences. Massachusetts also showed its gratitude by awarding Lee 6000 acres of land, located in the future state of Maine.

Sister Alice may have felt some relief bidding Arthur goodbye. She had lived in Philadelphia for nearly twenty years, and many personal problems had accumulated during that time. In 1760, when she emigrated to England, Alice believed she was putting her American troubles behind her. Two years later, she had married and returned to the colonies, her destination Pennsylvania rather than Virginia. It all had happened unexpectedly.

In London, Alice found a close friend in Anne Home, daughter of a prominent physician, Dr. Robert Home. Through visits at the Home residence, Alice was introduced to the medical community and thus to young Dr. William Shippen, Jr., of Philadelphia, come to complete his studies in Edinburgh and London. Fortunately for himself and Alice, "Billy" Shippen did not study perpetually. His diary shows that, although he worked diligently at medicine, surgery, and dissection, he managed to spend much time with families like the Homes. He also enjoyed London's theatrical fare.

Alice and Billy were married on 3 April 1762. As the parish record of St. Mary La Strand Church stated: William Shippen, "Batchelor," was wed to Alice Lee, "Spinster." The bride was twenty-six, nearly ten years older than Hannah had been when she married Gawin Corbin. Dr. Shippen was four months younger than the bride.

It was an affectionate union. Aware of this, Arthur Lee, who had been a student with Shippen in Edinburgh, advised his new brother-in-law: "My love to my sister, and if like her mother Eve, from your lips not words alone please her, add a kiss." As the years passed, the letters between Dr. and Mrs. Shippen show that they had a relaxed and candid relationship, even though they usually began their epistles with the quaint stiltedness of those days—"My Dear Mrs. Shippen."

The couple was very different in personality. While both were highly intelligent individuals, Alice was beloved for what one friend called "that heavenly mildness which is the characteristic of her soul." She came to be admired for "her extraordinary strength of mind, that is only exceeded by the strength of the affections of her heart." Her own daughter would speak of Alice's "masculine understanding."

On his side, Billy had an especially vigorous, outgoing nature. He delighted in human contact, which ranged from his distinguished work with students and patients to his pleasure in feasting, dancing, and drinking. An invitation to dine with the Shippens was cherished in Philadelphia, for Alice set a table to match Virginia's best.

In returning to America in 1762, Alice found herself in a colony where her husband's family was as significant as the Lees were in Virginia. Billy's prominent father, the senior William Shippen, himself had been a Pennsylvania physician, but now spent most of his time in country retirement. Consequently, Alice and Billy were able to move into the elder Shippen's imposing Philadelphia residence at Prune (now Locust) and South Fourth streets. She found the neighborhood was full of her in-laws.

Like the Lees, the Shippens had a strong founder. Edward, a merchant from Yorkshire, had established the clan in Boston during the 1660s. After becoming both prosperous and a Quaker, he removed to Philadelphia in 1694. There he and his descendants grew even more wealthy and prominent, although they drifted away from the Society of Friends. The Shippens tended to intermarry almost as much as the Lees. They lived luxuriously. Unlike the Lees, most Shippens were Tories during the Revolution. A Shippen wed Benedict Arnold and had to share his disgrace as a traitor.

An exception to much of this was Alice's father-in-law, William Shippen, Sr., He was the first family member to leave business and banking, exchanging these for the life of an apothecary and physician. An ardent patriot, he was a member of the Continental Congress. He also was a founder and trustee of the College of New Jersey (Princeton), a leading Presbyterian, and vice president of the American Philosophical Society. He was eager to have his talented son Billy as a partner, so when the young man graduated from Princeton, he was sent to England and Scotland in 1758 for the best medical training available.

Back in Philadelphia, Alice's husband showed as much interest in training physicians as he did in his own practice. Fascinated by anatomy,

Billy Shippen was the first professor of that subject in the new medical school of the College of Philadelphia (eventually the University of Pennsylvania). In this role, he had to weather suspicions about where he secured the cadavers for his students to dissect. He led in elevating midwifery into the science of obstetrics. As one of the first males to practice this specialty, Billy became renowned for his sympathetic care and success with difficult deliveries.

Once, he spent several days attending a woman in such dreadful labor that members of her family, the prominent Drinker clan, begged him to destroy the child to save the mother. "I opposed them all and persevered and made her the living mother of a very fine son, of which the town rings and I have gained much honor, besides the divine feeling of having done right and making many happy." At several moments in the ordeal, Billy realized how Alice's agony in childbirth was comparable.

Few women experienced more hardship with pregnancy than Alice. On the surface, she seemed to have an enviable existence as one of Philadelphia's prominent women. Yet she took most pleasure from the role of a mother. So it seemed tragic that, while her husband was among the region's leading authorities on obstetrics, Alice saw all but two of her eight infants die at birth or soon afterwards.

A daughter born to Alice in 1763 was christened Anne Home Shippen, but always called Nancy. Two years later, when a son arrived, he was called Thomas Lee Shippen, honoring Alice's father. The family spoke of him usually as Tommy. After these successful births, Alice seemed to be steadily pregnant for another ten years. Just as regularly, she saw each of these babies die. With every grief, the parents fixed more attention and hope upon Nancy and Tommy. Alice became increasingly depressed.

In 1772, Billy Shippen confided to R. H. Lee that Alice had gone to the seashore "to try what effect the salt water may have on her distressed mind and body which continue in a miserable condition. Her sufferings are inexpressible. God deliver her!" While Dr. Shippen was certain that his wife would regain her "happiness," Alice doubted it. She tried to forget her troubles by charitable deeds around Philadelphia, making herself, according to her spouse, "perfectly humble, thinking every one better than herself and every thing too good for her."

Then came war in 1776, and Billy was soon caught up in medical service for the Revolutionary army. Alice found herself alone in Philadelphia, Nancy having been sent to Mistress Rogers' school in Trenton and Tommy to Needwood Forest Academy in Frederick Town, Maryland, where his cousin George Lee joined him. By herself, Alice thought often of her brothers in their lonely European vigil, and so named a baby son after them. Born in August 1776, little William Arthur Lee Shippen soon died. Two years later, Alice went through her last pregnancy at age forty-two. In September 1778, Dr. Shippen sadly notified Richard Henry that Alice was "confined to her room and I am afraid will lose another patriot for me."

Before that final misfortune, Alice had been absent for a time from Philadelphia, refusing to submit to the city's occupation by British troops. Many members of the Shippen clan welcomed the English soldiers, which has confused some historians who have assumed that Alice, too, was a loyalist. Instead, among the Lees Alice appears to have taken the most judicious approach to Revolutionary issues. She found wrong-doing on both sides, and lamented the conflict. Nevertheless, she was outraged by the fall of Philadelphia and took refuge early in 1777 with Colonel Phil's widow at Stratford. She also spent time at nearby Chantilly with Richard Henry and his family.

Although Alice had not visited Virginia for seventeen years after she left the Potomac scenes, she and Billy had regularly exchanged letters with the Lees there. Supplies from Philadelphia were shipped south, and, as often, useful and appetizing products from the plantations were sent to the Shippens. To Richard Henry, Dr. Shippen wrote in 1768: "Nancy and Tom send twelve kisses apiece to your sons and daughters." He reiterated how much pleasure the "channel of communication" between the families meant to them—and he promised to fill R.H. and Frank's orders for a large supply of writing paper.

From Virginia, Alice wrote to her husband: "I feel I love in my very heart the true liberty of America, the liberty of saying and doing everything that is beautiful and proper." Alice's letters conveyed much affection, including assurance to Billy that she was "unalterably" his. She sent directions for her family's welfare, and asked Billy to be patient because reports of Tommy's illness at school had put her to the expense of sending a horseman all the way to Maryland to inquire after the lad. "You must not be angry. If you knew my feelings, you would not be."

She and Billy were distraught when there were no letters from each other. Dr. Shippen told Tommy: "I love her dearly and beg she will write me." Conceding she was "miserable" without Billy, Alice soon was impatient in Virginia. "Oh, when shall I have you all to myself?" she asked him. By late spring 1777, they were reunited, after which Alice stood beside her troubled mate as, in her words, "good for nothing doctors and commissaries" put his career in jeopardy.

Billy Shippen's professional difficulties are a vivid illustration of how the early history of medicine in Philadelphia was not entirely a matter of healing. It was marred by disagreement and jealousy between strong and colorful personalities, and Dr. Shippen was as much involved here as in the lecture hall or dissecting laboratory.

Capitalizing on rumors about Billy's lavish style of living, his enemies were in hot pursuit when he became General George Washington's medical commander. The appointment came to Dr. Shippen at least in part because his Lee brothers-in-law were powers in the Continental Congress. The fact that Washington had often lodged at the Shippen house, where he could be sure of good Virginia cooking, gave Billy a certain advantage over his competitors.

Shippen's full title was impressive: Director General and Chief Physician in the medical department of the American army. The pomp did not spare Alice three years of watching as professional animosities and politics, as well as her husband's errors of judgment, tarnished his name. The spectacle doubled the misery Alice already suffered from knowing how her brothers in Europe and Virginia were being vilified.

Finally, at Billy's request, a court-martial trial was held from March to May 1780 in Morristown, New Jersey. It crept at a snail's pace while charges were heard involving Billy's alleged malpractice and administrative dishonesty. Foes such as Doctors John Morgan and Benjamin Rush claimed that Billy had hampered physicians in properly caring for hospitalized troops. It was charged that he tolerated frightful health and medical conditions, and that he had personally profited when acquiring supplies for the army. The testimony seemed endless. Billy grumbled: "It is very mortifying to have every boy, formerly my pupils, asked what they know against the Surgeon General."

Through it all, Alice stood unwaveringly beside her husband. In her judgment, "such villains" as those opposing Billy were a "disgrace to the present age." Indeed, these miscreants "do not appear once in a thousand years to scourge mankind." The Lee brothers, themselves beleaguered, rallied beside Alice and Billy. Richard Henry advised Dr. Shippen to hold fast against "the wicked enemies of our country." Given R.H.'s own woes, it was not surprising that he should warn Billy their foes might well be victorious, at least until "virtue learns to be as industrious as vice, and men in general come to prize the former more than the latter."

While the controversy surrounding Dr. William Shippen remains murky, the evidence is clear that Alice's mate was not blameless. He allowed his fondness for self-indulgent living to distract him from duty and also to take injudicious, though technically legal, advantage of his powers of procurement. While General Washington expressed confidence in his good friend Billy, the latter's acquittal by one vote was hardly a resounding vindication. Even so, it was enough for Billy, who felt he could resign his post in triumph.

By the autumn of 1780, he was back with Alice in Philadelphia. Billy resumed teaching and practicing medicine, announcing he was unstained and his foes "reprobated." He talked of suing them for defamation, but he soon cooled down. After all, he told Tommy, "nothing preserves the health of the body [more] than an easy, pleasant, and good humored mind."

Meanwhile, Alice made ready to welcome Arthur, purring happily at being restored to "the cheerfulness of our fireside." She hoped that politicians would not hinder her husband from teaching, proudly reminding others that "he is the father of the College of Physick in America, and the foundation he lays for medical knowledge is of the greatest public utility." There was no hindrance, and Dr. Shippen went back to his professional tasks.

After Arthur departed for Virginia, Alice faced new domestic excitement. The Shippen household had the ways of teenagers to contend with, as well as the suitors who pursued her daughter. The wishes of Nancy Shippen, along with those of her brother Tommy, now dominated the interests of Billy and Alice. With their other children dead, the indulgent parents allowed their youngsters to become spoiled, self-centered persons.

Earlier, Alice had trouble allowing Nancy to grow up. When the daughter attended Mistress Rogers' academy in Trenton, Alice hovered impatiently nearby. Her daughter was not to tie fashionable ribbons around her shoulders. To do so "will certainly make her crooked," Alice wrote. To Nancy herself, Alice said: "I would do anything in my power that would assist in your improvement—much depends on your being improved. Neglect nothing that will make you agreeable to Mrs. Rogers and your school fellows."

The mother wished particularly to know "how you improve in humility." Nancy must overcome sloth, for it was industry "which makes so great a part of a female character." And if Nancy did not measure up to "expectations," her "Mama" would not send her "pretty things." Alice implored Nancy to remain "my dear girl who I love and always will love while she behaves well." For Alice, this included "how you have improved in holding your head and shoulders, in making a curtsy, in going out or coming in a room, in holding your knife and fork, in walking."

Evidently Nancy succeeded in pleasing her mother. Alice informed Tommy: "I am now happy in your dear sister" who was "as attentive, obedient, and affectionate—all as you or I could wish." Billy helped the cause by reminding Nancy that her mother "wishes to make you one of the finest women in Philadelphia. This should excite your love." Such a prospect certainly excited Nancy's luxury-loving father.

Billy wished to have a "fine" Nancy who could make a prosperous marriage. Money was always needed in the Shippen residence since Billy depended upon his medical practice and lectures for income. Any hope for wealth rested on a prospective legacy from his well-to-do father, and the elder Shippen lived almost as long as Billy. Nancy could not expect to bring a large dowry to her marriage.

Even so, Miss Shippen might reasonably hope to marry well. She was beautiful, educated, and her lineage on both sides was among the best that America offered. At age sixteen, she was also a merciless coquette. These credentials brought many suitors, including General Washington's nephew Bushrod. Apparently he had no chance against two competitors, Colonel Henry Beekman Livingston and a French diplomat, Louis Otto.

Livingston had recently resigned from the Continental Army. Some said he did so to woo Nancy, while others claimed he left in anger at being passed over for higher rank. The Colonel was from one of New York's wealthiest families. His father, the famed Robert R. Livingston, was deceased, but Henry's mother, Margaret Beekman Livingston, was very much alive and kept a sharp eye on the 163,000 acres constituting the Livingston manor along the Hudson. She worried over her son Henry's ways with women, which had become scandalous, and she hoped that a good wife might domesticate him. Henry seemed convinced that Nancy was certainly a desirable mate, but events proved he had no intention of abandoning his sexual adventures.

Louis Otto, Nancy's other favorite suitor, was a handsome foreigner who was attached to the French legation in Philadelphia. He could point to a title back in Europe and call himself Count, but at the moment the distinction brought no money. Even so, Otto wished to marry Miss Shippen, in spite of Nancy's childish toying with the rivals. Otto's beguiling passion survives in his letters: "I shall ever adore you, ever love you." He tried to convince Nancy that she preferred him, and that only wealth kept Livingston in the race.

The Frenchman feared that Nancy would "sacrifice your inclination to your duty." Evidently Nancy was quite willing to let Otto believe this, and implied to him that it was her parents, rather than she, who favored Livingston. Nancy's talk led relatives and friends of the Shippen (and thus legend) to believe that family pressure took Nancy away from her young and handsome Count. Actually, Alice and Billy wanted their daughter to make the choice.

Nancy's brother Tommy pulled for Livingston, whose brave military record and great wealth appealed to the fifteen-year-old lad. Tommy was willing to overlook one shortcoming in the Colonel, which was his dislike of the Lee family. The prejudice was formed "by the insinuations of [Silas] Deane, with whom," Tommy reported, "I believe, he was rather closely connected." To overcome this anti-Lee sentiment, Tommy advised his father they must let "Mamma . . . make a proselyte [of him], as I am sure no body can withstand such solidity of reasoning as Mamma possesses together with such a torrent of elegant language, especially in a matter where she is so perfect [a] master of the subject."

Almost to the moment of her wedding, Nancy flirted with these two swains. Dr. Shippen sent Tommy, away at school, a description in late January 1781: "On Monday she liked L——— and his fortune. On Tuesday evening when O——— comes, he is the angel. L——— will consummate immediately. O——— not [for] three years. L——— has solicited the father and mother. O——— is afraid of a denial. In short, we are all most puzzled." Billy doubted that Nancy was genuinely perplexed in choosing between Otto and Livingston. "She loves the first and only esteems the second."

Nevertheless, the wealthy Colonel Livingston won. Neither the bride nor Alice left a record of their feelings when Nancy married Henry on 14 March 1781. After a week of festivity, Colonel and Mrs. Livingston, accompanied by Dr. Shippen, traveled to the groom's Hudson valley estate. The father of the bride was a bit abashed at his role, carefully explaining to relatives that Nancy had insisted he come along "to see her fixed in her own mansion." Telling Richard Henry that he hoped "it will prove a happy connection," Billy proudly pointed out that his new son-in-law was brother to the Chancellor of New York.

Immediately, the marriage turned ruinous. Nancy became pregnant at once, while her husband reinstated several former mistresses, by whom there were already illicit offspring. For a few months, Nancy tried to ignore the truth and to appear cheerful. Her parents urged that she remember "it should be your first care to please and make your husband happy." Said Billy: "Show the world you have all the good qualities of a Shippen and of a Lee without one of their bad ones."

By October, Nancy had enough of her husband's unspeakable behavior. She found asylum with her sympathetic mother-in-law, Margaret Livingston, who resided nearby in the clan's famous Claremont. Nancy insisted she had tried everything before giving up. Livingston, however, had other ideas. "Cruelty," Nancy called his strategy when he refused to allow her to leave him unless she signed away all her dower rights. Hearing this, Alice urged that Nancy disregard the threat and return at once to Philadelphia. "You must expect nothing from me unless you come here."

Nancy obeyed, putting behind a marriage of less than a year which had utterly broken down. She and Colonel Livingston remained estranged for the rest of their lives, causing many unpleasant episodes. Henry was intensely jealous of Louis Otto, who he claimed led Nancy into adultery, allegations strengthening the Colonel's campaign to take custody of his daughter Peggy, to whom Nancy gave birth on 26 December 1781.

At this point, the matriarch, Margaret Livingston, stepped in. Herself disturbed by Nancy's youth and renown as a flirt, Henry's mother insisted upon rearing Peggy. The Shippens chose to comply, since Grandmother Livingston, whom everyone called the "Old Lady," was Peggy's only hope for a sizable inheritance.

After parting from Livingston, the eighteen-year-old Nancy began a journal which overflows with juvenile self-pity. Alternately, Nancy displayed pride in obeying her parents, anger over the fickleness of all lovers, and affection for her daughter. She called her husband "Wretched, unhappy man." Could he not see that only his brutality had put her to flight? Recording an imaginary conversation with Livingston, Nancy made as her last words to him: "And now you say I left you because I loved another."

So aware were the Shippens of the Colonel's accusations that even Billy agreed Nancy must be kept strictly under control. She was not to see Louis Otto, who continued writing to her. The treatment led Nancy to condemn "cruel custom" in her journal, while Alice urged her daughter "not to murmur but be resigned to the will of providence." Keeping his eye on the practical aspects of the muddle, Billy decreed that little Peggy must continue in the care of the Old Lady. No blunder must deny the baby a share of the great Livingston fortune.

The Shippens hoped for a time that Nancy's marriage might be patched up, so a reconciliation was attempted. In May 1783, a "sobbing" Alice sent Nancy to the watchful care of Mrs. Livingston, where the estranged couple would meet. "If you don't find your husband altered for the better," Alice warned Nancy, "don't let your love for our sweet baby tempt you to throw yourself into misery." Nancy noticed no change, wrote a letter of separation, and within a few weeks was back in Philadelphia. The circumstances brought Billy Shippen to repeat his favorite refrain: "It matters not what the world will say."

Tiny Peggy was left with her grandmother, Old Lady Livingston. Nancy could trust her to keep the little girl safely away from the Colonel, who continued to rage about Nancy's supposed liaison with Louis Otto. Nancy soon was telling everyone about Henry's "jealousy and unmanaged passions." Hoping to soothe their daughter, the Shippens relented a bit in the watch they had set over her. Nancy was released to re-enter society, but restrictions carefully governed how gentlemen might call.

When one of these was Louis Otto, Dr. Shippen always remained in the room, although Nancy professed feeling nothing more than friendship for the suitor. Nancy seemed indifferent when the Count was assigned to New York, and she began happily to attend parties, even though "My Papa was not pleased with me for keeping such late hours." When Nancy was obliged to remain at home, Alice tried to inspire her by reading aloud from a favorite author, Hugh Blair of the University of Edinburgh, whose five volumes of sermons offered plenty to occupy them.

Of Alice, Nancy said in January 1784: "She is a woman of strong sense, and has a generous heart, and a great share of sensibility"—an eighteenth century term meaning a high capacity for refined emotion. "Sweet sensibility! source of a thousand heaven borne sensations," said Nancy, "for the wealth of the Indies I would not be without thee."

But such powerful sensibility proved Alice's undoing. When Nancy celebrated her twentieth birthday during March 1784, Alice, who was forty-eight, began a withdrawal which rarely relented for the next four years. She explained that her retirement from society was to face what seemed her unworthiness and to make herself acceptable either for death or for continuing in a sinful world. There were other concerns that burdened Alice: Nancy's failed marriage; Tommy's growing up; a disillusion with the social posturing her life entailed; and sorrow over the continued decline of the Lee family name.

Such anxieties probably drew in some degree from psychophysiological impulses. Of these, perhaps the most important was that as she neared age fifty, Alice knew she was no longer capable of bearing children, a capacity of the greatest importance to her. For Alice, the maternal role was God's supreme calling for a female. Thus, she viewed the six little graves of her babies in Philadelphia's Arch Street burying ground as Heaven's reproach.

Also, Alice may have seen in Nancy's disastrous wedlock the punishment due a mother for allowing a daughter to enter the embrace of a lecher. And when Alice tearfully watched her granddaughter Peggy taken off to be reared by Old Lady Livingston, this could only be another mark of Divine disfavor. So it was that in 1784 Nancy observed how her mother became "more indifferent about worldly matters than ever I saw her."

From whatever combination of promptings, Alice began stressing her unworthiness in God's sight, while Billy noted that his wife's thoughts were focused on "futurity." Alice decided she must leave Philadelphia for seclusion at the country property of the elder Dr. Shippen, a refuge appropriately called Mount Peace. Nancy offered a sort of benediction: "Dear, good woman. She has had severe trials. I pray God they may be of use to her."

Thereafter, when Nancy was not visiting daughter Peggy in New York, Billy ordered her out to Mount Peace as companion for Alice. The role soon bored Nancy, who resented spending her time sitting beside a silent parent. What was it "that distresses her," Nancy wondered. "Nothing I could do would raise her spirits." Often Alice would retire to her room where she "spent the evening in earnest prayer." When Nancy complained to her father about "how hard it is to be alone with Mamma," she reported: "I made him angry."

And so the time passed. An elderly lady was found to assist Nancy in looking after Alice. Tommy visited with his mother when he was home from the College of William and Mary. But regardless of their efforts, the family could see no improvement in Alice. "She is so miserable," Nancy reported. "She spends all her time in crying, groaning, and praying day and night." Arthur Lee arrived and tried to cheer his sister, disregarding her protestations that she wished to be left in solitude. If Alice consented to reappear in Philadelphia it was usually for one night, after which she ordered a carriage and set out for Mount Peace, insisting on riding alone.

Meanwhile, Nancy amused herself with thoughts of her daughter, by playing the harpsichord, and at the chessboard. She was good with the game, and was astonished one evening when General Horatio Gates beat her. Occasionally, she made her mother's refrain her own: "I am deprived of all hope of ever being more happy in this world—The next I leave to *Heaven*." These thoughts were discarded when Old Lady Livingston announced that Peggy could begin spending part of each winter in Philadelphia.

This good news may have been a sign to Alice that she could return to life. During 1786, there were indications leading Dr. Shippen to predict that his wife might yet "come right." But progress was slow, and Alice often kept to her country refuge, returning Billy to despair and leaving Arthur to complain to his discouraged brother-in-law: "About my sister you never say a word to me." Nevertheless, 1787 was Alice's last year of serious withdrawal. She turned up more frequently in Philadelphia, where a visit from an old friend found her even "gay and agreeable."

There were occasions when Alice's gloom reappeared, but from a new cause—her son Tommy's latest venture. He was now in England, ostensibly to study law. Alice believed London's vice surpassed any sinfulness Williamsburg or Philadelphia could muster. Tommy's claims of virtuous behavior did not entirely reassure his mother—nor his father, who nearly broke under the alarm aroused when Tommy told of a bout with venereal disease. Alice was spared this news.

After a summer and autumn of variable spirits in 1787, in December Alice tumbled down the stairs. She was so badly bruised that she was ordered to bed. Billy often sat beside her. One day, after dinner, he read aloud the latest letter from Tommy in England. Alice's response gave Billy his first clear view of the oppressive burden she had carried.

Listening to her husband repeat Tommy's words of gratitude for all she had done for him, Alice wept. Rather than thank her, she announced her son should curse her. When Billy reminded her of how tenderly she had watched over Tommy's youthful years, striving to make him "the admiration of all strangers," Alice startled him by saying that precisely this aim had been her sin. She had filled the young man "with false pride" and thus led to his ruin.

Alice's assertion encouraged Billy to test some treacherous psychological waters. Deliberately, he tried a treatment in which he first agreed with Alice in condemning her role in the family. Then he switched tone to remind her how she had recently spent years in repentance. This led to the final step, by which Billy told Alice that, in view of her penitent state, he as her husband now forgave her, and assured her that God also did. As a concluding flourish, Billy recited for Alice words about a contrite heart being all the Heavenly Father required "of the greatest sinner."

Billy's strategy satisfied Alice, who began to talk calmly of all the pains she had once regrettably taken to prevent Tommy from being a devout Christian. By April 1788, her improvement seemed remarkable. Billy informed Tommy: "I begin to entertain hopes that your mother will be one among us again." As if to prove this, Alice took up reasserting herself as the lady of the house in Philadelphia.

Nancy, who had been running things in the Shippen residence, was pushed aside with the justification she was too severe with the servants. Alice announced she "would manage them now more gently and as well." At Christmas 1788, Alice presided as of old over a grand family dinner, and Nancy, her father noticed, was learning "to be the daughter again."

Near this time, Alice composed a document she called her "Covenant of Grace." Its contents probably explain how she replaced guiltiness with peace of mind. The "Covenant" began: "I, a poor lost child of the first Adam and wholly lost in myself by reason of my great sins and rebellion against my divine maker." Alice then chronicled the shame of her offenses. especially those of "my heart." But even these, she avowed, could be overcome by acknowledging that Christ could save her—"he to be the all, the glory, and I all the shame. He to be mine, and I to be his, forever and forever."

It was as if Alice, a daughter of the Lees and Ludwells, and inheriting their worldly pride, had been lifted from this family mire. She said she took the Gospel of Love as her guide. The worldly Billy Shippen was much impressed, predicting that his rejuvenated mate would govern the family "with more moderation and beneficity than before." In a letter to Tommy, Alice stressed that persons should be judged less by their deeds than by their motives. It was, she said, "the thoughts, the affections, the temper and frame or inclination of the mind which makes the grand difference between the happy and those who are not so."

Pondering this, Tommy remarked to Nancy that "it does not appear to me so strange that our dear mother should have taken herself from the world." By this means, she had learned to "indulge more extensively in the heavenly works of benevolence." And now, watching Alice's new mood and behavior, Tommy thought it likely that their mother's daily satisfaction would derive from "making those who are oppressed with care happy." Tommy proved an apt prophet, as his own tragic story eventually testified.

~ 10

"The World Seems Crazy"
1780–1797

Alice's seclusion at Mount Peace occurred at the same time her brother William struggled with his own enforced retirement. He and his wife Hannah had remained in Europe when Arthur sailed for America. They did not wish to expose their children to a wartime voyage home. There were now three youngsters: William, Portia, and Cornelia. A second son, Brutus, had recently died. The last birth had been that of Cornelia. With her arrival, Hannah's difficult childbearing days ended at age forty-three.

Stuck in Brussels, repudiated by Congress, and given no chance to defend himself, William should have been miserable. And, indeed, he was often wrathful over what he considered the many injustices done him, as well as over the victory of his enemies. But he also recognized the pleasure in domesticity, and pledged that "my family and books will employ my whole time, until some business is undertaken." William preached that "the care of a wife and family is amply sufficient to employ a man's whole time."

He spoke often about "my tribe" and particularly of his daughters. "Little Portia would win your heart, were you here," he informed Arthur. "She is so good and begins to lisp her words so sweetly." Son William had "all the fire and vivacity of his grandfather [Ludwell], with too great a portion of his feeble constitution."

Virginia was rarely out of William's thoughts, and for more than sentimental reasons. There were the 10,000 English pounds which planters owed him in debts dating back before the war. More important, of course, was Green Spring. Neither Hannah nor William had seen the plantation since she had inherited it, and the hazards of war had prevented them from receiving any income from it. Briefly, he talked of selling the property, as Richard Henry now advised, but then dismissed the idea.

One reason for retaining Green Spring was William's worry over the hardship its sale would entail for the slaves. He seemed especially concerned about the blacks, ordering that the "most promising and ingenious lads" be apprenticed to various trades. Some women should be taught to weave. Pregnant slaves ought not be overworked "or oppressed in any manner." The entire group must "be treated as human beings whom Heaven has placed under my care not only to minister to my luxury, but to contribute to their happiness."

At last, in September 1783, William arrived with his son to take personal command of Green Spring. Hannah and the girls were to delay their arrival until the plantation could be set in order, including repairs to the now tumble-down mansion. William oversaw that effort while also chasing after payment of the many debts owed him. His neighbors insisted on sending him to the Virginia Senate, but he did not remain long. There was too much to do at Green Spring. To relatives at Pecka-tone, William wrote: "I have been so miserably disappointed in work men that it is not of my power to say when the carpenter work will be done."

Amid the sound of saws and hammers in the autumn of 1784, William heard dreadful news. His dear Hannah had died in Ostend on 18 August while preparing to sail to the home she had left twenty-five years before. It was, said William, "a loss that at any time of life is generally not easy to be repaired and in my case perhaps it is impossible." Relying on his good friend and European business associate, Edward Browne, William directed that Hannah be buried in London with her parents. Most of the furniture in Brussels should be sold, and daughters Cornelia and Portia sent to Virginia.

He awaited impatiently for the appearance of "my sweet babes." Hannah's last request was that the girls grow up in the United States under the care of Frank and Becky Lee at Menokin. She had believed that "no woman educated in England could live happily in America or hope to be married [there]." As proof of his late wife's wisdom, William pointed to just such a learned lady in Green Spring's vicinity. She had wealth and was "tolerably handsome," he noticed, yet she had offers of matrimony only from "swindlers and adventurers."

The summer of 1785 passed with no sign of William's daughters, but it brought evidence of a worsening problem for him. His weak eyesight began to fail rapidly. He tried occupying himself by enlisting in efforts to strengthen the newly independent Episcopal Church. Insisting that Virginia had once been "remarkable for religion and piety," or so William recalled, he now lamented that upon his return to Virginia, he had found the Commonwealth gripped by "dissipation, immorality, and vice."

Soon, even this spiritual contribution seemed more than William's enfeebled vision permitted, causing him to wonder if he would even be able to see his daughters when, in September 1785, came the good news that Portia and Cornelia were finally on their way. The message contained one alarming detail. William's daughters were being accompanied by a Miss Haynes, an English friend of Hannah's.

William stewed over what was to be done with Miss Haynes, it being too late to stop her from making the voyage. He feared that she had matrimony with him in mind. William claimed his health was too precarious for him to take another wife. "My exit would leave her in a most disagreeable situation." Nor could he imagine Miss Haynes relishing "such close retirement as mine where few strange faces appear."

On 29 November, the two young women and Miss Haynes reached Green Spring. William found his daughters "all that a fond parent can wish." After a brief reunion, they were taken to Menokin and put into the loving custody of the childless Frank and Becky. Then William escaped the awkward presence of Miss Haynes by maneuvering her into the post of governess on a neighboring plantation. People who had greeted Portia and Cornelia had been impressed by their education, and naturally gave the credit to Miss Haynes.

But Miss Haynes had not been the girls' governess, a detail which William chose to keep to himself, He preferred to let rumor award the good lady "much Eclat." After all, he insisted, "it was not my business to put a stop to this prevailing idea." What Miss Haynes thought of the arrangement is unknown, although William phlegmatically asserted that she ought to be delighted. She was employed "at extravagent wages for this country."

Now, crippled by arthritis and nearly blind, William looked and felt much older than his forty-six years. At the end of 1785, with his daughters safely fixed, his son maturing nicely, and his finances slightly improved, William said: "I am perfectly contented to shake hands with the world and bid it a final adieu." He predicted that friends in England would "hear again *of me*, before you will hear *from me*." However, William was to survive at Green Spring for another decade, although his physical state did not improve.

William kept his son with him to serve as his sight and to learn about business and farming. Young William's presence was consoling, as was the elder William's close friendship with brother Frank. His relations with Arthur became somewhat strained when the usually tactless youngest brother demanded his money back after purchasing some wine through William. "I can't help being surprised that you are making this proposition to me," William responded, refusing to budge. He spoke of how

Arthur had found the same wine quite palatable when he drank it at Menokin.

There continued to be many unpleasant barriers facing William in collecting the money owed him, for numerous records had been lost, either in London or in Virginia. None of this, however, promised as much grief for the master of Green Spring as when he received a message in 1787 from Hannah's sister and his first cousin, the neurotic Lucy Ludwell Paradise. Tommy Shippen, who was in England at the time, called Lucy "mad" and "the strangest woman without doubt that God ever formed."

Lucy announced that she and her husband would embark at once to visit Virginia and particularly to see Green Spring, the ancient Ludwell family seat. After the Paradises arrived, the ten weeks of reunion went much better than the lonely William anticipated. Afterwards, Lucy began a royal procession of visits with other Lee cousins, doing so in interesting times, for it was now 1788 and Virginia was deciding whether to ratify the proposed Federal Constitution. Unfortunately, the issue made it the poorest possible moment to call at Chantilly, where Lucy found Richard Henry in a state of alarm. His latest plans for America were miscarrying.

During the 1780s, the master of Chantilly was more than ever leader of the Lee family. William took care to have a cordial relationship with Richard Henry. Frank deferred to him, and Arthur depended upon his guidance. Nor did the nation itself have to suffer long without R.H.'s attempts to lead it. He was back in Philadelphia in 1784.

When R.H. and Frank had left Congress in the hands of Benjamin Franklin's supporters in 1779, Richard Henry tried to be cheerful about his retreat. He insisted to Billy Shippen: "It is an honor to have been a principal object of this faction." Still, though he kept his seat in Virginia's legislature, R.H. was rankled by the memory of insults suffered by the Lees from friends of Silas Deane. As a southern agrarian, Richard Henry suspected that merchants from the mid-Atlantic region, led by Robert Morris and other Franklinites, were pillaging the new republic in order to line their pockets.

In part, it was to do battle against these enemies and to vindicate the Lee name that Richard Henry agreed to return to Congress in 1784. He found generally the delegates in Philadelphia were pleased to have him back. The Revolution had triumphed, and members of Congress knew that, as one of its early leaders, Richard Henry Lee had shown great valor in dangerous times. This respectful attitude quickly brought him election for one year as president of Congress.

In effect, this office made Richard Henry Lee the chief executive of the United States of America, and no honor did more to gratify his hunger for recognition. The Lees and Shippens rushed to congratulate him. Tommy Shippen saluted his uncle on being "rewarded for his glorious exertions." Now there was hope "that wisdom and virtue will still characterize the conduct of America." The family, of course, considered Richard Henry to be "the most virtuous" of the nation's sons, driving away "clouds of corruption."

When Congress moved its residence to New York City in January 1785, Richard Henry preferred to keep his personal business in Philadelphia. So he called upon Alice's son Tommy to run errands among tailors, pharmacists, and vintners. Proper attire, strong medication, and fine wines appealed to Congress' President Lee, which meant, for example, that Tommy was to fetch "the very best black silk net breeches, with silk gaitors." Care must be taken to have "the thighs long but not large—I wish the silk to be fine, stout, and strong." Uncle R.H. explained that such splendid trousers suit "my station," as did "black silk stockings and white shoes and knee buckles."

Richard Henry sent a challenge to his Philadelphia tailor, Mr. De Barthold. He must "convert the old President into a young Beau." As R.H. gleefully put it: "If for the good of my country I must be a Beau, why I shall be a Beau." In buying stockings, Tommy was directed to remember that the presidential foot was very tiny. When a sizable bill arrived from De Berthold, Tommy Shippen was sent to urge that the tailor be patient. Money, R.H. predicted, should arrive any day from Virginia.

Tommy's chores were endless, including selling Richard Henry's horses when the latter discovered an excellent reason to remain longer than expected in New York. By a change of policy, Congress began paying the residential expenses of its president. A delighted Richard Henry selected a house on the street where Old Lady Livingston was living during the winters with Nancy's daughter Peggy. The "little darling," as her distinguished kinsman called her, often visited him, searching his pockets "with the greatest freedom imaginable." Tiny Peggy was merely one of many guests received by the president of Congress.

During his year as executive, Richard Henry used his fine quarters to entertain grandly. He promised Dr. Shippen that "the best champagne should be plentifully at his call." When Tommy Shippen visited the house, he found Richard Henry "in a palace and think indeed he does the honors of it with as much ease and dignity as if he had been always crowned with a royal diadem." Sentinels guarded his uncle's door and "crowds of obedient domestics run to his call and fly at his command," while Richard Henry took the keenest pleasure in "a profusion of the delicacies and luxuries of good living [which] crowns his hospitable board."

Dinners at the president's house were impressive, even by Richard Henry's standards. He wrote delightedly to wish that his brothers and Billy Shippen could join him in "the black fish, sheep's head, and sea bass," all to be washed down with "Champagne, Claret, Madeira, and Muscat." Meanwhile, a report on Lee's social life came from an improbable witness, the eighteen-year-old son of an old ally, John Adams.

During much of July and August 1785, Richard Henry had as a guest in the executive mansion John Quincy Adams, who had left his father practicing diplomacy in Europe while the son returned to the United States to begin study at Harvard. Stopping first in New York before going on to Boston, young Adams had been so earnestly besought as a guest by "the President," for so the youth preferred to call R.H., that he had reluctantly settled into a several weeks' stay in Lee's residence.

While J.Q. had seen much elegance in France, Holland, Russia, and England, he was nevertheless made wide-eyed by the style in which "the President" lived. Like Tommy Shippen, Adams was especially taken by Richard Henry's lavish dinners, of which three per week were customary. According to Adams, the guests usually numbered twenty-five, all male. Once each week, the host insisted his company remain for what John Quincy found to be interminable concerts of music.

Such lavish living exacted a price in health from the presidential person, especially in view of Richard Henry's already chronic gout and dysentery. To ward off these attacks, Tommy was sent to procure what the Uncle called "Widow Diarrhea syrup." Said the president impatiently: "I assure you that it is very necessary for my health." At times, R.H. seemed more concerned about "my bowels" than public issues. On 13 August, according to young Adams, "the President" planned a gala sailing party, trusting it might restore a measure of comfort. Alas, Richard Henry was too "unwell" to go aboard.

Of course, as congressional president Richard Henry kept more in mind than his ease. While he was in the chair, Congress passed the Land Ordinance of 1785 by which America's vast western acreage was to be surveyed in rectangular sections and sold at prices and in quantities within reach of the average citizen. With Lee family encouragement, Virginia had turned over to the new nation the state's claim to much of the western land.

However, such congressional triumphs were rare, bringing public opinion increasingly to suspect the Articles of Confederation lacked power to keep order and prosperity. Richard Henry approached the subject more cautiously, so that when his term as president ended, he joined those who opposed discarding the Articles and writing a new constitution.

Amid the constitutional crisis, Richard Henry had to bear a family burden in the person of Arthur. Now back in America, the youngest brother was no asset to R.H.'s latest political venture. Indeed, Arthur made new enemies for the Lees. This might have been avoided had he kept a pledge he announced after leaving Paris. Arthur had promised to sit quietly on the sidelines, preparing a history of the Revolution. But when he failed to receive the manuscripts and anecdotes he begged of George Washington, Arthur stopped the project. He left only a few pages intended mostly to put a favorable light on his activities in London before 1774.

For Arthur, America was too full of enemies, dead and alive, to allow him to linger in his study. In 1781 he was sent to the Virginia House of Delegates from Prince William County, thanks to the power there of cousin Henry Lee. Many relatives in the legislature then saw to it that Arthur went in 1782 as a delegate to the Congress which was soon to move to New York. There he vexed his colleagues, particularly Thomas Jefferson and James Madison. They suspected, for good reason, that Arthur confused the public interest with avenging himself upon Benjamin Franklin, Robert Morris, and their associates.

Arthur became a pathetic figure in Congress, perpetually indignant, paranoid, self-centered, and often confused. His stands were rarely on the merits of issues, but as opposition to whatever his foes might favor. Amid his raging, however, there was always time for Arthur to remember the interests of the Lee family. He supported an early attempt to move the national capital to the banks of the Potomac, where his relatives owned much land.

Yet even the Lees were mystified by Arthur's campaign in 1783 to have the Northern Neck secede from Virginia and join Maryland. After this, the influence of cousin Henry was not enough to save Arthur. He lost his seat in the General Assembly, which left him ineligible to be a representative in Congress.

Before that happened, Congress devised a way to be rid of Arthur's obnoxious presence. In 1784, he was named one of the commissioners sent into western Pennsylvania for new attempts at persuading the Iroquois Indians to relinquish title to the area north of the Ohio River. Arthur faced the undertaking with typically strong opinions. The native Americans, he said, were "animals that must be subdued."

While on this assignment, Arthur fell ill in Pittsburgh at Christmas

1784. He used the time to write in his journal, mostly about the female sex. There had been no new development on this front, even though Arthur devoted himself at least as much to romantic ventures as to political vengeance. He was fond of saying that each male should "submit with all speed to that government which is the only legal one in the world—the government of the petty coat."

Arthur now despaired of finding a wife in Virginia, where he claimed only young persons married. Should he migrate to Kentucky, he wondered? There he owned 10,000 acres purchased with money paid for his services abroad. But frontier life was too risky. Should he return to England? He believed his funds would allow a comfortable existence in London, provided he remained a bachelor. But would he distress his family if he became a citizen of a monarchy?

With these thoughts Arthur meditated away the time in Pittsburgh, his mind skipping as usual from one determination to another. Finally, he decided to continue living in New York, except for pleasant visits with the Shippens in Philadelphia. Hereafter, he pledged, he would "take the world as I find it—to remain in the midst of this odd chapter of accidents." The hindrance to this plan was that Arthur must find a new occupation, since he had been forced out of politics.

Here, Richard Henry as president of Congress doubtless was a great help. Steadfast in looking after the younger brother. R.H. worked a miracle and secured Arthur's appointment as a member of the newly created Board of Treasury. Observers like James Monroe and Thomas Jefferson were aghast, foreseeing that Arthur would destroy this agency in the course of pursuing his enemies.

Taking office in July 1785, Arthur actually worked quietly in the scarcely demanding assignment until the creation of the new federal government in 1789 once again left him unemployed. Thereafter, President Washington carefully avoided naming Arthur to any post, though he had made it plain he wished at least to be a justice of the Supreme Court or Treasury Secretary.

When his career grew quieter after 1785, Arthur had more time for his brand of romance. He always claimed to be in love, but usually with at least two women. Reluctant to plead his own case, he relied on others to carry messages to the adored, some of whom were as young as seventeen. Since most of the community knew about these strange antics, no woman took Arthur seriously. The aging swain, now past forty, had to watch as those women he fancied were easily won by his rivals.

Arthur's only steadfast adviser in affairs of the heart was his niece, Nancy Shippen Livingston, whose own record in such enterprises was hardly convincing. Arthur liked to rehearse his theories before Nancy.

He informed her "that to captivate any or all of your sex, [a suitor] must apply, not to their reason or their interest, but to their fancy." All that a man needed for success was to keep attractive objects in front of women. These trinkets would "beguile them of anything." Such a strategy "will win every daughter of our mother Eve." In another mood, Arthur announced that a woman's greatest achievement was to produce a "man-child" because it enlarged the "slaves" surrounding women. "[Men] are born only to adore you."

When his own romance was not uppermost, Arthur tried to ease the marital problems of Nancy Livingston. Once again, his clumsy ways eventually botched his intentions. Arthur knew that one cause of Nancy's unhappiness was giving up her daughter Peggy to be reared by her mother-in-law, Margaret Beekman Livingston. Since he was often in New York until 1789, Arthur made a point of visiting Old Lady Livingston, who found her guest a less alarming fellow than Silas Deane's propaganda had led her to expect.

Eventually, Mrs. Livingston concluded that Arthur was decent and harmless, which brought her to ask Nancy: "From whence has that gentleman so many enemies? (This in confidence to you alone.)" Nancy replied that such a question was "as interesting as it is difficult to answer." Unfortunately, Nancy read to Arthur the Old Lady's letter inquiring about his critics. By doing so, she violated her mother-in-law's insistence that her question about Arthur be kept secret.

Immediately, Arthur rushed to the Livingston house to make his own explanations. This awkward confrontation of her mother-in-law was an example, conceded the embarrassed Nancy, of her uncle's need to "gratify a foolish, false pride." To the Old Lady, angry at having her request for confidence betrayed, Nancy could only say that her uncle seemed "to flatter himself with the prospect of convincing your family of his having enemies without any just cause."

Meanwhile, Arthur's brothers were facing some of their enemies in a new political war. By so doing, the period from mid-1787 to mid-1788 saw the family make its most important contribution to the nation since the adoption of the Declaration of Independence. And yet no Lee sat in the Constitutional Convention which gathered in Philadelphia midway through 1787. Richard Henry had been offered a seat, but he, like Virginia's governor Patrick Henry, was wary, and chose to remain aloof. Being a member of the General Congress, Richard Henry excused himself on the ground he ought not be a delegate to a gathering whose work Congress must eventually judge.

Therefore, as a new constitution was created in Philadelphia, Richard Henry was in New York, leading Congress in passing a statute of towering significance, the Northwest Ordinance of 1787. This legislation created the basis by which new states were to enter the Union on terms equal with the older ones. Furthermore, with Richard Henry's exertions, the Ordinance prohibited slavery in the region north of the Ohio River.

A monumental accomplishment, the Northwest Ordinance has often been lightly regarded because attention, then and now, turned toward the deliberations in Philadelphia. Richard Henry hoped the Convention would produce worthwhile results which, according to him, must then be studied and acted upon by Congress. He pointed out that the Articles of Confederation called for such a procedure. To do otherwise could turn the nation's future to "the intemperate part of the multitude."

For once Arthur was correct in a prediction. He announced that the constitutional crisis would make "wise men groan." Brother R.H. became a good case in point. It was not so much the proposed Constitution which alarmed him as the extra-legal method by which it was approved. Richard Henry was outraged when a majority of congressional delegates agreed that a new plan of federal government should go directly to the states for ratification. And when R.H. insisted that Congress send along its own amendments and a bill of rights, his colleagues humiliated him by brushing aside his motion without debate or a vote. It was done, said the bruised Lee, "with a most extreme intemperance."

Congress, he claimed, had fallen to "a coalition of monarchy men, military men, aristocrats and drones, whose noise, impudence and zeal exceeds all belief." Since Congress would not even hear "the patriot voice" warning that the proposed Constitution endangered liberty, Richard Henry returned to Virginia determined to sound the alarm there and across the country. But even here, he would not carry the day. He could not even win his own family to the anti-ratification cause.

Billy Shippen hurried a bulletin to Tommy in London: "Your uncle Frank Lee thinks the new form of government must be adopted lest we may not get so good a one." Cousin Harry Lee was a delegate to Virginia's ratification convention and spoke strongly in favor of the Constitution. Arthur, of course, did not desert Richard Henry, but he failed in seeking election to the ratification convention. This meeting took place during June 1788 in Richmond, Virginia's new capital. When he was urged to attend, Richard Henry blamed his pesky gout and intestinal disorder for keeping him at Chantilly.

There, on the Potomac, he was working against outright ratification long before the convention assembled. During the winter and spring of 1788, R.H. wrote influential friends in many states urging them to support changes in the proposed Constitution. These efforts led to his being mistakenly credited as author of the famous *Letters from the Federal Farmer*, considered the most influential argument for modifying the controversial document. Recently, scholars have shown Lee's views to have been significantly different from those of the publication. Nor did Richard Henry or any family member ever claim he was the author.

The writer who signed as "Federal Farmer" was probably Melancton Smith of New York. He argued more calmly than Richard Henry with his famed hyperbole usually could. Few came out so bluntly as Richard Henry when he spoke of the campaign for ratification as another "conspiracy" against American liberty. While many of his letters were shared in private, Richard Henry's most significant epistle, sent to Virginia's governor Edmund Randolph, was intended as a public document and was printed by Mathew Carey in the *American Museum*.

Here, as elsewhere, Lee explained why the proposed Constitution menaced freedom. Mainly, he called for adding to the document a guarantee of mankind's traditional rights. He stressed the freedoms of speech, religion, press, elections, and petition. As means to these ends, R.H. urged a limit to the power of the proposed federal judiciary and executive, and he suggested improvements in advising the president. Fearing a dangerous alliance would develop between the president and the Senate under the new Constitution, Richard Henry called for installing more authority where the people sat—in the House of Representatives.

It can be argued that Richard Henry Lee did more for improving constitutional government in America than most men attending the Philadelphia Convention. His hue and cry about the proposed document's shortcomings slowed the haste for ratification. It was in significant measure due to Richard Henry that supporters of the Constitution pledged a bill of rights would be the first order of business under the new government. In hesitant states, these assurances probably tipped the balance toward adoption and thus restored life to the infant Union.

Although Virginia had ratified the Constitution without making amendment a condition, by the summer of 1789, Richard Henry's voice of caution was predominant in the state. Consequently, he and William Grayson were elected the first Unites States Senators from the Old Dominion, entailing a sweet victory over James Madison, who had piloted the ratification forces. This success was not enough to prevent Richard Henry from worrying over the new republic when he reached New York to take his seat in the Senate.

Had all liberty fled to Europe, he wondered in 1789 when the French Revolution began. He informed brother Frank that the Constitution's first ten amendments, containing the bill of rights, had been passed, but "much mutilated and enfeebled." In a memorable line, Richard Henry warned Frank: "It is too much the fashion now to look at the rights of the people as a miser inspects a security [money], to find out a flaw." He told cousin Charles Lee of his fear that civil liberties must be won all over again.

Although Richard Henry was elected president *pro tempore* of the Senate, little of what happened in that body pleased him, including such innovations as the federal judiciary system, the banking plan, and the method of handling state debts. His dismay added to his increased physical debility. When the government moved to Philadelphia, R.H. asked Billy Shippen to locate lodging for him very near the state house, "that my gouty feet may sustain no injury from the wintry weather." In October 1792, Richard Henry resigned as Virginia's first and senior United States Senator, citing the "feeble state of my health."

Arthur had ached to enter the new federal government, but he was defeated in his bid for a seat in the House of Representatives. Nor could Richard Henry persuade Governor Patrick Henry to find a rewarding public position for Arthur in Virginia. It left the youngest brother adrift. He did not even own a home. "The world is all before me and I am not yet clear where I shall fix my future residence," he told Frank.

In the autumn of 1791, he purchased a country place with 565 acres near the town of Urbanna in Middlesex County. From there, Arthur could look across the Rappahannock River to Richmond County, where his sister Hannah Corbin had spent her last years. He named the property Lansdowne, after his friend the Earl of Shelburne's estate, where Arthur once spent time happily. Predictably, these memories, along with rural life, were not enough to brighten his outlook. He remained convinced that the world was deteriorating—"could we see things as they really are, we should only sicken at the sight."

Hoping to make Lansdowne less lonely, Arthur peppered his niece Nancy Livingston with new requests for advice and help as he sought favorable attention from a variety of women. He claimed that his aim was to bring all females to appreciate "that the space within their arms was celestial," a spot that was the source of "divine pleasure." Appropriately, Arthur announced that a woman should admit no male into her embrace "unless he was animated with the divine enthusiasm of Love."

A home and wife were "balm of hurt minds," Arthur said. "Tis love that makes the blossom bloom. Tis love that pours out all the music of the groves. Tis love that animates, sustains, and blesses all creatures." Marriage, he announced, meant that "we die, it is true, to a single life . . . but we arise by a change almost as great as that of regeneration."

Still, Arthur could not push himself to pass through that wondrous change. He never proposed marriage, seemingly satisfied that he had done enough by asking Nancy to convey messages to the ladies of New York or Philadelphia. Once or twice, Arthur recognized that he was all talk. Of one woman he admired from afar, he said: "She, like me, will dream away her life in imaginary joys; and lose the real happiness of matrimony, in the fanciful pleasure of the imagination."

And so Arthur Lee came to the end of his life. "I am now cast off with as much disgrace as they can fix upon me," he confided to Tommy, as he reviewed his career. He said that his labors "have only ruined myself without benefiting the public," but he believed he had merely done his duty. Arthur insisted that had he to do it over, he would once again abandon his "brilliant prospects" in London for service to the American people.

Accustomed to indoor life, Arthur did not prepare himself prudently for working around his trees and other plantings in early winter. During one such outing, he caught a cold which developed into what the family called "a violent pleurisy." He died on 12 December 1792, just short of being fifty-two. His cousin Light-Horse Harry Lee gave as generous an estimate of him as was possible. "His loss to the public was not so great as it would have been had the community been in the fashion of availing themselves of his talents." Years later, John Adams wrote of Arthur: "This man never had justice done him by his country in his lifetime, and I fear he never will have by posterity."

In his will, Arthur requested that, should it be convenient, his remains be placed "in the vault of my dear parents," one of the rare occasions he ever spoke of them. The weather proved a hindrance, so that the deceased's hope to be interred at the family's Burnt House Field cemetery had to be denied. Arthur was buried in the garden of Lansdowne, where visitors can still find the spot.

Richard Henry was named his brother's sole executor. The estate was surprisingly sizable, considering Arthur's claims of poverty. He left the bulk to Richard Henry and thereafter to the latter's son, Francis Lightfoot Lee, for whom Arthur was godfather. Many smaller bequests were made to numerous nieces and nephews, with Arthur's gold snuff box, encrusted with diamonds, going to brother Frank. A diamond ring and "gold sleeve buttons" were given to Frank's wife, Becky.

Upon Richard Henry, as executor, rested the thankless responsibility of reminding Billy Shippen of the debt Arthur had claimed his brother-in-law owed him in the amount of 1,662 pounds. After tactfully pointing out this obligation, Richard Henry told Alice's husband that he loved him too much to quarrel. In the interest of family harmony, Richard Henry suggested that claims between the Shippens and Arthur's estate be canceled.

This peaceable outlook characterized the final months of Richard Henry's life. Having left the Senate, it became easier for him to be light-hearted. His nephew Tommy Shippen remembered Uncle R.H. in his late years as often being "of a gay and cheerful disposition, and very fond of promoting mirth, and of seeing every body pleased and happy." The nephew particularly recalled R.H.'s advice that a husband must learn to "take hints without waiting for express desires."

A more tranquil mood entered Richard Henry's last letters. In one of these, written to cousin Richard Bland Lee, who was a congressman, the enfeebled statesman pleaded that America avoid another war with England. Such a step "must inevitably put our existence as a free people to the most eminent hazard." Repeatedly, R.H. emphasized that he was an American before he was a Virginian. "I know no country but the United States." And he certainly still knew how to practice American politics. Though dying, he managed a letter to President Washington, recommending a neighbor for a government job.

On 19 June 1794, Richard Henry Lee died at Chantilly. He was carried down river to the Burnt House Field burying ground and laid beside his first wife, Anne Aylett. Two years later, his second spouse, Anne (Gaskins) Pinckard, joined them. On his tomb are inscribed words uttered by Thomas Ludwell Lee in 1776 when he implored Richard Henry to come home from Philadelphia to guide the drafting of a constitution for Virginia: "We cannot do without you."

As was true all his life, Richard Henry had little wealth and many debts when he died. Chantilly sat on land leased from the owners of Stratford. The deceased was not far from the mark in saying he had grown both gray and poor in his country's service. To meet these debts it was necessary to have a public sale of R.H.'s possessions. The auction was held at Chantilly on 28 October 1794, and a second at the Westmoreland County court house on 22 April 1795. Even the library had to go to the highest bidder. Relatives and friends gathered to purchase remembrances of their dead leader. Frank took away a double-barreled gun for ten pounds, it being only one of many weapons offered for sale. Light-Horse Harry gave ten shillings for a stack of straw.

Although Richard Henry was sixty-one at the time of his death, he left his widow Anne with offspring who were still children. Their youngest sons were Frank, who was twelve, and Cassius, who was fifteen. R.H.'s daughters had married well, by Virginia standards. Two selected Lee cousins as mates, and three chose more distant relatives, a Washington, a Corbin, and a Turberville. R.H.'s son Ludwell married Flora Lee, daughter of Colonel Phil.

It was Flora and Ludwell's son, the second Richard Henry Lee, who sought in 1825 to revive the repute of his grandfather by publishing two volumes of memoirs. The books were frankly aimed at "rescuing the name and honor of Richard Henry Lee from oblivion, of making it revered as it ought by a country which truly owed him more than almost any other man." The grandson gathered letters and recollections, hoping that "the character of Mr. Lee," which "adorned the infancy of the republic," would eventually "cast a light and glory on the maturity of its destiny!" Despite this campaign, in which the Lee family joined enthusiastically, a satisfactory biography of Richard Henry Lee has never been written.

Even less is remembered today about the next Lee brother to die. William survived at Green Spring for a year after Richard Henry's death. He was sightless and dependent upon his son. William had journeyed to New York in June 1789 for cataract surgery, but the trip was fruitless. Although the procedure, which was then called couching, was performed upon the one eye in which some vision remained, the patient returned to Virginia unimproved. Thereafter, William spent summers in the mountains, drinking the spring waters which were becoming a fashionable attraction in the region.

A few weeks before he died, William heard from Frank, who grieved over the blind brother's "distressed situation," saying how "it gives me pain when I reflect how little it is in my power to assist you." Actually, there was one bit of help Frank did provide. This was to calm William's suspicion that he was becoming destitute. No matter that he was comparatively wealthy, William Lee sometimes believed his prosperity was an illusion and he feared he would awaken to find himself penniless. He worried especially that he might impose poverty upon his children, an anxiety which may have had its roots in William's long and unsuccessful struggle to receive his own inheritance from Colonel Phil.

Frank shrewdly reassured his brother: "As to worldly matters, I think you should make your mind easy on that score. You will at all costs leave a sufficiency to your children to make them happy, unless they are much wanting to themselves, in which case millions would be insufficient." Then Frank closed his letter with a charming statement of the calmness which had come to distinguish him from his three brothers. "The world seems crazy and we old people must scuffle with it as well as we can for our few days of existence."

William died on 27 June 1795, and was buried beside his Ludwell grandparents in the old churchyard at Jamestown. He left a lengthy will, dated in 1789, which began: "I, William Lee of Virginia, late alderman of London. . . ." The bulk of his vast real estate, slaves, livestock, and financial holdings passed to his twenty-year-old son William Ludwell Lee.

Although there were no restrictions upon the bequest, the father did urge that his son take legal steps to drop the name Lee "and bear the name of William Ludwell only, that the family name of Ludwell so ancient and honorable both in England and America, from which he is lineally descended, may be revived." Young William rejected the advice, remaining a Lee during his brief life.

The daughters of the deceased, Portia and Cornelia Lee, were given generous bequests, these to revert to their brother if the girls married at less than age sixteen. Nor must they accept husbands before they reached twenty-one without their guardians' consent. Portia and Cornelia, who were eighteen and fifteen when they were left orphans, continued briefly to live with Uncle Frank and Aunt Becky at Menokin.

On 17 January 1797, Frank died, preceded in death just ten days earlier by Becky. She had been nursing her husband and caught his severe cold. Frank was sixty-two, Becky less than fifty. Thereafter, for thirty years they rested in the local parish graveyard until their remains were moved to the Tayloe estate at Mount Airy. Far from any road, the family cemetery sits in a grove of cedar trees, surrounded by a pasture usually filled with grazing cattle—which makes the rare visitor take care on the long walk to the graves. Under the trees, an inscribed stone announces that beneath it is buried a Signer of the Declaration of Independence.

Menokin, the house Frank and Becky loved, was built on property that reverted to the Tayloes. Ludwell Lee, Richard Henry's son and Frank's godson, received most of Frank's slaves, cattle, and other possessions. A notable exception was the gold snuff box "given to me by my ever lamented brother Arthur Lee," which Frank directed should go to his nephew and namesake, Francis Lightfoot Lee, Richard Henry's son.

Frank also took pains in another last respect. He had spoken often of his gratitude toward Alice and Billy Shippen for taking Becky and him into their home during sessions of the Continental Congress. It was one of Frank's few regrets that he would die unable, he believed, to repay the Shippens for their kindness. Shortly before his last illness, Frank wrote to sister Alice mainly to remind her "of my affection."

In Frank's will, the Shippens were left fifty guineas "to be laid out in a piece or pieces of silver plate." Frank intended this, he said, as a "small testimony" of great esteem and gratitude toward the Shippens, who, long before, had developed a special fondness for Frank. His niece, Nancy Shippen Livingston, wrote lines of tribute to "Thou sweetest of all the Lee race/That ever adorned our shore."

Nancy's poem, composed some years before Frank's death, could serve as epitaph for this lonely survivor of the Lee brothers: "Thy temper's as soft as the dove's/When she warbles aloft in the air,/And thy converse enchantingly sweet/When engaged in discourse with the fair./But when learning engrosses thy thought/Then thy genius shines brighter and best/ And shows that thou surely wilt be/The adornment to all in the West."

Once upon a time, all the Lee brothers from Stratford, except Colonel Phil, had yearned to brighten North America by rising to continental prominence. Only briefly did any of them achieve this goal. After their brilliant days of valor in 1776, Frank, Richard Henry, and their brothers were brought by unhappy circumstances to deplore what was happening in the western hemisphere. But unlike R.H., Arthur, and William, Frank learned to live with a Republic commanded by men and ideas the brothers mostly opposed. While others might feel the sting of failure, Frank merely said "the world seems crazy," and was content to be with Becky and his books. Indeed, as Nancy recognized, Frank was "the sweetest of all the Lee race."

11

"Last of the Stratford Lees" 1786–1817

It happened that Alice Shippen's son Tommy was visiting Virginia when Uncle Frank died at Menokin. From there Alice heard the sad news that she was, as Tommy put it, "the last of the Stratford Lees." Of all the family who grew up at Thomas Lee's proud house on the Potomac, she was now the only survivor. Astonishingly, Alice lived two more decades, long enough to see a new generation come to humiliation at Stratford. But by then, Alice had also watched the sorrows of her own children multiply. Neither her son nor her daughter would brighten the lives of their parents.

One of the causes for Alice's bout with depression in the 1780s had been the tug-of-war over Peggy Livingston, Alice's granddaughter. "Poor little Peggy," Uncle Arthur Lee had observed, "it should be flattering to her to know what a contention there is for her company." Not only Nancy and Old Lady Livingston wished to have the six-year-old, but Nancy's husband Henry Livingston was still demanding to have her. Again, he urged reunion with Nancy, claiming he had reformed.

Momentarily, Nancy listened sympathetically, so that, in 1785, Henry came to Philadelphia to press his case, and Nancy wrote in her journal: "Thank God [I] am reconciled to him." But she spoke prematurely. Her husband soon departed shouting he had been rejected, while Nancy called him "inflexible." It left her, she said, "a wretched slave, doomed to be the wife of a man I hate." Henry resumed his blustering talk about Nancy's alleged infidelity, and how this made her unfit as a mother. Meanwhile, the harem he kept under his roof continued to flourish.

Then, in 1787, New York eased slightly its restrictions on marital separations and divorce. Livingston immediately proposed a legal parting and Nancy was agreeable. Advised by her father and Uncle Arthur,

Nancy informed her husband that before any talk of separation could proceed, "You will oblige me so far as to settle a portion of your estate on our dear little girl, that she may be in some measure independent." On his part, Livingston was willing to discuss maintenance payments only after Nancy agreed to give up her dower rights.

The discussions dragged on for two years, part of the debate being whether a legal separation or a divorce should be sought, and whether to do so in New York or Pennsylvania. Uncle Arthur urged Nancy not to assume a divorce could be gotten "with as much nonchalance as of a discarded lover."

Acknowledging this, Nancy bluntly informed her husband that she must bring to the divorce proceedings "proof . . . of your living with another woman." As for herself: "I am totally indifferent about your opinions of my character, as the innocence of my conduct will be always a shield against any malicious attack that may be made on my reputation." The words sounded like Nancy's adviser, Arthur Lee, who called her battle "the cause of humanity—and in that cause the female voice is irresistible."

Nancy retained Aaron Burr as her attorney, while Livingston said he would seek the famous James Wilson as counsel. Nothing came of these preparations. "How uncommonly wretched is my situation," Nancy told her mother-in-law, as it became clear that Henry was not sincerely intending to free her. With his wanton existence, her husband had no reason to marry again and could gratify his jealousy by keeping Nancy from finding happiness in a second husband. Nancy continued to be "Mrs. Livingston" for the rest of her life.

Once her own spirits were restored, Alice did what she could to encourage her daughter. "My dear Nancy," she said, "I flatter myself you have happy days to come, but you must not let pride, but truth and candor be the judge. Take them, my dear, to your bosom, make them your choice companions." This was much like encouragement Alice was giving to Tommy, whose future for the moment seemed promising enough to offset the lamentable career of his sister.

While Alice had been in retreat at Mount Peace, her husband had sent Tommy to England for legal study. Eager that his only son succeed, Billy believed his chances would be improved by going abroad. And since Grandfather Shippen would pay the bills, Tommy's father and the Lee uncles agreed the trip should be made. Only Tommy was reluctant, but he departed in July 1786 after turning twenty-one. He was handsome and shared Uncle Richard Henry's striking height of six feet two inches.

Time would show, however, that the ambition that marked most of the Lees and Ludwells did not affect Tommy. He had his father's love of ease, but with a willingness to do only what was absolutely necessary to supply that comfort. This trait was not visible enough before 1790 to alarm his kinsmen. Instead, the youthful Tommy was hailed by Uncle R.H.: "He does honor to us all, and I doubt not but that he will be both honorable and useful to his country."

Uncle Arthur agreed, and proposed to follow the nephew's European pilgrimage closely. "He is a great favorite with us all," Arthur told the proud Dr. Shippen. In turn, Tommy spoke of the inspiration he took from his uncles' example. Before leaving for England, he toured Virginia with various Lees, including "the old Squire." Being with them, Tommy told his father, "instructed and warmed me." The experience "has fired me with a virtuous ambition."

The Lee relatives emphasized that when in England, Tommy must learn the family's genealogy. Richard Henry urged him to visit Shropshire, "near Shrewsbury," where R.H. believed "the elder branch of our family lives . . . and possess undiminished the old original family estate." Tommy was also advised to call upon their relative, the Bishop of Chester. Another good turn would be for the nephew to haunt the bookstalls. Richard Henry stressed that he wished the young man to purchase "very valuable and well approved books in any science."

Grandfather Shippen sent a different sort of instruction. He warned Tommy about the two temptations that ruined many young men, "gaming and wenching." The first of these Tommy avoided after reaching London on 4 August 1786. He became something of a specialist in the second. Settling into rooms at the Inner Temple, young Shippen proceeded to avoid serious study, preferring to go out into society, to travel, and to chase women.

There was some profit in this schedule. Tommy often visited with his parents' old friend and now Minister to Great Britain, John Adams, and his wife Abigail, who described Tommy "as genteel, well-bred, [and] promising a youth as any one from our country." More often, however, Tommy's journal described romantic encounters, some with married women, as well as listings of expenditures for what the reluctant scholar delicately termed "Venus."

Although Tommy sent assurances to his mother that London was no more sinful than any city, and that he was regular in church attendance, he tended to be more relaxed with his father. Dr. Shippen knew well enough what a young man's fancy might lead to, and perhaps he thought a bit of worldly experience would season his son.

If Tommy did not speak to his parent directly about what the youth described in his journal as "raging lusts," rumors nevertheless reached Philadelphia concerning the escapades of young "Mr. Shipping," as Abigail Adams called him. Dr. Shippen immediately sent warnings about the "danger from women." "Take care, my dear son. Excess produces the most painful diseases of body and mind." And when Tommy confessed he had caught one of those disorders, his father dropped his own worldliness with a thud and sent more fervent pleas.

"As you love me, as you wish the evening of my life may be pleasant and happy, as you wish not to blast the hopes of your family and country, I beg on my knees, I beg you will avoid a repetition of such complaints in the future. They will, though slowly, yet certainly destroy you." After this outburst from his father, Tommy's letters were less forthcoming. Nevertheless, he had to write often to Dr. Shippen, for the young man always needed money.

Usually, the funds were sent promptly, along with Billy's reminders to Tommy that he was to be "an honor and ornament to your country," and that "to be really great, we must also be good." There was a special reason for the parent's emphasis. Billy hoped to see Tommy take an important place in American government. In 1787, he began sending the son advice on strategy. Since Billy anticipated that the proposed Constitution would be adopted, he urged that Tommy say nothing on the subject "unless you think 'tis a good and safe system." Dutifully, Tommy sent a letter endorsing the Constitution, which his father showed around Philadelphia. The result, he reported to Tommy, was that important citizens "declared you had more sense than all your uncles and that you would be a very great man."

Uncle Arthur was so proud of Tommy that he overlooked the young man's support of a change in constitutions. After his nephew returned to America in 1788, Arthur assured Lord Shelburne that Tommy had survived Europe without "adopting any foreign follies." He reported that the young attorney had begun practicing law in Philadelphia. The uncle did not know that Tommy immediately disliked the drudgery of legal practice, and was even less comfortable with his parents' efforts to push him into marriage.

Consequently, Tommy was happy to accept an invitation to make another tour of Virginia, this time guided by Uncle Arthur. They set out in the autumn of 1790, first paying their respects at Mount Vernon. The parlor atmosphere there may have been chilly since other guests included Thomas Jefferson and James Madison, neither an admirer of Arthur Lee. In his carefully sentimental reports to his parents, Tommy observed that Martha Washington's soul "overflows" with "the very essence of kindness."

Then nephew and uncle began visiting one Lee mansion after another. What Alice was eager to hear, of course, were her son's comments about Stratford, which he obligingly called "the seat of my fathers." Until recently, the plantation had been the residence of Colonel Phil's daughter Matilda, but she was now deceased. Her husband-cousin, Light-Horse Harry Lee, was absent, so Tommy and Uncle Arthur toured the house by themselves and lodged with Uncle Richard Henry at nearby Chantilly.

Tommy acknowledged the "venerable magnificence" of the Stratford buildings and the "happy disposition" of its grounds, but he was most impressed by the portraits of "dear mother's forebears." His uncle had trouble pulling him away, particularly from the likeness of the man whose name Tommy bore, Alice's father Thomas Lee. His portrait, according to his grandson, displayed "a blend of goodness and greatness, a sweet yet penetrating eye . . . a heavenly countenance." Begging his parents not to think him "extravagant," Tommy confessed wanting "to kneel" before the likeness of Thomas Lee.

At Chantilly, Richard Henry offered "a most hearty" supply of crab, fish, fowl, and liquor. Then the travelers were off to Menokin to visit Frank and Becky, whom Tommy found "as happily situated as it is possible in this world to be, except [for] their want of society which they have in themselves only." From there, Tommy and Arthur moved to the James River for stays with Uncle William at Green Spring and with friends in the Williamsburg area.

This proved the most important part of the itinerary. Stopping with Carters and Byrds at Westover and Nesting plantations, Tommy met a seventeen-year-old widow who within a matter of days had "robbed him of his heart"—at least that was what Nancy heard in Philadelphia. When her brother returned from Virginia he was engaged to Mrs. John Bannister.

Before her brief marriage, Betsy Bannister had been Elizabeth Carter Farley. Her mother, Elizabeth Byrd, was not only from the notable family at Westover but also a granddaughter of King Carter. Betsy's father was James Parke Farley of Nesting. Given her distinguished lineage, Tommy could reasonably expect his fiancée to bring welcome wealth with her. They were wed in Virginia on 11 March 1791, Tommy exclaiming: "Hail me the happiest of men." Betsy told Nancy Livingston: "Your brother, your incomparable brother, is all our fondest hopes would have him."

Still smarting from her own disheveled marriage, Nancy replied to her new sister-in-law: "May you meet no disappointment, no abatement of your happiness." But Nancy struck a graceful note when she described her gift to Betsy as "a wedding night cap, simple and plain, only calculated for one who needs not the aid of ornament." A warm greeting came to Betsy from Alice, who had not made the wintry trip to attend her son's wedding. "We are all ready to receive you in our hearts. Our arms are wide open to embrace and give you every proof of friendship. . . . Methinks I see you forever blessing and blest."

Tommy agreed with his mother. He, too, was reassuring, telling Betsy: "Our prospects are fair and bright," adding "God forbid that any thing should happen to blast them." And for two years no threats appeared. Tommy proudly told his father that Betsy's income would make them reasonably independent, though he predicted, accurately, that occasionally they would have to ask for Shippen help. With obvious relief, Tommy now began a career as a country gentleman, ignoring his father's hopes that he be a brilliant lawyer and statesman.

The couple purchased a farm in Bucks County, about seventeen miles from the center of Philadelphia. They named the place Farley, after Betsy's father's family, whose wealth made this refined life possible. Before they took possession of the farm, the newly-weds lived in town with Alice and Billy Shippen. It was here that their first child, William Shippen III, was born.

Tommy proudly prepared a listing of persons who "were attentive to Mrs. S in her first lying in on 29 January 1792 and the order in which they paid their attentions." It was as much a chronicle of national as Philadelphia society. First to call was Mrs. Washington, wife of the President, and next was Mrs. Adams, wife of the Vice President. Soon the President himself appeared, followed by Alexander Hamilton, General Knox, the governor of Pennsylvania, and then less notable persons.

The euphoria caused by the birth soon diminished. Within a year, Tommy's health began to break. Mainly, his disorder was tuberculosis—pulmonary consumption, his physicians called it. What was more vexing for a time were painful hemorrhoids. While Tommy crept into invalidism, Betsy proved to be strength incarnate. "Ill-fated wretch!" Tommy called himself, while Betsy busily anointed his posterior with a salve made of hog's lard and opium. "It was," said Tommy, "the most degrading situation."

Nor did life improve after August 1795, when Tommy and Betsy finally were able to live at Farley, their rural estate. With them went little William as well as a second son, named after his father. Despite the pleasure in his surroundings, Tommy's journal remained more an account of disease than of an effort to be a country squire. The diary documented in excruciating detail his highly personal health problems.

The pages elaborated on the author's worsening cough, his fight to breathe, the frequent times he was bled, his dependence upon laudanum (an alcoholic tincture of opium), his medication's disastrous effects upon his gastro-intestinal system, and his morbid outlook as he lounged in his green silk dressing gown. All these were mercilessly described for the curious, whom Tommy expected would be his descendants.

His wife, parents, and sister soon could see that Tommy had little hope of surviving. All toiled to cheer him. He and his family spent winters at Alice and Billy's spacious Philadelphia house, where Alice could assist Betsy in caring for the invalid. When warm weather took them out to Farley, Tommy's parents made almost daily trips, bringing food and gifts. Billy Shippen's old enemy, Dr. Benjamin Rush, was called in as Tommy's physician, which meant even more copious bleeding and doses of laudanum.

The heroine of the sad drama continued to be Betsy, Tommy's indefatigable mate. Despite preoccupation with himself, Tommy recognized his wife's achievement. "She has done more than any mortal but herself could have done." Occasionally, he felt well enough to report: "I slept in *my lady's* chamber last night." Usually, Tommy was reduced to making diary entries like the following: "My dear wife comes and sits on the bed with me, marks her sheets there, attends to my castle building, entertains me with her conversation, then she assists me at my bath." His journal left a testimonial: "My sons! when you read this, if your mother be alive, remember to draw an impressive lesson of all you owe *her* of respect and love." Never, he said, did Betsy "forget anything that can give me pleasure."

Evidently at the close of 1796 there was momentary distraction for Betsy in a gift brought out to Farley by Alice. It was a huge box of shoes just arrived from England. In it were three dozen pairs, a sight which Tommy said elated Betsy. "Lord, what a display of shoes!" Some were made from queen's silk, others from Spanish leather, and yet more from embroidered leather. Soon afterwards, Betsy hastened to show off her favorite pair when she attended a party at the residence of retiring President Washington. Tommy heard "she [was] much caressed."

When Dr. Rush permitted, Tommy welcomed many callers. Since Philadelphia was still the federal capital, the company could be very distinguished. One day in January 1796, Vice President John Adams appeared. "I never knew him half as communicative or agreeable in my life," Tommy observed. "At last, he seems to have given up old England, and to believe she is on the decline." Another time, Tommy's cousin, Attorney General Charles Lee, brought "the famous Mr. John Marshall of Richmond" to amuse the invalid with talk about legal subjects.

Mostly, Tommy's companions during the sad vigil were, besides Betsy and his parents, his sister Nancy and her daughter Peggy. Apparently the mother and daughter sang duets for the family, usually choosing hymns, after which Alice would read from the Bible or from books of sermons. Sometimes after food or refreshment, Tommy would smoke a "segar" if he felt up to it. He could occasionally consume much wine, along with oysters, lobster, fish, and fowl. This was mostly the case when Betsy's mother and her entourage, which included slaves, arrived for visits from Virginia. The assembly at Farley then often numbered thirty persons.

Tommy's spells of improvement grew shorter, and the relapses were more miserable than before. "Oh, what a divine medicine is opium," the patient wrote, "and how like a true friend in that you are never so fully sensible of its value as in its absence." When laudanum brought less relief, Dr. Rush prescribed a change in climate during the cold weather. Leaving their boys with Grandmother Alice, Tommy and Betsy made two trips to Virginia and the Carolinas, the first lasting through the winter of 1796–97.

Aside from Alice's uplifting letters to Tommy, there is no record of her feelings during this unhappy time. Apparently, she bore up well while her son was away, giving a gala dinner party in January 1797. Billy tried to encourage Tommy by describing how lighthearted the Shippen household had been. Alice was highly successful in serving a wonderful Virginia meal, her proud husband reported, adding that at table he had on his right the Vice President-elect. "Jefferson was great," Billy wrote Tommy afterwards.

Traveling in Virginia, Tommy had to be content with a stringent diet provided by his concerned relatives. They prescribed a formula said to have benefited Uncle William Lee in his last days: "mutten, suet, and milk." This menu was hardly the only reason for the invalid's frequent emotional breakdown in letters to his parents. Tommy admitted he now found misfortune difficult to bear, especially as he had come to believe, "I am forgotten and neglected by everybody in the family." He told his father: "I am wretched and oppressed." Fortunately, "My old friend the laudanum bottle stands by me, and gives me all my strength and all my spirits." He mused over how his wife, parents, and children would go on living "after my poor, wornout thread is broken and cast away forever."

Nevertheless, Tommy survived the first trip to Virginia and the Carolinas, returning in the spring of 1797 to Philadelphia for what would be his last summer. He had a library of 800 volumes at Farley which he looked forward to enjoying. That year, a particular favorite was Rousseau's "new *Eloise*." Thinking that her son might relish a political essay read aloud, Alice asked a visitor from Virginia, Burwell Bassett, to do the honors as the family listened. The luckless Bassett proved a dull reader, to Tommy's amusement. "Betsy fell fast asleep; Mrs. Dunbar

[Betsy's mother], much as she is devoted to Bassett, yawned and held her head in her hand; my mother gave a forced attention."

Once again, as winter began in 1797, Betsy and Tommy set out for Charleston, where friends promised haven and sunny weather. As usual, Tommy soon found he had left home without sufficient cash. Little help could come from his Virginia relatives, for as Tommy told his father: "There is nothing on earth they won't give you but *money* and that they really have not to give—so that if you do not send me one hundred dollars by this night's post, I shall be quite down in the mouth." The funds arrived, and the invalid reached Charleston. This time, there was no relief.

On 4 February 1798, Tommy had a last chat with Betsy. "He looked at me with the most benign countenance," she reported to Alice. Tommy said that the soft Carolina climate made up for his "thirty years of pain." After assuring his wife that he was prepared to die, he uttered his last words, which, according to Betsy, were: "I am now completely happy. I have been two hours in sweet converse with my God. His arms are open to receive me." Tommy then asked Betsy to sing some Psalms. "I have seen a new light. I am a new man."

A few moments later, Thomas Lee Shippen died at age thirty-four. He was buried in Charleston. On hearing the news, Alice wrote at once to Betsy: "Oh, could I clasp him in my fond embrace!" But she had the solace of Betsy's narration of Tommy's closing sentences. Such faith, said the mother, truly showed "how much glory may be won in a short life."

Thus consoled about Tommy, Alice could give more attention to her daughter-in-law: "I will weep for you, my dear Betsy. Your loss is infinite." It was not, however, indefinite. Betsy soon remarried, this time to George Izard of a South Carolina family who were once political allies with the Lees. Betsy brought him to live at Farley, which had always been her property since Virginia money had purchased it. Izard served as a general in the War of 1812 and was named by President James Monroe to be governor of Arkansas. Betsy had a long marriage with Izard and gave birth to three more children.

Her new life made Betsy content to have her Shippen sons reared by Alice. The arrangement was a happy one, with the lads devoted both to grandmother and mother, and the two women remaining close friends. Alice's favorite grandson, young William Shippen, became headstrong at age thirteen, obliging his mother to remind him how his grandparent "has borne with your infantile humours. She has supported you on the bed of sickness. She has gratified your most extravagant wishes . . . and now has to bear with the most unpardonable insolence."

Actually, it was not her grandsons but her daughter Nancy Livingston who made Alice's old age difficult. Betsy complained that her sister-in-law relished "tormenting her mother." Nancy had become a troubled personality, and for cause. She remained estranged but not divorced and thus was denied another mate. She watched widows like Betsy readily remarry, often more than once. It meant that Nancy saw any chance for romantic happiness vanish. When the diplomat Louis Otto, once a rival for her hand, became a widower, he briefly resumed his suit, until an unavailable Nancy saw him take another wife and return to Europe.

For years Nancy feared retaliation from Colonel Livingston, leaving her anxious and highly strung. Always looking over her shoulder, Nancy fancied Henry might at any moment raid the Shippen residence to rush away with Peggy or with furnishings he claimed as his. Nancy admitted she was "constantly on the watch and in continual fear of every stranger I see, but that he should be the one commissioned to carry her [Peggy] off." Just before he died, Tommy observed of his sister: "Was there ever such a creature? She suffers a thousand deaths instead of one."

Actually, Nancy had some basis for alarm. While Peggy was living in New York, her grandmother became inattentive, so that the Colonel slipped into the mansion at Claremont and hustled Peggy away. She stayed with her father just long enough for other male Livingstons to call as a delegation and demand that Henry release the girl. He did so, but the lesson was not lost upon the Livingston family and Nancy.

In 1793, when Peggy was visiting her mother in Philadelphia, word arrived that Colonel Livingston "has thrown his mistresses out." Fearing this was another subterfuge to allow her husband to appear in Philadelphia feigning reform, Nancy hurried her daughter away from town to a hiding place. Grandmother Livingston agreed with this precaution and sent money to pay for the costs of keeping Peggy out of sight.

Her threatened security so undid Nancy that she began suspecting Alice would believe Henry's talk of repentance and help him find Peggy. In panic, Nancy decided that she, too, must disappear, so she set out for New Jersey. To her horror, whom did she spy following her to the ferry but Henry Livingston. Catching up to her as she boarded the boat, the Colonel implored his wife to listen, promising any concession if he could see his daughter.

The ensuing scene alarmed the captain and crew who finally persuaded Livingston to depart. After this, Nancy and Peggy remained in seclusion for two years. At that point Peggy became sixteen, and finally safe under the law from custody of her father. But the ordeal had left the emotions of daughter and mother sadly scarred.

In 1801 the Old Lady, Margaret Beekman Livingston, died, bequeathing an annuity sufficient to keep both Peggy and Nancy in comfort. A friend of Nancy's extended congratulations, saying that Mrs. Livingston indeed had been "a good old lady" who "well knew the persecution you have endured on account of your marriage." Seven years later, when Nancy's father died, she and Peggy did not fare as well. In his will, Dr. Shippen took note of Grandmother Livingston's generosity and chose to leave most of his property to Tommy's son, the third William Shippen.

His decision left Nancy outraged and served further to weaken her relationship with her mother. Nancy threatened to sue the newly widowed Alice, whom she thought was dawdling in choosing which parcels of real estate to sell to derive much needed cash from Dr. Shippen's legacy, thereby delaying Nancy's receiving what little was coming to her. But Alice seemed unperturbed, rejoicing that, like her son, her husband had died in Christian faith.

Not only that, but Billy Shippen had been reconciled on his deathbed with his venerable professional and personal enemy, Dr. Benjamin Rush. The latter attended Billy in his last illness, "introduced by an anthrax"— a poisonous boil. Rush recorded that the patient, age seventy-two, confessed that his hope "was founded on the merits of Jesus Christ." The two elderly physicians forgave each other, and Rush claimed he prescribed for Billy "with a sincere desire to prolong his life. Peace and joy to his soul for ever and for ever."

Nevertheless, Benjamin Rush felt he must be candid about Alice's late husband. "He had talents, but which from disuse became weak and contemptible. He was too indolent to write, to read, or even to think." Others, less harsh than Rush, spoke of Billy's genial spirit, his love of food and drink, and his pleasure in society. Many women recalled his gentle care at childbirth. Alice, meanwhile, left no comment concerning her husband of over forty years.

The second of Alice's grandsons, Thomas Lee Shippen, Jr., died in August 1810, while a student at Princeton. For the remaining seven years of her life, Alice devoted herself to the surviving grandchild, William, whose success as a medical student gave her much satisfaction. More important, however, since Nancy was sulking over money, grandson William became the person upon whom Alice could pour her maternal love.

Alice took her greatest pains in guiding William through a religious conversion. Her admonitions were much like those she exchanged fifty years before with her sister, Hannah Corbin. "Say to your maker, say to yourself—if I must perish, it shall be at Christ's feet, trusting Him and using the means he has appointed for my restoration and eternal happiness." Just before she died, Alice wrote to her grandson: "I wish I could be appointed your guardian angel," she said, and "use all my influence to prevail on you to turn your back on this poor, wretched world."

William responded pleasingly. Alice told him: "You have been so kind to me always, especially since your dear grandfather left me to your care." Shortly before she died, Alice stressed again to her grandson "what a comfort" he had been and how he had borne out his grandfather's "judgment in placing this confidence in you." Another time the grandmother wrote: "My dearest, sweetest William, you have been the sweetest, best child to me. Mrs. Livingston has been a bad one. This is the last testimony of your . . . affectionate grandmother, A. Shippen."

Alice continued to send letters after 1816, but they had to be penned by others when she duplicated brother William Lee's experience and became "perfectly blind." Despite this infirmity, Alice often changed residences, living mostly with friends and relatives. Her daughter-in-law Betsy had to brace herself for Alice's stays at Farley, since the elderly lady insisted on bringing her own furniture to every location. But no matter where she camped, Alice centered her thoughts on young William.

On 25 March 1817, Alice Lee Shippen died at eighty-one "without a groan" after "a fit of asthma." So said Betsy, who watched at the bedside as Alice's "immortal spirit took its flight." She departed as she had lived, Betsy reported to William, imploring blessings on her dear ones. According to "her wish," her remains joined those of her husband and six infant children.

Many years later, when the Arch Street cemetery was renovated, what was left of the Shippen monument and the bodies was removed. The stone over Alice's grave had said: "Endowed with great talents, she was also a liberal friend of the poor, a Sincere Christian. Hark, the trumpet sounds and the tombs burst. Awake, arise, the Savior of the world calls."

Preparing for Alice's funeral, Betsy told her son: "I have taken all the [burial] arrangements out of Mrs. Livingston's hands for reasons which I need not assign on paper." When Nancy and Peggy, who were now regarded as eccentrics, spoke of attending the service in silk dresses, Betsy forbade them to appear except in traditional black worsted. They complied.

Alice's grandson William, to whom she had left her entire estate, also resented donning customary mourning dress. Again, Betsy squelched this rebellion. "What do you imagine the amiable Blairs and Livingstons would say if *you* were not to pay this *last* mark of respect to your departed Grandmother? She who idolized you from your birth is insensible to all the follies and ceremonies of this poor world, but the living must conform."

Betsy herself survived but nine years more, dying in June 1826. An obituary asserted that "her wit was like the playful lightning of a summer evening—it illumined but did not wound." The notice failed to mention a serious side which had led Betsy to decline ever residing in Virginia or South Carolina. "I am so strenuously opposed to living in a slave country," she had insisted. And she wept when she inherited slaves—"those poor old Black people." When her son William selected a Virginia woman as his wife, Betsy was dubious about his choice, observing of females from her own state: "Their manners, habits, nay very *ideas* are different."

Betsy had even more sobering advice for her physician-son. Speaking from her experience in three marriages, she warned: "I would not have you imagine that little Cupid's torch is to be forever burning. Far from it, my dear child. The heavy chains of Hymen soon put the little God of Love to flight, and then wretched is the man who does not find his wife forebearing in her temper, affectionate in her manners, *sensible* in her conversation, neat in her person, and pious to her God."

Meanwhile, Nancy and her daughter Peggy took their peculiar ways into old age, but there is no truth in the legend that the pair lived as hermits. Nancy found a cause which kept her rushing around Philadelphia. She and Peggy busily sought donations to the Domestic Missionary Society, with the goal of evangelizing slaves. Predicting that emancipation would soon come for all blacks, Nancy foresaw a society which was "one fold under one Shepherd among the civilized nations of the earth." She also campaigned to convert Jews to Christianity. As she aged, Nancy's days were often spent putting the first five books of the Bible into verse. She also composed hymns, one of which she entitled: "Tis Good for me to be afflicted."

Nancy Livingston came to the end of her punishing life on 23 August 1841. She was broken and infirm at seventy-eight. Her daughter and companion Peggy lived on to age eighty-three, when she died on 1 July 1864. To be together in death as in life, the daughter was placed in her mother's tomb. Not only did she emulate Nancy's habits, Peggy also professed the same religious outlook. As a young woman, she had dedicated herself to "singlehood," believing "that though utterly vile and worthless in [our]selves, [we] are complete in Christ." She got on well with her cousin Dr. William Shippen, although she was quick to scold when he profaned the Sabbath by writing letters.

Alice Lee Shippen's relatives had enjoyed reminding her she was longest to survive of the remarkable family that had arisen at Stratford. She had lived forty-three years beyond her brother Colonel Phil's death. During that time, a second line of Lees had come to prominence. These cousins grew up at another Potomac mansion, Leesylvania. Most of them respected the venerable Alice, calling her "dear Aunt," and often visiting her in Philadelphia.

Among these rising Lees, the kindest to Alice was Lucy, the daughter of Light-Horse Harry. "You must be the best Aunt in the world," Lucy said. Alice became a sort of second parent to the younger woman, whose own mother had died when Lucy was small. They shared many comments on the fortunes and misfortunes of the Lee family. Alice warned Lucy that she must not rely upon family bonds. "There is no such thing as natural affection," to which Alice added: "You are yourself proof of its falsehood, as well as your dear brother." Alice was speaking of Lucy's father, Light-Horse Harry, who by then was a fugitive from society.

After Lucy married Bernard Carter, Alice recommended the study of the Lee genealogy. "I have observed with surprise that genius runs in families," she remarked, and urged that Lucy believe "the Lees are no contemptible family." However, Alice did not leave it at that. "I hope it is not family pride that makes me write this," she added, knowing nevertheless that it was more hope than assurance which lay behind her comment.

~ 12

From Leesylvania to . . . 1754–1794

Back in 1754, Alice's cousin Henry Lee II had left Lee Hall for Prince William County, where he established a new home he called Leesylvania. Like Stratford, it sat majestically on the Potomac and was surrounded by 2000 acres. This property had come into the family when Richard the Scholar married Laetitia Corbin. Henry's legacy also included twenty slaves, much livestock, and nearly 3500 acres in Fairfax County, situated near where the District of Columbia would be established.

After reaching his majority in 1750, Henry practiced law for three years in Westmoreland County. He did not, however, choose to live at Lee Hall where his mother resided. Separation did not prevent Mary Lee from sending Henry frequent reminders that he ought to marry. She even arranged an "entertainment" at Lee Hall for him and his lady-friend of the moment, a Miss Benson. The mother painted a charming picture of wedlock—"the felicity that holy state can admit . . . is certainly one of the happiest this side of the grave."

Felicity with Miss Benson was not in store for Henry. He may have hesitated because of Uncle Thomas' dictum that a Lee should find a prosperous wife. If so, Henry was remarkably successful. His marriage took place in the same auspicious setting where Uncle Thomas had wed Aunt Hannah, the mansion at Green Spring, the James River residence of the prosperous Ludwell clan. There, on 1 December 1753, Henry Lee married a famous beauty, Lucy Grymes.

Lucy was born on 26 April 1734 in Richmond County, which was adjacent to Westmoreland. Her late father was Charles Grymes, from a distinguished family. Lucy's mother, Frances Jenings, also had an impressive lineage, being the daughter of Governor Edmund Jenings and Frances Corbin, sister of Laetitia Lee, the wife of Richard the Scholar.

The match was a triumph for Henry, so much so that his chums decided it was time to stop calling him "Buck." One candid friend even sent Henry an expression of amazement at "the success of your amour." Such astonishment at Henry's winning Lucy must have stemmed, in part at least, from the competition for the lovely Miss Grymes. She was considered "the lowland beauty," and could count a youthful George Washington among her admirers.

The bride and groom soon set out for the latter's inheritance in Prince William County. At Leesylvania, their plantation at Freestone Point, Henry began a career typical for his family. He served creditably in local government and commanded Prince William County's militia, an especially important task during the Revolution. He served as presiding justice for the area, and had many terms as a burgess and, after 1776, as a delegate to the General Assembly. Henry also sat in the various Virginia conventions of that era, and was for a time in the senate, the legislature's upper body.

Few of Henry Lee's letters survive, and not any of Lucy's, which is doubly lamentable since she was prominent in the only exciting Leesylvania occasion we know about. In 1767, Henry wrote in obvious dismay to the Squire, reporting that two local slaves had been caught in an attempt "to poyson" Lucy. One black, named Harry, belonged to Leesylvania. The other, Gawin, worked at the nearby iron foundry owned by Colonel John Tayloe, Frank Lee's father-in-law. A disgusted Henry complained that Tayloe's foreman was seeking to get Gawin pardoned, even though the latter was said to be ringleader in the plot. Henry predicted that "as he [Tayloe] is a great man, I suppose it will be done."

Nothing else is known about the cause or the result of this ominous affair, nor, for that matter, about any other extraordinary event at Leesylvania. Instead, Henry and Lucy Lee are mostly remembered through the glittering promise of their several sons. And it is with them that the Lee family story moved dramatically in another direction.

For a time, it appeared that the Leesylvania brothers would keep pace with the sons of Stratford in the race for fame and achievement. Five males and three females were born to Lucy and Henry. Of these, the lives of two sons are especially important for the clan's history. These were the eldest, Henry Lee III (Light-Horse Harry), born 1756, and Richard Bland Lee, born 1761. Their careers were to be tragically entwined.

Before concentrating on Harry and Richard, the stories of their three brothers, Charles, Theodorick, and Edmund Jennings Lee, deserve summary. Of these, Charles became the most successful. Born in 1758, he graduated from Princeton in 1775, going thereafter to Lee Hall as aide for Uncle Squire in the naval office. Charles quickly discovered he preferred the life of a student and removed to Philadelphia for legal schooling, remaining while the Revolution ran its course.

As a young scholar, Charles dismayed his parents by his expensive habits. Replying to the son's plea for funds, Henry grudgingly agreed to send more money, but observed how needless the expense would have been, "had you taken my advice [and] applied your hours wasted in idle pursuit of dissipation to Coke-Blackstone, etc." Next time, Henry expected Charles to report "application and frugality."

Charles finally was admitted to the bar in 1794. Before that occurred, he held a collector's post in Alexandria and served briefly in the Virginia legislature. In November 1795, that fond neighbor of Leesylvania, President Washington, appointed Charles to be Attorney General of the United States. It was a last moment selection, for Washington was about to leave office. Charles retained the position under President John Adams.

As he was about to step down from the presidency in March 1801, Adams named the Attorney General to be one of several new judges on the federal circuit bench. When these "midnight" appointments were nullified by Congress in 1802, the staunchly Federalist Charles Lee entered political oblivion. He practiced law, making the most of a close friendship with Chief Justice John Marshall. Before he died in 1815, Charles had a professional role in the impeachment of Justice Samuel Chase, the trial of Aaron Burr, and the famous case of *Marbury vs. Madison*. His first wife, Anne Lee, a daughter of Richard Henry Lee, had died in 1804.

Charles' brothers Edmund and Theodorick seem to have had more quiet lives. Edmund Jennings Lee married Sarah Lee, another child of Richard Henry. They lived in Alexandria, where he was both an active layman in the Episcopal Church and the town's mayor. He died in 1843 and Sarah in 1837. Most obscure of the brothers was Theodorick, who remained a farmer until his death in 1840.

Lucy, Mary, and Anne Lee were the three daughters of Leesylvania. Lucy did not marry. Anne became Mrs. William Byrd Page. The marital fortunes of Mary Lee, the third daughter, introduced a man who complimented the Lee family by asking for three wives. This was Philip Richard Fendall, a distant cousin from the Maryland Lees, who took Mary as his third spouse in 1791. His first wife had been Sarah Lettice Lee of Maryland. For his second bride, Fendall went to Stratford to wed Elizabeth (Steptoe) Lee, Colonel Phil's widow.

Except for Richard Bland Lee, to whom we turn presently, the brothers and sisters from Leesylvania learned to distance themselves from the eldest sibling, Henry Lee III. Yet Harry's story had by far the most auspicious beginning of anyone in his generation of Lees. He was sent to Princeton in 1770, at age fourteen, which at the time was customary. The school was selected perhaps because cousin Alice Shippen's husband Billy and his family helped to found and sustain the institution. Billy and Alice kept a parental eye on Harry while he was at Princeton.

He did well at the college, as its president John Witherspoon attested. Billy Shippen saw so much promise in Harry that he predicted the lad would be "one of the first fellows in this country. He is more than strict in his morality. He has a fine genius and is too diligent." From Leesylvania, Henry and Lucy followed all of this with interest, and the father traveled to New Jersey for Harry's commencement in 1773. In Harry's class was another young Virginian, James Madison.

After leaving Princeton, Harry intended to study law in London's Middle Temple, a plan ruined by the colonial break with England. Instead, he entered the war in 1776 as a captain in a unit of Virginia dragoons commanded by his cousin, Colonel Theodorick Bland. Soon, Harry had a commission in the Continental army where his love of horses helped him excel as a cavalry officer.

He also had the approval and timely assistance of the family's intimate friend and neighbor, George Washington. The General recognized young Lee's expertness in drawing loyalty, discipline, and courage from a troop of light dragoons. Joined by his men, Harry became a specialist in surprising the enemy through sudden raids which ended as quickly as they began.

In April 1778, with Washington's prodding and while Harry's cousins Richard Henry and Frank Lee were still highly influential, Congress put an independent partisan corps under Major Harry Lee's command. Including both cavalry and infantry, the unit became known as Lee's Legion and its commander as "Light-Horse Harry." The legion's skill in swift movement and lightning-like attack demonstrated Harry's undoubted talent for leadership and assault. Success, however, appeared to depend on whether Harry and only Harry was in charge.

Light-Horse Harry Lee's military career is as difficult to appraise today as it was in his lifetime. He certainly inherited more than his share of valor, proving to be an able, if sometimes erratic, soldier. He was admired by those astute commanders, George Washington and Nathanael Green. This advantageous notice reflected more than family connections. Yet, controversy followed and still follows many of Harry's military feats. The most debatable was the attack he led in New Jersey at Paulus Hook in 1779, after which Virginia officers charged him with grave errors of command, bringing about a court-martial.

Although Lee was acquitted, emerging with Washington's continued backing and the praise of supporters (and cousins) in Congress who ordered a medal struck in his honor, Harry's pride and confidence never recovered from this experience. Thereafter, his rage fed on the realization that others doubted his judgment, accomplishment, and character. Harry seemed preoccupied more by those he considered his American enemies than by the English foe. Unable to accept criticism, Harry did not recognize that he was often opposed by fellow officers mainly because he was arrogant, vain, imperious, ambitious to a fault, and painfully sensitive. He quarreled easily, a trait which in time forced another appearance before a court-martial.

Certainly at least a few of Harry's loudest foes spoke from envy, while others assailed him simply because he was a member of the controversial Lee family. But Harry insisted that everyone of his critics came from these camps. This blindness kept the young officer in a near-perpetual fury, and he refused to be calmed even by soothing from so sage a friend as his superior, General Greene.

Generals Washington and Greene had their patience taxed often enough by Harry's headstrong ways. There was, for example, Harry's appalling decision to decapitate the corpse of a deserter he had executed. He ordered the head displayed among his troops to encourage their obedience. George Washington had given Harry permission to make short work of any deserter, but this grisly excess distressed the commanding general. Still, since Washington considered Lee's Legion to be an asset, he overlooked the prevailing dislike and mistrust of Harry. But even Washington might have agreed when Alexander Hamilton, speaking of Harry, regretted the "Julius Caesar or Cromwell in him."

Not the least of Nathanael Greene's great achievements during the Revolution was his patient sympathy for Harry Lee. Even so, there were times when even he spoke bluntly to his junior officer. He did so, for instance, after Harry complained once too often at being denied supplies he claimed he deserved, and at seeing others receive commendation and promotion he insisted were properly his. Harry probably never saw the point in Greene's reply: "I have run every risk to favor your operations, perhaps more than I ought; clearly so, if I had not my own reputation less at heart than the public service in general, and the glory of my friends in particular."

Back at Leesylvania, Harry's father sympathized for a time with his controversial son. When brother Charles expressed fears for Harry's reputation, Henry Lee replied in 1779 that, while he agreed some of Harry's recent activities "cast a shadow" over the son's earlier achievements, he predicted this soldier offspring would emerge stronger than ever. "I flatter myself it will not be in the power of his enemies to pluck from him those laurels they cannot acquire."

Having been promoted to lieutenant colonel, Harry was ordered in March 1780 to take his Legion to the southern front. They were to support General Greene's defense of the Carolinas and Georgia against Great Britain's generals, Charles Cornwallis and Henry Clinton. Nothing about his southern assignment pleased Harry, so that by January 1782 he was ill, disheartened, and angry. His Legion's participation in many encounters had brought as much complaint as commendation.

And now that Cornwallis had surrendered at Yorktown and the war was concluding, Harry was bored by a soldier's life. The army organization was beginning to restrain him, while his critics grew louder. The conclusion Harry reached was that he and his free-wheeling style of command were no longer welcome. At age twenty-six he chose to resign his commission, announcing his decision to General Greene in a childish letter marked by self-pity.

He complained of "the indifference with which my efforts to advance the cause of my country is considered by my friends." He spoke of "the persecution of my foes." He said he was "disgusted with human nature,"—a refrain other Lees were repeating at the time. He then accused Greene of denying him due recognition. To all of this, General Greene calmly suggested: "Give yourself time to cool," and urged his young associate to remain a soldier. While he often did not understand Harry's personality, Greene consistently praised his contribution to the Continental army's success.

Unmoved by Greene's encouragement, Harry Lee left his troops as spring began in 1782. Some observers saw him depart as a hero, full of dash and courage. Others considered him a surly quitter, who could not abide any rein on his whimsical and injudicious ways. The confusion was caused by Harry's gravely flawed character, which led him to behave as if his talents set him apart from rules governing other mortals. He continued in this style for the rest of his life. Eventually, a friend of the Lee family offered an explanatory epitaph that, despite its harshness, seems sadly close to the mark: "Light-Horse Harry Lee a fool was born, a fool he lived, and a fool he died."

Ironically, as Harry left the army, he seemed for the moment to behave very prudently by finding a way to avoid the usual uncertainties of a soldier re-entering civilian life. Instead of returning to Leesylvania, he would establish himself at that other Lee capital, Stratford, thanks to an alliance he had created within the Lee family while on an earlier leave from the Legion. At that time, he had proposed marriage to Colonel Phil's daughter Matilda Lee, who had accepted him. She was eighteen, while Harry was eight years older. They were second cousins.

As we have seen, Matilda's father died in 1775 without leaving a will. An only son, born at the moment of Phil's death, died in 1779 after tumbling down a high flight of stairs in front of Stratford's main door. The lad's fate left three women, Matilda, her sister Flora, and their mother, Elizabeth Steptoe Lee, each with a portion of the estate at Stratford, as well as much land elsewhere.

Colonel Phil had been nearly forty when Matilda, his first-born child, arrived. His letters to his brothers showed his delight in the little girl and how he sought to cultivate her musical ability. Matilda apparently grew into a lovely young woman, whom Billy Shippen found especially charming, since he saw her resemblance to the beauty and grace of his wife Alice, Matilda's aunt. Evidently for good reason the young mistress of Stratford was known as the Divine Matilda. In addition, maturing without a father apparently gave her a shrewd and independent outlook which would serve her well in her brief marriage.

Harry arrived to claim his bride and her wealth on a beautiful early spring afternoon. Matilda and the family were enjoying the sun and listening to music on the rooftop patio between Stratford's great chimneys. Days of riding had tanned the young colonel to the shade of an Indian, so he was not at first recognized. Otherwise there was nothing physically striking about his build and height. What did impress observers was how Harry's orderly and companion, a white man named George Weldon, was allowed to kiss his master's hand.

It turned out that Weldon remained at Stratford for the rest of his life. The same could not be said of Harry Lee. He and Matilda were wed in April 1782. For a time, Harry seemed settled in Westmoreland County, trying to encourage the trustees of Colonel Phil's estate to make decisions to his and Matilda's advantage. The commissioners, of whom R.H. Lee was one, did not move fast enough to suit the impatient Harry, as he made clear in complaints to Richard Henry.

At first, Harry had basis for dismay. Elizabeth Lee, his mother-in-law, was alloted for her lifetime that part of Stratford which included the magnificent house. Then Harry had a bit of luck. Elizabeth Lee had recently wed Richard Fendall. While the couple intended for a time to live at Stratford, after Harry married Matilda and moved in with them, the Fendalls decided that they preferred to live in Alexandria. They departed, taking Matilda's younger sister Flora with them. Mrs. Fendall and Flora left their shares of the estate to be managed by Harry.

What ensued was tragic for Stratford. Harry became a compulsive speculator in real estate and other get-rich-quick schemes. As his debts mounted, he began selling those parcels of Stratford land over which he had jurisdiction through Matilda. By 1789, Stratford plantation contained about 4000 acres, down from the 6,595 at the time of Colonel Phil's death.

In that year, Mrs. Fendall died, which meant that her portion of the Stratford property, which included title to the manor house and outbuildings, reverted to Matilda as Colonel Phil's eldest daughter. Being Matilda's husband, Harry now could claim to be master of the place. But it was not for long. The next year, 1790, the frail Matilda died in childbirth. There was barely time for her to prevent what would likely have been the extinction of Stratford.

During her eight years with Harry, Matilda watched as he approached financial responsibilities with much the desperate urgency and incessant movement that had characterized his military style. Unfortunately, this civilian strategy failed, so that by the time of Matilda's death, Harry had lost her confidence and that of most other members of the Lee family. Unlike William Lee, who received full title to Green Spring at the demise of his wife Hannah, Harry was denied ownership of Stratford.

During her last moments, Matilda directed that a deed of trust be drawn, putting Stratford and her other properties in the hands of cousins Ludwell Lee and Richard Bland Lee until her children came of age. By now there were three heirs: Philip, Lucy, and Henry. Harry was treated courteously and allowed to continue living at Stratford with his offspring.

This generosity was probably a mistake, especially since one of the two trustees was Harry's compliant younger brother, Richard. Whenever a chance appeared, Harry found ways to chip at the property, so that an even smaller amount of land surrounded the great house when the estate passed in 1808 to Matilda and Harry's son Henry, who earlier had become heir at the death of his elder brother Philip. These parcels of Stratford had been sacrificed to Harry's mounting indebtedness from speculative land ventures.

Certainly, Harry Lee was not the only American at the time who was misled by delusions of quick wealth. But he, more than most, showed how these dreams could become a mania. When one scheme after another failed, it meant that he must contrive other "sure things" to cover his losses. Ironically, Harry had named what would prove to be one of his greatest failures after his wife. He hoped to build a thriving commercial and industrial center on land purchased at the falls of the Potomac. He christened the town Matildaville, but it remained no more than a costly dream. There were many other investments, in ventures extending to Kentucky, Pennsylvania, North Carolina, and Georgia. The deals sometimes involved thousands of acres.

Closer to home, Harry hoped for huge returns from residential lots in the new federal city of Washington. There he had joined with a gambler every bit Harry's equal, Robert Morris and his building company. Morris bedazzled Harry with talk of profits upwards of hundreds of thousands of dollars. Ultimately, the plan produced a jail term for Morris and more anxiety for Lee. He had put $40,000 in the scheme, later protesting the amount had been merely a loan to Morris. Hardly so, for Harry had accepted a share of District of Columbia realty from Morris.

Not even Harry's hero, George Washington, was safe from his protégé's zeal. Harry paid a debt to Washington with what today would be called a bad check, since Harry knew the paper was probably worthless when he passed it. He said the guiltiness he felt and the stinging rebuke received from Washington were his greatest mortifications in life. Thereafter, when President Washington considered Lee for assignments in federal military service, he warned his advisers that while Light-Horse Harry might be reliable as a soldier, he was not dependable in economic matters.

As the years passed, Harry's creditors grew louder in their impatience, and he scrambled more frantically trying to sell, buy, or borrow his way out of trouble. His surviving letters include a cryptic note which sums up his plight as he searched for more time or money: "Sir: Another day has passed—no letter—I pray you to tell me when shall my torture cease." Harry's need to stay ahead of his creditors forced him to measures that caused many contemporaries to consider him a cheat or a swindler. The stories his neighbors told about him reflected this.

It was said that one astute citizen sent his son into the world with three warnings. He should stand no stallion, own no sawmill, and "have no dealings with Harry Lee." Another tale had Harry arrive at a friend's plantation with the claim he had lost his horse. The obliging acquaintance lent Harry a steed and a slave to ride along to lead the mount back. Weeks passed with neither the slave nor the two horses reappearing. When the footsore black came limping back, he told his master that Lee had sold both of the borrowed horses. When the astounded owner asked: "Why didn't you come home?" the slave relied: " 'Cause General Lee sold me too."

Along with everyone else, members of the Lee family had to learn that Light-Horse Harry was not to be trusted. From Green Spring, cousin William Lee sent chiding letters when Harry failed to pay some debts. Then there was the whereabouts of several casks of fine wine which William had arranged for shipment to Stratford. After waiting several years for payment, a frustrated William directed Harry to turn any remaining casks over to Richard Henry. Also, William asked when he would be paid for all the wine "which I know you have disposed of upwards of two years ago[?]"

This was Harry's style—to be forgetful or oblivious of regulation. Even his father had to learn about Harry the hard way. In 1786, a year before his death, Henry Lee was assured by Harry that the latter had merely overlooked some debts owed to the parent. They would soon be paid—or so Harry claimed. Henry Lee left no indication whether he believed his son. But the chilly treatment accorded Harry by his father's will showed how discouraged the parent had become.

The document carefully alloted all properties, slaves, furniture, cash, and other tangibles among Henry's wife and all the children except Harry, who was to receive none. The finest pieces of realty in Virginia went to the younger sons, with the leavings going to Harry, which meant a bit of land near Lee Hall and an acreage in Kentucky. Then came the father's stern order: "It is my will and desire that my son Henry shall hold all that I have given him free and clear from any debts and legacies." The concerned parent took pains to reiterate that Harry should have "no part" of the slaves bequeathed to the other heirs. Harry was also reproached when his father denied him any role in carrying out the will.

Not that Charles Lee, who was Henry's choice as executor, was thereby freed from worries over his older brother. One of those who owed money to the estate was William Lee. Fearing this was his only chance for payment of the money Harry owed him, William told Charles that his own obligation to Henry Lee's estate would be paid "by an order on your brother Col. H. Lee." William said he knew Charles would understand why this step was necessary.

Of the numerous family growing up at Leesylvania, none stayed to make the place a residence, despite its magnificent view of the Potomac. When Henry Lee died in 1787, he left the house to Lucy his widow for her lifetime, and thereafter to their second son, Charles. Lucy died in 1792, and was buried beside Henry near their home. In need of money, Charles mortgaged the 2,040 acres to William Lee. Soon afterwards, the residence at Leesylvania was destroyed by fire, and eventually the acreage was sold. Thanks to encouragement from the Society of the Lees of Virginia, in 1985 the Commonwealth established Leesylvania State Park at the site of Henry and Lucy's home.

Henry Lee lived long enough to see his third son, Richard Bland, fall under Harry's spell. The Revolution had begun when Richard was ready for school. He was sent to Chantilly to be educated with the tutors employed by Richard Henry Lee. Three years later, in 1779, Richard matriculated at the College of William and Mary, it being a safer location as long as British redcoats were lurking near Princeton. He graduated in 1781, and returned to Leesylvania. His father gave him a start as a landed gentleman and politician, and soon Richard was a congressman and appeared bound for success.

Unfortunately, Richard seemed willing to leap at Light-Horse Harry's every command, even to pouring his own resources and those of his wife down the various ratholes Harry pointed out. The relationship had begun in 1786 when Harry was already expecting Richard to help him out of financial pinch. In time, Richard's trusting nature cost him everything, including his reputation.

Usually, Harry had the grace to warn his brother when he had written checks against him. "Be assured I should not have drawn on you for a shilling could I have encompassed the needful by any resource in my power." But, having done so, there was no turning back. "Be ready, for you must take [pay] it up." Occasionally, there was no time for courtesy. Harry forwarded bills beyond his means to Richard for payment with only the words: "I owe it."

Richard and Harry's collaboration embraced more than fiscal matters. The brothers became allies in politics. In the 1780s, Harry served for three years in the Continental Congress. There he stoutly supported the trend toward stronger national government, even though he was pitted against Richard Henry Lee. Meanwhile, Richard Bland Lee sat as a delegate from Loudoun County in Virginia's General Assembly, where Harry charged him with looking after both their interests.

As partners in statesmanship, Richard was not always successful in championing Harry. The latter made it difficult for Richard by taking an awkward stand on an issue of concern to Virginians. This was whether Spain should open the port of New Orleans at the Mississippi's mouth for use by American farmers west of the Alleghenies. Legislators from Kentucky, which was then still part of Virginia, were vocal in Richmond, demanding their commerce be free to go down the Mississippi. Even so, as a delegate to Congress, Harry Lee joined the faction that bowed to Spain's wish that New Orleans be closed. His vote might have been encouraged by a loan of $5000 made to him by the Spanish government—which he never repaid, although Madrid pursued him.

When news of Harry's capitulation to Spain reached Virginia's General Assembly, he was swiftly rebuked and his seat in Congress taken from him. Immediately, the thin-skinned Harry's famous anger flared, and he complained bitterly to Richard: "A community ought to be tender of the reputation of her servants. I expected delicacy as well as justice from my country, or I never would have risked a reputation dearer to me than life in the precarious tenure of a democratic assembly." Muttering that he would not forget those who had criticized him, Harry turned his wrath upon Richard: "It is wonderful that you should have been silent on the head [Harry's censure]. It proves their cunning or your lethargy."

It turned out that Harry's purse as well as his pride were threatened by his loss of the congressional seat. Billy Shippen reported that "Harry is much mortified, having taken a large house in New York for the winter." Since he had paid an expensive rent, Harry wanted to remain in New York. So, suddenly, he announced his switch in favor of opening the Mississippi. After this change of heart, the representative who had been elected to replace Harry in New York decided he did not desire the job after all. Harry could remain in the seat (and his large house) for another year.

This was in 1786. Two years later, Harry entered a new controversy in which eventually he made an even more spectacular change of sides. As a delegate in 1788 to Virginia's debate over ratifying the federal Constitution, Harry argued that a strong national government was essential. Doubtless, Harry knew that his stand aligned him with his hero, George Washington, whose certain election as president meant that Harry might thereby hope for his own political advancement.

But soon after Washington's administration began, Harry experienced another disquieting change of view. At first he had applauded as President Washington's policy steered toward a stronger central government. Then, suddenly, Harry began declaiming that it would be better to shed blood than see the national authority suffocate the states by the policies of the nation's first President. It was an astonishing transformation. Only those who knew Harry's character might guess that his switching horses stemmed once again from financial embarrassment.

Late in 1789, Harry had approached Alexander Hamilton, who had been named secretary of the treasury, to ask for what was privileged information about government securities then circulating at woefully low prices. It was rumored this paper might be restored to full value under a soon-to-be-proposed federal funding policy. If Harry had been told in advance what was to happen, he could have made a fortune, so that his inquiry to Hamilton was an obvious impropriety. The Secretary told him so, a rebuke which may explain why the easily offended Harry began indignantly (but only for the moment) to oppose anything Hamilton endorsed.

At this point, Harry had no national forum in which to express his outrage, holding only a Westmoreland County seat in Virginia's General Assembly. Nevertheless, he used this audience with such effect in denouncing the Washington administration that his colleagues believed Harry had actually converted to anti-federalism. Consequently, on 2 November 1791, the legislature elected Light-Horse Harry Lee governor of Virginia, a largely ceremonial office wherein an incumbent usually could expect three annual terms.

Meanwhile, brother Richard's political behavior under the new federal government was even more colorful than Harry's. With the adoption of the Constitution, Richard had stepped into national prominence. In 1789 he was the first person elected from the northern Virginia district to the new federal Congress. He represented an area which included among its constituents the president of the United States, otherwise a farmer at Mount Vernon.

At the outset, Richard took his seat as an ally of Washington and those who eventually formed the Federalist party. In doing so, he assumed he was also in step with his brother Harry, whom he knew had been pleading during the ratification debates for a stronger central government. Quickly, however, controversy arose in Congress over public finance, the subject about which Harry had improperly approached Treasury Secretary Hamilton.

Mainly, the disagreement was over the nation's credit. Hamilton insisted that it was necessary for the federal government to fund the national debt and assume the debts of the states. These included paying off notes the states had issued, the subject which had so tempted Harry. To some onlookers, including many in Virginia, Hamilton's plan seemed to threaten the integrity of the states, besides being unfair to those members of the Union, like Virginia, who were conscientiously trying to pay their obligations.

The ensuing maneuverings resulted at first in defeat for Washington's administration. In April 1790, Congress narrowly voted against assuming the states' debts. Among the defectors from the administration was Richard Lee, who had learned that his constituents and his brother Harry now opposed the rise of strong federal government. Although Hamilton and Washington were dismayed by the defeat, they saw that victory was still possible if only four congressmen could be persuaded to change to a yea vote, should the matter be reopened. Bringing this to pass produced one of the most significant early deals in federal politics.

Hamilton knew that Virginia very much wished to see the permanent seat of the federal capital built on the Potomac. Since he could deliver the votes in the House of Representatives to make this possible, Hamilton set out to see if he could offer this plum to Virginia congressmen in exchange for their switch to support paying state debts. As the first step, Hamilton brought the secretary of state, Thomas Jefferson, to believe that continuation of the Union depended on the assumption plan succeeding. If Jefferson could find two Virginia congressmen to change their votes, Hamilton pledged to round up enough backing to place the capital on the Virginia border.

One member of Congress, James Madison, wished to switch, but he feared the wrath of his constituents. It made Jefferson turn instead to Richard Bland Lee. He invited him and Alexander White to be his dinner guests. Both men represented congressional districts abutting the Potomac. Probably to no one's surprise, Alexander Hamilton also turned up for a place at Jefferson's table.

In a gentlemanly fashion, the Virginians were told where the capital would be if they shifted their votes on the state debt question. Richard agreed readily, perhaps thinking what a boost this might be for property owners like Harry who had investments along the Potomac. Congressman White eventually went along, but not before suffering violent indigestion in his host's presence.

The Treasury's financial program was adopted, and in 1800, as planned, the nation's government moved to the banks of the Potomac and the new federal City of Washington was created. At that time, the District of Columbia was designed to include the town of Alexandria, Virginia, which had been part of Richard's congressional district. But when these plans were announced, Richard's constituents rebelled. Convinced that by assuming the debts of the states the new federal government was becoming a threat to local authority, Richard's neighbors saw that he was defeated for re-election.

Nor did Harry Lee fare any better. He, too, became the center of controversy after once again shifting his support, this time back to federal power. It was now difficult to know where Harry stood, and in 1794 he was removed as governor before the close of his term. Thereafter, except for Harry's brief stay in Congress during 1799–1801, these two brothers from Leesylvania retreated to private life. Their knack for getting into trouble accompanied them. Eventually, even the companionship of courageous wives was not enough to prevent calamity from overpowering Harry and Richard.

~ 13

. . . Calamity
1794–1827

Richard Bland Lee's first campaign for a wife failed dismally. He sought to win a daughter of King Carter's grandson and namesake, Robert Carter of Nomini Hall, a great Potomac estate situated near Lee Hall. At Christmas time 1790, Carter loftily rejected Richard's suit. Ostensibly, the reason was Carter's disagreement with Congressman Lee's political views. Perhaps equally harmful to Richard's cause was that Carter knew all about the Lees and the rising problem at Stratford. The prospect of a daughter married to a brother of Harry Lee could not have appealed to the Carter family.

After this rebuff, Richard wasted no time in trying his luck elsewhere. The result was impressive. He found a mate in the Philadelphia residence of Stephen Collins, one of the city's most successful merchants and financiers. One wonders if Richard knew that Collins was numbered among Harry Lee's impatient creditors and that as recently as August 1790 a discouraged Collins had reminded Harry: "I have wrote you several letters on the score of your note to me . . . and yet you take no notice of it."

Fortunately for Richard Lee, Stephen Collins was kind by nature and deferred to his daughter Elizabeth's wishes that Richard be allowed to court her, even if he was Harry's brother. Miss Collins was an unusually attractive and intelligent woman of twenty-five when she first welcomed Richard's visits. The Collinses were good friends of Alice and Billy Shippen, and Elizabeth was one of Dr. Shippen's admiring and admired patients, a relationship which may have helped foster her union with the Lee family.

Richard and Elizabeth were married on 20 June 1794 with the Episcopal sacrament, which caused the Society of Friends to remove Elizabeth from its membership. Stephen Collins presented the bridal couple with a gift of a thousand dollars. A month later, the pair arrived at Richard's Virginia plantation, called Sully, reached only by grueling carriage or horseback ride from Alexandria. It was a large place, inherited from Richard's father. Today Dulles Airport stands on some of the land.

As a bachelor often away on political duty, Richard had been content to live in a log hut. It was there that Elizabeth set up housekeeping, although Richard could show her an unfinished but handsome dwelling nearby which would soon be their home. The house still stands as a historic site, and was the setting in which Richard hoped to overcome the sting of being rejected by the voters. Like most Lees, it was not easy for him to forget that he had been ousted from Congress because he differed with the majority.

Richard told his brother Theodorick that it was particularly galling to be libeled by enemies "who never felt a nobler motive than the indulgence of private motive, or the gratification of an inordinate personal ambition." He would be consoled, Richard predicted, by having time now to oversee his farm, as well as the work of tenants to whom he rented much of his other property.

Although she was a Philadelphia heiress, Elizabeth tried to enjoy life on a Virginia plantation. After being "mistress of Sully" for only a week, Elizabeth reported that she rode out every day with Richard to inspect the farm and its workers. The jaunts were especially necessary for her, she said, since she had no one else to talk with at Sully. What she saw on these outings challenged her Quaker origins, for the Virginia countryside was dominated by slave labor.

Nevertheless, Elizabeth made an effort to appear unperturbed in letters written to relatives in Philadelphia, although she obviously was straining when, after she and Richard had visited all the slaves, she tried to picture chattel bondage as charming. Her husband, Elizabeth reported, assured her he approached his slaves "not as a master or tyrant, but as a friend or father." This impressed the new Mrs. Lee, who observed that when Richard appeared at the slave quarters, one saw only "joy and gladness."

"There is nought that wears the appearance of slavery around him," Elizabeth proudly assured her Philadelphia kinfolk. All the blacks were neatly clothed, well fed, and happy. In fact, one venerable slave congratulated Elizabeth upon getting " 'so good man. He no let me want anything all my life. I die content.' " But the bride's euphoria quickly evaporated, and she discovered that by no means all the laborers were satisfied and that some even ran away from Sully.

Soon there was company of sorts for Elizabeth at Sully when Light-

Horse Harry arrived looking for aid and comfort. He, too, had recently been turned out of office, and he, too, had recently been married. The story Harry could tell about his career as governor was nothing less than unique in Virginia politics, nor was there anything ordinary about the manner by which the widower-governor sought a new wife. Even Harry's entry upon his duty as governor was unusual, for the new chief executive had been surrounded, not by legislators but by creditors heartened their quarry was employed. They hastened to congratulate—and dun him.

Governor Lee replied stiffly to one group of creditors in a letter of December 1791, thanking them for their salutations "on my election to the chief magistracy of my country." (In that day, Virginians called the Old Dominion their "country.") As to the request for payment, the Governor could offer only the evasions for which he was famous: "The arrangements I have made for the completion of the other subject of your letter will not produce the end as soon as I had expected; before March it will be in my power to finish the business, when you shall hear from me."

Harry brought his children—motherless for the moment—to reside in a ramshackle Executive Mansion in Richmond. However, the governor's thoughts were not often of home. Becoming chief executive made him head of the Virginia militia, a post he hoped would lead to action and renewed fame. He also sought any command he might wangle in the federal army. This resulted in what the governor considered a personal slight. In 1792, President Washington passed over Harry and put General Anthony Wayne in charge of troops battling the Ohio Indians. Harry had wanted the appointment desperately, and he reacted wildly.

Though he was governor of Virginia, Harry immediately began to negotiate with the government of revolutionary France for high rank in that troubled nation's army. It would be a new start, he thought, and likely to bring him the recognition for which he hungered. He seemed undeterred that the bloodiness of the French Revolution was causing discord in the United States. Earlier, Harry himself had expressed alarm at what was going on in Paris. Nevertheless, astounding though it seems, Governor Harry Lee of Virginia prepared to emigrate and receive the rank of major-general from the French government.

President Washington was one of those who emphatically cautioned Harry against such a dubious move. Even blunter advice came on 20 April 1793 from cousin William Lee at Green Spring. William was incredulous "that you intend to quit your present honorable and dignified situation to go in search of adventures among the savage cannibals of Paris." The uncle said he refused to heed such absurd reports, knowing that Harry would surely see that God would soon punish "that detestable city."

At the last moment, Harry was dissuaded from going to France by the outcome of his pursuit of marriage. Matilda's death had not kept him long from thinking about the delights, as he put it, of "every sweet nymph." By 1793, such interest led his attention to rest upon Maria Farley, who resided with the Charles Carter family at Shirley, a plantation on the James River near Richmond. Maria was a cousin of the Carters as well as the younger sister of Betsy Farley, who had recently married Tommy Shippen.

The governor pursued Maria ardently, the campaign taking place before all the Carters, and particularly Ann Hill Carter, Maria's close friend and the twenty-year-old daughter of the master of Shirley. Quickly and emphatically, Maria rejected Harry's avowals of love and proposals of marriage. Undaunted and evidently unembarrassed, the governor immediately turned his attention upon Ann and asked her to be his wife. A distant relative of Ann observed that by proceeding thus, Harry Lee discarded "decency and delicacy."

Charles Carter may have had twenty-one children by two marriages, but this did not diminish his special affection and concern for his daughter Ann. Nor did he need to be a descendant of King Carter to be wary of Harry Lee. Carter was one of Virginia's richest men, a fact opening Harry's motives to suspicion. Nevertheless, Ann was said to be in love with the governor, a man seventeen years her senior.

For Charles Carter, this marriage was preposterous. He refused to grant his consent, choosing as his basis that Harry was about to resume a soldier's career and would do so in Europe. Learning of the Carter family's objections, Harry again used his talent for changing his mind and announced he now realized the plan to join the French army was "madness." Charles Carter found he had lost the ground selected to defend his daughter.

Gracefully, Ann's father agreed to her becoming the First Lady of Virginia. As for the wedding date, he told Harry, "we think the sooner it takes place the better." Ann was promised as a "dutiful and loving wife," and her father admonished Harry that "we flatter ourselves that you will be to her a most affectionate and tender husband."

Ann Carter and Harry Lee were married at Shirley on 18 June 1793, after which the governor escorted his bride to Richmond, taking with them the relieved comment of President Washington, who commended Harry for abandoning the "field of Mars" for "the soft and pleasurable bed of Venus." But Harry did not linger with Ann. She discovered at once that her husband would be an irregular companion, often away from home. Not that this deprived Ann of the satisfaction of children. She and Harry were to have six youngsters, these to join Matilda's three orphans.

The latter awaited Ann in the governor's house when she arrived after her wedding. Presently, Matilda's eldest son Philip died, perhaps when Harry was away on a mission to Pennsylvania. He had gone there to overpower unhappy citizens who threatened in late summer 1794 to take up arms against a federal tax on whiskey. In thus leaving Virginia, Harry demonstrated anew how quickly his political principles could change. The whiskey tax uproar convinced him he must stop opposing a strong national government. He now began speaking emphatically of the need to strengthen federal power. If force was the price needed to assure such authority, Harry suddenly was for it.

As titular commander of the Virginia militia, Governor Lee told President Washington that he and his men were eager to join in suppressing the Pennsylvania rebels. Accordingly, Virginia troops were called to federal duty, and Harry was made a major general. Off the Virginians went, intending, under the leadership of General Lee, to fight other Americans. This venture did not please many members of Virginia's legislature, who charged that Harry had taken their sons and neighbors into what could prove to be civil war fought to force citizens to bow toward the federal capital. Once again, Harry found he marched out of step with his constituents.

After debating whether to censure the absentee governor, the legislature chose instead to declare that by his behavior Light-Horse Harry had vacated his office. A new chief executive was elected, and the deposed governor reappeared in Virginia both indignant and mortified. Nor had there been opportunity for heroic leadership in Pennsylvania, since no battle occurred. Only one benefit came from this otherwise embarrassing episode. Harry thereafter had the satisfaction of being addressed as General Lee.

Leaving the governor's residence, Harry took Ann and the children to Stratford, where Ann had her first baby, whom Harry named Algernon Sydney Lee. Meanwhile, Elizabeth Collins Lee gave birth to her first child, but not at Sully. During the winter of 1794–95, she accompanied Richard to Philadelphia for his last appearance as congressman. There, a daughter named Mary was born in May 1795. The next summer, 1796, the two new mothers, Elizabeth and Ann, first met each other when Harry left Ann and tiny Algernon at Sully while he went in search of prosperity.

The two sisters-in-law were soon close friends, and they talked of the day when their children, cousins of course, would marry. They even held a mock engagement ceremony. Soon afterwards, Elizabeth's infant died, quickly followed by Ann's son. The tots were buried together "near my chamber window," Elizabeth reported to her brother. "I indulge myself a thousand times a day in viewing the spot that contains two of the loveliest babes that ever breathed."

Elizabeth studied the two graves with a philosophical eye. The sight of them, she said, "will ever serve as a check on those expanding hopes and prospects that in our happy moments we know no bounds to." There would be five more children for Elizabeth, including a second Mary, who lived barely longer than her predecessor. However, of the sturdier four, two boys and two girls, three inherited Elizabeth's powers of longevity and lived well beyond the Civil War. Ann's maternal future also included five more youngsters, all of whom survived their parents by many years.

While Richard Lee sought to succeed as a country gentleman at Sully, Harry seemed undiscouraged by his dismaying experience as governor. He was soon back as a political figure, proclaiming his support of strong central government and the Washington-Hamilton policies. His strategy was to attack his fellow Virginian, Thomas Jefferson, who was emerging as the voice of opposition to federal power. The strain between Jefferson and the Lee family went back to Revolutionary days and the Continental Congress. Now, Harry thought he saw in Jefferson personally a great national danger, and he set out to display him as such.

He began this campaign while still governor by transmitting hearsay to President Washington in August 1794 concerning Jefferson, who had recently resigned as secretary of state. As Lee told the story to the President, Jefferson allegedly had been heard saying that Washington would be a good chief executive if only he had better advisers around him. The inferences were twofold: that Jefferson believed Washington by himself was incapable of wise governance, and that the Hamilton faction was bent upon national ruin.

Harry's rumor-mongering was reprehensible, for it was apparent that he sought mostly to ingratiate himself with the President. Washington was not deceived and assured Jefferson that he paid no heed to Harry's tale. Harry was undaunted. He may have cut a pathetic figure, but he was persistent, going about condemning Jefferson as a partisan leader aiming to destroy the principles of the Revolution which brave men— like Harry—had fought to sustain.

One of Harry's charges was that Jefferson had been cowardly and incompetent as governor of Virginia during the Revolution. Another attack was possible when Harry exhumed an old story about how a youthful Jefferson had made sexual advances to a married woman. Jefferson tried to brush Harry's assaults aside, calling him a "miserable ter-giversator" and the Lee family a group of insects.

Alas for Harry, Jefferson and his Republican party won the presidential election of 1800. Their victory meant Harry's political ruin. A year before, he had taken a seat in Congress after a narrow victory. His single term was during an anxious time when America feared war with France. Criticism of federal policies led the apprehensive Adams administration to suppress opposition by such measures as the Alien and Sedition laws. It was legislation Harry supported, while announcing he was ready as a major-general to fight France, the nation he had so recently prepared to serve.

Harry's term in Congress had one memorable moment. George Washington died suddenly, late in 1799. In a eulogy for his beloved commander, given at Congress' memorial service for the deceased, Harry's words, while for the most part unremarkable, included lines the public came to relish. He announced that the late President had been first in war, first in peace, and first in the hearts of his countrymen.

Other than coining this refrain about Washington, there was little worth noting about Lee's brief career in Congress until an episode at the close of his term. In 1801 the House of Representatives had to break the tie in Electoral College voting between Jefferson and Aaron Burr, a stalemate possible under the Constitution until the Twelfth Amendment was ratified in 1804. Burr had been slated by Jefferson's party to be Vice President. As a die-hard Federalist, Harry was the only congressman from Virginia who hoped to mortify the Jeffersonians by voting to make Aaron Burr President. He did so, even though Alexander Hamilton himself urged all Federalist congressman to reject such a desperate tactic.

Out of office for good in 1801, Harry found that his financial troubles had worsened. He was reduced to selling off such precious property as the land on which Richard Henry Lee's Chantilly had stood. The acreage happened to be among those omitted from the trust Matilda Lee had created to protect Stratford from Harry's desecration. Chantilly itself had been pulled down not long after Richard Henry died.

By 1802, pressure from his creditors had driven Harry to dispose of nearly all the cherished Lee acreage in Westmoreland he could touch. These sad measures brought no significant relief, leaving him hopeless in his indebtedness. As lawsuits tightened the noose, Harry told one friend how he regretted the havoc he created in the lives of relatives and friends. It ought to be the other way around, he said. Properly, it should be he who must bear the Lee family "upon my shoulders like Orpheus." Yet

The Lees acclaim this portrait as that of their Founder, Richard Lee I. He probably sat for it in London around 1662. Richard was then at the peak of his career, having created a personal kingdom of land and commerce in Virginia and in England. He also had many sons to whom to leave this gain, which death obliged him to do in 1664. Legend says the artist was Sir Peter Lely. A closer look, however, suggests that the canvas is not in Lely's style. Possibly, it is a copy painted in the 1690s from an original, for the portrait bears intriguing signs of the school of Sir Godfrey Kneller, who worked after Richard's death. *Private Collection, New York; Thomas Feist, photographer.*

According to family tradition, Anne Constable, who became Mrs. Richard Lee I, joined her husband during 1662 in having her portrait painted. Soon afterwards, she became a widow who obeyed Richard's will which directed her to sell their new home near London and return to her plantation on Virginia's Northern Neck. There, surrounded by what was still wilderness along the Chesapeake Bay, she remarried and finished raising her large family. *Private Collection, New York; Thomas Feist, photographer.*

By an unknown artist, this likeness shows the Scholar, Richard Lee II, probably after he retired from public life at the end of the seventeenth century. He then devoted himself to his splendid library at Machodoc, his plantation on the Potomac, where he particularly enjoyed reading books of a pious nature. Although he was said to have mastered Latin, Greek, and Hebrew, Richard had been no recluse. His valorous career in Virginia governance more than earned him the respite in his study. Public service also cost him his health, as the face in this portrait suggests. *Courtesy of Catherine Lee Davis; Thomas Feist, photographer.*

Soon after this portrait of her was painted, perhaps by an itinerant artist, Laetitia "Lettice" Corbin Lee died in 1706, leaving her husband Richard the Scholar to grieve for a spouse he called "a most affectionate mother." At her marriage in 1674, Lettice Corbin had come to the Lees bearing land and wealth, thanks to the success of her famed parent, Henry Corbin. *Courtesy of Catherine Lee Davis; Thomas Feist, photographer.*

Forty years after his death in 1750, this portrait of Thomas Lee, builder of Stratford and briefly governor of Virginia, deeply moved his grandson Thomas Lee Shippen. Upon beholding his famous forebear's likeness, which he saw when first visiting Stratford, Tommy said he wished to kneel in admiration, so impressed was he by the countenance of his grandsire. Since then, the portrait has continued to inspire respect, although the artist's identity has been disputed. Now, thanks to the observation of Graham Hood, the painting of Thomas Lee can with some assurance be attributed to Charles Bridges. The sixty-year-old Bridges came to Williamsburg in 1735, remaining for ten years to paint in the capital and across the Old Dominion. Signs of Bridges' technique and style, including outfitting his subjects in the dress and wig of bygone days, mark this portrait of "President Lee," so known for his leadership of Virginia's Council of State. *Private Collection, New York; Thomas Feist, photographer.*

This likeness of Hannah Ludwell Lee probably was painted by Charles Bridges. Hannah Lee was mistress of Stratford and mother of numerous amazing children. She inherited the dynamic personality associated with her Ludwell and Harrison forebears and grew up at the renowned James River plantation called Green Spring. Eventually, Hannah's son William Lee came to own that property. In their mother, William and his siblings evidently had a model of aggressiveness matching that of their father, who considered his wife a true partner. When Thomas Lee died in 1750, he asked that his remains carefully be placed as close as possible to those of Hannah in her grave. *Courtesy of the Robert E. Lee Memorial Association.*

Charles Willson Peale painted this likeness of Richard Henry Lee during 1784, probably when the latter become president of the American Congress. Election to that office was one of the two highest moments in Lee's colorful life. The other was when he arose in the Continental Congress on 7 June 1776 to move that Britain's colonies in America should become independent. But there were many discouraging times for Richard Henry, one of which began soon after he pushed for independence. Political maneuvering denied him a privilege he had clearly earned, that of drafting the Declaration of Independence. Disappointment and misgiving over this and other aspects of the new Republic burdened Lee's later career. *Courtesy of Independence National Historical Park Collection.*

The portrait which inspired this sketch of Francis Lightfoot Lee evidently burned early in the nineteenth century. It was probably painted around 1780, just when "Frank" Lee said farewell to his years of Revolutionary service in the Continental Congress where he had been one of the signers of the Declaration of Independence. A quiet, unassuming person, extraordinary for a Lee, Frank may have been the most beloved member of that generation in the family. He was a public servant whose contribution deserves to be better known. Personally, Frank preferred to be at home on his plantation, called Menokin, near the Rappahannock River, where he cherished the company of his wife Becky Tayloe Lee. *Courtesy of the Virginia Historical Society, Richmond, Virginia.*

Tradition claims that this drawing by an unknown hand is of a youngish William Lee. The subject's attire, however, which would have been appropriate only after 1800, suggests that the likeness is probably that of William Ludwell Lee, William's son. The elder William Lee died in 1795, and his son in 1803. William Lee was another of the famed offspring of Stratford. He had been elected sheriff of London and an alderman for that city before leaving his mercantile business and going to France in 1777 to serve with his brother Arthur as a diplomat for the new United States. After the Revolution he became a widower and lived on his late wife's property, Green Spring, a fabled Virginia plantation. His son William Ludwell Lee inherited the estate. *Courtesy of the Virginia Historical Society, Richmond, Virginia.*

Youngest of the Stratford brothers, Arthur Lee sat for this portrait by Charles Willson Peale in 1785. He was nearing the end of a career, mostly served abroad, in which he had become one of the most controversial figures in the Revolutionary era. The necessity of defending Arthur against his many detractors strengthened his family's alienation from the new American Republic. Among the Lees, where unusual personalities predominated, Arthur's nature was the most troubling, and thus prevented him and America from a larger use of his undoubted talent. *Courtesy of the Virginia Historical Society, Richmond, Virginia.*

Uncertainty shrouds the date of this early photograph of Stratford, taken by Huestis Cook. One claim makes it 1862. Whatever the date, which more likely is late in the nineteenth century, the field of corn barely visible behind the mansion adds to the unkempt air lurking about the property. When this picture was taken, it was long after the Lees had lost Stratford. The plantation's greatest days were before 1775, the year its second master, Philip Ludwell Lee, died. His successors so harmed the estate that the last Lee to own Stratford, Henry Lee IV, dismissed the place as worthless. Indeed, he and Light-Horse Harry, his father, had nearly made it so. *Courtesy of the Robert E. Lee Memorial Association.*

If Stratford was one capital for the Lee Family, the Shippen residence in Philadelphia was another, particularly during the turbulent Revolutionary years when the Lee brothers were serving in the Continental Congress. Richard Henry and his brothers had two remarkable sisters, one of whom was Alice Lee. In 1762, while in England, she married Dr. William Shippen, Jr., who became a noted Pennsylvania physician. This is a sketch of their home at the corner of South Fourth and Locust streets, a fashionable address in the exciting days around 1776. At Shippen House, the Lees and others from the Old Dominion enjoyed Alice's fine Virginia-style meals. Later, alas, the house became a place of much sorrow. *Courtesy of the Robert E. Lee Memorial Association.*

Henry Lee II established the Leesylvania branch of the family, a line named for the plantation Henry created on the Potomac upstream from his cousins at Stratford. This like-
ness was painted by Alice Matilda Reading from a miniature now lost. It appears to picture
Henry Lee around 1754 when he and his bride, the famed beauty Lucy Grymes, settled at
Leesylvania. While Henry Lee can claim being the father of Light-Horse Harry and grand-
father of Robert E. Lee, he also deserves to be remembered for his courage during the
Revolution and for his legislative career. Like his older brother, Richard "Squire" Lee,
Henry took seriously the family's tradition that Lees were born to lead. *Courtesy of the
Virginia Historical Society, Richmond, Virginia.*

The Gilbert Stuart portrait of Henry Lee III, known as Light-Horse Harry, is of uncertain date. It is said to have been painted shortly before Harry's misguided career took him to jail for debt in 1809. A few years later, Harry fled the United States in disgrace and roamed among the Caribbean islands. In 1818 he managed to reach Cumberland Island, off the coast of Georgia, where he died in anguish, probably from abdominal cancer. Later, Harry Lee was reinterred with his son, the revered Robert E. Lee, in the Lee crypt at Washington and Lee University. Visitors to the spot are now encouraged to remember Harry's flamboyant contribution as a cavalry officer during the American Revolution and that he was an early governor of Virginia. *Courtesy of Fitzhugh Lee III.*

In the French style, this painting is supposedly a likeness of Ann Hill Carter, who in 1793 became Light-Horse Harry's second wife. Ann probably sat for it in 1800, when she was in New York while Harry was briefly a congressman. At that time, women honored the memory of the recently deceased George Washington by wearing his miniature as a mourning piece. Unknown for years, Ann's portrait, like so many Lee family canvases, may have been sold, for it strayed as far as Italy before eventually returning to Virginia. Growing up as one of many children in the great Carter family of Shirley on the James River, the beautiful Ann Carter Lee had the courage to remain loyal at Stratford while her husband dashed about. After the birth of Robert E. Lee, Ann left Stratford forever, taking her family to live in Alexandria. Briefly, Harry tagged along before going into exile. *Courtesy of Washington/Custis/Lee Collection, Washington and Lee University, Lexington, Virginia.*

From an early portrait of Richard Bland Lee, this copy is said to have been painted by a descendant, Alice M. Reading. It probably pictures Richard when he was a young congressman aiming for a career in American politics. Soon, however, Richard was forced by the voters to retire from public life. He then allowed himself to be entangled in the misfortunes of his brother Light-Horse Harry, so that eventually Richard lost Sully, his handsome plantation near Alexandria. His last years were crushed by debt and unhappiness. The painter of the original portrait is unknown. *Courtesy of the Virginia Historical Society, Richmond, Virginia.*

This painting by Alice Reading pictures Elizabeth Collins, wife of Richard Bland Lee. Matching her sister-in-law Ann Carter Lee's experience, Elizabeth found that marriage to a member of the prominent Lee family brought much trouble. But again like Mrs. Light-Horse Harry Lee, Mrs. Richard Bland Lee came to display such courage in the face of personal adversity as to earn ranking among the truly valorous members of the Lee clan. Elizabeth Collins Lee lived until age ninety, and for years was considered one of Washington society's three leading widows, joining Dolley Madison and Louisa Catherine Adams in that role. *Courtesy of the Virginia Historical Society, Richmond, Virginia.*

Ann McCarty Lee, the subject of this portrait and once mistress of Stratford, perhaps sat for the unknown artist before she sailed in 1829 with her husband to Europe. There she died pathetically in 1840. Her marriage to Henry Lee, son of Light-Horse Harry and Matilda Lee, became one of Virginia's great personal tragedies. Beginning life as a wealthy heiress, Ann McCarty fell into drug addiction after losing her only child. Afterwards, her husband disgraced the name of Lee. Both Ann and Henry Lee remained secluded abroad and were buried in France. *Courtesy of the Robert E. Lee Memorial Association.*

Dedicated in 1890, this monument needed no more identity than simply "LEE." Now, more than a century later, it still requires nothing beyond that solitary word to receive universal recognition. The majesty of the monument as well as that of its surroundings should be visited to be appreciated adequately. Where else could General Lee properly stand but here? He guards the gateway to the magnificent Monument Avenue in the South's most sacred city, Richmond, Virginia, once capital of the Confederate States of America. Lee's presence has drawn countless visitors and inspired many admiring comments. One of the most thoughtful responses to the monument was made in 1905 when the American/English man of letters, Henry James, visited Richmond. For James, beholding Lee astride Traveller was all the reward he needed to compensate for a dreary trip into Virginia. James called the monument a "precious pearl of ocean washed up on a rude bare strand." He sensed in Lee "a kind of melancholy nobleness." With this perception, Henry James put perfectly into words not only the spirit that history has bequeathed to Lee, but also what time has bestowed upon many of his Lee ancestors. In the foreground is the author, photographed during one of his frequent strolls to the Lee Monument when he was a resident of Richmond.

While in Baltimore during 1838, Robert E. Lee had his portrait painted by William Edward West, of which this is Stratford's copy. At the time, Lee was a lieutenant in the Corps of Engineers and would soon undertake military assignments that often took him away from his wife and growing family. Distressed at having to leave the rearing of his children with a wife in whom he lacked confidence for that purpose, and dismayed by his seemingly slow progress in the army, the glamorous young man in this painting would soon be prematurely aged by his bouts with melancholy and frustration. *Photograph by Richard Cheek for the Robert E. Lee Memorial Association.*

While it seems certain that this daguerreotype pictures Mary Custis Lee, there is some question whether the child shown is Mildred Lee, Mary and Robert E. Lee's youngest child, or possibly Robert E. Lee, Jr. The type of daguerreotype and the appearance of the two subjects, however, suggest 1847 or 1848 as a probable date for the picture. The youngster is most likely Mildred Lee. Perhaps the likenesses were taken to cheer Robert E. Lee, away at the time fighting in the Mexican War. He would return in 1848, aghast at the progress of his wife's rheumatoid arthritis. Mary Custis Lee was facing what became near total invalidism. *Courtesy of the Virginia Historical Society, Richmond, Virginia.*

This photograph of Stratford, Robert E. Lee's birthplace, shows the house's south façade today as it greets its many visitors. Owned and opened to the public by the Robert E. Lee Memorial Association, Stratford Plantation with its great house affords a unique trip back to the eighteenth and early nineteenth centuries. So vivid is the impression made by the house that patrons, led by costumed interpreters, can be pardoned for thinking they hear murmurs from Thomas and Hannah Lee or Colonel Phil, the trio who built and were the proudest owners of the property. In the garden near by, visitors can view the grave of Betsy McCarty Storke. She restored the plantation to a dignified and useful place in Westmoreland County, after later Lees had defaulted on that responsibility. In America, no great family's house witnessed such extremes of joy and lamentation, hope and despair, as when Stratford watched the Lees rise and fall. *Photograph by Christopher Cunningham for the Robert E. Lee Memorial Association.*

this could not be, he admitted. "My necessities are such that every day's gain in time is momentous to me."

Any hope that Harry might draw upon the great wealth of his father-in-law vanished in 1803 when Charles Carter revised his will. He did so, Carter admitted, because "I am apprehensive" as he viewed the future of his daughter, Ann Carter Lee, Harry's second wife. Carter took pains to assure that all property bequeathed to Ann and her children should be "solely" theirs. If not, Carter predicted "they may be destined to come to want." Ann's bequest was placed in a trust, and Carter carefully excluded any Lee family member from serving among its managers. This step was necessary, Carter noted, if Ann's inheritance was to be safe from "possession or molestation from her husband, General Lee."

By 1804, Harry was concentrating on staying beyond reach of lawyers and unsympathetic relatives. His brother Charles Lee put the family's view of Harry succinctly: "I remain disappointed by him." Another clan member was less restrained. This was William Hodgson, a businessman of Alexandria who had married Portia Lee, William Lee's daughter. By then, Portia owned half of Green Spring, property that her husband believed Harry Lee had cheated of more than 5000 pounds sterling—at the time, both English pounds and U.S. dollars were cited in financial matters. When Hodgson set out to make Harry pay, the result was an unpleasant family tangle.

For a time, Portia's spouse tried being patient with Harry, until the latter was caught in a falsehood. Immediately, Hodgson lost his temper. "Do you suppose I can put up with such treatment?" he asked, adding, "Taking the whole together, you have nothing now like kindness to expect." Thereafter, Hodgson's many letters to General Lee began with a terse "Sir." There were no replies from Harry's hiding places, even when Hodgson promised that should the fugitive appear to discuss the debt, no one "would molest you by any legal process during your journey."

Harry had good reason to fear being apprehended. For instance, one of his creditors was Nathaniel Pendleton of Alexandria, who contended Harry owed him $25,000. Hearing that Harry was planning on slipping through Fairfax County unnoticed, Pendleton and his lawyer sought to set a trap for him. "I will give $250 to have General Lee arrested in Fairfax," said Pendleton, "because I think his brothers and Ludwell Lee would not let him go to prison." Since Pendleton evidently knew Harry well, he doubted his plan to catch him would succeed. "I expect he will produce as much delay as possible."

Portia Lee, William Hodgson's sister, recalled one occasion in 1804 when Harry managed to appear in Alexandria. He turned up for dinner at the home of relatives where, as usual, he sought to dominate the talk. On this occasion, he loudly deplored " 'the d_____d lies' " he said were circulating about women associated with males in the Fitzhugh clan. " 'I do *not* like [to talk of] these things myself,' " he insisted, but announced that he had undertaken to question the Fitzhughs on the delicate subject.

" 'I like to know the truth,' " said Harry, as if the Old Dominion did not buzz with rumors about his own behavior with females. Cornelia may have had Harry's repute as a lady's man in mind as she listened to his pious pronouncements, for she seemed to smile as she related the dinner scene to Elizabeth Lee at Sully: "Now did you ever hear of such a man as General Lee? I could not help laughing heartily to think of his interrogating a gentleman on such a subject."

A favorite haven for Harry was Sully. There, or sometimes at Stratford, he would confer with Richard about ways to get out of debt. Often, however, Richard found he was alone in trying to represent Harry and himself before their creditors. One such occasion brought him to face the implacable William Hodgson. The latter hoped to be met by truthfulness from Richard instead of Harry's evasions and falsehood. Finding the master of Sully no more dependable than his brother, Hodgson chided Richard for being part of "circumstances certainly not very correct." He had discovered Richard was trying to pay debts with security "which proves worth nothing."

Stung by Hodgson's rebuke, Richard complained of being spoken to in a style "such that one gentleman has no right to address to another." He resented, Lee said, being treated as if he were "a common cheat." To this, Hodgson replied that he had assigned no motive to Richard's actions, although he clearly implied that should the shoe fit, Richard must wear it. "If the plain recital is disagreeable, I am not to blame." Hodgson suggested that Richard re-examine his own "conduct."

Elizabeth Collins Lee watched the havoc Harry was causing among his relatives, and foresaw that it would soon threaten Sully. Feeling she had to confide in someone, Elizabeth shared her uneasiness with her Collins relatives in Philadelphia. She told her mother and brother that Harry Lee "has produced to us anxiety and unhappiness." The Lees were left, she said, forlornly to hope that "the General [would become] a better and more honorable man" than they had seen for some time.

Harry's circumstances grew no easier. In 1808 his son Henry became twenty-one. Under Matilda's arrangement for Stratford, on reaching his majority young Henry should take command of the property, although his father might continue to live there. As impractical as his father, young

Henry may not have realized the problem he had inherited. Under his father, Stratford had become decrepit, ill-kempt, and idle, bearing no resemblance to the grand estate which had matured while Colonel Phil was alive. Most items of value in the house had been sold, and the building had to be barricaded against sheriffs and bailiffs trying to serve papers and make collections.

Obviously, Stratford was no hiding place for Harry when the law was after him. Nor was haven to be found anywhere by 1809, so that Light-Horse Harry Lee had to surrender to the authorities. Until early 1810, he was incarcerated for debt, first in the Westmoreland County jail, and then in the Spotsylvania County prison. To justify his sad record, Harry explained that his financial buccaneering had been designed "for the good of my children." This goal "and this only [was] worthy of the pain and suffering I undergo."

Hoping to escape the discomfort of jail, Harry announced that he was ready to make a deal. Pledging to "cooperate" by surrendering his few remaining assets, Harry asked in return to be granted "a small farm (2 or 300 acres only)." He would willingly serve as his creditors' tenant "or in any way safe to them." Surely, he claimed, this "small favor" was not too much to request. His creditors thought it was, and Harry remained in jail, using the time to write his *Memoirs of the War in the Southern Department of the United States.*

Published as two volumes in Philadelphia during 1812, this work had value as a narration of the campaigns in Virginia, the Carolinas, and Georgia. Even so, the book was marred by Harry's puffery of himself. He also could not resist mounting renewed attacks on Thomas Jefferson and on the system of American political parties which Harry claimed Jefferson had created.

Finally, as the only means of going free, Harry formally admitted before the law that he was an insolvent debtor. What was left of his resources was then turned over to bankruptcy officials who began untying a knot in which each strand seemed to lead from one obligation to another. For all of the loans and support Richard had provided, the only compensation Harry could offer him were the rights to the *Memoirs.* Loyally claiming it was a "worthy" book, Richard peddled subscriptions for it, but found the response disappointing.

After his release from imprisonment, Harry was penniless and no longer capable of financial adventuring. He returned to Stratford, made his wife pregnant again, and followed her and her children to Alexandria in 1810. There Ann's modest income from her father's will and the support of other Carter relatives afforded a new life for all but Harry, who was fitful and unhappy. He seemed to think about little but assailing those he claimed were the cause of his downfall, which still meant Thomas Jefferson and his followers.

Harry's pugnaciousness nearly cost him his life. In July 1812, he went to Baltimore to aid a friend, Alexander C. Hanson, a journalist who strongly opposed the War of 1812, which he and Harry blamed on the Jeffersonians. Once in town, Harry was soon leading Hanson and other supporters against a crowd bent upon squelching opposition to the war. The Hansonites holed up in a house and prepared to shoot it out with the mob.

At this point the police arrived, and prudence momentarily prevailed. The Hanson allies accepted sanctuary in the Baltimore jail, an angry group of foes tagging along. Finding the authorities indifferent, the gang broke into the prison and beat and knifed Harry and his associates, Harry barely escaping death. Badly slashed and bruised, it was eleven days before he was able to speak. Eventually, he was carried to Alexandria, broken in body and spirit.

As soon as he could travel, Harry went into exile, departing the United States in May 1813. In doing so, he ignored protests from his youngest brother Edmund Jennings Lee. With Richard Lee now himself impoverished, Edmund had assumed responsibility for the sizable bail required under Virginia's insolvency law to free Harry from jail. When Harry sailed away in 1813 to roam among the Caribbean islands, the bond was forfeited. Said Edmund Lee: "If I am obliged to pay this money it will be almost my ruin."

Edmund pleaded with the court to postpone a decision on collecting the bail, arguing that Harry was merely temporarily absent in search of improved health. Meanwhile, Edmund had to fend off troubles Harry had caused on another front. In this case, Edmund found he was hailed into court in Kentucky through confusion over ownership of property. The litigation arose because Harry had sold some land in 1795 to one party, and then proceeded to sell the same property to Edmund in 1806. When these fraudulent tactics were discovered, Edmund again was in court. It was a sad time for the Lees.

Meanwhile, Harry went from island to island searching, he said, for enough strength to return to his family. He tried such spots as Barbados, Havana, Guadeloupe, the Windward Islands, Port-au-Prince, and others. His letters to Ann Carter Lee had a stilted, embarrassed, even mawkish tone. Only occasionally and briefly could Harry sound sincere. At one of those moments, he confessed to Ann: "God of Heaven, how cutting to my heart [is] the knowledge of your situation." He assured her he would not permit "your self privations," and spoke of buying a house for her someday.

In letters to others, Harry's old flair would shine through. He sent President Madison "some very fine madeira five years old," and told his Princeton classmate: "I embrace the opportunity with delight, happy always whenever I can in any way administer to your accommodation." There were many letters of exhortation to the eldest son of his marriage with Ann Carter, Charles Carter Lee, always known as Carter. After the latter became a student at Harvard, Harry sent him lengthy messages of counsel and encouragement, stressing particularly the value of familiarity with classical literature, which Harry always professed to enjoy.

Harry Lee seemed never to appreciate that his career was more a solemn warning than an inspiring example for his children. His guidance for his son Carter usually became pompous and high-flown, suggesting that Harry's capacity for deluding himself had carried him beyond conscious hypocrisy. A typical letter, that of 8 August 1816, stressed that Carter should "love virtue and abhor lying and deception." The lad must "dwell on the virtues and labors of the world's great men which history presents to view. Admire and imitate them." Harry assured Carter that "the wise and good are by our God beloved, but those who practice evil he abhors." Never, never should the son imitate "the low, vulgar" examples in life.

The path to glory, Harry advised Carter, would come by his "watching his tongue and his purse . . . never suffer want or temptation to induce the wanton disbursement of the last." Here, ironically, was the most oft-repeated theme of Harry's messages. Reappearing in one guise or another, it stated: "Avoid debt, the sink of mental power and the subversion of independence."

Curiously, many of Harry's letters to his family evidently were never dispatched. In 1831 a trunk of the General's personal effects, which included the unmailed epistles, reached Carter Lee from the West Indies. The son read and re-read his father's inspirational messages, calling them indisputable proof "of the sublimity of his temper and the nobleness of his sentiments."

At the start of his exile, in 1813, Harry Lee was still physically handicapped from his narrow escape in Baltimore. His mental state is harder to understand. He seemed more relieved than depressed at having to leave America, and yet he sincerely may have expected to return and begin life anew. However, his health did not improve, and actually grew more precarious. By 1818, even Harry seemed to realize that his symptoms were grave and that he was unlikely to live much longer. He decided to return to Virginia.

Given a cabin to himself on a schooner bound for New England, Harry set out in February 1818, prematurely old at sixty-two and in pain. Apparently, he suffered from a malignancy in the lower abdomen. At sea his condition worsened, so that the captain put him ashore on Cumberland Island, off the coast of Georgia. There, appropriately, he was given shelter by Mrs. James Shaw, the daughter of his former commander, General Nathanael Greene, who himself had hoped to spend his last days on Cumberland Island. Death intervened, and Greene was buried in Savannah.

In his final hours, Harry received medical treatment by the physician from the frigate *John Adams*, flagship of the U.S. fleet on patrol nearby. Nothing could be done to help Harry, so that his remaining moments were horrible and his screams brought shudders to those who heard them. When pain gave him some reprieve, he was so enraged by his plight that he abused the kind souls who had taken him in. Finally, death took him on 25 March 1818.

General Harry Lee was given a military burial in full pomp, with crossed swords placed on his breast. Navy musicians played a solemn march, and cannon on the *John Adams* were fired as Harry's corpse was lowered into the earth. And there he rested, far from his family, for nearly a century. His son Henry arranged in 1832 for a headstone to mark the grave. Another son, General Robert E. Lee, visited the spot in 1862 and 1870. Then, one hundred years after Harry went into exile from Virginia, he was returned to the Old Dominion.

By action of the Virginia legislature, with the approval of members of the Lee family, Harry's remains, "found in a most remarkable state of preservation," were removed from Cumberland Island and brought to Lexington, Virginia. It was Memorial Day, 30 May 1913, when the body was interred in the Lee mausoleum beneath the chapel of Washington and Lee University, a place created to honor Robert E. Lee. Here, with his wife Ann Carter Lee and their famous son and his family, Light-Horse Harry Lee rests today.

Appropriately, it was Harry's faithful brother Richard who took word to Ann that her husband was dead. "May God support you," said he, adding with singular appropriateness: "may you find abundant confidence in the virtues of your excellent and promising children." Richard knew exactly what—and what not—to say. Harry's son Henry, however, saw no reason for restraint, writing extravagantly to his step-mother about his "noble sire," praising "the lofty and gentle spirit of the departed hero—his affection as a husband, his tenderness as a father, his ardour as a friend, and his misfortunes as a man."

At Harvard, another son, Carter Lee, was assigned the task of composing a valedictory poem for the Class of 1819. He chose to include a few lines about his father, largely to honor his parent's Revolutionary heroism. But he also extolled Harry's "hapless virtue." Sang the poet of his parent: "His was the soul so dauntless as to dare/The attempt to free his country, but despair/Made him an exile amiable and kind."

Richard Bland Lee found his last years only slightly less tortured than Harry's. The tragedy had familiar episodes, as when Richard was discovered to have used his wife Elizabeth's property covertly as guarantee against foreclosures on his own land. Learning of this, Elizabeth's brother Zaccheus Collins said, "I was surprised and perhaps a little hurt." He vowed that Richard must make restitution, with interest. None of this had been known to Elizabeth.

Finally, desperation prodded Richard to implore Elizabeth's mother and brother for aid. Zaccheus Collins replied that they were "so very reluctant to fall into your plans." He suggested that Richard try his Lee relatives. But these cousins limited their help to words of encouragement for Richard's wife. One of them promised to pray that the Almighty would take particular care of Elizabeth "through all your troubles."

Elizabeth had never hidden from her Collins relatives how "the last five years have produced to us anxiety and unhappiness." No one, she admitted, had suffered more "embarrassments" from Harry Lee's financial dealings than the residents of Sully. As a sad example, Elizabeth's mother had enjoyed visiting Sully, but soon she refused to reappear in Virginia and became nearly estranged from her only daughter. Mrs. Collins never hid her dismay that Elizabeth and Richard had become so deeply enmeshed in the schemes and debts of Light-Horse Harry.

"I well know her suspicions," Elizabeth conceded to brother Zaccheus as early as 1804. Even in her last illness Mrs. Collins refused to see Richard, believing that her son-in-law's presence would fetch only "unpleasant consequences." Zaccheus Collins told Elizabeth that life in the Lee family demanded of her all the "fortitude and wise judgment which . . . are so remarkable in the character of my sister." In turn, Elizabeth recognized that Richard's deceit meant she must rely upon her brother rather than her husband. She reverted to her Quaker tongue to tell Zaccheus that her plans must be "between thee and myself."

She made this decision in 1808. After three more uneasy years, the moment she dreaded came. Against Elizabeth's remonstrance, a desperate Richard sold Sully to the second Francis Lightfoot Lee, R.H.'s son. Elizabeth said he was giving the property away at $18,000. Young Frank payed off the mortgage held by Justice Bushrod Washington. After this sorrowful moment, Richard and Elizabeth lived for a time in Alexandria before settling in Washington, where the only recourse was for Richard to throw himself on the mercy of President Madison.

He begged that the President consider him for a public job, acknowledging that he had been ruined by "indiscretions of a beloved brother." Should the President hear unfavorable opinions about him, Richard asked for the privilege of rebuttal. Any appointment given him he pledged would receive "*all* my time." Madison complied, naming Lee to the commission which settled claims of property damage in the War of 1812. Later, he was appointed judge of the District's orphan court.

These positions did not prevent creditors from haunting Richard. He thought of migrating to Kentucky, thus shifting the burdens away from Elizabeth. He made a trip to the Bluegrass, hoping somehow to find value in lands in the area foisted on him by Harry. Much cast down, Richard confessed in 1819, "I shall be obliged to leave my family to their fate as my agency can no longer be useful to them." Only word of his appointment to the orphan court induced him to return to Elizabeth.

Back in Virginia, Richard found that debts and law suits still faced him. There were more accusations by creditors who claimed they had been betrayed by the team of Harry and Richard Lee. In 1825, Richard wrote to James Madison, now in retirement, asking his help in being appointed clerk of the Supreme Court. It was a pathetic plea, in which Lee stressed his poverty, his age, his infirmity, and his debts of $50,000. He assured Madison that all this was due to the imprudence of others.

The misery of his last years brought Richard to concur in the pessimism which had overtaken his cousins from Stratford. He spoke of the "frail passions" which seemed to control humankind, and the likelihood that these emotions would make impossible a true republic in America. "The more freedom, the more danger," he said. Thus spoke an aged and destitute Federalist who had lived to see the rise of Jacksonian democracy. Richard's last letter, written to a son studying at the University of Virginia, contained two pieces of advice the excellence of which the father had learned the painful way: the son should avoid melancholy and seek to be frugal.

Richard Bland Lee died 12 March 1827 at age sixty-five, suffering much physical pain at the end. He was taken for burial to the Congressional Cemetery in Washington. Soon afterwards, his widow Elizabeth reviewed the price of being part of the Lee family. Had she been imprudent by remaining loyal to the Lees, she wondered. Musing along these lines in a letter to her brother, Elizabeth regretted that she had been obedient in all the transactions Richard and Harry Lee had put in front of her. Recalling how "in vain I read or reasoned," she admitted that in the end "I *signed.*" Now she was left to ponder "to what extent *my hand* has prostrated my poor children."

There was little romance in Elizabeth's review of her career with the

Lee clan. "Oh! I have been unfortunately and peculiarly situated for many years," she confided to Zaccheus. "No friend near, no advisor." Only the "self-interested" had swarmed around her, and she had been left "unable to resist what was ever pressed upon me." Elizabeth particularly remembered the episode when her husband had begged her to surrender property back to him which earlier he had placed in her name so that creditors could not touch it.

Once Elizabeth began unburdening herself, the words would not cease. "I have done all to pay debts and save credit, but alas! to no effect. Many must suffer." Nevertheless, she pledged to her brother, "you will find me strong in mind and willing to submit." Elizabeth reminded herself that other families had been greatly blessed, only to fall into calamity. Apparently, she said, "it is the will of God that the proud family and name of *Lee* should be among the number."

❧ 14

Refuge in Alexandria
1794–1858

While Harry and Richard Lee were heaping calamity upon themselves and others in the Lee family, their wives sought to keep their marriages intact. In doing so, Elizabeth Collins Lee and Ann Carter Lee made the town of Alexandria a refuge. By the 1790s, Alexandria was an attractive and bustling river port. While the town was placed for a time within the newly created District of Columbia, it remained Virginian in spirit.

Alexandria was a plausible rallying place for the Lees. Beginning with the first Richard, the clan had patented much property along that section of the Potomac. By the late eighteenth century, Lees were taking up residence on family plots in the town, producing many relatives to greet Elizabeth Collins when she arrived in July 1794, the bride of Congressman Richard Bland Lee. The city-bred Elizabeth was delighted when she and Richard spent winters in Alexandria. It was difficult for them to resist the hospitality of kinsmen whose large houses seemed always to have room for more Lees.

Ready to welcome Elizabeth in Alexandria were Richard's brothers Charles and Edmund with their wives Anne and Sarah, who were themselves Lees. The two women were sisters, coming to the city from Westmoreland County, where they had been daughters of Richard Henry Lee. Charles and Edmund lived in adjacent houses, and next to them was the residence of Richard Fendall, whose second wife had been Elizabeth Steptoe, the widow of Colonel Phil, and whose third spouse was Mary Lee, the sister of Charles, Edmund, Richard, and Harry. Fendall himself was descended from Richard Lee the Scholar.

These Lees, and others to come, had settled centrally in the city, with addresses along Washington, Oronoco, Prince, Duke, and Cameron streets. If she walked out a bit, Elizabeth soon approached the residence of Ludwell Lee, another son of Richard Henry. He had married his first cousin, Flora Lee, who had grown up at Stratford and was Colonel Phil's daughter. Ludwell Lee's Alexandria home sat on the prominence where today stands the Masonic Memorial to George Washington. Proceeding downstream, Elizabeth could visit Mount Vernon, which Richard Henry Lee's grandson, John Augustine Washington, would eventually inherit.

Life brightened considerably around Alexandria with the arrival in 1797 of two young female Lees. They were Portia and Cornelia, William Lee's orphaned daughters. After Frank and Becky Lee died at Menokin, where Portia and Cornelia had been living, the young women declined their brother's invitation to join him at Green Spring. Young William Lee was busily pulling down the decrepit remains of the original house, considering replacing it with one designed by Benjamin Latrobe.

This improvement was not enough to lure the sisters, who found Green Spring's neighborhood quite dull, since Williamsburg was no longer Virginia's capital. There was little along the James River to compare favorably with life around Alexandria. The villagers of Williamsburg had, according to Cornelia, "a locality of manners, if I may so express myself, that renders their society only insipid." They lacked "that secret charm . . . which attracts and attaches."

But even in comparatively sophisticated Alexandria, Portia and Cornelia must have been looked upon as somewhat unusual. They were a contrast to most of the women in the city, for the sisters had spent their early years in Brussels and in London. Both had been well tutored in literature and the graces, which delighted the bookish Elizabeth. She took the young women to live at Sully, where they were company for the lonely mistress of the plantation.

Portia Lee was now age twenty. Cornelia was seventeen and evidently a highly talented and independent-minded person. She saw that books were always carried out to Sully, where she read aloud to the children. Cornelia took special pleasure in the writings of the gloomy Englishman William Cowper, whose religion-based views concerning human nature and society would later influence Cornelia's life.

The happy rural days for Elizabeth and the sisters lasted only two years. In May 1799, Portia was married at Sully to William Hodgson, an Alexandria merchant, who then took his bride to live in town. The bridal couple induced Cornelia to come along for a time. She remained until the autumn social season was about to begin, when she retreated to Sully. Portia regretted her departure, calling Cornelia "my dear and saucy sister."

Actually, Portia Hodgson was herself a strong person. She announced she was determined to keep uncontaminated by the "gadding and dissipations" which she felt shaped the lives of most women in Alexandria. Since her husband wanted her with him in society, the loyal Portia reported to the envious Elizabeth, stuck out at Sully, "It is my duty to be contented in *any situation* with the worthy man to whom I am united." Still, having to traipse around town left *"little,* indeed *no* time for the useful and rational occupations of life." In Portia's opinion, "the pale looks and heavy eyes" which accompanied late hours of partying made living in Alexandria "pernicious to health."

When an errand took Hodgson out of town, Portia loudly lamented the departure of "my good man," and added: "I miss him inconceivably." Portia here uttered what doubtless was an unintended pun, though it was surely a prophetic one. As soon as her husband returned from his first business absence, Portia became pregnant. Upon arriving in Alexandria during the spring of 1800, Cornelia reported to Elizabeth that Portia was "getting quite lusty," but that "the event cannot take place till the last of the summer."

Both Portia and Cornelia's letters, and particularly Cornelia's, witnessed candidly to the misgiving with which women in that day necessarily had to confront childbirth. It was, as Cornelia put it, "this dreaded event." And, oh, she added, might the "little bantlings" which resulted be worth "every pang" they caused. Pregnancy was a subject which Cornelia, still unmarried, conceded put her "out of humor with myself."

It was a fearfully hot August in 1800 when Portia awaited apprehensively the arrival of her first child. From Sully, Elizabeth sent messages of reassurance, but Portia was not easily soothed. "As to the *approaching affair* being a *frolic,* I am convinced not all the determination in the world can make it so." But being "heartily tired of my present situation," Portia conceded that she was ready to face "the *worst,*" if only "to have it over." It was a *"Black Monday,"* she confessed, and "my side pains me most severely."

The male world, as Portia watched it, seemed to go on unperturbed by her discomfort. Disregarding his wife, William Hodgson gave a large dinner for a group of gentlemen, obliging Portia to hide in her room. "They will not even have a *peep* at me, that's certain," she told Elizabeth. "I shall eat my chicken solitary and *alone.*"

Portia was not solitary for long. Within a few days, Cornelia penned a short bulletin to the folks at Sully. "Rejoice—Portia has a fine son." Now the attention switched to the infant's christening, and to giving thanks for Portia's abundant supply of milk. Seven more times this new mother would pass safely through the "dreaded event." Portia lived to be sixty-three.

The boy child born that torrid August in 1800 was named William

Ludwell Hodgson, thus honoring both his grandfather and uncle. Portia and Cornelia had remained close to their brother William. Still a bachelor, William continued to give all his energy to Green Spring, and to improving the lot of its slaves. He made many trips to Alexandria and Philadelphia, always, Cornelia said, "with a head and hands full of business." Other relatives referred to William as "amiable, genteel, and well-informed."

William Lee relied upon Portia and her husband for guidance, naming Hodgson, along with "my dearest sister Cornelia," as his executors. Portia and Cornelia visited Green Spring in October 1801, pleased with how "handsome" the new mansion was and taking walks along some of the paths they had once followed with their father. The sisters, however, noticed how the Lee family name no longer seemed to mean much beside the James and York rivers. In Yorktown, they had to wait two days for William's carriage to pick them up, for no one noticed them or offered help.

Then, tragically, the sisters found themselves very much part of James River life. William died on 24 January 1803, one day beyond his twenty-eighth birthday. Ill but a short time, he died "with great fortitude" and "with a firm reliance on the merits of our blessed redeemer." His admiring brother-in-law William Hodgson asserted: "In him the poor have lost a friend." Since William had wished to be interred beside his father and other Ludwells in the Jamestown churchyard, the burial was postponed until better weather. On 15 February, the eminent Bishop James Madison, uncle of the future President, officiated at the service.

William Ludwell Lee's will provided for the emancipation of his slaves, the education of the younger blacks, and a generous bequest to improve public education in the Williamsburg neighborhood. The bulk of his wealth, however, was left "to my dear sisters Portia Hodgson and Cornelia Lee." This was important news for the Alexandria community, as it placed the two young women among Virginia's wealthier persons. Elizabeth Lee informed her Philadelphia relatives that in addition to being "the best girls in the world," Portia and Cornelia were now "among the richest." Their brother's bequest gave them an estate valued at 50,000 pounds.

Now the sisters were obliged to visit their jointly held estate at Green Spring. They had acquired, as Portia's husband put it, "more land than can be well attended to." William Hodgson sought at once to place the plantation under better discipline. He ended William Ludwell Lee's kindly practice of encouraging all his neighbors "to come hither during the fruit season and take what they pleased." The freed slaves would be allowed to work the land formerly assigned to them, but only, warned

Hodgson, "as long as I think they deserve it." And hunters must be kept off the property, particularly if they had dogs. "Every one caught will be instantly destroyed."

Such was the rigorous view of Portia's husband, the efficient executor. Leaving such matters to him, the sisters let the sight of Green Spring lead to reflections on the troubled Lee family. The "inflictions" suffered by relatives, Portia said, tempted her to withdraw from the "unfeeling world." But Green Spring was a poor spot for retreat, being "cold, dreary, deserted."

Cornelia Lee had her own personal concern. She was twenty-three and single when she found herself a woman of wealth. She did not like the prospect, saying it made her vulnerable to many worldly pressures, including marriage. Acknowledging that she feared the pain and danger of childbirth, Cornelia admitted she had hoped quietly to enter spinsterhood. But now that she was rich, she predicted men would pursue her. She told Elizabeth: "I have lost that sweet content I before possessed. Suspicion appears now to be necessary, and most of all I suspect myself."

There were moments when Cornelia felt her new money might be a reason to flee from Alexandria, which seemed suddenly populated by males clamoring for her attention. Cornelia knew she was no beauty, and admitted that her mirror always reminded her of her "blemished face." There was no doubt, she said, why men now tried to tell her how attractive she was. "Oh, what a miserable, mercenary world it is we live in," she sighed to Elizabeth. All of Alexandria seemed intent on her marriage, Cornelia announced.

"The longer I live," she said, "the more knowledge I gain of the human heart, the less reason I find to be pleased with my discoveries." Even Portia and William Hodgson joined the campaign to bring Cornelia to the altar. Before the period of mourning for brother William had ended, the Hodgsons gave a dinner featuring Cornelia, to which a number of Alexandria gentlemen were invited. Cornelia complained that the affair bored her, keeping her from the reading she preferred. Guests, she noticed, "give me no pleasure."

This indictment included John Hopkins, a Richmond businessman now often in Alexandria. He had once been a financial associate of Cornelia's father and was twenty years older than she. It was apparent that Hopkins had known Cornelia for a long time before he discovered her charms. "I suppose every body will mark him as my intended," Cornelia reported to Elizabeth. "However, I care not." She had no time for the multitude who seemed "determined to have me married, whether I will or no."

Cornelia could enumerate many reasons to avoid marriage. "I feel not the least inclination to enter the holy estate of matrimony, and sincerely believe it will be better for me if I never do," she confided to Elizabeth on Christmas Eve 1803. For Cornelia there was the instructive example of an acquaintance who had married into the Fitzhugh family, and now sat helplessly while her "worthless husband" philandered.

"Poor woman," said Cornelia, "bitter indeed has been her earthly portion," for all her husband's relatives "revile her as the cause of his imprudencies." What most annoyed Cornelia, apparently, were the "grave, demure looks" which sinners were prone to wear. "Oh, how I dislike hypocrisy. Milton says it is the only evil which walks unseen."

Then something changed Cornelia's mind about John Hopkins and marriage. Perhaps it was the sight of Portia and Elizabeth increasingly caught up by the problems and joys of their children and husbands. Looking back, Cornelia realized that with her mother's early death and the separation from her father, she had matured without the strengthening "shield" of genuine family life. "The Father of us all in his good pleasure" had willed the importance of marital life, Cornelia conceded. Now, it remained to see what God's decrees of "love and mercy" would produce for her.

On 19 October 1806, Cornelia Lee made the change she dreaded, marrying John Hopkins. The ceremony, held at Portia's house, took place at sunset. A guest reported about the bride that "her gown, while expensive, was neat and simple." She wore one white flower at her cap. Observers said Cornelia looked "remarkably well," and that she joined enthusiastically in the dancing which went on until well after midnight.

Elizabeth and Richard had to miss the wedding, but Cornelia sent a cryptic note: "The knot is tied and my fate and fortune irrevocably fixed." For a time, Mr. and Mrs. Hopkins lived in Alexandria, where Cornelia promptly became pregnant. As the birth neared, she shared her anxiety with Elizabeth, who was still hanging on at Sully. Said Cornelia: "I am sorry to feel that an event which gives much transport to many a female bosom is none to me. I never at any time viewed it as a subject of rejoicing."

Furthermore, Cornelia mused, why should anyone wish to perpetuate the race in a world so full of perplexity and care? Who should "feel anxious for the introduction of other beings on this scene of trial," she wondered. But, having discovered, as Cornelia put it delicately, how "things are so" between male and female, she confessed she could see why humanity had babies "with alacrity."

A daughter, named Portia, was born on 30 August 1807, after Cornelia safely passed through what she described as "those pangs which pronounced me a mother . . . a trial sometimes perilous and always painful." Any personal peace was now gone forever, she admitted, for the child meant "an anxious mind and broken time." Cornelia vowed to find some charm in motherhood. "I can truly say that in the midst of perplexity and unhappiness, I have ever thought it was for my good and [was] wisely ordered so."

Evidently Cornelia and John Hopkins were a happy pair. Perhaps an older man whose interests were in business proved a wise choice by Cornelia. A mutual friend told Elizabeth that it was best for women to avoid intellectually disposed males as mates. Men "who are much engaged in abstract studies have seldom an inclination to all the minute affections and attentions of domestic life, and she who wishes for an adoring husband cannot calculate to find one in a learned man."

There are few surviving letters from the years after Cornelia's first child was born. She did tell Elizabeth how she was coming to be content as a mother, as well as a wife. Recalling how often she had said she never wished for offspring, she now feared that, with every childhood illness, God might be preparing to take a child away. It would be a fitting punishment, Cornelia conceded, for "inwardly vaunting my own strength; to show me what a poor creature I am and how little I know myself."

There were three more daughters born in the Hopkins household, but Cornelia did not live to see her babies become young women. Her last child arrived in April 1818. Soon afterwards, the dangers of pregnancy caught up with Cornelia at age thirty-eight. She never recovered from this birth and died in Richmond on 24 July 1818, four months after her cousin Light-Horse Harry was buried on Cumberland Island. In a last note to Elizabeth, Cornelia lamented how woes seemed never to cease for the Lee family.

It had been soon after Cornelia's wedding that Elizabeth found herself no longer mistress of Sully. Instead, she was one of the Lee family members in Alexandria who welcomed Ann Carter Lee, the now deposed mistress of Stratford. As Light-Horse Harry's courageous wife, it was Ann's turn to find asylum in Alexandria. If any person needed refuge and friendship, it was she. And yet no family member responded to an ordeal with more dignity and patience than Ann Lee.

Despite her calamitous marriage, Ann apparently never wavered in seeking to make the best of it. Often tempted and even encouraged to leave the vagabond Harry, she remained loyal to her role as wife. How enduring was the love she may once have had for her husband is a secret Ann took to the grave.

After leaving the governor's house in Richmond, Mrs. Harry Lee found herself often alone with her growing family in Westmoreland

County. Her eldest son Carter remembered her as an excellent chess player. Since he learned the game quickly, the two passed much time over the board. Even so, when compared with Shirley and Sully, the remote location of Stratford brought a life of near-imprisonment to the once-gregarious Ann.

Her correspondence with Elizabeth was thus all the more important to her, especially when Ann had nothing more to talk about in exchange for news than "a very fatiguing ride on horseback." In 1799, Ann was reduced to begging for word of what went on in Alexandria. "So confined is the sphere in which I have moved for the last six months that I am almost totally ignorant of every occurrence beyond the distance of fifteen or twenty miles." Except for an occasional visit by a Carter relative, Ann said her motto at Stratford had become " 'the world forgetting, by the world forgot.' "

There had been a season of happiness in 1798 with the arrival of a son to replace the Algernon Lee who had been buried at Sully. This infant was named Charles Carter Lee after Ann's father. "From the superlative beauty of his father and mother," Ann quipped, one would assume these qualities would descend to the lad. "But alas! my dear," Ann informed Elizabeth, "he inherits neither the charms of the one nor the other." Even so, he was healthy, "and (his mother thinks) very sweet."

Five years later, Ann's messages were rarely so light-hearted. "Fate has probably forever severed me from [you]," she lamented to Elizabeth. Claiming that she was becoming an invalid, Ann renewed her pleas that Elizabeth send reports of family doings in Alexandria. It was the one place where she knew she could find cheer—"Oh! that I could [be] there." But now she had two more children to keep her at Stratford, a daughter Anne, and a son, Sydney Smith, whom the family called Smith. Ann wondered if these youngsters would ever know their relatives in Alexandria.

In April or May 1806, Harry reappeared at Stratford and Ann again became pregnant after a barren period of four years. It was an unwelcome condition, as she admitted to Elizabeth. The next months were especially dismal, since Ann's father, Charles Carter, died. His children were left to feel, as Ann bluntly said to Harry, "that our best hopes are buried in the grave of our blessed and dearly beloved friend." Now, "the eyes which used to beam with so much affection on me were veiled forever!"

Writing from her parents' plantation at Shirley, Ann went on to urge her husband to recognize how, with her father now dead, "your afflicted, fatherless wife can now only look to you to smooth her rugged path through life, and soften her bed of death!" But Harry seemed incapable of providing even the most elemental of Ann's needs, which at that point was a coach to carry her in her pregnant state from Shirley back to Stratford. Ann pleaded with Harry: "You will certainly bring a conveyance for me . . . do not disappoint me, I conjure you."

Partly, Ann's anxiety came from recalling how she had been compelled to give birth to her previous baby while traveling. Five years before, Harry had been unable to return Ann to Stratford in time, so that the infant had been named Smith after the family who provided his mother with shelter. Since then, Harry had so stripped Stratford that there was no durable carriage left. Ann barely managed to reach Stratford in time.

The trip through the wet and chill had given Ann a severe cold, adding to her dread of the approaching birth. A week before the baby was born, Ann wrote a discouraged letter to Elizabeth, who was also in advanced pregnancy. Sending wishes for Elizabeth's success, Ann acknowledged that she regretted they both were to have babies. Her infant arrived on 19 January 1807. She named him Robert Edward after two of her brothers.

Aside from her condition, the dilapidated state of the mansion at Stratford and its grounds was cause enough for Ann's pessimism. Also, the whereabouts of Harry at the time are unknown. Her narrow survival of Robert's birth meant no omen of better times. Unbelievably, conditions around Ann could and did worsen, for in April 1809, her debtor husband began his year in prison.

To overcome these mortifying circumstances, Ann was encouraged by her Carter relatives to leave Harry. Her reply reflected the steel in her character, as when she responded to an invitation from her brother-in-law, Dr. Carter Berkeley, who lived in Fredricksburg, a town which lay between Stratford and Alexandria. He was the bereaved husband of Ann's sister Mildred, who had recently died. Berkeley urged Ann to bring her children and live with him and his youngsters, a proposal Ann graciously declined in November 1809. She gave two reasons.

First, Ann said, "Mr. Lee constantly assures me his intention is to live with his family after his release from his present situation." But even if Harry wandered away again, Ann admitted she still would not join Dr. Berkeley. She must, she said, "have my own house." And since she was inclined to live in the city, Ann offered to take in the Berkeley children. She was determined, she told her brother-in-law, "to fix myself permanently, be it ever so humble a manner, and must indulge myself in at least making the attempt."

Ann spoke of remaining at Stratford until Harry was set free. He had implored her, she reported, not to move out. "This he says is for the mutual benefit of Henry [Harry's son and Matilda's heir to Stratford], myself, and himself." Ann made certain her relatives knew that, while she had agreed to this condition, she had given no other pledge. Ann had reserved to herself "the right of choosing my place of residence afterwards."

The selection apparently was not a difficult one, for shortly after Harry emerged from prison, Ann took her children and headed for Alexandria, with the bankrupt Harry tagging along. She had located a house in town which relatives made available. Just as important for Ann was the warm welcome she received in Alexandria from both the Lee and Carter sides. Especially pleased to see her was Elizabeth, along with Portia and Cornelia.

In February 1811, Ann's last baby was born, a daughter who was christened Mildred. Weak though the ordeal left her, Ann at least had pleasing company. Elizabeth reported to her own family: "I am sometime every day with Mrs. H. Lee." Others called Ann "Mrs. Harry" or "Mrs. General Lee." There was good reason for this. So many Lee men and women lived nearby that the neighborhood must have seemed a perpetual family reunion. Wives each needed something more for identification than "Mrs. Lee."

The setting in Alexandria would have irked Harry Lee. He found he could not step beyond his wife's front door without expecting to meet the accusing—or pitying—look of a brother, sister, or cousin. As his final refuge, the Caribbean islands at least spared Harry the sight of a Lee on every corner. Ann's oldest son Carter could recall an occasion or two when he accompanied his father to where the parent might socialize with a few veterans of Lee's Legion. Here, at least, the old commander could temporarily escape encirclement by his Lee connections.

Ann had remained only briefly in a small house on Cameron Street, near Christ Church, before she was rescued by a distant Lee kinsman, William Henry Fitzhugh, who lived in the country on his huge estate, Ravensworth, in Fairfax County. Fitzhugh also owned a large residence at 607 Oronoco Street in Alexandria, whose comfort and beauty can still be appreciated by visitors today. He turned it over to Ann and her children, putting them even more squarely amidst the community of Lees.

Next door, on the corner of Oronoco and Washington Street, lived Cornelia Lee Hopkins and her husband. Across Oronoco resided the Widow Fendall, who was Harry Lee's younger sister Mary. A path through Mrs. Fendall's garden led to Harry and Mary's brother Edmund Jennings Lee's home. Somewhat further away was another of Harry's brothers, Charles Lee, who lived near the academy and dancing school. Just outside of town on the river, one could find Portia Lee with her husband, William Hodgson. As Carter Lee vividly remembered: "we had a large family circle" in Alexandria.

When Ann and her family arrived, the community was an impressive place. With a population of 7500, Alexandria had prospered as a commercial center. From around the world ships came to trade at its wharves. The enterprise made it possible for Ann's children to get a sound education in town, where there was even a community library to supplement the volumes found of shelves of some homes, at least those along fashionable Washington Street. There were also thirty-four taverns in Alexandria.

Some of Ann's children, including Robert, were entrusted for a time to family schools supported by the numerous Carters. The girls went to Shirley, while the boys attended at Eastern View, the Fauquier County home of Ann's sister Elizabeth, who had married Robert Randolph. But the great intellectual event for the family was the matriculation at Harvard in 1815 of young Carter Lee. This was thanks to the generosity of Ann's brother, William Carter.

Only two letters apparently survive of those Ann sent to Carter. These date from May and July 1816. In the first, Ann stressed how the postwar economic depression had reduced her income from the Carter trust. She admonished her son to cut back on his social spending, and particularly not to subscribe to balls. The family on Oronoco Street was having to practice great frugality, Ann said, and Carter must do the same if he was to remain in college.

Ann admitted to a shortage of horses, so that trips to Ravensworth were impossible. Nor could funds be found for Carter to come home for holidays. "You must wait till better times." Meanwhile, Ann acknowledged that her health was poor—"my old complaints," by which she probably referred to the slowly developing tuberculosis that seems to have caused her death.

At first Carter did not take his mother's cautioning very seriously. He sent no accounting of his expenses, making another maternal admonition in order. Ann asked him if he realized that his mother and brothers and sisters had to debate each evening how best to spend their few cents for the next day's food? The family's annual income had dropped from $1440 to $605. Then, as if realizing she was too much a materialist, Ann addressed higher matters. She begged Carter to prize his good reputation and the lofty expectations his family placed upon him. "Disappoint them not, I entreat you."

Finally, Ann allowed a glimpse of her principal worry. She feared Carter would fall away from the Christian faith into some heresy such as Socinianism. Would she not then be to blame for agreeing to let him go to a college where these abominations were taught? "Oh! pray fervently for faith in Jesus Christ," Ann implored. "He is the only rock of your salvation and the only security for your resurrection from the grave." The letter closed: "Farewell, my dear child."

And, indeed, Carter did fare well at Harvard. Faculty records show he was a good student, and he was never fined for misconduct. He brightened 1818, the year his father died, by the remarkable feat of winning both the Bowdoin Prize and the Boylston Prize, the former for an essay on *Paradise Lost.* Unaccountably, Carter was not present for the final College examinations, but he was later quizzed in the president's presence and declared passed, thereby joining the sixty-one other members of the Class of 1819.

While Carter was at school, Ann received an occasional word or two from Harry's Caribbean retreat. Her husband sometimes shipped presents to his family and particularly to Carter, clearly his favorite. Harry took pride in having an offspring at Harvard. He showered gifts and advice on the young man, telling him: "I shall especially mark my eldest boy not only because he is first in the order of nature, but because he has been from the hour of his birth unchangeably my delight." Harry did ask Carter to "hug my dear Robert for me and kiss little Mildred." The father also expressed concern for "your dear and afflicted sister Anne." She suffered from tubercolosis of the bone and eventually had to have an arm amputated.

It seemed a special distress to Harry that daughter Anne refused to write to him. He deemed her attitude "mortifying to me" and, he predicted, eventually "to herself pernicious." Anne was ordered to send him a letter. The younger children Harry admitted were strangers to him, especially the baby Mildred, whom "I know nothing about, nor ever shall." He remembered a bit about little Robert—"was he as good as ever?" he asked Ann. "It is his nature, he always seemed to me to be a copy of my brother Edmund."

To Ann, Harry sent such items as a pair of spectacles, "the best sort," adding, "which I hope you may live long to use." He also dispatched such items as six bottles of brandy, a half-dozen bottles of madeira, a box of coffee, and some brown sugar. The money for these presents as well as for Harry's living expenses probably came from relatives. Since he himself had no resources, Harry could only fall back on his old habit of glib promises when he assured Ann that he intended to buy a house for her, "but I must defer that."

How often Ann replied to her husband's letters is unknown. Evidently one reached him in 1817, drawing a puzzled response from Harry. He wondered if her letter "does most honor to your heart or head." This, he admitted, "I am at a loss to determine."

After Harry died in 1818, Ann lived another eleven years, long enough to launch in life the children she had reared. Upon graduating from Harvard, Carter took up the practice of law in New York City. In 1828, sister Anne was married to William Marshall, a clergyman who eventually became a lawyer and jurist. In 1829, when their mother died, Smith Lee had a good beginning in the U.S. Navy, and Robert E. Lee had just graduated from West Point, though he was not eager for a soldier's career. Ann's youngest child, Mildred, was yet unmarried when her mother entered her last illness.

As Ann Lee's strength diminished, she spent many days in the quiet of the Fitzhugh estate at Ravensworth. It was a princely domain of 22,000 acres. The owner, Ann's cousin William Fitzhugh, had a beautiful and attentive wife, Anna Maria Sarah Goldsborough, who made Ann welcome. Both the Carter and Lee family lines led to Ravensworth. William Fitzhugh was the great-grandson of Richard Lee, the Scholar.

Two of Ann's few surviving letters come from the time of her invalidism. They were written to Smith Lee, away at sea. No letters by Ann to her son Robert or to her daughters are known to exist. To Smith, she matter-of-factly explained that her disease was proceeding inexorably and would soon result in her death. Then, after reporting much family gossip, Ann admitted that what she wanted most was to have her sons beside her. "Alas, Alas, I wish I had my little boys Smith and Robert living with me again."

While Smith could not leave his naval assignment, Robert was home from West Point in time to be with his mother when she died. Legend claims that he was the main comfort and aid for Ann. Judging from her two letters to Smith, however, she had no favorites among her children. All of them, and not Robert alone, were attentive as she declined. Two years after her death, Carter Lee said: "The semi-menial offices I used to perform for my mother afford the most satisfactory recollections of my life. Were I to have a picture of myself taken, it would be with a market basket on my arm."

Two days before she died at Ravensworth on 26 July 1829, Ann Hill Carter Lee prepared her will. To her daughter Anne Lee Marshall, she left a female slave, Charlotte, and the latter's four children. Mrs. Marshall also received half of her mother's wardrobe, a tea set, and other personal effects. Mildred Lee, the youngest child, was given a male slave, a carriage, horses, a piano, and half of her mother's wearing apparel. The most important decision, however, concerned the financial side of

Ann's estate—trusts bequeathed by her father and sister Mildred. Ann reconstituted these in an annuity for her daughters. Each would receive the income from approximately $10,000.

What remained went equally to Ann's sons. At the time, it seemed a modest legacy, mostly 20,000 acres of what was considered worthless land in far-western Virginia. The land was further disadvantaged by an accumulation of unpaid taxes. Also, the young men received six residential lots in the District of Columbia which no one would buy at any price. Of greatest value was Ann's gift of thirty slaves to be divided among Carter, Smith, and Robert. Except for these blacks, the brothers received little to help them begin life. Their mother had taken pains that her Carter legacy, which had kept her independent, should pass to a new generation of Lee females.

Once Ann was buried at Ravensworth, her son Carter had the unhappy task of closing the family's household, recently removed to Georgetown. He oversaw selling the furniture while Robert and Mildred went off to visit relatives. "I am left to myself to reflect on how melancholy it is that there will soon be no longer a roof under which we can be gathered as our home," Carter lamented. Now the scattering of the family "seems to complete the overthrow of that domestic happiness which after all the heart appears most to rely on." He noted how both friends and relatives had been in tears upon leaving the late Ann Lee's residence.

After Ann's death, her devoted sister-in-law Elizabeth, widow of Richard Bland Lee, lived for another thirty years. She entered unexpected poverty when her wealthy brother Zaccheus died intestate in 1831. The generous bequest he had pledged to Elizabeth was tied up in litigation and ultimately claimed by Zaccheus' son-in-law. Elizabeth sent word to her children: "*I need not tell you now to avoid expense.*" Even so, she became a much-admired lady of Washington, despite what her son called "straitened circumstances." There were three elderly widows who presided over society in the federal capital: Mrs. John Quincy Adams, Mrs. James Madison, and Mrs. Richard Bland Lee.

Just past her ninetieth birthday, Elizabeth Lee died on 24 June 1858, and was buried beside her husband in Washington's Congressional Cemetery. By then she had known sadly that Sully had brought misfortune to another generation of Lees. In 1811, Francis Lightfoot Lee, son of Richard Henry, had purchased Sully from the near-bankrupt Richard. Young Frank was well-off financially, having been his Uncle Arthur Lee's chief beneficiary.

Frank had not inherited a strong mental constitution and suffered from melancholia as a young man. Even so, after Tommy Shippen's death,

Frank was considered by many to be the Lee clan's brightest prospect. But then came blows which broke him—the deaths in rapid succession of his two wives, who were sisters. In 1819 he began a rapid descent into gentle, but hopeless insanity. There had been time for him to arrange for other Lee family members to care for his five children and for Sully.

These arrangements failed. While the kinsmen he named as trustees doubtless acted with kind intention, their negligence nearly ruined Frank's resources, so that Sully had to be given up. Frank spent the rest of his life in shelters for the mentally ill, mostly in Pennsylvania. He was brought back to Virginia in 1849 at age sixty-seven, a calm, child-like person who enjoyed being well-dressed. He died at an asylum near Alexandria in 1850.

Like Ann Carter Lee, Frank left a son bound for fame. This was Samuel Phillips Lee, whom Frank had named after one of his school masters. Phillips Lee made a brilliant marriage to the daughter of Francis P. Blair, a powerful figure in the Jacksonian movement. He then became one of the North's most courageous naval officers during the Civil War.

Ann Lee's son Carter would be an elderly farmer before he could witness the achievements of his kinsmen General Robert E. Lee and Admiral Samuel Phillips Lee. Their records were established in time to ease some particularly painful memories Carter had carried for thirty years. These were left by his half-brother, Henry Lee, who became master of Stratford in 1808. A decade later, Henry brought infamy to the family's name. Pondering the tragic lives of his father and his brother, Carter was once forced to concede: "I have never felt so sensibly the utter demolition of the fortune of the race of Lees."

~ 15

Farewell to Stratford
1787–1829

Light-Horse Harry Lee left a record with some redeeming features. Compassionate friends remembered his brave Legion in the Revolution. Others recalled his plea for the federal Constitution's adoption, or his stirring eulogy of George Washington. Unfortunately when Harry's son Henry Lee died, in 1837, there was nothing edifying in his past. This grandson of Colonel Phil and son of the Divine Matilda at Stratford earned a derisive title as "Black-Horse Harry Lee." His family called him Henry.

Two children had survived from the union of Matilda and Light-Horse Harry. Lucy Grymes Lee, the elder of the pair, and Henry Lee, who was fourth in descent to bear that name. Both appear to have had serious personality disorders which spoiled their lives.

Stuck in the limited province imposed upon a nineteenth-century woman, Lucy's escapades were necessarily more limited than her brother's. In a step Lucy apparently considered a lark, at age seventeen she married Bernard Moore Carter. He was Ann Carter Lee's brother, so the wedding made Lucy a sister-in-law to her step-mother, and an aunt to her half-brothers and sisters.

The wedding took place at Sully in 1803. While the bride acknowledged the groom was certainly handsome enough, he was, Lucy said, "such a fool!" The marriage proved catastrophic, so that Lee family lore speaks very cautiously of Lucy Lee Carter. We hear only of a difficult nature, a long estrangement from her husband and children, and even an attempt to burn down her own home.

Little can be recalled about Lucy. Clearly, when she married Bernard Carter, Lucy took a harmless eccentric as a husband. At the time of their marriage, Bernard's father, Charles Carter, gave him title to Woodstock, a lovely estate in Fauquier County. It remained Lucy's home until 1817, although not Bernard's. Around 1812, he left Lucy and the children and began wandering for several years in Europe, a practice which soon became his habit and an annoyance to Lucy, who liked to report on this and other troubles to Alice Shippen in Philadelphia. While Lucy conceded her husband had some admirable qualities, she said his absence had become "a mortification and vexation." Because of Bernard, Lucy claimed she had "suffered beyond measure. . . . It has taught me the vanity of all human calculations and made me look to a higher power than man for comfort and assistance."

Still, Lucy admitted to Alice that she yearned for her mate. But when he returned finally, she found she could not live with him. After Bernard settled 22,000 English pounds on her shortly before 1820, Lucy moved to Philadelphia. There she remained for the rest of her long life, often referred to by the family as "our unfortunate cousin Mrs. Carter." She died in 1860.

Amid her troubles, Lucy wished aloud that she could turn to her brother Henry for help. However, as she admitted to Alice in one of the greatest understatements a Lee ever uttered: "My brother is so situated I could not expect much assistance from him." When Alice's daughter Nancy observed in 1820 that there was something "unstable" about the makeup of certain Lees, she probably had Henry Lee particularly in mind. By then his errant behavior had become a sensation.

We know virtually nothing about Henry as a youngster. He was born at Stratford on 28 May 1787. When his mother Matilda died in 1790, Henry soon went to Richmond with his father, where they lived in the Governor's house and where the lad was soon introduced to his new step-mother, Ann Carter. Then it was back to Stratford, where Henry grew up, surrounded by an increasing number of half-sisters and brothers, the eldest being Carter Lee, eleven years Henry's junior.

There being no funds in 1806 for an education such as his father had received at Princeton, Henry was sent to a struggling place called Washington College in the mountain village of Lexington, Virginia. He did not remain long, proceeding to the College of William and Mary, where he may have studied until 1809. From his schooling, and perhaps even more from his father's tutelage, Henry developed an interest in literature. He came to be considered a proficient writer.

When Light-Horse Harry was clapped in prison in 1809, Henry returned to Stratford, which was now his by his mother's will. For three years, commencing in 1810, records show a Henry Lee as one of Westmoreland County's delegates to the General Assembly. This probably was the twenty-three-year-old master of Stratford, who served until the

War of 1812 began and Henry was commissioned a major in the infantry. He was assigned as a military aide to a distant kinsman by marriage, General George Izard, who had married Tommy Shippen's widow.

After peace was declared, Henry returned to Virginia and found that both he and Stratford were impoverished, obliging him to cast about for a career. At least one Lee tried to help. Uncle Richard Bland Lee asked President Madison to give Henry a job, asserting that his nephew's preference was to go abroad as secretary in some American embassy. The president was informed that Henry was "an accomplished scholar, familiar with ancient and modern classics, a master of polite literature, and of the French language."

Uncle Richard took pains to emphasize that this younger Henry Lee was "of a correct and high toned honor and morality." Madison was urged to remember "the great services in war, and especially in the war of our Revolution by his father, whose errors and misfortunes have placed his son in a situation very different from that which his early expectations gave him a just right to hope." Finally, as if knowing a diplomatic assignment would be out of Henry's reach, Richard Lee intimated that just about any job would do, even if it took the nephew to the western territories.

Upon receiving no response, Uncle Richard again approached the President, remarking that Henry was inclined to re-enter military service. He wished to be named the army's adjutant general. Learning this slot was filled, Richard announced his nephew would accept the post of deputy adjutant general. "He is very anxious to get into some active employment in which he might be useful to his country." Meanwhile, Henry used the title of Major, and continued to do so until he died.

Uncle Richard's labor in Henry's behalf was not entirely fruitless. The nephew was offered a job, admittedly a lowly one, as assistant inspector general for the army's southern division. This Henry rejected, choosing instead to campaign for Congress in 1816. He proclaimed to the voters that he ran from "no sordid motive." If elected, he would seek to restore the "pure patriotism" of the founding fathers. His targets, Henry said, were the public debt, extravagant politicians, and party strife. All of these, the candidate warned, led to "the fate of those nations that have loaded mankind with misery, and heaped all history with ruins." The electorate rejected Henry's plea.

Hardly handsome or an impressive physical specimen, Henry Lee was said to have been an agreeable conversationalist. In those early days, his relatives seemed to enjoy his visits. His brother-in-law Bernard Carter returned from abroad to say how "I long much to embrace you." This message must have arrived just as Henry turned his thoughts to another sort of embrace. He had married a distant cousin, Ann Robinson Mc-Carty, perhaps the richest heiress in Westmoreland County.

The McCarty-Lee nuptials in March 1817 appeared almost too good to be true, as indeed they soon proved. For generations, the two clans had been neighbors. Thomas Lee and Daniel McCarty, Ann's forebear, were brothers-in-law. The 2000-acre McCarty estate, Pope's Creek (later Longwood), lay along Stratford's western boundary.

As it turned out, the wedding brought not one but two women to Stratford. After Henry took Ann as wife, he soon acquired her younger sister Elizabeth "Betsy" McCarty as his ward, replacing her step-father as guardian. Ann was born in 1797 and Betsy in 1800. Their father, Daniel McCarty the younger, died in 1800. In 1802, when their mother, Margaret Robinson McCarty, married Richard Stuart, of Cedar Grove, in Prince George County, he took custody of Ann and Betsy.

Soon, Margaret McCarty Stuart died, so that Ann and Betsy went in 1808 to live with their maternal grandmother, Margaret Rose, who lived near Stratford. Thanks to a generous income from Ann and Betsy's inheritance, Mrs. Rose could see that her granddaughters received tutoring in all subjects. Eventually, she sent the young ladies to Philadelphia "for the purpose of finishing their education."

Both Ann and Betsy evidently were attractive, intelligent women, accustomed to having the best the world offered. Ann's wedding dress alone cost 105 pounds. To Stratford, Ann carried beautiful furnishings as well as money. The eighty-year-old mansion suddenly had a new lease on life. Ann also brought her sister Betsy with her, these orphaned sisters being close friends. By November 1817, Betsy had enjoyed living at Stratford so much that she chose to remain and petitioned the court to have Henry Lee succeed Richard Stuart as her guardian. Lee posted a $60,000 bond as assurance for accepting authority over Betsy's wealth, which Stuart dutifully turned over to him.

Although Henry's success in matrimony offered through Ann's wealth the means to restore Stratford, the new husband was more inclined to be indolent and enjoy high living. He paid no attention to a friend who implored that he "Rouse from your lethargy." One achievement did please Henry, however. It was his becoming a parent when a daughter was born to Ann early in 1818. The proud father invited the world to come and see the baby girl. "She is said to be beautiful."

To learn what happened thereafter requires cautious steering through gossip, legend, and a few manuscripts. As late as 28 June 1820, Henry was in high spirits, inviting a female Lee cousin to visit Stratford. He arranged a ride for the guest by Richard Stuart, Ann's step-father, with whom he seemed on good terms. Then the cheerful days at Stratford ended when Henry's daughter ran onto the mansion's high stoop and tumbled down the long stairs to her death. Her fate was exactly that of Colonel Phil's son forty years before.

Later that summer of 1820, when Ann could not recover from grief over her daughter's death, she made morphine her main consolation. Henry evidently took his solace in the company of his ward and sister-in-law Betsy McCarty, by then age nineteen. Soon Betsy believed herself pregnant by her guardian and notified her step-father, Richard Stuart. He rushed to Stratford and took Betsy to her Grandmother Rose's house, where she had lived before entering Major Lee's custody after her sister's marriage.

The most persistent story claims that eventually Betsy had a still-born child. Actually, no one knows what happened. The limited evidence implies that Betsy never was with child, or if she was, she did not remain so for long. On the other hand, there is no doubt adultery took place at Stratford. Henry never denied his guilt, and the episode was enough to ruin him.

On 27 February 1821, the Westmoreland County Court responded to a request from Betsy that she be officially taken from Henry's protection and restored to the care of her step-father Richard Stuart. This because, as the court sternly put it: "Henry Lee hath been guilty of a flagrant abuse of his trust in the guardianship of his ward Betsy Mc-Carty." Betsy referred to Stuart as "my kindest and dearest friend," and assured him that his comfort had helped her out of a state "almost distracted and overpowered."

Betsy agreed to follow Stuart's instructions, which were to say and do nothing while she wrestled with guilt. "For my sake I do not ask you to love me," Betsy told her Stuart relatives, adding that "I have only deserved that you should despise and forsake me." She hoped they would "think of me with some affection for my mother's sake, who tho' she (as an angel) must blame, still loves and pities her unhappy child." Calling herself an "unworthy sister," Betsy nevertheless closed a letter to her step-father with a hint that her spirits might even then be reviving: "At the next opportunity you have," she requested, "send me Hume's history from the reign of Mary of England."

Betsy had plenty of time to read, for the havoc wrought by her relationship with Henry Lee had only begun. Proceedings in chancery court lasted over several years as Betsy and her advisers sought to retrieve her wealth, which had been placed in Henry's care. There were also the tireless efforts of many in the Lee-McCarty circle to humiliate Henry—who proved difficult to mortify. In fact, Henry tended to talk freely of his affair with Betsy McCarty.

Later, he told a friend: "I am fully sensible of the enormity of my sin and not afraid, as you shall see, to acknowledge it in all its dimensions." But, said Henry, his offense was absurdly magnified because of Virginia's unenlightened statute, which held that sexual intercourse between a couple who were in-laws was legally incest. Had this not prevailed, Henry believed that the public would have been less severe with him.

Was it not understandable, Henry asked, that "when thrown together and no barrier of blood between them," a husband and his wife's sister might allow "unguarded intimacy" to "surprise" them into adultery? Yet Virginians could not see it so, Henry conceded, since his behavior had been shown through "the eye of prejudice" to be a "mountain of atrocities." He found all the commotion in the Old Dominion to be hypocritical. If he must have his sins paraded about, would it not, Henry wondered, "be just to ask who is guiltless, to inquire if there never was adultery before or never will be again[?]"

Henry did not mention that the outrage over his relationship with Betsy McCarty had been intensified by his subsequent tactics. The public soon learned that Henry tried to hustle a friend into marrying Betsy a few months after she had escaped from Stratford. Evidently, Henry's premise was that, if Betsy could be persuaded promptly to take a husband, her behavior with Major Lee at Stratford would be seen in a different light. Henry was sure Miss McCarty should appear attractive to some suitor somewhere. It was a simple proposition as Henry saw it—whoever wed Miss McCarty would be comfortable for life, thanks to her wealth.

With this in mind, Henry apparently set out to find a bachelor who fretted over modest means, but who had influential contacts. The latter were of great importance for Henry's plan. In exchange for doing a gentleman the favor of helping arrange a marriage to the well-fixed Betsy McCarty, Henry expected whoever fell in with the plot to assist in Stratford's legal and financial troubles, for Henry now faced a suit seeking to recover Betsy's funds which he had squandered while serving as her guardian.

Henry must have completed his design during the summer of 1821, when he entertained a guest who became the candidate for Betsy's hand. This friend was Robert Mayo, who at age thirty-six was still trying to find a way to avoid the drudgery of ordinary toil. Mayo lived in Richmond, springing from one of Virginia's distinguished families. His grandfather William Mayo had laid out the town of Richmond in 1737. Although Robert Mayo had been educated as a physician, graduating from the University of Pennsylvania and studying with Dr. Benjamin

Rush, he preferred the career of a writer. In 1819 he published four volumes called *A New System of Mythology*. Dr. Mayo's background was ideal for Henry's purposes. It also helped that he seemed neither particularly bright nor principled.

Henry was quite frank about needing Mayo's help in persuading a Richmond attorney to defend him, just as he was candid in explaining his predicament. "Recent events have," he wrote to Mayo, "shattered my amicable and social relations." Now, "for one transgression, one fatality rather, I am left in total darkness." Only Mayo, Henry said, had shown him "warmth and benevolence."

The distinguished Virginia congressman, Philip P. Barbour, had been retained as attorney for Betsy. This was stern opposition, so that Henry hoped Mayo might persuade Benjamin Leigh to serve as counsel for the defense. Also, Mayo was instructed to arrange a loan to assist the master of Stratford. Repayment would be certain, Mayo was assured, since Henry intended to file a countersuit for personal injury from "the peculiar pressure and persecution in which I labour."

As for Mayo's interest in wooing Betsy, Henry promised the aid of both himself and Ann, whom he stated was enthusiastic about the idea and hoped to welcome Mayo to Stratford often. While awaiting just the right moment to recommend Mayo to Betsy, Henry claimed that Ann entertained herself happily at the piano "and seems to forget our late calamity in the melody of her music. I hope to God you may make her forget them forever." To further impress Mayo with the urgency of arranging financing for the Stratford inhabitants, Henry said that without the loan, even the piano must be sold to gratify "the beggarly villainy around me."

Henry assured his friend that he was making arrangements for Mayo only "out of duty to my wife." Dr. Mayo obviously was so edified by these protestations that he resorted to subterfuge for borrowing the money Henry urgently needed. Deceit was necessary, Mayo had to admit, since Major Lee's name was so besmirched in Richmond that openly arranging a loan for him was proving impossible. Someone with a clear repute must be found who would be willing, in lieu of Henry, to contract for the funds.

In the autumn of 1821, Mayo insisted that the campaign for Betsy McCarty's hand begin. He announced to Henry: "I would consider myself the happiest man in the world could I be so fortunate as to interchange a favourable impression with Miss McC." Apparently astonished at this zeal, Henry hastened to caution the impatient suitor. He told Mayo that word had it Betsy's mood was still "so unsettled and alarmed."

Any romantic gambit would be imprudent, Lee admonished, and

"received with great suspicion," particularly if he, Henry, were involved. An effort by him to help Betsy find a husband would be attributed "to the very worst motives." Mayo was told to stand back until the young woman became her own boss. Henry pointed out that Betsy would be twenty-one on 9 December 1821. Until that anniversary, Henry suggested that Mayo use the time to round up letters attesting to his character.

Then came what Henry reported was a favorable development. Betsy and her grandmother had invited Ann to visit, "if she would consent to see her sister." Ann had accepted at once, for her "resentment" of Betsy, Henry announced, was now "overpowered by her sorrow for her misfortune." The sisters were reunited; Henry confiding to Dr. Mayo that the pair "fell into a tête-à-tête of much affection and intimacy."

This unexpected opportunity allowed Ann to tell Betsy of the interest expressed in her by the Richmond physician, who was eager to be "a suitor for her hand." The information, according to Henry's account of Ann's visit, left Betsy "surprised and astonished." The good news, Henry notified Mayo, was that Betsy found the prospect appealing. Her family felt otherwise.

Whether such a chat between Betsy and Ann actually took place, or was a story concocted by Henry, is unknown. Clearly, this version of a reunion among sisters allowed Henry to keep Mayo on the hook while advising him to remain calm until the Northern Neck grew tired of repeating vile stories about Betsy's lost honor and about what Henry delicately called "our recent domestic calamity." Furthermore, said Henry, the McCarty family felt time was still needed for Betsy's "moral and religious advancement" to move her toward social rehabilitation. To her relatives, an immediate marriage would not help the cause.

At this point, Henry evidently lost control of the situation, and his protégé ran amuck. Instead of devoting himself, as Henry wished, to raising money for Stratford's debts, Mayo decided he must speak to Betsy in his own behalf. Though he had never met young Miss McCarty, he wrote to her saying all he could think of was her beauty and amiability, and of how their lives together would be the envy of the universe. Mayo sent poetry he had composed in Betsy's honor, as well as a listing of persons who would attest to his sterling character. Also enclosed was a message to Mrs. Rose, the grandmother. The indefatigable Dr. Mayo then posted more love letters to Betsy.

Once begun, Mayo would not subside. Ann was induced to send one of the suitor's letters with a note of her own addressed to "dear Grandma." She expressed her endorsement of the doctor's reputation. A reply came the same day. Mrs. Rose was blunt. She returned Mayo's letter and said that Betsy was not interested. Then she added some thoughts of her own. "No man of character would make such proposals to Betsy," she said, adding with remarkable understatement that it was indeed "a piece of strange conduct in a total stranger." Clearly, said the grandmother, Mayo was only interested in "a poor ruined girl who has a comfortable fortune at her own command."

Relentlessly, Mrs. Rose demolished the basis for Henry's plan by advising everyone to understand that it would be a huge mistake to think that Betsy's family "would be glad to get her off on any term." As for the grandmother, she pledged to keep Betsy from risking "her temporal and eternal welfare by throwing herself into the arms of an adventurer." As if this were not enough, Betsy sent a note to Ann, acknowledging her entire agreement with Mrs. Rose. "I believe it would be madness in me to marry any one."

Out of the rubble of his plan, Henry sought desperately to keep Mayo's help. He had to report Mrs. Rose's view, but he tried to soften the news by assuring Mayo that "your conduct in this affair I must be allowed to say has excited my warmest respect." Nobly taking the blame, Henry announced that the obstacle was himself. Betsy's family, he admitted, associated Mayo in their minds with the infamous master of Stratford. They see me, said Henry, "as the lurking demon of what they therefore consider a hellish plot." Mayo was advised to be patient.

No such sober message could stop Mayo now. He renewed his shower of letters upon Betsy, talking wildly of her enchanting power and of his love. Suspecting Henry was encouraging this, Grandmother Rose forbade any communication between her residence and Stratford. Henry called this "a violent and I fear inveterate excess of puritanical bigotry," a condition the Major diagnosed as a "lamentable disorder." He had to admit, however, that even Ann considered the project futile, and refused to read any more of Mayo's letters.

Henry's scheme collapsed. Mayo lost interest in helping with Stratford's legal and financial problems, although his yearning for Betsy McCarty seemed to deepen. He announced that his character had been "too deeply implicated" to quit the chase now. Unlike Henry, Mayo commended the grandmother's zeal and predicted that she would soon be his ally. As for Betsy, the suitor believed her to be eager for him and that she was siding with her family merely out of admirable meekness. Having been banished from the field, Henry dryly said: "I am charmed by your enthusiasm and I wish you success."

On 4 April 1822, Mayo arrived in Westmoreland County, setting up watch outside Mrs. Rose's residence in the county seat of Montross. He reported to Henry that he glimpsed Betsy through the window, "the most lovely figure I ever beheld." Suitably inflamed, he knocked at the door, but was told by a servant that Mrs. Rose was ill. Mayo then asked if he could come in and write a note. At this point and in full health, Mrs. Rose appeared and confronted him in a manner Mayo admitted was "positive and inflexible."

The grandmother was, in fact, so clear that Dr. Mayo gave up the campaign and retreated to Richmond, where he expressed mystification at his reception in Montross. A moment alone with Betsy, he claimed, would have assured her that "there was more to my credit than the interested motive—a sincere regard for herself."

Robert Mayo remained in Richmond until 1830, becoming editor of a newspaper allied with Andrew Jackson's political cause. He was rewarded with a post in the federal Treasury. In Washington, he found a woman willing to marry him. They had two children, while Mayo built a reputation as a colorful and independent personality. He continued to write, but broke with the Jacksonians, having earned the scorn of the old General himself, who claimed that Mayo stole some letters and handed them over to enemies of the Democratic party.

Meanwhile, even before Mayo was turned away by Grandmother Rose, Henry Lee was compelled to pay his debt as Betsy's former guardian by selling Stratford. The Lee mansion went finally out of the family's hands in June 1822 when it was purchased by William C. Somerville of Maryland. He and Henry had become acquainted during the War of 1812. The sale marked the start of a pitiful odyssey for Henry and Ann.

Leaving Westmoreland County, along with numerous debts and much gossip, they lived for a time in Washington. Their only dependable income was from hiring out the thirty slaves, who were all that was accessible of what had been Ann's wealth. The legend about Henry and Ann claims she broke with him at this point and went to an obscure spa near Nashville for seclusion and to overcome her addiction to morphine. Henry is said to have sought forgiveness and reconciliation, and that finally he succeeded. Eventually, so the story goes, Ann triumphed over her drug dependence.

This tale is a garbling of fact and fiction. Actually, Ann and Henry were inseparable, and he seems to have tried to help her recover her stability. Henry's sister Lucy also supported Ann. "Let me entreat you, my dear Ann," Lucy wrote, "to exert yourself to be as tranquil and cheerful as you can." She stressed how self-control "is the best and only palliative." "My heart is greatly affected at your misfortune, my dear Ann." So, too, did Ann's own kinfolk grieve, for contrary to family lore, her relatives kept corresponding with Ann.

Life away from Stratford grew no kinder for Ann, leading her in

1825 to write what must have been an alarmingly melancholy letter to Grandmother Rose. The Rose household replied, sending a letter to Gadsby's Hotel in Washington, addressed to Mrs. Ann R. McCarty Lee. The message implored the granddaughter to try again to rise above her despair. Mrs. Rose did not skirt the primary concern, however. She wanted to know if Ann had fallen further into her habit of taking opium, that "dreadful, sinful practice." Come home to Westmoreland County, Mrs. Rose urged. The grandmother was ready to embrace Ann if she would give up narcotics. "Come to me without delay," she pleaded.

Ann apparently never returned to Westmoreland County. Her husband reappeared long enough in 1824 to cast his vote for Andrew Jackson in the presidential election. At that time, Henry probably arranged with one of his few friendly neighbors, Richard Brown, to act as his agent in local business. But Brown was more than that. He was a solitary voice in the county for the beleaguered Lee couple.

Brown sent word to Ann "that all her poor neighbors about Stratford make unceasing inquiries after her and that they still have a grateful recollection of her kindnesses to them and that they desire most sincerely her health and happiness." To Henry, Richard Brown asked soothingly (and at length): "Are you never to be forgiven for one sin? And is that single act of your life to give a license for all kinds of abuse and calumny to be hurled at you by all that are base enough to attempt your destruction by every species of falsehood and defamation, and can such slanderers receive the countenance of the virtuous and enlightened part of the community?"

Henry might have preferred that Brown's letter stop at this rhetorical point. But his friend went on to report he often recalled how promising Lee's talent and career had been "before your tragical affair with Miss M." Nor was there much solace for Henry in the way Brown closed his long letter: "I can only deplore the catastrophe that has blasted prospects so bright as those you held and forced you from the society of early friends and the home of your ancestors."

More typical of the response Henry's plight drew was that from a long-standing acquaintance who had moved to South Carolina and thus was out of touch with local affairs in Virginia. The friend, Rockfort Clarke, wrote that he had only recently learned how Henry had "wasted your inheritance, neglected your business, and employed your talents irregularly." If this was true, Clarke implored Henry to reform. He must "tread steadily in the right path," and make the Bible his standard. Clarke promised to beseech the Holy Spirit to enter Henry, enabling him to "conclude your life on the purest principles."

Henry left no comment about such advice as he sought to be a journalist and writer. One of his first projects was to defend the memory of his father, Light-Horse Harry, by preparing a history of the Revolutionary battles during 1781 in the Carolinas. This was to refute what Henry considered the recent shabby treatment of his parent by a biographer of General Nathanael Greene.

In 1825, with the help of Chief Justice John Marshall, Henry received a modest appointment in the postal service under John Quincy Adams' administration, a job he promptly lost when the public learned of it. Henry claimed enemies in Virginia had reported him to the Adams camp as being a Jackson spy. That was not hard to believe, since Henry had written propaganda for Senator Jackson's side in the campaign of 1824. At this point, Lee's notoriety attracted Jackson himself, who proved sympathetic with the luckless Lee. They had a bond of sorts, for Henry had been assigned to the southern front at the time Old Hickory won his fame at the Battle of New Orleans in January 1815.

Lee recounted his plight and his views to Jackson, stressing how he had been persecuted for the General's sake. In turn, Jackson made Henry acquainted with his chief advisers, Duff Green, the Washington journalist, and Major William B. Lewis, who were planning the General's run for the presidency in 1828. Since laudatory biographies written about candidates were then an important part of electoral huckstering, Jackson's high command chose Henry to prepare one about the Hero of New Orleans. To do so meant that Henry and Ann must go to Nashville, where the budding biographer could work with Jackson's papers at the candidate's residence, The Hermitage.

The opportunity was providential. Ann had not shaken her dependence on morphine, so that going to Nashville allowed her to reside just a mile from The Hermitage at a new watering place where miracles were reported to occur. This was the "Fountain of Health," whose springs had erupted in December 1811 as a result of the so-called New Madrid earthquake whose effect had rocked areas as far east as Nashville. The resort welcomed guests who could pay a dollar a day. Ann and Henry were encouraged to expect astounding results, for the Fountain of Health was said to have benefited sufferers from "ulcers of the liver, gonorrhea, jaundice," as well as diseased feet, persistent dysentery, and nearly every other known malady.

Unfortunately, Ann's disorder did not respond, and she grew worse. She and her husband arrived in Nashville during the spring of 1827. A year later, Henry told brother Carter Lee that Ann had been shifted to the care of a physician. Nor was there better progress to report concerning Jackson's biography, to the disgust of the sponsors in Washington who had begun advertising the forthcoming work. Duff Green sent messages to Henry urging that he appreciate how he was expected to "render a great service to your country." Green delicately reminded the sluggish author that a successful biography of Jackson would encourage the public to identify the name of Lee "with the illustrious citizen now the first in the affections of the American people."

Green also pointed out that, by finishing the biography, Henry would be defending a noble man against slanders of desperate enemies. When even this last telling point failed to stir Henry, Green became severe: "My dear sir, do you recollect the purpose for which you undertook to write out this work?" And did Lee not see the threat his failure posed to "your own *reputation* as a man of *business* as well as a man of letters[?]" Green's pleas availed nothing, and the biography was never completed, although Henry did contribute to the Jacksonian effort in 1828 by composing campaign letters and other documents.

During the election furor, Henry had news from Virginia which must have startled him. William Somerville, who had purchased Stratford from Henry, had died recently at Lafayette's home in France while enroute to a diplomatic assignment for Secretary of State Clay. He had departed on this mission before fulfilling one of the responsibilities which came with buying Stratford—the new owner was legally liable for part of Henry's debts, since the court still sought restitution of Betsy McCarty's property.

Somerville's heirs later argued they did not know of this obligation when they dallied in coming to claim Stratford. Unfortunately for them, faced by this seeming indifference, Westmoreland County officials had seized Stratford, announcing that on the fourth Monday in March 1828 the property would be auctioned and the proceeds used to help pay Major Lee's debt.

The sale took place on the stipulated day and at the Westmoreland County court house, scene of many Lee triumphs and sorrows. Stratford brought a bid of $11,000, paid by Mr. and Mrs. Henry D. Storke. What should have stunned Henry was that Mrs. Storke was none other than the former Betsy McCarty. In 1826 she had married into the respectable Storke family of Westmoreland County. Now, two years later and through an astonishing quirk of fate, she returned to Stratford as its mistress. She kept the role for fifty years.

Betsy Storke and her husband had no children. After his death in 1844, Betsy remained at Stratford, while also playing an important part in the Stuart family circle created by descendants of her step-father. At Stratford, Betsy used her understanding of herbal medications to become a famed healer in the county. When she died in 1879, she was buried in the garden at Stratford. Her will left the property to Stuart relatives, who, in 1929, sold Stratford to the Robert E. Lee Memorial Foundation.

On learning who had bought Stratford, Henry Lee tried to shrug off the news. He told his brother Carter that when Henry and Betsy Storke paid $11,000 for the property, it was a price "really eleven times more than it is worth." He announced that if he could find the means, he would establish a plantation in Louisiana, and be an absentee owner, living in Cincinnati.

This hope was as much a pipedream as Henry's expectation of receiving a distinguished political appointment from his benefactor, Andrew Jackson, the new president of the United States. Given Henry's failure to complete the campaign biography, the victorious Jackson command did not feel greatly obliged when Henry asked for a choice job out of the spoils being distributed by Old Hickory's cohorts. The leaders in dividing the patronage were Duff Green and William Lewis, both of whom were disappointed by Henry's sloth.

Nevertheless, a hopeful Henry and Ann returned to Washington after the election, bearing a lock of the new President's hair given to them by Rachel Jackson shortly before the First Lady-elect died. They made the trip aware that they were now wholly dependent upon the generosity of the Jackson administration. In April 1829, Henry learned that the President had named him U.S. consul at Algiers.

When Henry's brother Carter, who had grown increasingly close to Henry during the latter's tribulations, heard the news, he was incredulous. "What can you promise yourself?" he asked Henry. Surely there was no wealth, fame, or ease in this pitiful spot? "But for the name of the thing," Carter said, "I would rather be an overseer of your negroes." He wondered if Ann were willing to go on such a humble assignment. Carter may not have realized that Ann's addiction probably made any foreign location agreeable to Henry, who must have dreaded exposing her weakness to the gossips in Washington and Virginia whom he believed sought further to embarrass the couple.

Asking Carter to handle their affairs in America, Henry and Ann headed for the Barbary Coast in August 1829, leaving as if Henry were making a triumphant journey to become American minister at a great foreign court. With a grand flourish, Henry announced to his faithful friend Richard Brown in Westmoreland County that he was rewarding him by choosing his son George F. Brown as an aide.

In a scene reminiscent of his father's scrambles, Henry got away just in time, embarking from New York. According to Carter, who had not appreciated what headaches he would acquire by representing his brother, creditors were pressing the new consul. "Write me whether you will not be by that time out of reach of the legal process," Carter urged Henry.

Sister Lucy Lee Carter was the only other family member to take an interest in Henry's departure. She went to New York to visit with her brother and his wife, but left early rather than go through the anguish of a final farewell. Lucy said she was certain they would never meet again. Events soon proved her correct.

~ 16

Hiding in Paris
1829–1840

As she said goodbye to Henry, Lucy Carter urged that he "treat Ann with the utmost tenderness. It would be well to humour her peculiarities if she has any. Then they would wear off." Lucy chose to add: "If I have said anything offensive, you must forgive me for it, as be assured the best motives dictate what I have said." For themselves as Lees, Lucy said she could not avoid the conclusion "that we are both unfortunate."

Henry's brother and agent, Carter Lee, was more concerned that Henry live prudently while abroad. He warned Henry to manage within his salary. What little income there was from the rental of Ann's slaves must go to helping pay creditors in America. Ann's property must be sacred, Carter admonished: "It would be *wrong* in you to attempt to diminish it."

At least Henry now had a steady, if modest, stipend as an employee of the United States government—or so the consul in Algiers and his brother assumed. But this security vanished in March 1830 when the United States Senate, by unanimous vote, denied Henry Lee his federal appointment. The senators discussed the nomination in secret session, using materials apparently supplied by Virginia's senator John Tyler with the aid of Ann and Betsy's uncle William Robinson. Thanks to Tyler and Robinson, evidently Henry's adultery with Betsy was graphically recounted on the floor of the Senate.

And there was more. Robert Mayo reported that a distorted story of his attempt to woo Betsy was also dragged into the debate, and "other things were also said too horrible to mention." Mayo implored Henry to return at once and confront "this most foul scandal that has been industriously circulated against you." Carter Lee was more realistic, seeing Henry's case as hopeless since "the whole administration party deserted you and made you a ready sacrifice." Better now to rise above politics, Carter cautioned. It would be preferable to "hunt bears in Missouri."

A more optimistic Richard Brown in Westmoreland County rounded up a few neighbors to sign an address to President Jackson in behalf of Henry, and he rushed to defend Henry before Senator Tyler. Coming away disheartened, Brown warned Henry that the entire Jackson command seemed unfriendly, including even the President.

These distressing reports from America left Henry believing he had but one steadfast supporter, his wife. "Mrs. Lee, faithful and true as ever," Henry told Carter, "refused to separate from me." According to Henry, Ann said she "preferred danger with me to danger without me." The pair departed Algiers after hearing from Secretary of State Martin Van Buren that Commodore David Porter would be the new consul in Algiers.

Henry and Ann lived in Italy during the remainder of 1830 before settling in Paris in February 1831. Briefly, Henry spoke of returning to America. Ann, however, said: "I shall return very unwillingly." She complained of having no friends except brother-in-law Carter Lee, and she confided in him that her sole wish was to be *"with my dear Mr. Lee and to make that my happiness."* She had sent her maid back to the States. "You have no idea what a relief it is to me to have no little black imp to scold."

Ann's attitude allowed Henry to drop talk of defending himself in America. Besides, as he admitted, the cost of a voyage was beyond him. He made life in Paris a matter of husbandly honor. "Mrs. Lee dreads returning to the cruel state of desertion and discourtesies she has on all hands . . . been exposed," Henry told Carter. The mistreatment they shared, Henry said, "I disregard on my own account. I cannot be indifferent to it on hers. She was formed for the quiet affections of social life and in her own country she had been cruelly denied them. I therefore feel it more my duty than it is my inclination to gratify her by another year's residence abroad if I can."

Henry continued insisting it was Ann's dread of the "persecutions" awaiting her in the United States which detained him. So, he asked Carter to begin supplying money for their stay. He also approached his friends the Browns in hope of a regular remittance. This strategy did not deceive Carter Lee. He knew that Henry was hiding behind Ann's skirts, which made Carter's task the more awkward when he found it impossible to supply the exiled pair with the financing they requested.

The annual income from the work of Ann's thirty slaves, which amounted to $700, remained too little to support the Parisian style in which Henry and Ann preferred to live. Consequently, until his death in 1837, Henry's letters from Paris mingled pleas for loans with promises of impending success from his projects as an author and warnings that he was nearing debtors' prison. He fell back upon every resort to raise money, paying no heed to Carter's pleas that the exiles return to some asylum in western Virginia. The wilderness harbored no sharp tongues. Surely, urged Carter, Ann "has sense and fortitude enough to reconcile her mind to the dictates of prudence."

Henry only exhorted Carter to try harder, although there was little money the younger brother could locate, especially after he found properties Henry told him to sell had been sold or mortgaged years earlier. At times, Carter's supply of patience wore thin, obliging Henry to send fresh pleas, such as, "I am not able to see how I shall escape the jail which has been grasping for me for years." The pitiful words would refresh Carter, making him begin still another search for funds. He even sent Henry some of his own scant resources.

For a time, Henry had similar success with George Brown, the young neighbor from Westmoreland County whom Henry had taken to North Africa as his secretary. Brown had remained on assignment in Algiers, so he was nearby to receive frequent pleas from his former boss. Like Carter Lee, Brown was stirred by Henry's begging, particularly when a loan of even a few dollars could draw highly colorful gratitude, as when Henry told Brown how the arrival of his remittance "actually took me from under the gallows and I can never thank you too much." Brown was assured that he would be repaid as soon as Henry received "nigger money" from selling Ann's slaves, a step he blamed Carter for being "soft-hearted" in resisting. Finally, they were sold in 1835 for $9000, a sum far from sufficient for Lee's debts and needs.

Eventually, the Brown family balked at sending more cash. Immediately, Henry lost his temper, accusing his friends of "incorrigible laziness or total alienation." The attitude hardly benefited Henry's cause, putting him back at Carter's feet: "I am without money, without friends, without credit, and without hope. I bear up with all the fortitude in my power and labour on my work." Yet when Carter extracted a promise from a New York newspaper to pay handsomely for a series of articles by Major Lee about European events and scenes, Henry shied away from this challenge.

It was not exactly laziness that made Henry resist the hard work of a journalist. While in Paris, he produced an amazing amount of writing. Unfortunately, it was largely of a self-serving character. There were three projects. One was a long, rambling letter to the Jackson administration in which Henry defended himself and accused the politicians of betraying him. Another project was a book that violently attacked the memory of Thomas Jefferson. Finally, Henry wrote a biography of Napoleon, the purpose of which was to show how Light-Horse Harry Lee and Napoleon, and, by extension, Henry himself, were much alike in character and fate.

His rebuke of the Jacksonians, written to Major William B. Lewis on 26 July 1833, disclosed the extent to which feelings of persecution had weakened Henry's powers of reasoning. Henry announced that his letter was a call from "unmitigated exile." Mostly, it reviewed the wrongs he fancied had been done to him by the Democrats. The tirade was momentarily relieved, perhaps unintentionally, at the point when Henry paused to assert a fondness for children. Contending he should have been a schoolmaster, Henry added: "I do not mean for young ladies."

Since the letter was mostly a listing of how he had been wronged, Henry should have sent it to someone else, for Major Lewis had sought to help Lee. Such benefaction did nothing to diminish Henry's wrath. "I was not so blind," he said, "nor so stupid as to be insensible to the strong evidence of indifference toward me. . . . Yet I did not complain even to my wife." Most annoying, Henry grumbled, had been Jackson's support for men whom Lee considered his own moral inferiors. He singled out particularly Edward Livingston, the Secretary of State.

The longer the letter stumbled on, the angrier Henry obviously became. He even put words in President Jackson's mouth by surmising that Old Hickory had said, upon learning that Lee's appointment to Algiers had been rejected, " 'We shall [leave] him a prey to popular odium and private hate.' " As for his having been told to come home so that some other job might be found for him, Henry likened such a fate to that of Haman, the Biblical figure who sat at the king's gate hoping for a scrap of bread, while the Jacksonian command "have feasted to their surfeit."

"Had I been a connection of Jefferson," Henry asked, "do you suppose I would have been so deserted?" The question disclosed part of why rage so consumed Lee. He was now convinced that Thomas Jefferson and his friends had brought down both Henry and his father. And yet, as Henry insisted to Major Lewis, was not Jefferson a more flagrant adulterer than Henry had ever been? Though he wished to dismiss his affair with Betsy McCarty, Henry found it useful to stress that "while mine was the crime of a private man," the moral offenses of many public figures went ignored.

"My treatment shows that a man who is surprised into adultery is, if he aspires to a humble office, to find the indifference of his friends conspires against him with the persecution of his enemies." After seemingly endless reiteration of sentiments like these, Henry put down his pen. At his request, however, Ann Lee made a transcript of the letter for her husband's file. This was an unusual step, as Henry admitted when he warned Major Lewis that a copy would exist. One wonders what Ann thought when she read the lines in which Henry spoke lightly of his adultery at Stratford.

Henry was so enraged no one probably could have persuaded him that even if Jackson had seriously wished to give him another appointment, Henry's own follies would have doomed such generosity. After Henry published a diatribe against Thomas Jefferson in 1831, no politician could have helped him. Consisting of 237 pages of hate, the work was entitled *Observations on Writings of Thomas Jefferson*. It had a second edition prepared by Carter Lee in 1839, fulfilling a pledge Carter made to Henry before the latter's death.

Rarely has American writing seen more malice and acrimony than when Henry Lee wrote about Thomas Jefferson. His wish, Henry acknowledged, was to produce "an overwhelming answer to Jefferson's detestable calumny." "Jefferson's slander on my father," Henry said, "had seriously depressed his reputation."

Henry explained to Carter that he was willing to take any step needed, including vilifying James Madison, in order "to show that Mr. Jefferson had slandered my father." Their parent, Henry reminded Carter, "was never spared by his enemies nor supported by his friends." The author's determination to return evil for evil justified Madison's observation that Major Henry Lee was "a vial of rage."

It might easily have been different. Three days before Jefferson died on 4 July 1826, Henry had gone by invitation to Monticello to study letters which the dying patriot wished him to see. Henry was preparing a new edition of his father's memoirs of the Revolutionary campaign, and Jefferson hoped that by examining manuscripts at Monticello, Lee might make revisions in Light-Horse Harry's work that would offer a less caustic view of Jefferson's service and courage as governor of Virginia. General Lee's memoirs had strongly implied that Governor Jefferson had been inept and a coward.

Jefferson's strategy momentarily succeeded, so that a deeply stirred Henry Lee came down from Monticello prepared to soften his father's asperities. He did so in the new edition of Light-Horse Harry's recollections by describing Jefferson as an illustrious patriot. The admiration was short-lived. In 1829, Jefferson's grandson published a volume of his forebear's letters, bringing to everyone's attention an episode involving Light-Horse Harry which, until then, had not been widely known. This was the occasion in 1794 when Harry had passed second-hand accounts to President Washington purporting to show Jefferson saying that Washington could be manipulated by dishonorable advisers.

Readers of this edition of Jefferson's letters were not allowed to mistake whom Jefferson was talking about when, in defending himself to Washington, he condemned Harry Lee as a "miserable tergiversator who ought indeed either to have been of more truth, or less trusted by his country." Jefferson's editor-grandson made clear that his forebear considered Lee a "slanderer," an "intriguer," and one who sought "to atone for sins against you [Washington] by sins against another."

When he read this, Henry proclaimed that to assail Jefferson had now become simply "a defense of my father's memory." Honor-bound, he planned a rejoinder which he said would have three purposes. First, to refute Jefferson's charges against Harry Lee. Second, to extol the latter's virtues. Finally, to show that Jefferson had ruined many characters and was unworthy of public respect.

The book's thesis was simple: not Jefferson but Light-Horse Harry merited the people's veneration. Henry insisted his father had never resorted to deceit or falsehood, and always "manifested in his language on all occasions, peculiar delicacy for the feelings and reputations of others." Over and over, Henry's pages claimed that his father invariably displayed "virtue, ability, and patriotism, unalloyed by selfish or sinister designs." Jefferson, on the other hand, was stripped by Henry of all merit. Not even the third President's intellectual ability escaped unscathed. "His diction was anything but refined," and his religious views were "jejune and vapid skepticisms."

Thus did Henry rant, holding up his father as saintly, and making Jefferson a satanic contrast. Even Light-Horse Harry's financial woes were polished into the dignity of "visionary speculations," whose unfortunate results enabled Harry Lee to display valor "in bearing up against the weight of distress and ruin." Harry's life showed "a degree of fortitude [which] could not be witnessed without admiration."

Henry concluded the assault by calling down "shades of dishonor" upon Thomas Jefferson, while "reflections of glory" should "irradiate" Light-Horse Harry Lee. In doing so, Henry introduced the name of Richard Henry Lee as another noble figure maligned by Jefferson—because, Henry implied, Richard Henry Lee was the real drafter of the Declaration of Independence. Richard Henry was "vastly" Jefferson's inferior in "pretensions," but he was "greatly his superior in merit."

After Henry's glorification of his father was published in the United States, Carter Lee sent optimistic reports of the book's prospects. These were evidently based on the response of a few inveterate Federalist Jefferson-haters in New England, and some vague expressions by Chief Justice John Marshall, who was never an admirer of his distant kinsman from Monticello. But soon it was apparent that copies of the book could not even be given away.

Of course there was some praise for the volume from Henry's relatives. Carter said he was "deeply moved and charmed by it." He reported that Ludwell Lee (whose father was lavishly praised in the book) had observed one could never be too severe with Jefferson. A brother-in-law was reputed to have said that Henry had demonstrated Jefferson was "a self-seeking, anti-Washington, backbiting Devil, and not a man." And Uncle William Fitzhugh reportedly shouted about Jefferson after reading the book: "What a damned scoundrel."

The most memorable comment about the Jefferson book to reach Henry came from his cousin Zaccheus Collins Lee, a son of Elizabeth and Richard Bland Lee. Writing in 1833, Collins urged Henry to continue assailing Jefferson's memory. If Henry kept up the good fight, Collins predicted that "however prostrate and o'er clouded may be the fortunes of our house, it may yet boast an aristocracy of talent and patriotism, which poverty and slander can never tarnish or take away."

Praise from kinfolk aside, even Carter Lee was alarmed in 1834 by the widespread disgust Henry's book caused. He urged Henry to be more moderate in the future. "You are hardly aware of how prone you are in your writing to bestow unnecessary censure." For example, Carter inquired, "where was the necessity of any reflections on Mr. Madison in your late work[?]" This assault was unwarranted, Carter lamented. And now Madison was saying how he thought his efforts to help General Lee "would have spared him from an attack from any of his children."

The accumulation of such comments was one reason Carter published a second edition of Henry's Jefferson volume in 1839. Hoping he might redeem something from the book's wreckage, he explained what Henry's motive had been. In a new foreword Carter insisted that the commentary on Jefferson "was forced on the sons of General Lee." To those who complained about the acrimonious tone of the book, Carter replied, in Henry's justification, "as the provocation was *infinite,* his severity could not be *excessive."* Carter urged everyone to appreciate "the feelings of a son at witnessing an unprovoked outrage upon the memory of his father."

After completing his tirade against Jefferson, Henry lived long enough to write another book. This was the first volume of a biography of Napoleon, published in 1835. The second volume was finished but left in manuscript at the author's death. Carter encouraged his brother in this project, but sternly advised him to drop plans to make the biography an attack on Sir Walter Scott, whose pen had treated Napoleon severely. Wondering why Henry was always on the rampage, Carter warned his brother that his approach displayed "more of the partizan than coolness becoming a historian."

His words were wasted, for Henry's *The Life of the Emperor Napoleon* was little more than an effort to undo Scott's biography of the Frenchman. So high was Scott's standing at the time among readers in England and America that Henry's remonstrance was foolhardy at best. Meanwhile, his praise of Napoleon elevated the French leader to sainthood. Consciously or not, Henry pictured the repute of Napoleon as being as badly mauled as Light-Horse Harry's had been—or, for that matter, as Henry's was.

Henry could have had all three—Emperor, father, and self—in mind when he wrote of "a man whose character in rising to a level with the noblest examples of any former age, provoked and encountered the vilest prejudices and passions of his own." He condemned Scott's "bigoted and fantastic zeal," which were adjectives Henry used when speaking of his own persecutors in the United States. He also assailed "the timorous and clandestine manner" in which Walter Scott "dips his pen into the nameless and noisome receptacle whence he derived this slander."

A thousand copies of the biography reached America early in 1835, but were detained at the customs office until $300 could be found to pay the duty. Since Carter was in Tennessee at the time, the burden of distributing the book fell upon his younger brother, Robert E. Lee. When the latter found no dealers interested in stocking the book, he took the time to read it and sent his observations to Carter. Henry's book might be well-written, Robert asserted, but it was mostly "acrimony." To be precise, "It labors to make Napoleon too perfect and squints toward Jacksonism, which however pleasing to the friends and admirers of these heroes, ought to be lost sight of in a true and impartial history."

More astute by far than Carter, Robert warned that he did not take seriously the few persons who had stopped him on the street to speak well of Henry's book. He noted mildly that those who talked with a member of the Lee family about Henry's book could hardly be expected to say anything "in its dispraise." By May 1835, Robert reported that Henry's book was getting nothing but bad reviews. Passing this on to the author, Carter again scolded him for his "severity" which was his "besetting sin" as a writer.

Carter tactfully confined his own remarks about Henry's *Napoleon* to the volume's many typographical errors. In Paris, Ann Lee suffered a variation of this problem. Like his father, her husband wrote in an illegible scrawl, which he then handed to Ann for transcribing. She struggled with the Jefferson book and the first volume of the Napoleon biography before giving up. Henry reported that she "swore" never to copy his hand again.

Then came even worse news about *Napoleon.* Carter learned that Henry had misrepresented the cost of publishing the book. The expenses actually involved an additional $4000, which Henry had neglected to point out to his brother. Furthermore, it had required 8000 francs simply to provide paper and printing for 2000 copies, of which 1000 were shipped to the U.S.

These revelations brought Carter to the end of his rope. He told Henry that both of them had now exhausted their resources. Carter wondered if he should visit Westmoreland County, where perhaps the Brown family might be coaxed into another contribution. It was only a forlorn hope, and Carter admitted he could hardly expect any success from such an excursion. The one benefit would be to allow him "a melancholy look at Stratford."

With very little money arriving from America and expenses mounting in Paris, Henry found no one willing to lend him money. The banking firm of Rothschild was becoming impatient, as Henry and Ann switched from one dwelling to another, some located in the countryside beyond Paris. The two hoped to keep one jump beyond angry landlords. When Henry went in search of loans, he was followed by Ann's affectionate notes. One reminded him to bring her a pair of new shoes. "I am very lonesome," she said, and anticipated the moment when "I shall see you and kiss you again."

In 1836, the pair's loneliness seemed about to be relieved with news that Henry's half-sister Mildred Lee Childe and her family were coming to Paris. The prospect offered another advantage, for Edward Childe was from a well-to-do New England family. Henry immediately used money he did not have to offer his brother-in-law a handsome leather bound volume as a welcoming gift.

Gleefully, Henry reported to Carter that Mildred had paid a call. This was enough to encourage Henry, for most of his Lee relatives, except for Carter and Lucy, had turned away from him. Upon seeing Mildred, Henry said to Carter: "Any resentment which I might have of it disappeared at the thought that our meeting would please you." The result, Henry hoped, was encouraging. "I am, of course, devotedly attached to her and she tolerant of me."

Henry spoke too soon. The Childes seemed to wish nothing more to do with the unfortunate Henry and Ann. Less than a year later, Mildred and her husband refused even to appear in the funeral procession that followed Henry Lee to his grave. Beside him at the moment of death, which came when he was forty-nine, had been only Ann and a very distant cousin, Charles Randolph, who was in Paris at the time.

At Ann's request, Randolph reported to Carter that Henry had died on 30 January 1837, the cause being influenza and an acute case of hiccuping. The death had been an unpleasant scene, the stricken man suffering great chest pain and gasping for breath. Henry had not been able to recognize Ann. The news did not surprise Carter. Henry had written about being in poor health, of being white-haired before he was fifty, and of developing a most unattractive paunch.

Charles Randolph was horrified by the circumstances in which Ann found herself. He described her as alone and penniless. The failure of the Childe family to come to her aid made Randolph indignant. He claimed they acted "in a most shameful manner." What he may not have known was that Mildred and Edward Childe paid most of Henry's final expenses, including those for the burial they had chosen not to attend.

It seemed to Randolph, who probably heard the refrain from Ann, that her friends in America, and particularly Carter Lee, must hasten to her aid. "Poor lady!" said Randolph, "she can't remain here." The widow, however, had other ideas. With her dependence upon morphine unabated and complaining of no support in America except Carter Lee, Ann refused to budge. She begged Carter: "Come to me." She spoke of being unable to leave her "dear" husband's lonely grave, a spouse whom she contended had died with no idea of how destitute he had left her. Ann assured Carter that Henry expired knowing "in you I should find a friend and protector."

Ann's pressure on Carter never relented. "Oh, if poor Mr. Lee could see me now. . . . I am abandoned of heaven and earth," was a typical refrain in her letters. She reported having few francs, many debts, poor health, an impatient landlord, creditors who "tormented me incessantly," and a frightening American consul at Paris, John C. Brent. Not only did the exasperated Brent have Ann on his hands, but also he worried about consular funds he had lent to Henry in an unguarded moment.

Meanwhile, Ann kept pleading with Carter for money and that he come to Paris. It was a trip Carter promised several times to make but never did, causing the tone in Ann's letters to become more shrill. "I am but a sad spectacle," she wrote from Passy late in 1838, "and not one you would like to contemplate. I have been much changed by grief and sickness." She wished she could describe to Carter "how many other torments I have to suffer!" "I must have clothes. I must try to make myself a little more comfortable." "My head aches so dreadfully when I write."

The Widow Lee did not like to admit that she could apply for help to her half-brother Richard Stuart. She claimed, evidently without truth, that she had written about her distress to her Stuart relatives, who never "sent me a sous." And anyway, she said, they would only mount a tirade "against my husband for having spent my fortune." Ann insisted she could hear Richard Stuart say how "he has been humiliated and mortified that I who ought to be so independent should be so reduced to begging."

With Carter irresolute and Ann immobile, Robert E. Lee decided at the end of 1839 that he must intervene. Apparently he did not know the main reason why Ann refused to come home—her drug addiction. Even so, Robert studied the situation realistically. It was he who arranged to have the many unsold volumes of Henry's biography of Napoleon auctioned—the pile went for eighty cents apiece. He then candidly shared with the Stuart family what he knew of Ann's fiscal plight, a step toward what Robert deemed the obvious way to help her. In his judgment, the Stuarts should bring Ann home and care for her.

Robert acknowledged to Richard Stuart, Ann's half-brother, that until recently he had understood Ann's resources were adequate for her needs. But now Ann had notified Carter that she must have $1200 per year sent to her. Her physician (who apparently was supplying her with drugs) had obligingly written attesting to the costliness of Ann's frail health. After giving Stuart these essentials, Robert volunteered that possibly he and Carter could each come up with $100 per year for Ann. Brother Smith Lee could contribute little or nothing from his naval pay. Robert then closed his letter, leaving unasked the obvious final question—would the Stuarts annually provide a thousand dollars, the balance needed by Ann?

The Stuart reply was swift—and contained an unexpected counterproposal. The family asserted Ann should return to Virginia. Richard Stuart said he had written to her, inviting her to make her home with them. But there was a condition. The Stuarts informed both Ann and Robert that upon her reappearance in Virginia, she must reclaim her McCarty landed inheritances which her husband had improperly sold. As Richard Stuart candidly stated it, Ann's patrimony in Westmoreland County was still legally hers, for she had "unlawfully" given Henry disposition of it.

The Stuart response obviously startled Robert Lee, who could not have foreseen the suggestion of legal action to recover Ann's property. This litigation would surely create a sensation, resurrecting all the stories of how Henry Lee had misused his wife's resources. It was a prospect Robert called fraught with "harm," even though Richard Stuart pledged the family had no intention of reproaching the memory of Henry Lee. This hardly reassured Robert, for Stuart went on to recall that Henry "had been forced by the inquiry of his creditors to dispose of her property."

It was also disquieting for the Lees when they learned that the Stuarts wished to involve Betsy Storke at Stratford in their plans to redeem Ann.

Apparently sensing how this would freshly ignite gossip about the Lee family, Robert decided to suspend negotiations with the Stuarts. The best alternative was to send Ann what little money could be raised in America and implore her to be frugal.

To Carter, Robert acknowledged he could now appreciate why Ann wished to avoid a return to Virginia. After advising his brother not to mention the Stuart plan for Ann to reclaim her property, Robert urged that Carter explain to their sister-in-law how careful with money she must be. (It seems that Robert himself never wrote to her.)

Surely, said Robert, "if the matter was plainly stated to her, so as to show her the situation of her affairs and of your own, that unless she is entirely changed from what I recollect her, she would see the necessity of yielding to circumstances." No matter how the Lees might wish to aid one "still dear" to them, Robert insisted that Ann must be compelled to realize "there was no way of relieving [her] from a most painful situation."

The crisis soon ended. On 27 August 1840, Ann McCarty Lee died at age forty-three. John Brent, the American consul, was precise in his report to Major William B. Lewis, who had been trying to help Brent deal with Mrs. Lee. "She was reduced to a state of remarkable debility, but her last moments were tranquil and apparently without pain. She had been, as you know full well, for many years past addicted to the immoderate use of opium and laudanum, which with other constitutional causes, have brought her to the grave." The physician attending her attributed death "to the use of the drug in question."

Brent observed that despite efforts to help Ann with her addiction, she paid to support persons who supplied her with the drug. These individuals, said Brent, were "morally responsible" for her end. Even when she had been informed that she must die unless she escaped her dependence, Brent told Lewis that it was "advice she positively refused to accept." Thus, there were many debts, which Brent bluntly insisted now must be shouldered by Ann's family.

After arranging for an Episcopal burial service, Brent paid for a cemetery plot where Ann's remains would rest for ten years. Thereafter, the space would be used by another corpse, unless, as Brent pointed out, Ann's relations chose to invest in making the location perpetually hers. Soon after this, John Brent himself died, leaving his heirs to press Carter Lee for payment of the money the late Consul had advanced to Ann and Henry. There was nothing left but to take the route Robert E. Lee had hoped to avoid, that of reclaiming and selling some of Ann's land inherited from the McCarty side.

The McCarty sisters, Ann and Betsy, shared a story that ought not to be forgotten, leaving us to hope that more of their manuscripts might come to light. For the present, Ann's torment can just be glimpsed, and Betsy's is virtually beyond sight. Their personalities are little more than shadows, and their thoughts about the Lee family remain a mystery. Each was to be a mistress of Stratford in a grotesque drama. For Ann, the old Lee mansion witnessed the crumbling of her dignity and the beginning of a terrible degradation. What we know of her suggests that Ann McCarty Lee gave way to flaws in her nature which a happier marriage might have suppressed. Her adult life seems rarely to have been more than a display of weakness and self-pity.

For Betsy, Stratford was a more complicated place. At first, it meant humiliation. But thereafter, what might her thoughts have been when she returned as mistress of the house? Or, after she concluded fifty years there as an admirable neighbor for Westmoreland County? Betsy's peaceful grave in the beauty of Stratford's garden seems a fitting commentary on her life, while it also hints that occasionally there is some justice in human existence.

After their deaths, Ann and Henry vanished from the family story, although whispers about them persisted. Henry's hopes that his attack on Jefferson and his eulogy of Napoleon might salvage his family's reputation went unfulfilled. Elsewhere, however, a rehabilitation of the Lees was already under way at the time Henry died. Led by Henry's half-brother Robert E. Lee, the family's restoration began at Arlington, a residence new to the Lee chronicle. It too sat on the Potomac, with a commanding view of the federal capital. The enormous irony of Arlington's location and perspective would not be apparent until April of 1861.

～17

Longing for Arlington
1829–1846

Although his birthplace was Stratford, Robert E. Lee was from the Lee-sylvania side of the family. Yet neither of these ancestral locations meant to him what Arlington would. This was not surprising since Robert kept only a vague and often confused understanding of his family background. He called himself the "reverse" of a genealogist.

Once, Robert asked cousin Cassius Lee to locate the Lee coat of arms for him. He inquired because he remembered seeing a family tree at Uncle Edmund Jennings Lee's house in Alexandria. As a result, Cassius Lee soon found himself explaining to Robert such elementary family facts as who Colonel Phil was, as well as assuring him that since the Stratford Lees could claim a family crest, it belonged as well to the Lee-sylvania branch.

But these were trivial interests for Robert. His consuming concern was always the physical and moral well-being of his wife, children, and other relatives. The unhappy careers of his father Light-Horse Harry and his half-brother Henry must have strengthened Robert's determination that duty, self-denial, and discipline should characterize his life and those of his dear ones. He preached these attributes with an intensity unmatched by other Lees.

Consequently, we know a great deal about how Robert's children grew up under his training. Unfortunately, few reliable accounts survive of Robert's childhood and youthful experiences. One must take cautiously the testimony of many aged relatives and friends who eagerly came forward after Robert's death to stress that the mark of nobility was upon him even as a lad. Nevertheless, these observations after the fact, when combined with glimpses dating from his boyhood, show Robert worked hard at being good. Even his father, faraway in the West Indies, remembered this quality in him.

No boyish letters by Robert exist, but those written when he was a young man seem typical of most fellows his age. He had a sense of humor, a capacity to tease, a delight in the graces of young ladies, a fondness for gossip, and an affection for his relatives. These features have been nearly smothered by persons who produced recollections to prove posthumously that Robert had been comprised entirely of religious dedication, impeccable deportment, and a devotion to study.

Possibly the most down-to-earth description of a very young Robert was offered by brother Henry. In an 1832 letter, Henry recalled how "sheepish and shamefaced" Robert tended to be as a boy. "I remember arriving at Alexandria once when he was in that condition. He was the last of the three children that came to greet me and then he approached slowly with his mouth skewed up inordinately and his face kept directly ahead." It turned out that Robert had lost a tooth and was trying to hold a substitute in place. When he did not succeed, Henry remembered how the other youngsters shouted: " 'Oh poor Robert, he has dropped his bone tooth.' "

Of Robert's brothers and sisters in Alexandria, only Carter Lee remains more than a blurred memory today. While nearly all of his letters to Robert have been lost, many of Robert's replies are available. Remembered for his songs and stories, his wit and high good humor, Carter was usually the center of any social circle. There was much of his father in him, for even in old age Carter was still chasing dreams of wealth—and generously offering Robert a share in the deal. The latter was obliged to be the voice of caution and reason for the two. Nevertheless, Carter had a rare gift. He could sometimes perceive himself clearly. After reaching his mid-thirties, Carter foresaw only an "insignificant" destiny. "I am amused and amusing, and what else can I say for myself?" he asked.

Unlike Carter, Sydney Smith Lee, Robert's second brother, apparently was a quiet person not given to writing letters, a shortcoming Robert deplored. Born in 1802, Smith grew up with "Rose" as a nickname. The affectionate Robert would begin his epistles to him with "My darling Rose." About all that can be said with much assurance about Smith Lee is that he was considered the most handsome of the brothers and sisters, and that he went to sea at age fifteen, rising to command the steamer *Princeton* and to join Matthew Perry when the U.S. Navy made its celebrated visit to Japan in 1853. Later, he was in charge of the Naval Academy at Annapolis and of the Philadelphia navy yard before the Civil War began. In that conflict, Smith joined Robert in siding with Virginia.

Robert's sister Anne Kinloch Lee, born in 1800, was said to be the talented sibling of the group. Carter Lee called her the most interesting of all "my mother's children." It was she who refused to write to her father. As a child, she had to have an arm amputated. Perhaps for this reason, Anne's marriage was delayed until she was twenty-eight. On the other hand, she may have chosen to wait until her younger sister Mildred was old enough to care for their invalid mother.

Anne was wed in late June 1826 to the Reverend William L. Marshall of Baltimore, three years her junior. A family member claimed it was necessary "for political reasons" to keep the marriage a secret until July 1829, which was when Anne's widowed mother died. If this is true, the cause is unknown, unless Ann Carter Lee had opposed the marriage. Anne went to live in Baltimore, where her husband soon decided to give up "parsoning" and become a lawyer. This decision may have reflected the success of the Marshall family as barristers, for Anne's husband was a cousin of Chief Justice John Marshall.

While William Marshall was succeeding as a lawyer and jurist, Anne became increasingly the victim of emotional and physical disorders. Her mother had once described her as having a very delicate temperament. In 1840, when one of Anne's sons was run over and killed by a wagon, a collapse was not unexpected. Her brother Robert hastened to visit her, finding that the accident "appeared to crush in her all desire of life and hopes of happiness."

Anne lived until 1864, however, although always an invalid. She did not survive to see another of her sons, Colonel Louis Marshall, decorated for gallant service against the South. To the enormous pain of Robert E. Lee, the Civil War divided him from his sister and her husband. After the war, Judge Marshall joined Louis in going west to settle in California. Thereafter, as Robert sadly remarked, there was no further word from the Marshalls.

The baby of the family, Mildred Lee, had been born in 1811, after her parents had exchanged Stratford for Alexandria. She was not yet two when Harry took up his exile in Barbados, so she never knew her father. At age twenty, Mildred received a proposal of marriage. Since she was an orphan by then, Mildred's eldest brother Carter had to represent the family in dealing with the suitor, Edward V. Childe. The latter was a twenty-seven-year-old Boston attorney who had just returned from four years in Europe to take up his inheritance. Daniel Webster gave Childe a warm endorsement, as did Charles Lyman, one of Carter's chums from Harvard days.

Despite Childe's references, Carter said he consented reluctantly to the marriage, preferring not to surrender his sister to a stranger. But, conceding Mildred was now old enough to make a choice, Carter accepted Mr. Childe on behalf of the family. In Paris, where Henry Lee received word of the negotiations, he commended Carter's decision, consoling him with a cryptic caveat: "The happiness of marriage is altogether a matter of accident, not of judgment."

After Mildred and Edward were married in 1831, the groom announced that, in view of his wealth (he had an annual income of $2000 and expectations of much more), he could give up the law and seek a life devoted to literature. In 1833 Edward sailed from Boston to England, leaving Mildred, who was pregnant, to follow as soon as possible. She wasted no time and thereafter resisted all efforts by her husband and other relatives to coax her into returning.

Mildred lived a restless life, moving from city to city in Europe, although she always came back to Paris as headquarters. The existence did not please her husband who, in 1844, wistfully told his brother-in-law Robert of wishing to re-establish his family in the United States. Mildred, however, refused absolutely to hear of it. So Edward visited America without her, but only for brief stays. Then, in 1856, Mildred died in Paris at age forty-five. Her children considered Europe their home and remained there, while Edward Childe settled in the United States.

Along with Robert, these two sisters and two brothers constituted a closely knit branch of the Lee clan. And it is here, within these family ties, as well as in his marriage and his religious faith, that Robert is most approachable. When his thoughts were of home, wife, children, and the welfare of his soul, Robert's usually contained personality could sometimes break loose. Since most writers have featured Lee as a soldier and battle commander, the roles that demanded he repress himself, the inner Robert has rarely appeared in history and biography.

As a result, the enduring importance of Arlington for Robert has often been disregarded. Although young Robert and his brothers did visit Henry Lee at Stratford, more often they were rambling about the grounds of Arlington, since the property was just a short distance up the Potomac from Alexandria. Arlington was the home of George Washington Parke Custis, Martha Washington's grandson and the adopted son of George Washington. Known as "the child of Mount Vernon," Parke Custis had lived at George Washington's home until his grandmother Martha's death in 1802. At that point, he established himself at Arlington, the name he gave to land bequeathed him by General Washington.

Friendship and kinship meant that Ann Carter Lee and her children were especially welcome at Arlington, allowing Mr. Custis to replace Harry Lee as the father in Robert's life. Of Arlington, Robert said in 1854, "my affections and attachments are more strongly placed [there] than at any other place in the world." Mr. Custis, he asserted, "has been for me all a father could, and whom I never cease fondly to regard and love as such."

Other members of the Lee family had been drawn to Arlington as soon as Parke Custis created it. Cornelia Lee visited there in 1804, reporting it had a "really lovely situation," although the road to the newly begun house was nearly impassable. She found young Parke Custis so busy caulking a boat that he took no time to offer "eatables," although he did provide "a glass of excellent wine." Cornelia considered Custis "the greatest figure you ever saw," and predicted that his residence "will be a very showy, handsome building when completed." Custis aimed to have the front of his dwelling resemble an Athenian temple, and he succeeded, massive columns and all.

G. W. P. Custis was a personality quite unlike any of the Lee males. Most of the public usually joined Carter and Henry Lee in chuckling when the name of Parke Custis was mentioned. He was known for painting huge canvases depicting historic scenes. He also composed epic poems. In neither enterprise did he display talent. Custis also enjoyed music, theater, and literary talk. His only sustained practical interest was in breeding sheep.

Custis' distractable nature led to a general mismanagement of the agricultural properties he had inherited elsewhere in Virginia. He looked to these plantations to pay the costs of operating Arlington, where the mansion seemed to take forever to finish. Custis intended that Arlington should keep alive the nation's appreciation of his illustrious step-father. He reverently displayed the first President's memorabilia, which youths like Robert Lee were encouraged to study.

The mistress of Arlington was even dearer to Robert than the master. Mrs. Custis and Robert were distant cousins and developed a close mother-son relationship. Born in 1788, Mary Lee Fitzhugh was the great-great-granddaughter of Richard Lee the Scholar. Her father, William Fitzhugh, ended his days in Fairfax County, near Arlington and Alexandria, on a 22,000-acre estate called Ravensworth. His wealth passed to Mary's brother, William Henry Fitzhugh. It was he who took such an interest in Robert's mother and her family when they sought refuge in Alexandria. Later, it was at Ravensworth that Ann Carter Lee died and was buried.

Two years after his mother's death, Robert returned to Arlington and married the only child of that household, Mary Anna Randolph Custis, whom he called "cousin." While Parke Custis may have been a poor businessman, he was worldly enough to hesitate when Robert asked for Mary's hand. The young man's credentials were less than overwhelming. Custis knew everything about the Lee family's recent troubles, including the poverty imposed by Light-Horse Harry's dealings. It meant that 2nd Lt. Robert E. Lee must rely upon his modest army pay to support a wife who was accustomed to luxury.

Indeed, young Lee could promise little more than affection and diligence to Miss Custis. He was a handsome, well-built officer of twenty-two, nearly six feet tall, and with black hair. Robert had graduated second in his class from West Point, where his career had been exemplary. His choice for service was the Corps of Engineers, by which he was sent first to Cockspur Island, near Savannah. He was not yet engaged to Mary Custis when he went to Georgia in 1829, where his companions included the attractive sisters of Jack Mackay, a friend from West Point whose family lived in Savannah.

Legend claims that Robert tried to win one of these Georgia belles. If so, that campaign ended after his furlough in 1830 led to the announcement of his engagement to Miss Custis. Her father had finally given his consent. Love must have had much to do with Robert's choice of cousin Mary. A shared interest in sketching was about the only similarity between them. She was tiny, hardly handsome, usually unkempt, so disorganized that she could be called scatter-brained, and, by 1830, intensely religious. Thus, the prospective bride offered a vivid contrast to the man she would marry.

The match puzzled Henry Lee in Paris. He was certain "that Robert cannot be older than Miss Custis." Henry was nearly correct. While the family Bible states Mary Custis was born 1 October 1808, which puts her eighteen months junior to Robert, the entry shows signs of tampering. Meanwhile, there was nothing ambiguous about the date of a letter Cornelia Lee Hopkins wrote on 4 December 1807, nor about a comment it contained: "Mrs. Custis has a daughter who from her size might be mistaken for six months old. Her name is Mary Anna Randolph." Perhaps some later member of the Lee family altered the Bible record, for a prejudice of the day held that wives properly must be younger than their spouses.

After his betrothal, Robert returned to Georgia in the autumn of 1830, leaving Mary to vacillate over their wedding date and to confess "I wish you were here today to amuse me. . . . I wish for you very often, though I am still *content.*" Mary reported that her mother no longer considered it necessary to read Robert's letters. "So you are perfectly at liberty to say what you please," Mary advised her intended, adding, "trusting your discretion to say only what is right."

Here Mary moved to a favorite topic—the welfare of her fiancé's soul. This was her *"true"* interest for which "my petitions are daily offered to my Heavenly Father." Mary implored Robert not to "banish" Christian faith from his heart. She described praying ceaselessly that God "may turn your heart to Him." When he did so, "I should have nothing more to wish for on earth with regard to you." Carter Lee, who happened to be around Arlington at the time, said that Mary had "a little of the over-righteousness which the blue lights [revivalist sects] brought into Virginia." He hoped the approaching marriage "will cure her mind of this disorder."

Thirty years later, Mrs. R. E. Lee recalled every detail of how her religious conversion took place before her wedding. She remembered that gradually she grew more aware of her acute "sinfulness," but was reluctant to "give up *all* for God." It was, she said, the grip of Satan, who kept whispering to her to forget God. But then she began dissolving into tears and prayer, until ultimately "I was made to feel willing to give up *all,* even my life if God should require it." Thereafter came "joy and peace."

Robert brought no such religious experience to the occasion when he and Mary were wed at Arlington on 30 June 1831. The minister dwelt heavily on the words of the rite, making Robert assert, half-jokingly, that he felt his "death warrant" was being read. Then, after days of feasting at Arlington and Ravensworth with friends and relatives, Robert and Mary left to take up housekeeping at Fort Monroe on Old Point near the mouth of Chesapeake Bay. Carter Lee saw them go, hoping that Mary's "rosy cheeks" would inspire Robert with thoughts derived from Arabian tales.

Instead, the couple seemed drawn more to their worries. Mary still fretted over her spiritual state, and Robert was concerned about his professional future. In her journal, Mary moaned that her mind was "a sink of corruption." Not long after her wedding, she wrote: "What have I to say, O Lord, save that I am still the unworthy recipient of all thy boundless mercies. I am thine. Save me from self, from sin, from the world and every fatal delusion." She especially prayed to be released from indolence and "this torpid state."

While Robert attended Episcopal services with Mary, he distressed her by showing "but little respect for the preacher." To her mother, Mary confided: "I cannot but feel that he still wants the one thing needful [religious faith], without which all the rest may prove valueless." Mary proposed to pray for her husband's conversion, an accomplishment she feared would demand "that faith which can remove mountains."

And so the couple settled into army life. From the outset, there were dismaying developments. Mary fell ill soon after reaching Fort Monroe, a preview of a career of physical disability. Robert assured Carter he was trying to restore a bloom to "the roses" in Mary's cheeks. He did not report that he was also seeking to train Mary in efficiency and self-discipline, a futile task over which even his patient nature despaired. Mary acknowledged to her mother: "Robert says he wishes you would send [summon] me home . . . he does scold me early and late."

Accustomed to having her way, Mary also expected attention. But Robert was busy with the usually dreary duty of an engineer, which at the moment meant heaping rocks near Fort Monroe. It left his wife to complain: "I do not walk much for Robert has not a great deal of time to go with me." However, Mary hastened to note her spouse did have admirable qualities. She told her mother that Robert was "tender and affectionate" and that "he spends his evenings at home instead of frequenting the card parties which attract so many. . . ."

Meanwhile, Robert kept hoping Mary would turn her concerns to domestic improvements. Nor did he always confine his complaints about Mary to her or her mother. After experiencing three years of marriage, he warned expected guests that "Mrs. Lee is somewhat addicted to *laziness* and *forgetfulness* in her housekeeping." She did her best, Robert acknowledged, but "in her mother's words, 'the spirit is willing but the flesh is weak.' "

His scoldings of the hapless Mary probably helped Robert endure dissatisfaction with himself. Doubts about his career vexed him, as his letters to brother Carter show. Robert worried about continuing as "an indifferent engineer." He often spoke of resigning his army commission, and later confessed that had he found an alternative sufficient to support and educate his family, he would have been a civilian long before 1861.

In 1838, Robert confided in his close friend and fellow engineer Andrew Talcott that his idea of happiness would be to settle "in some quiet corner among the hills of Virginia where I can indulge my natural propensities without interruption." Again, to Talcott: "I am waiting, looking, and hoping for some good opportunity to bid an affectionate farewell to my dear Uncle Sam. And I seem to think that said opportunity is to drop in my lap like a ripe pear."

If only he had some money, Robert lamented. Then he would indeed break free. To brother Carter, he complained: "I suppose I must continue to work out my youth for little profit and less credit, and when old be laid on the shelf." He avoided mentioning what should have been the encouraging example of his associates, such as Andrew Talcott, who did resign their commissions and enter civilian life to become prosperous engineers. It was simply that Robert did not try very hard to escape the army.

While he chafed constantly, he held back from the risks of leaving a secure spot. He made an art of stressing how devoted he was to duty and of reminding his family to be faithful to theirs. "I am obliged to forgo my own inclinations to follow Uncle Sam's," Robert would say, adding that he hoped his offspring would never have "reason to think I had preferred my own ease and comfort to their welfare and interest."

Consequently, Robert E. Lee's career became a paradox. At two points in his life he showed daring and imagination. These were on the battlefields of the Mexican War and the Civil War. But across the longer stretches of time, he seemed lethargic and inclined to stick with what was familiar and at hand. This outlook was encouraged by Robert's wife. Two months after they were established at Fort Monroe, Robert tried to persuade Mary that they should exchange the army for farming in western Virginia. She would not hear of it. Her aim was to remain close to her parents and Arlington.

When Mary became pregnant in 1832, she retreated to Arlington. Once back at home, she soon decided that she and Robert must make the place their residence. Robert was not so sure. "But are you right in this[?] We ought not to give others the trouble of providing for us always." Would not the two of them be happier "situated by ourselves," he asked. "I know your dear mother will be for giving you *every* thing she has, but you must recollect *one* thing and that is that they have been accustomed to comforts all their life."

Robert announced that he and Mary must "content our wishes to their smallest compass." This being her mate's decree, Mary set out to enlarge their means by trying to arrange a promotion for her husband, one that would change his assignment to Washington, merely across the river from Arlington. When Robert heard of Mary's scheme, he scolded again. "Molly, let me *charge* you *not* to say or do anything that would make persons believe that I *have* or *would* apply for ————'s situation, or even that I expect it. Keep *quiet,* Molly, and let things have their own way."

As Mary awaited their baby at Arlington, Robert remained alone at Fort Monroe trying to be cheerful during the spring and summer of 1832. He teased Mary about how he was called upon to escort other women at the post. "Think of that, Mrs. Lee! And hasten down if you do not want to see me turned into a Beau again." When Mary showed no interest in being away from Arlington, Robert's attempts at humor gave way to melancholy.

In June he told her "I am in a dull humour this evening and cannot be roused." He could not understand her reproof that they must be patient in separation. "You say every thing is for the best, though I must acknowledge it sometimes passes my poor comprehension to understand it." Why, he asked, were her letters so brief. "And what *fatigues* you so much? Did I not tell you, Molly, to be *careful* and did you not promise?" Robert warned that after they were reunited, he would keep a *"remarkably* tight rein" over her.

Himself a practitioner as well as preacher of self-denial, Robert soon patiently accommodated to Mary's pleas. He agreed that probably it would be best if they established Arlington as their family capital. The advantage of this location had become apparent when Mary was pregnant again soon after their first child, a son, was born in September 1832. To be near by, Robert accepted assignment in the chief engineer's office in Washington. It was not long before his love of Arlington matched Mary's, leaving him dismayed that military orders often took him away from the Custis residence.

Usually, Mary and their rapidly growing family could not accompany Robert on his army assignments. Consequently, the frustrations, not only of separation from wife and children, but also of his snail-like progress in the army, made Robert yearn for Arlington all the more. When he was stationed at St. Louis in 1837, he told Mary that his mind turned "forcibly and longingly to all at dear Arlington."

Upon returning from St. Louis, Robert spoke of being elated at making "my escape from the West." While he admitted seeing a "grand" future for places like Missouri, Robert preferred "the Ancient Dominion." He told cousin Hill Carter such was his delight upon re-entering Virginia that "I nodded to all the old trees as I passed, chatted with all the drivers and stable boys, shook hands with the landlords, and in the fulness of my heart—don't tell Cousin Mary—wanted to kiss all the pretty girls I met."

Robert admitted he often day-dreamed while on duty away from Arlington. He wrote to Mrs. Custis of having envisioned what he would do if he ever had an annual income of $20,000. The first step would be to put Arlington "in apple-pie order." But would such wealth make him and his dear ones too happy, he wondered. Conceding that it might, and thereby distract them from striving toward a better world in the hereafter, Robert announced they must be content "with what has been allotted."

In one respect, certainly, Robert and Mary had a generous allocation. Their children were numerous, despite Mary's illnesses and Robert's long absences. The child born in 1832 had been called George

Washington Custis Lee, and given the nickname Boo. Next to arrive was Mary Custis Lee in 1835. After her came a second son, William Henry Fitzhugh Lee, born in 1837. His nickname was Rooney. He was followed by two sisters, Annie born in 1839 and Agnes in 1841. Then it was time for a Robert E. Lee, Jr., in 1843. The last child, a daughter born in 1845, was named Mildred after her father's sister.

After Mildred's birth, Robert took stock of his family. "Upon my soul," he told Mrs. Custis, "if this thing goes on so regularly, I shall in good time equal King Priam. I do hope in *that* event, that Mamma will be satisfied, for from present appearances, she will stop at nothing less." Would his wife be content with fifty offspring? Robert teased. "I wish to arrange this matter satisfactorily to all parties and that some limit be fixed which shall in no event be exceeded."

Mary, too, must have begun to feel there were enough babies. At first she had been thrilled by maternity, describing little Boo as the "most joyous creature I ever saw." To her mother, Mary exclaimed how "the first sound that greets my ears in the morning . . . is his little sweet voice cooing and singing beside me." Four years and a second child later, Mary heard less pleasing noises: "My brats are squalling around me so that I cannot write more. You know how such music puts all our ideas to flight."

The birth of her second child had physcially and emotionally devastated Mary, leaving her bedfast and suffering from agonizing pelvic abscesses during the summer and fall of 1835. It had caused "the most exquisite pain," Mary reported, and when she emerged from the ordeal she considered her appearance so disgusting that she grabbed a scissors and cut off her hair. When it grew back rapidly, she threatened to have it shaved. "I expect on my return to find her bald," Robert said.

When Mary did not regain her strength or spirits, and instead caught the mumps, Robert took time in August 1836 to take her on the first of what would be many stays over the years at one or another of the mineral springs in the mountains of Virginia. Mary insisted that drinking the water improved her, but the chance to visit with numerous friends and cousins was perhaps a superior benefit. By that time, such spas had become favorite summer retreats for Virginians of means, no matter that their physical complaints were less than serious.

Mary's illness in 1836 became even more alarming when she developed what Robert called brain fever. It "seemed to overthrow her whole nervous system," leaving her "much shattered" and with a "restless anxiety, which renders her unhappy and dissatisfied." From this point, Mary apparently never fully regained health, although there were to be five more births.

This mounting number of youngsters was itself enough to leave Mary feeling tired and stupid, as she described herself. She spoke of being in "a constant state of wretchedness." "All the children together keep such a clamour that I can scarcely get a moment to think or read." For Mary, family responsibility was an obvious strain, causing Robert's letters to become even more supervisory, with hints that he considered his wife little more than a child herself. He felt compelled to monitor every aspect of her life, as well as their children's.

Consequently, the feature of a soldier's career which most vexed Robert was that his wife and offspring were often out of his sight. There was, however, comfort in knowing that Mary's mother could be in charge in his stead. Robert's relationship with Mrs. Custis evolved into the kind of mutual respect and confidence which ought to have existed between husband and wife. They became allies out of a need to see that Mary and her children were properly governed when Robert was absent.

He was quite candid with his mother-in-law about how Mary tended to do only what suited her. "It requires much earnestness to induce her to conform to what she is not herself impressed with the necessity of." Sounding much older than thirty-two, Robert announced that "young women, you know, will not be advised." Therefore, as it would be "useless" and "a waste of time" simply to make suggestions to Mary, Robert directed Mrs. Custis to "*make* her do what is right."

What Robert feared most, as he conceded to his mother-in-law, was that Mary's "discipline will be too lax, too inconstant, and too yielding." Their children must have "moral and mental improvement," so that they could "live to be the happiness of us all," brightening "the fading days" of their parents. Leaving the most precious responsibility a male could have, his children, with such a female as his wife always troubled Robert. Mindful of his own experience in growing up, he liked to intone: "A child learns all that it has of good from its mother."

When Robert praised the "good," the first attribute he had in mind was the one his father and his half-brother Henry conspicuously lacked—self-denial. He pleaded that his wife and children join him in striving to attain this virtue. It was advice he gave copiously, even late in life. After he became the famous Confederate commander, to those parents who wrote to him requesting guidance in raising a child, Robert replied with words such as: "Teach him that he must deny himself"—the same lesson Robert sought to impart to his own youngsters.

In 1837, while in St. Louis working to control the Missouri River channel, Robert received reports that five-year-old Boo was becoming headstrong. Immediately, the father rushed orders to Arlington that the boy be diverted at once from "self-will and obstinacy." It was parental "duty," Robert explained to Mary, to "counteract" these unhappy qualities and to show the lad "that he *must* comply." Mary was advised to hold the warning of an unbending father before the son.

"You must assist me in my attempts," Robert said, urging that Mary and he combine "the mildness and forbearance of the mother with the sternness and perhaps *unreasonableness* of the father." Disciplining the children, said Robert, "is a subject which I *think* much on." Increasingly, those military assignments which separated him from wife and offspring meant in Robert's mind that he was betraying the obligation of guiding his youngsters toward wholesomeness.

Yet even when the children were gathered around him, Robert never felt confident that he was a sufficiently stern mentor. He was badly shaken by an event which took place at Fort Hamilton at the end of November 1845. To this post, near New York City, Robert had brought part of his family, including his second son, eight-year-old Rooney. The lad was given many warnings, including that he must not go alone to the stables. Rooney disobeyed and began lurking near where feed for the horses was cut up. One day he extended a hand too close and had the tips of its fingers chopped off.

This event undid Robert, who was at once angry, guilt-ridden, and compassionate. The father used this act of willfulness to impress his eldest son Boo, who had been a great worry to his parents now that he was away at school. Rooney's damaged hand was described to Boo as a warning and edification. Robert stressed particularly how Rooney's sin had brought incalculable anguish to his parents. "You see the fruits of his disobedience," the father wrote. "He may probably lose his fingers and be maimed for life. You cannot conceive what I suffered. . . . Do take warning."

The next letter Boo received again emphasized Rooney's—and also his father's—plight. "If children could know the misery, the desolating sorrow with which their acts sometimes overwhelm their parents," Robert told Boo, "they could not have the heart thus cruelly to afflict them. May you never know the misery I now suffer, and may you always be preserved to me pure and happy." As encouragement for the lad, Robert commended Boo's recent high marks in school. "You cannot give me more pleasure than does this assurance of your good conduct and progress in learning."

Next, the afflicted Rooney himself was pressed into duty. Boo received a letter in his father's penmanship, but which Rooney was supposed to have dictated. Said the younger brother: "I hope neither of us will disobey our parents in the future," to which Robert added: "This severe lesson must never be forgotten by children." He reminded Boo that now the family had two "disfigured" youngsters, for before Rooney's accident, little Annie had blinded one of her eyes with a scissors. According to Robert, her mishap, like Rooney's, was the consequence of "inattention and disobedience," leading him to admonish Boo: "If you ever require to be strengthened or confirmed in the path of rectitude, let the fate of these two be there before you."

Months later, the memory of Rooney's accident still preyed on the father: "The thought of his injury comes over my spirits like a withering blight and I feel as if I could have sacrificed my life to have saved that dear hand." Since this was impossible, Robert campaigned anew for Mary to appreciate the imperativeness of controlling the children, especially since there had been another alarming development. Robert's namesake, little Rob, was becoming disobedient. Now, groaned Robert, all the children needed curbing. "You must therefore set seriously to work upon the dear little creatures," he begged Mary. She must "see what you can make of them."

Bringing up righteous children was only one aspect of Robert's concern as a parent. Another asked whether he had enough money to send them properly into life. To Robert, financial worries seemed relentless. He brooded over what he considered an inadequate income, as well as over his need to sustain a reputation for honesty and probity. Never far from his mind was the unenviable name the Lees had earned from his father's behavior. When brother Carter Lee displayed some of Light-Horse Harry's casual ways with finance, Robert was quick with a rebuke. "It is unpleasant to give checks on banks and not have there funds to meet them," he pointed out. He was always aware, Robert said, that "people may think I am endeavoring to *swindle*."

Often, Robert seemed to feel he must treat Carter as he would an older son. Carter had left New York and an abortive legal career to try developing the wilderness property he and his brothers inherited in western Virginia, particularly in Hardy County. An inn, a spa, a plantation—all were planned by Carter despite the remonstrances of Robert, who patiently kept pointing out the uselessness of these acres. He urged Carter to be realistic. "It is a hard case that out of so much land, none should be good for any thing, and a provoking one, too."

Nevertheless, Carter regularly begged Robert for loans or offered him opportunities for investment. Robert's defense was artful: "If I had a thousand for every hundred dollars I have, I should not have enough for all the demands upon me for money." As for Carter's latest scheme: "If it were not for the pain I feel at the trouble and vexation of your situation, I should have to laugh at the grandeur of your plans."

Still, there were moments when Carter was handy for Robert. One of these was after the death in 1842 of Uncle Bernard Carter, their mother's brother, who had spent most of his life wandering in Europe and America. Bernard made a will which named Robert as executor. It was a tribute which Robert found unbearable after "my dear uncle's" heirs began a family quarrel.

Claiming that he knew nothing of investment matters (which was false modesty) and that the army kept his whereabouts uncertain (which was true), Robert renounced his executorship in favor of brother Carter. The hapless Carter had scant success, leaving the heirs to more squabbling and begging Robert to act as honest broker, an honor he steadfastly declined.

In 1843, Robert tried to set a good example before Carter by announcing: "I can be content to be poor, with the knowledge of being able to pay my debts and that no one has a just claim against me that I cannot meet." He would laughingly insist that the only dubious ventures he made were purchases of lottery tickets from which he had no expectations save what luck might bring. Usually, the thrifty Robert put spare dollars in the James River and Kanawha Canal Company, an early favorite of George Washington. He also purchased stock in the Bank of Virginia, claiming "the state of Virginia will never turn swindler."

For years, Carter remained one of Robert's worries. The older brother failed in two attempts at election to the legislature, undertaken despite Robert's warning that it was "better for you to stay at home for a few years and get all your affairs fixed." Paying no heed and complaining about the "poverty which has been holding me down all my life," Carter next tried plantation life in Mississippi. Again, he failed.

He considered being an attorney in New Orleans, but abandoned that plan to hitch his ambition to a Whig party triumph in 1844. That broke down. Then, finally, came a successful move. At age forty-nine, Carter married Lucy Penn Taylor, whose lineage was almost as distinguished as Carter's own. They settled near Richmond in Powhatan County on what apparently was Taylor family land. The couple called their farm Windsor Forest, and there Carter soon was prospering and happy as a husband and father. He retained his interest in literature and tried to prove one could be both a poet and a farmer.

This ambition caused Robert the soldier to tease Carter about civilians having no grasp of what hard work involved. Ironically, though, while he never reached distinction in letters or agriculture, Carter spent his last years in the manner for which his brother Robert often said he yearned—tilling a small farm, surrounded by his family, and far from politics and the army. Carter's domestication may have added to Robert's discontent with himself, as, nearing age forty, he foresaw nothing but many separations from his children. His absences grew longer, he sighed, just when the youngsters' need for parental and academic supervision increased.

There were more self-reproaches for Robert after a national economic depression forced the army to reduce its officers' salaries. Robert's was cut by nearly half, wringing from him the acknowledgment: "I never was poorer in my life, and for the first time I have not been able to pay my debts." But soon afterwards, in 1846, the outbreak of hostilities between the United States and Mexico dramatically diverted Robert from his domestic troubles. The war brought experiences which abruptly changed his life and outlook.

❧ 18

"My Country" 1846–1861

By serving in the Mexican War, Robert E. Lee was parted from his family for two years, 1846 to 1848, an interval that affected him more than any other experience before 1861. He did not approve of the war, confiding to Mary his belief that America's incitement of hostilities "disgraced" their country. As a staunch Whig, he shared the partisan view that the war with Mexico was a Democratic scheme.

Believing he would die in Mexico, Captain Lee prepared his will before leaving Arlington. The document displayed how fruitful his discipline and economy had been. By living on his soldier's pay, and by evading Carter Lee's costly gambles, Robert could list $38,750 in stocks and bonds, notably shares in the Bank of Virginia. His slave Nancy and her children, all of whom he had inherited from his mother, were to be freed as soon as possible—both Robert and Mary were supporters of the American Colonization Society. His share of worthless western land he noted only in passing.

All of Robert's estate was left to Mary, and after her decease to their children equally. He pointed out that, with a sightless eye, daughter Annie "may be more in want of aid than the rest." She must therefore "be particularly provided for." In a letter to Mary, written 13 August 1846, Robert urged that the income from the stocks and bonds, usually amounting to $2000 per year, be used to educate their children.

The will completed, Robert headed for Mexico, keeping messages streaming back to his family. Enroute, he sent Mary a cheerless reminder of "the heavy responsibility" she now had for the children. Emphasizing his sense of impending death, Robert shared his last wish with her. As his widow, Mary must make their youngsters "more obedient."

She should be firm with both boys and girls, and maintain them upon an *"undeviating course."*

Though he soon became accustomed to being in a war and therefore thought less of dying, Robert's instructions to Mary were unchanged. He continued to exhort her to "teach them [children] to love me and bring them up so that they will be an honour to you and bring satisfaction to themselves." Nor were the youngsters spared, although Robert now advised the daughters apart from the sons. The young males had reached a stage where they merited different treatment.

The boys were directed to seek self-improvement. "I shall not feel my long separation from you if I find that my absence has been of no injury to you. . . . But oh how much I will suffer on my return if the reverse has occurred!" Could the lads not see, their father asked, that upon them depended "whether I shall be happy or miserable. . . . You must do all in your power to save me pain." They should "pray earnestly to God to enable you to keep his Commandments and walk in the Laws all the days of your life."

When Robert wrote to his four daughters, he did so in a spirit typical of men in his day. Like most of his contemporaries, Robert saw women as created to be the male's comfort and help. The female's duty was at the hearth and in the nursery. Since his wife was increasingly an invalid and their daughters seemed bent upon becoming nearly as frail, Robert used the pitying terms "your poor mother" and "poor little thing" when describing Mary and his daughters.

There were, of course, less personal sections in Robert's family letters. He sent long descriptions of life in Mexico, which he wanted Mary to share with her parents and the youngsters. In many passages he continued to regret that the war was taking place. He spoke of being "ashamed" at how the United States "bullied" Mexico. The fact that the war brought him temporary (brevet) promotions left Robert unimpressed. To his father-in-law Custis he noted that other officers had received more recognition for less accomplishment than his. "I do not mention this in the way of complaint, but that you may not think I am overwhelmed with gratitude and obligation."

Even if his contribution went generally unheralded, Robert's service during the war proved paradoxically to be nothing less than an astonishing professional success. One acute observer has called Lee's performance in Mexico "magnificent." And, indeed, it led Robert's commander, General Winfield Scott, in 1858 to describe Lee as "the very best soldier I ever saw in the field." In the years following the war, Robert became known to a tiny circle of military leaders as possibly the finest of America's officers.

Yet Robert's twenty months in Mexico began inauspiciously, promising for a time to be a dull repetition of what he had been doing all along. During the autumn of 1846, he was with General John E. Wool's army in northern Mexico, where the greatest excitement coming Robert's way was the endless miles of road construction he had to supervise. He went on some reconnaissance excursions, but these did not bring him into danger.

Then, in January 1847, Robert's life changed when he was summoned to join a group of officers gathered at General Scott's side. In the next year Lee's brilliant leadership in reconaissance forays was crucial to the successful march of Scott's forces toward Mexico City. For example, it was Robert who found the route for the victorious assault at Cerro Gordo on 18 April 1847. As if this were not enough, in the ensuing battle Lee commanded the column that turned the tide in the United States' favor.

In his report concerning the battle, General Scott commended Robert's contribution above all others, choosing to write: "I am impelled to make special mention of the services of Captain R. E. Lee, engineers. This officer, greatly distinguished at the siege of Vera Cruz, was again indefatigable during these operations [Cerro Gordo], in reconnaissance as daring as laborious, and of the utmost value. Nor was he less conspicuous in planting batteries and in conducting columns to their stations under the heavy fire of the enemy." The recognition meant Robert had pulled ahead of such fellow officers in Mexico as P. G. T. Beauregard, Joseph E. Johnston, and Thomas J. Jackson, men who would be important in Lee's life during the Civil War.

Thereafter, Scott relied heavily upon Robert, having him brevetted major and later colonel for his "gallant and meritorious conduct." In August 1847, the commander expected Robert to chart a route across rough terrain that might lead the American forces directly toward Mexico City, avoiding other roads which were fortified by the Mexicans. Once again, Lee and his men discovered the way, after which Robert served valiantly for thirty-six hours in three engagements before Mexico City was taken. He seemed to be almost everywhere in behalf of General Scott, particularly at Chapultepec. The demands were so exhausting that he finally collapsed from lack of sleep.

When he was not in the field, Robert remained one of the officers closest to General Scott, absorbing lessons in military tactics and taking a significant part in shaping the strategy that brought the enemy's defeat. These few months gave the only practical battle training Robert received during his thirty years in the army before 1861. Working beside Winfield Scott in Mexico taught Robert how to plan attack.

While Robert's achievement in 1847 earned him the highest esteem of General Scott and other officers, it seemed to do little to enhance his professional career, and it certainly did not lift his spirits. He departed from Mexico more than ever disgusted by what he felt politics and preferment did to mistreat good men. Given the intimate size of the federal and military organization in the 1840s and 50's, one has to wonder if lingering rumors about Light-Horse Harry and Henry Lee were a barrier to Robert's advancement.

Robert himself merely said that in a system in which ability so often went unrewarded, it was better "for me to be classed with those who have failed." At the war's end, he repeated his old refrain: "I wish I was out of the Army," and he pledged: "I shall make a strong effort to leave it." It was in this mood that Robert returned home in June 1848. At Arlington, he watched his wife and children as they "devote themselves to staring at the furrows on my face and the white hairs in my head." Even the older children "gaze with astonishment and wonder at me, and seem at loss to reconcile what they see and what was pictured in their imaginations."

The profoundest change in Robert, however, was inward rather than visible. He returned having begun a religious pilgrimage that would dominate the rest of his life. While in Mexico, he had written to Mary's mother, in whom he confided more than to anyone, that when "I look back to my own life, I can find nothing to point to . . . I have done no good."

Such a confession had found the means of absolution by the time Robert was back at Arlington. He had discovered a haven, he announced, in which he could lay down his disappointments, his frustrations, and his anxieties. They could all be left in the unsearchable wisdom of God. Virtuous effort might fail, and evil seem to triumph, Robert conceded, but the ultimate good behind life's struggle would be disclosed in the next world, the goal toward which Lee now believed all mortals should deliberately hasten.

A year after he rejoined his family, Robert heard a remarkable sermon in Baltimore which lifted him to a final "blessed assurance." He told Mary he now was certain that only surrender to God would allow mankind to escape evil and calamity. "No one can be more sensible of these facts than I am. But it is so difficult to regulate your conduct by them. Man's nature is so selfish, so weak. Every feeling, every passion urging him to folly, excess, and sin that I am disgusted with myself and sometimes with all the world."

His efforts at self-improvement would be futile, he feared. "Even in my prayers I fail, and my only hope is in my confidence, my trust in the mercy of God." For Robert, this made the prospect of the tomb especially consoling. He assured Mary that "death will soon come to cure all our ills in this life." Meanwhile, he proposed to spend more time reading the Bible and the Episcopal prayer book, deriving "much comfort from their holy precepts and merciful promises, though I feel unable to follow the one and unworthy of the other."

Even with trust and obedience as their watchwords unto death, Robert conceded the course remaining before him and his family would not be easy. "God punishes us for our sins here as well as hereafter," he reminded Mrs. Custis. "He is now punishing me for mine through my children. It is there I am most vulnerable, most sensitive. As I feel I deserve it, I must bear it without complaint." He prayed for each child. "If they knew how much I love them," he wrote in 1852, "how I feel through them, I know they would spare me much."

As his daughters began their schooling near Arlington, Robert sent orders even to the teacher. She must not relent with the girls. "I cannot admit their assertion that 'they can't.' They *can* if they *try*. I say in addition they *must*." According to Robert's latest view, humans were so "weak, shortsighted, and ignorant of what is for our good that we must be *made* to do *right*. We will not do it ourselves, although we *know* we will suffer in consequence."

With religious fervor as his "new armor," Robert seemed refreshed in his vigilance over his rapidly maturing children. His outlook helped him when Custis (no longer called Boo), the eldest son, enrolled at West Point. Robert had hoped his own unsatisfactory experience in the army might discourage Custis, but once the young man had chosen, the parent cheerfully exhorted him, especially when Custis spoke of discouragement and despair.

"Why, man, when I am troubled," Robert told the son in 1852, "I think of you to cheer and support me. I feel as if I had somebody to fall back upon." Custis was reminded he must care for the family when, as Robert solemnly put it, "I am gone." The cadet should learn to take life as it came, and turn affairs "to your advantage." While sad thoughts were inevitable, they were beneficial. Robert assured the young cadet: "They cause us to reflect. They are the shadows to our pictures. They bring out prominently the light and bright spots. They must not cover up all."

As he reread what he had written, Robert evidently decided his son might see him as unduly optimistic. So he closed by admonishing Custis: "All that is bright must fade, and we ourselves have to die. Keep this in view and live to that end." This would require *"strength, fortitude, and capacity . . . a firm resolve* on your part, *persevering industry,* and a *coura-*

geous heart." Custis was assured that the temptation to relax "will grow feebler and more feeble by constant resistance." The cadet was also advised to think of "how *cruel* it is for young men by their neglect and inattention to bring upon their parents and friends the mortification and distress of their failure."

Before Custis had graduated, his father was appointed superintendent of the Military Academy, serving in the position from the autumn of 1852 until spring of 1855. During this time, the Lee family was together at West Point, except when the lure of Arlington was too strong, as in 1853 when Mrs. Custis died. She had made her will several years earlier, carefully leaving to her son-in-law a ring with "General Washington's hair and pearl initials." To the entire family, she gave a benediction: "May Heaven bless you all my beloved ones with all spiritual blessings of more value than those bands of gold and silver."

The more he pondered this irreplaceable loss, Robert said "the greater is my grief." Yet, he asked, why mourn? The departed "had gone from all trouble, care, and sorrow to a happy immortality! There to rejoice and praise forever the Lord and Saviour she long and trustfully served." It was held up as an edifying lesson for the entire family when Robert learned that Mrs. Custis died while murmuring the Lord's Prayer.

Hearing of this last moment, Robert announced: "We must discard all selfishness and all egoism, and so act and live as she would have wished. May our death be like hers and may we all meet in happiness." The first step, Robert suggested to his wife, would be that she display restraint in buying elaborate mourning wear. "I place little value upon the fashionable external woe." His advice may not have been necessary, for Mary was filling her journal with supplication and confession: "Oh, how I have neglected to *watch* unto prayer. Oh, my Father, forgive me."

As ninth superintendent of the United States Military Academy, Robert's hair began growing gray, thanks to worry over the cadets, each of whom he felt was entrusted to his personal care. The Secretary of War, Jefferson Davis, recalled how Lee had aged during the West Point years and how the superintendent fretted over his charges—even to seeking the reason whenever he heard that a student was not writing to parents at home.

Discipline was made as rigorous in cadet quarters as it was in the superintendent's residence. The fact that a son and a nephew, Custis and Fitz Lee, were then enrolled at the Academy deepened Robert's sense of personal concern for all cadets. Custis graduated first in his class in 1854, with a lad named "Jeb" Stuart standing second. Stuart would be General R. E. Lee's valued and colorful cavalry officer during much of the Civil War.

While at West Point, Robert oversaw important changes in regulations and curriculum. He devoted himself particularly to sharpening the measurement of good scholarship and strengthening the hand of the institution's academic board when it came to dismissing students who faltered in their work. These accomplishments were warmly praised by the Academy's board of visitors. Nevertheless, serving in this role gave Robert little satisfaction. As early as a year into his assignment at West Point he admitted: "I have less heart for the work."

He soon had a chance to escape. In March 1855, after Congress created several additional army regiments, Robert learned he was permanently promoted to lieutenant colonel and offered a transfer to the cavalry from the engineers. If he accepted, he would be assigned second command of the 2d Cavalry, whose headquarters was to be Texas. Lee accepted the move, there being more hope for advancement in the infantry and cavalry than within the engineers. Consequently, the Academy had a new superintendent on 31 March 1855, and Robert headed for Texas. For a time, he seemed elated and spoke of his pleasure at leaving the "confined and sedentary existence at WP." Once more, said he, events showed "how kind our Heavenly Father is to us. Always arranging for us better than we could for ourselves."

Except for one lengthy interruption, Robert was stuck in Texas from mid-1855 to early 1861. Much of the time he was miserable, assigned usually at Brownsville, sometimes at San Antonio, and obliged to follow another confined life, for he found himself shackled with responsibility for the army's Texas department. Alongside the paper work, Robert had to sit as a judge through the tedium of frequent courts-martial, when his thoughts often turned to family and Arlington.

Being away from home "was a just punishment for my sins," he told Mary. Yet he detected divine benefits from his ordeal. Robert interpreted his Texas assignment as Heaven's way of preparing his wife and children for his death. Since he was once again claiming that melancholy event was at hand, Robert talked of a deepened penance for his misdoings. If, somehow, "my sins may be forgiven," Robert foresaw that "the day of my death will be better for me than the day of my birth."

"A sincere repentance" and "that I may be patient" were the prayers Robert repeated in his letters from Texas. Over and over, he stressed how the Lees were "in the hands of a kind God," and that "we have only to endeavor to *deserve* more and to do our duty to him ourselves." He conceded the difficulty in this. Only God could provide strength needed "to give me resolution to deny my inclinations and a willingness to submit to any punishment for all my misspent time and the sins of my life he may think fit to inflict."

There was a small Episcopal parish in Brownsville where Robert attended worship, but even these services dismayed him. As a Virginian, he was impatient with the "high church" style of Texans, which reminded him of Roman Catholicism. Claiming that organized religion had perverted the "purity preached by our Saviour," Robert spoke of "an inward rebellion over which I have no control." He felt he was better off staying at Fort Brown and worshiping without distraction. But when a baby died at the fort, Robert dutifully read the Episcopal service for burial.

Thinking about the infant's death and the "anguish" of the parents, Robert told Mary he was nevertheless convinced there should be a feeling of relief whenever a child was called to Heaven while still "unpolluted by sin and uncontaminated by the vices of the world." Although parental sorrow caused by losing the baby was "dreadful," yet God imposed the grief "in mercy." The parents could rejoice that their infant "has been saved from all sin and misery here." Young couples at the beginning of marriage had Robert's sympathy. "It is sad to think how soon the clouds of disappointment darken the prospect of life's horizon. Yet how glorious the prospect of the life beyond the skies!"

News of his sister Mildred's death in Paris was relayed to Robert while he was in Texas. He seemed crushed, saying he had particularly yearned to see her again, as his memories of her were so full. But now he could console himself in what had become his familiar response to reports of death: "I trust that her merciful God . . . saw it was the fittest moment to take her to himself." He then added: "May a pure eternal life now be hers and may we all so live that when we die, it may be opened to us!"

Robert's unhappy mood in Texas shaped his effort to comfort Mildred's husband Edward Childe: "I do not even wish her [Mildred] return to this world of pain and care." Writing in January 1857, Robert send Childe a second letter, assuring him that "we can only look for happiness beyond the grave." To other relatives Robert was also urging that all eyes be fixed on the next world, for this life promised only grief. He was fifty years old.

By no means was every passage in Robert's letters to Arlington so lachrymose. While a melancholy mood predominated, there were paragraphs in which Robert sought to cheer his family by telling stories of Texas life. These portions showed Robert's remarkable talent for descriptive narrative, his ironical style, and his sense of humor. One such tale pictured Robert camped along the Brazos River on the Fourth of July 1856. He reported the only way to shelter himself from a fierce sun was "my blanket elevated on four sticks driven into the ground." Though he felt he sat in "the blast from a hot air furnace," Robert wryly observed he still managed to muster some ardent feelings "for my country."

When he was obliged to chase after the Comanche Indians, Robert's tales were often comical until they turned impatient, bringing him to grumble: "These people give a world of trouble to man and horse, and, poor creatures, they are not worth it." But when he was back at Fort Brown, Robert was not much happier. One drawback was the camp's social life, which the reclusive Robert deemed a waste of time. He reminded Mary: "I am a great advocate of people staying at home and minding their own affairs, and am indisposed to trouble strangers." Nor was it easy being alone, for Robert invariably faced an invasion of flies and mosquitoes, the former by day, the latter by night. Thanks to them, he had "no lack of animation." "I am so extremely awkward in catching them that they mock at my efforts."

Perhaps the brightest passages of Robert's Texas letters were those about cats, his favorite pets. In March 1857, he relayed news of the death by apoplexy of "Jim Nooks," a Fort Brown feline. "I foretold his end," Robert wrote. "Coffee cream for breakfast. Pound cake for lunch. Fretted oysters for dinner. Buttered toast for tea, and mice and rats taken raw for supper!" Alas, "cat nature could not stand so much luxury. He grew enormously and ended in a spasm." And then Robert applied a moral touch to close his story: "His beauty could not save him."

The cats, the Indians, the local society, and his religious meditations were never enough to keep Robert from worrying about the folks at Arlington. His greatest concern was his wife. At age fifty, Mary Custis Lee was no less erratic in her habits and dress than she had been in girlhood. Mindful of this, Robert's instructions about money matters became marvels of explicitness. Finally, Mary had heard enough. She told Robert in September 1856: "Altho' my accounts may not seem to you very clear according to your nice mode of keeping yours," she assured him that "there is no one more particular to pay all I owe to the utmost farthing. Do not be uneasy about me."

Mary's next letter was much less spunky. She notified Robert that, try though she might, she could no longer walk except for short distances and then only with a crutch. "I often suffer much pain and stiffness," she acknowledged, adding: "It is fortunate for you that you have not got me in your tent at present as I would be of very little service to you, and you would have but little time to wait on me." Mary, of course, did not wish to be in Robert's "awful" circumstances. "I cannot imagine how you preserve your health."

Actually, Robert's robust constitution had begun a premature aging. He sometimes mentioned pain, especially that which circulated down his arm—an indication of the onset of arterial disease, a malady which would trouble Robert during the Civil War and cause his death at age sixty-three. His letters to Mary did not, however, dwell on his physical state. He preferred to encourage a spiritual outlook in his crippled wife that might sustain her.

These messages usually closed with some version of the fatalism upon which Robert had come to depend: "All is for the best, though we cannot always see it at the time." Mary must be steadfast in prayer, and fret not over matters beyond her control. "Lay nothing therefore too much to heart. Desire nothing too eagerly, nor think that all things can be perfectly accomplished according to our own notions." Her "pure piety" would, Robert assured his spouse, enable her to bear "this painful affliction," as she bowed "to all the chastisements of our heavenly father."

Not easily consoled, Mary was often impatient. Why are "my active limbs . . . bound with rheumatism," she asked, "I cannot account for it." However, Robert's urgings eventually took effect. In her journal entries, Mary now wrote of one lesson learned—"to *bear* in *silence,* and in tearful prayer to look up to my God." How much easier this might be done, she admitted, if only she knelt with Robert beside her. In his absence, she said she must rely upon his letters and draw upon their austere encouragement, all the time awaiting the outcome of God's wisdom—Robert having advised Mary: "It may be a greater advantage than we imagine that our petitions are not granted immediately."

There should have been less comfort for Mary when Robert reported in August 1857 that a San Antonio widow found him attractive. After promptly explaining how only in politeness had he accepted the widow's invitation to look at the stars in her garden and stressing that his behavior remained entirely correct, Robert could not resist an admiring comment about the woman. Unfortunately, his words made the widow an uncomfortable contrast to the incapable Mary. "She would take care of a man finely," Robert mused at the memory of his hostess in the garden. "Those are the kind of women . . . a man wants in the army," he went on. She was "strong-minded" and had the benefit of "Texas habits." Robert did not elaborate on these habits.

Whether Robert wished to have strong-minded daughters is doubtful. His letters to them called mostly for dutifulness, as he set out to inspire the young women into constant attendance upon their invalid mother. Perhaps as a result of this strategy, none of Robert and Mary Lee's four daughters married. Annie died young. Agnes and Mildred heeded their father's command and remained with their mother. The exception was the eldest daughter, Mary, an early rebel who frequently escaped the family circle by visiting the Lees' many relatives and friends.

As her mother put it, "You know when Sister gets away from home, it is hard to get her back again."

Typical of Robert's exhortations to his daughters was a January 1857 letter to Mildred, his youngest child, who was eleven at the time. "Do not even *wish* for what you ought not to have or do, but try hard to be a truly good, as well as wise girl, and rigidly obey your parents and tutors." The special task she faced, Robert told her, was to "be particularly attentive to your mother. Now that she is in pain and trouble, it is more than ever your duty to assist and serve her." Robert conceded that "Perhaps God has thus afflicted her [his wife] to try her children."

Letters to the other daughters were similar in tone, although Robert would lighten them occasionally with charming stories about his cats and chickens. He rarely found it necessary to burden the women of the family with more profound subjects. Consequently, it was a weighty decision when little Mildred must have his permission to learn to dance. Robert reluctantly consented, hoping the result would be improved posture. He made clear he did not wish his daughter to dance when she was grown up, even though he admitted never seeing "any sin in the exercise."

Another popular youthful interest that dismayed Robert was the reading of novels. In his judgment, such writing was prone to "paint beauty more charming than nature and describe happiness that never exists." It left young people "to sigh after that which has no reality and to despise the little good that is granted to us in this world and to expect more than is ever given." Much worse, of course, was that fiction detained the young mind from developing a religious commitment.

One cost of his Texas assignment was that Robert was not at hand when Agnes and Annie confronted the salvation of their souls. From their parents the Lee girls early had been taught "there is no such thing as an indolent Christian." Each day must be given to Bible study, seeking grace "to overcome all your evil and sinful tempers." Bulletins concerning the results were regularly dispatched to Texas. In one, Agnes meant to be reassuring: "Do not be unhappy on my account, dear Papa, for I don't think I ever *can* do *any thing* to make you ashamed of me, though I know I am very, *very* bad and just the opposite of what I *ought* to be."

"Perhaps as I grow older, I may know how to do better," Agnes announced, and closed her letter: "Oh, I wish I could *kiss* you good night." A few months later, in the spring of 1857, happy news was sent to Texas. Agnes and Annie had at last passed through the deep religious experience both young women had hoped for. Annie predicted to her father, "I know you will rejoice," and she proceeded in six pages to depict how she and Agnes had poured out tears and prayers before God's throne, and how their supplications had been answered. Annie could now attest: "I do love my precious Jesus," and that it was "wicked in the last degree" to doubt Him.

The converts' father replied in elation to their announcement, joining Mary in praising the mercy of God which had roused the hearts of their children. "That ought to reconcile us to all the discomforts and affliction with which we are troubled." With this, Mary agreed. She reminded Agnes: "Think what a happiness to your poor mother to be able to present *all* her children at the *throne* of God and to be able to say 'Here I am, Lord, and the children Thou hast given me.'" Even young Rob Lee, who became a student at the University of Virginia, joined in encouraging the sisters. He would inquire: "How are you getting along with your God? My sister, neglect not him."

Report of his daughters' spiritual progress was much the best news Robert received during his years in Texas. On the back of one of his wife's letters he noted his joy "at the determination of our dear daughters to devote their hearts and lives to the service of Almighty God." This achievement by the young women was particularly welcome since it eased their father's dismay over their brother Rooney's distressing behavior.

When his turn came to try, Rooney (William Henry Fitzhugh Lee) had failed to be admitted to West Point. His second choice had been Harvard. There, according to his alarmed father, the young man was active in nothing but "running about amusing himself." This practice must stop at once, Robert ordered in 1856. As a father, he felt particularly chagrined. "People do not know the misery they entail in their children and society by bringing them up badly, and yet what have I done?" The son received the severest paternal censure possible from the Lee moral universe when Robert decreed that Rooney "thinks entirely of his pleasures and not of what is proper to be done."

During a lonely Christmas in Texas, Robert confessed to Mary that Rooney's shiftlessness caused much lost sleep, "and adds more than years to the gray hairs on my head." While Rooney might be well disposed, the young man had made the terrible mistake, according to Robert, of allowing his feelings instead of his reason to guide him. Unless Rooney developed "self-control," Robert announced, he would never have confidence in his son. "I have seen so many young men throw themselves away," he said, adding that the waste was because the youths would not deny themselves.

Robert's dismay over Rooney was heightened by the evidence he saw around him at Fort Brown of how other parents were failing. He observed so many "poor mothers" unable to control their children, or, worse, were indifferent to their offsprings' antics. "I have seen so much bad home training," Robert told Mary, "that I have become an advocate for infant schools where children can be gathered together under well trained instructors and taught to practice politeness, gentleness, courtesy, and a regard for the rights of others." A "selfish animalism" needed to be scourged from young people if they would begin to recognize the merit of *self-denial and self-control.*

Rooney left Harvard without his degree and took a commission in the infantry as arranged by his father's friend, General Winfield Scott. At first the lad had been reluctant to enter the army, claiming he preferred to take up farming. Choosing to avoid his father when discussing the future, Rooney looked to Mary for advice. He claimed that his father invariably discouraged him. Hearing of this excuse by Rooney, Robert became indignant. What had Rooney expected, he wondered—that his father would commend his errors? Robert scoffed at Rooney's ideas about farming: "If at 20 he is unable to be his own guardian, how does he expect to be so at 21?"

When Rooney entered the army, his father paid the debts left behind at college as well as costs for an outfit the son needed in military service. Then, just after the parents had turned Rooney over to "a merciful and tender" God, the young soldier notified them he was in love and wished to become engaged to be married. Rooney broke the news to his mother and asked her to inform his father. The young man's beloved was an orphaned cousin, Charlotte Wickham, who had been reared by her Carter grandparents at Shirley.

Mary did her best to calm Robert. "It is useless to say any thing, but let matters take their course." After all, "a virtuous attachment is often a great safeguard to a young man." Recognizing Mary's point, Robert allowed himself to be soothed. In a tender mood, he began to correspond with his prospective daughter-in-law, often using her nickname, "Chass." Actually, Chass received letters that were written by a hand practiced in sharing thoughts with young women, for Robert had recently begun exchanging messages with another youthful female relative, Martha Williams, known as "Markie." To her, Robert came to express himself in ways more relaxed and personal than to anyone else since the death of Mrs. Custis.

The letters to Markie differed from those Robert sent to his wife and children. In these, his sense of duty, worry, and guilt seemed to block a crucial part of himself. By contrast, as early as 1851 Robert was composing for Markie Williams such lines as: "If it were not for my heart, Markie, I might as well be a pile of stone myself, laid quietly at the bottom of the river." He assured her that at difficult moments his heart "always returns warmth and softness when touched with a thought of you."

To Chass he said: "I never thought my dear Charlotte, when I held you a girl in my arms, and felt arise the love I bore your mother, that you would ever be nearer and dearer to me than then." As an army wife, she would need much patience, while her husband must practice "self-denial." He predicted that Rooney would be "tender and faithful."

The engagement brightened the tone of Robert's letters to Rooney. He told "my dearest son" that "I always thought and said there was stuff in you for a good soldier, and I trust you will prove it." Now he must hold on to his "purity and virtue," including avoiding the use of tobacco. "You have in store so much better employment for your mouth. Reserve it, Roon, for its legitimate pleasures." As for Chass, whose parents had died from tuberculosis, Robert strove to believe reports that she had outgrown the disease.

Robert and Mary did not oppose a prompt marriage between the young couple, especially after Rooney announced he would conclude his brief military career and begin farming on land he had inherited from his grandfather Custis. The wedding took place at Shirley on 23 March 1859. It was the same house in which Rooney's grandfather, Light-Horse Harry, had married Ann Hill Carter. Mary was too infirm to attend, but Robert was present, being on extended leave from his Texas post because of Mr. Custis' death.

That sad event handed many festering problems to Robert. George Washington Parke Custis died on 10 October 1857. At first, Robert thought a two-month furlough would be adequate to carry out his father-in-law's will, in which Robert had been named executor. Instead, he had to request more time, which ultimately stretched his absence from Texas into more than two years. But even this was not long enough to meet the demands of the Custis estate.

The old gentleman's will must have seemed simple enough when he drew it up by himself. Even so, it left many years of vexation to Robert. The 1100 acres at Arlington, long since fallen into decrepitude, were left to Mary Lee for her lifetime, and thereafter to her eldest son, Custis Lee. The latter's two brothers each received 4000-acre farms in the Virginia Tidewater. Rooney was to have the rather famous one once home to Martha Washington in her early years. The place, called White House, was located in New Kent County on the Pamunkey River. Young Rob Lee was given Romancoke, a plantation in King William County. Both farms were at least as rundown as Arlington.

But there was more to the Custis legacy. Each of Robert and Mary's four daughters was to receive $10,000, money that their grandfather decreed should be paid out of income from the plantations. These were profits Robert foresaw as likely as getting blood from a turnip. The only hope for finding the money was that other bits of real estate, particularly Smith's Island located near the southern tip of Virginia's Eastern Shore, might be sold. But the will was ambiguous on this.

There was no uncertainty, however, in the document's statement that each of the Custis slaves, nearly two hundred persons, should be emancipated within five years. That was the same deadline Robert was given to fulfill all the other bequests. To make his task even more difficult, Robert had to pay the debts left by his father-in-law. These amounted to $10,000, the very sum which Robert estimated would, at the least, be needed to revive Arlington. In short, the Custis will handed Robert an impossible assignment. Dutifully, he set out to comply with it.

In addition to worries over estate matters, Robert's furlough from Texas was darkened by further decay in the health of his wife. Immediately upon her father's death, Mary had dispatched a plain-spoken letter to her husband in Texas. "I will do my best, but you can do so much better," she told him, adding "it is time now you were with your family." The wretched Texas natives "are not worth the trouble and expense they have occasioned. I think now your first duty is here."

On his return, Robert was inclined at first to agree, so shocked was he by the lamentable condition of both Mary and Arlington. He prepared to resign from the army, but the nearer the moment came, the more he hesitated. Finally, he chose to keep his commission, claiming it was time sons Custis and Rooney should be drafted into family service. He arranged that Custis was reassigned to the War Department in Washington, a post which should allow him to manage Arlington. As for the other plantations, Robert urged Rooney and Chass to take possession of White House. From there, they were to look after Romancoke until Rob reached his majority.

These were only partial solutions, for Robert realized funds must be found "to build up old Arlington, and make it all we would wish to see it." This task, along with other responsibilities as the Custis executor, left Robert almost as disheartened at home as he had been in Texas. "You see what a suffering set we are," he said to Custis in May 1859, after depicting the sorry state of affairs. Mary's "great" pain especially worried him. "Your poor mother," he confided to Custis, was "a great aggravation to me at this time, especially just as I am preparing for my departure for Texas."

Some embarrassing publicity he received in the summer of 1859 made Robert all the more impatient to return to Texas. It stemmed from his decision to hire out some of the numerous slaves at Arlington, where there was not enough work for them. So inept had been Parke Custis' management of the plantation that the slaves were unaccustomed to hard work. Among the slaves put to laboring elsewhere, two, a male and female, ran away. They were captured, whereupon Robert sent them further south in Virginia, beyond the temptation to dash for a free state like Pennsylvania.

A distorted version of this story was contained in letters to the editor of the *New York Tribune,* in which Robert E. Lee was pictured as a villain disobedient to the benevolent terms of his father-in-law's will. According to these reports, sent anonymously from Washington, Robert had ordered the two fugitives whipped, and when no one would flog the young woman, he himself applied thirty-nine lashes. Just as embarrassing was the claim of another letter that Mary's father, Parke Custis, had fathered fifteen children by his slaves. Many "dark yellow" grandchildren were depicted running around Arlington. Robert refused to reply to the slander.

Such allegations about his purported cruelty to slaves were circulating when Robert's return to Texas was further delayed in mid-October 1859. In his brevet rank of colonel, Robert was assigned to lead a Marine detachment ordered to suppress John Brown. He was the Kansan who, with his followers, had occupied the federal armory at Harper's Ferry in Virginia, hoping to incite a slave insurrection. While the emergency itself was soon resolved, its investigation kept Robert near Washington for several more months.

Finally, in mid-February 1860, Lee was back in San Antonio. His absence had hardly refreshed him, leaving him pondering life's two unhappy alternatives: home and military assignment. For now, the army appeared to him the more desirable. Although pledging that his affections remained at Arlington, Robert believed he was increasingly of little use there.

In a particularly morose moment on 27 August 1860, he wrote to daughter Annie that he did not know when he would return to Virginia. "It is better, too, I hope for all that I am here. You know I was much in the way of every body, and my tastes and pursuits did not coincide with the rest of the household. Now I hope every one is happier."

Robert was not much cheered when news arrived that Rooney and Chass had named their infant son after him. "I wish I could offer him a more worthy name, a better example," he replied to Rooney. The baby must seek to build up the Lee reputation, and "avoid the errors I have committed." To cousin Anna Fitzhugh at Ravensworth he admitted: "A divided heart I have too long had, and a divided life too long led. That may be one cause of the small progress I have made on either hand, my profession and my civil career."

"While I live," said Robert, "I must toil and trust." But where and how to do so seemed increasingly to elude him and his intentions wavered. At the close of 1860 he was again out of sorts with army service. He began claiming to his children that "my few remaining years" must be devoted "to your poor mother, whom I am afraid will never be relieved from her malady, and as life advances to its close will require more attention."

Lee's renewed impatience with military assignment was owing at least in part to America's deepening sectional crisis. In November 1860, Abraham Lincoln's election as President had brought several Southern states to secede from the Union. It was a disaster that Robert had begun predicting much earlier. Well before his return to Virginia in 1857, he was commenting on the mounting political danger. His interest was itself a measure of the gravity of the situation, for Robert had otherwise rarely spoken of intellectual or political matters in his letters.

From Texas, in 1856, he had asked eagerly for news of the presidential election of that year, trusting that "the Union and Constitution [are] triumphant." Hearing that James Buchanan was chosen, Robert said: "I hope he will be able to extinguish fanaticism north and south and cultivate love for the country and the Union, and restore harmony between the different sections." To his brother-in-law, Edward Childe, Robert marveled that many persons placed no value upon the "whole country."

There should be, he insisted, "no North, no South, no East, no West, [but] the broad *Union* in all its might and strength, present and future." For himself, Robert pledged, "I know no other country, no other government than *the United States* and their *Constitution*." While penning these lofty sentiments, Robert did take care on 27 December 1856, to explain his views on slavery to his wife. As with any other serious question, he resolved it through his religious faith.

Robert believed no one could cogently deny that bondage was a moral and political evil, and that it was a greater curse for whites than blacks. Yet the blacks were much better off in America than in Africa, Robert insisted. "The painful discipline they are undergoing is necessary for their instruction as a race, and I hope will prepare and lead them to better things. How long their subjugation may be necessary is known and ordered by a wise and merciful Providence."

In Robert's opinion, there was but one solution to the presence of slavery. Only Christianity, with its "mild and melting influence," would lead to emancipating the slaves, not the "storms and tempests of lay controversy." Christianity, Lee reminded Mary, was slow but sure. "The doctrines and miracles of our Saviour have required nearly two thousand years to convert but a small part of the human race, and even among Christian nations what gross errors still exist!"

While all should pray and work for gradual emancipation, Robert was prepared to leave the outcome to God. Surely, Robert said, radicals like the abolitionists must come to see what harm they caused by their wild talk of immediate freedom. "Is it not strange," he mused, "that the descendants of those pilgrim fathers who crossed the Atlantic to preserve their own freedom of opinion, have always proved themselves intolerant of the spiritual liberty of others."

Nevertheless, the political insanity Robert had feared did come inexorably to prevail in America. By late January 1861, Lee despaired that any human deed would save the Union. While still in Texas, he announced that "God alone can save us from our folly, selfishness, and short-sightedness." In writing to cousin Markie Williams, he spoke of seeing a "fearful calamity" ahead. If it came, he would "go back in sorrow to my people and share the misery of my native state." By his doing so, "there will be one soldier less in the world than now."

For Robert, disunion could not be justified, for it meant that George Washington's "mighty labours" would be wrecked by anarchy and civil war. He assured Rooney on 29 January 1861: "Secession is nothing but revolution." The Union, he insisted, was intended to be perpetual by its founders. Robert recalled that Virginians had considered secession to be treason when New Englanders talked of it during the Hartford Convention controversy. "What can it be now?"

Dreading the answer to his question, Robert foresaw a new Union based on sword and strife, a shameful arrangement replacing the old federal system built upon brotherly love. Such an enforced Union, Lee told Rooney, would have "no charm for me." And should civil war ensue, Robert announced there would be nothing left for him but to "mourn for my country."

~ 19

The General
1861–1865

Early in 1861, and still in Texas, Robert watched what he most dreaded, an unraveling Union. Then came orders that he appear in Washington. For once, he encountered no delays in the long trip home. He arrived at Arlington on 1 March 1861, where he joined Mary in praying that "designs of ambitious and selfish politicians who would dismember our glorious country may be frustrated and that our own state may act right and obtain the result promised in the Bible to the *peace makers.*"

Robert found Mary an even more advanced cripple, while their daughters seemed to grow frailer. Custis was nearly disabled by rheumatism, and Rooney had discovered agriculture posed unanticipated difficulties. It was such a dismaying homecoming that Robert's only encouragement were signs he was approaching the end of what he considered a lackluster life. At age fifty-four he could point to a steadfast military career, but few uninitiated observers standing outside the army would see it as very promising. There was little sign at the start of April 1861 that soon Robert E. Lee would have star casting in one of history's greatest tragedies.

Lee was not impressed when he was told in Washington of his belated promotion to full colonel. He knew it was a gesture by a War Department scrambling to strengthen the loyalty of officers from the Southern states. He was more stirred when his old friend General Winfield Scott encouraged him to remain with the Union. Taking this urging to heart, Robert went across the Potomac to Arlington to think about his future and that of Virginia.

During March 1861 he spent much time alone. He told daughter Mildred, who was away at school, that he and his beloved cat Tom were solitary companions. "The puss is well but melancholy." In fact, Lee had to report an alarming sign: Tom had become very belligerent and "carries on perpetual combat. . . . His face is much scarred and he begins to look like a veteran."

When the national crisis had deepened by early April, Robert tried to keep his paternal humor. He gently reproved Mildred on her poor spelling. "I noticed that you spelt Saturday with two *ts* (Satturday). One is considered enough in the Army, but perhaps the fashion is to have two." As for the endangered Union, Robert acknowledged his thoughts were too full to say much for the moment. He did, however, make the significant observation "that the business of a soldier is to defend his country."

No one knows the extent of the struggle within Robert as he saw war approaching between North and South. He paid no heed when the Confederacy offered him the rank of major general, a further indication that Robert was waiting to see what Virginia would do. He opposed secession, deplored the presence of slavery, and cherished the Union. But these avowals were shunted aside when the subject of loyalty to Virginia arose. Emotionally, he had to dismiss an abstract Union whenever he visualized federal power laying violent hands upon the Old Dominion. Robert seemed now to speak more earnestly of Virginia as his nation and that his sense of honor required he defend "my country" against foreign [Federal] invasion.

Robert and family were stunned upon learning a Virginia convention, gathered in Richmond to consider the crisis, had voted on 17 April to adopt an ordinance of secession. (On 23 May the voters would approve the step by a margin of four to one.) Agnes told Mildred, "I cannot yet realize it, it seems so dreadful." The words probably echoed what had been the conversation during mid-April among the Lees at Arlington. Likely, Agnes was repeating dinner talk when she asserted that Virginia "had to take one side or the other, and truly I hope she has chosen the right one."

On 18 April, before he knew of the convention's decision for secession, Robert rode from Arlington into Washington where he had been summoned for what would prove to be one of the most momentous conversations held in the capital. First, Lee stopped to talk with his admired—and admiring—old commander and fellow Virginian, Winfield Scott, now general in chief of the Federal army. Scott's regard for Robert was as towering as ever. Recently, he had described Lee as the best soldier in Christendom. Proposing to assure that this talent was on the Union's side, Scott wanted R. E. Lee to be his second in command.

While there is no record of what exactly passed between the two comrades, Scott later emphasized how he had indicated that if Lee remained with the federal government and stood by "the old flag," the younger man would be placed at the head of the entire U.S. Army, subject only to Scott himself. General Scott knew that his wish had been accepted by President Abraham Lincoln and Secretary of War Simon Cameron.

After hearing this, Robert left Scott and went to visit with the President's trusted associated Francis Blair, who was authorized by Lincoln to sound out Robert's willingness to lead a Federal army, and if so, to make Lee an all but official offer of the command. Conversing with Blair in his residence across Pennsylvania Avenue from the White House, Robert heard what Scott had predicted. The president and the secretary of the army wished Lee to lead a large force—perhaps 100,000 men—then being raised to assure that federal authority prevailed across all the land. In Lincoln's view, this of course included those Southern states who now considered themselves out of the Union.

With typical succinctness, Lee later described what was said when his turn came to speak: "I declined the offer he [Blair] made me to take command of the army that was to be brought into the field, saying as candidly and courteously as I could, that though opposed to secession and deprecating war, I could take no part in an invasion of the Southern States."

The meeting between Blair and Lee remains one of those points in American history where even scholars are tempted to speculate concerning "what if. . . ?" Indeed, the lives of countless citizens on both sides of the Mason-Dixon line, to say nothing of Robert E. Lee himself, would surely have been altered if Lee had agreed to remain with the Union and accept the assignment put before him. Had he done so, the ensuing war between North and South might well have been as brief as some on both sides had expected.

After concluding the interview with Blair, Robert returned to General Scott's headquarters to report what had happened. The chagrined Scott confessed he was not surprised. Even when Scott told Lee that his decision was a fearful mistake, Robert stood his ground, though the temptation to relent must have been enormous. After all, he had been taken to a mountain-top and shown a breathtaking prospect—one in which Robert would have exchanged the recent tedium of Texas duty for command of the Republic's entire army.

Recognizing that this vista left Lee outwardly unmoved, General Scott advised him not to delay if he was bent upon resigning his commission. If Robert had any remaining reasons to hesitate, these were removed on the next day, 19 April, when he heard the by now stale news that Virginia's convention had voted to join the other seceded states. On 20 April, sitting in an upstairs room at Arlington, Robert wrote the few words by which he gave up his commission in the United States Army. He then walked down to tell his wife what he had done, after which he began letters seeking to explain his decision to relatives and friends.

One of Robert's most moving statements went to his sister, Anne Lee Marshall. With her family, Anne would support the Union cause, as did certain other members of the Lee clan. The heaviness of Robert's spirits weighed in his remark: "Now we are in a state of war which will yield to nothing." The South was undertaking revolution, he frankly conceded, adding that he opposed this step and had urged peaceful resolution of the conflict. Nevertheless, he had been compelled to decide "whether I should take part against my native state."

His letter to Anne went on: "With all my devotion to the Union, and the feeling of loyalty and duty of an American citizen, I have not been able to make up my mind to raise my hand against my relatives, my children, my home." Knowing Mrs. Marshall would disapprove of the resignation of his commission, Robert implored her to "think as kindly as you can, and believe that I have endeavored to do what I thought right." The epistle closed: "I shall love you till death." Robert also wrote to Smith Lee, saying he wished he could have talked with him again before resigning. "I am now a private citizen, and have no ambition than to remain at home."

On the next day, Sunday, 21 April, Robert was met after church services in Alexandria by several men apparently sent from Richmond to alert him that the Old Dominion wanted R. E. Lee to command the state's army as a major general. On Monday, Robert set out for the capital, leaving Arlington forever. He realized that news of his appointment had preceded him, for people gathered along the train route to chant his name as the cars passed. Upon reaching Richmond, Robert found that the vice president of the Confederacy, Alexander H. Stephens, was also there, and that Virginia had invited the Confederate States of America to make Richmond its permanent capital.

Once Lee chose to remain with Virginia, events passed beyond his management. The next morning, Tuesday, an official delegation escorted him to the capitol where he was formally notified by the assembled convention that the Old Dominion wished him to take leadership of its troops. He accepted, although slightly flustered by the praise he heard from those gathered in the House chamber. Robert made little reply except to stress his trust in "Almighty God and an approving conscience." He did not go on to remark that it was a summons by Virginia and not the Confederacy that now made him draw his sword.

For four years Robert was compelled to be apart from his family.

But his thoughts often turned to home. No matter where battle took him, he rarely failed to write to members of his family. Every interest of theirs drew his wartime attention—whether Mildred should study Latin at school; how a slave should be treated; or to which mineral spring Mary should go for her rheumatism. His letters to family members were variations on a single theme: "I am very anxious about you."

His anxiety had deepened when, soon after he went to Richmond, he learned Mary was reluctant to leave Arlington. The property's location just across the Potomac from Washington made it immediately appealing to the Federals. In the face of this danger, Mary finally agreed to flee, explaining no less than to General Scott that, were it not for the worry she would cause her husband, she would refuse to abandon her home. "I would not add a feather to his load of care."

Angrily, Mary abandoned Arlington to its fate, leaving behind much precious Lee, Custis, and Washington family memorabilia—as well as Tom, Robert's affectionate cat. Robert informed Mary that she and he had been obliged to surrender her birthplace because "we have not been grateful enough for the happiness there within our reach, and our heavenly father has found it necessary to deprive us of what he has given us." He bemoaned "my ingratitude, my transgressions, and my unworthiness."

Despite Robert's effort at humility, the thought of how Arlington had been invaded and occupied by the enemy distressed him. He managed to talk cheefully of hoping Tom the cat would lord it over the Yankee invaders who took up residence in the house. "He will have strange things to tell." Mostly, however, Robert was reduced to commenting that Arlington was now "so desecrated that I cannot bear to think of it. I should have preferred it to have been wiped from the earth, its beautiful hill sunk, and its sacred trees buried, rather than to have been degraded by the presence of those who revel in the ill they do for their own selfish purposes."

With such explosions, Robert would usually try to calm himself through his technique of self-reproach, insisting anew that because he was such "a poor sinner," God had found him "unworthy" to retain Arlington. When Mary continued to moan over the property, Robert tried to help her realize that "it cannot be helped and we must bear our trials like Christians."

After leaving Arlington, Mary and her daughters paused first at Ravensworth, but Robert warned that the Fitzhugh estate was unsafe, it being only ten miles from Arlington. He urged his brood to keep on the move. Bowing to his insistence, Mary and the others left Ravensworth (where, by the way, Mrs. Fitzhugh remained safely throughout the war) and became nomads, usually living with relatives or friends at places like Shirley, until settling in Richmond in 1864.

The loss of Arlington made Robert and his family look wistfully toward Stratford. In the summer of 1861, Annie and Agnes visited the Stuart cousins down in the Tidewater and were taken to see the house where their father was born. Probably unaware of the scandal forty years earlier involving their Uncle Henry Lee, Robert's daughters reported enjoying their visit with Betsy McCarty Storke, the widowed mistress of Stratford.

Hearing of their trip, Robert made a startling announcement: "It has been always a great desire of my life to be able to purchase it [Stratford]." Perhaps there was still a chance, he speculated. "Now that we have no other home, and the one we so loved [Arlington] has been so foully polluted, the desire is stronger with me than ever." He shared a few recollections of Stratford with Annie and Agnes, especially of the chestnut tree which he said his mother had planted.

Before he discarded the thought, Robert mentioned to Mary his wish to buy Stratford. It was, he told her, the only setting other than Arlington "that would inspire me with feelings of pleasure and local love." While Stratford was "a poor place," Robert hoped there was sufficient productive soil for his family to "make enough cornbread and bacon for our support, and the girls could weave us clothes." It seems to have been only a momentary yearning, for Robert left no further mention of Stratford.

Watching his family bounce from place to place worsened the gloom war imposed on Robert. He became annoyed with the Southern people, whom he felt displayed little sign of "self-denial and self-sacrifice." Even his own dear ones, Robert admitted, seemed oblivious that everyone must "prepare for the worst." He doubted that he and his relatives would ever be reunited. "God only can give me that happiness. I pray for it night and day," he told Annie and Agnes, and then added: "but my prayers I know are not worthy to be heard."

There was another reason why Robert's self-esteem dwindled. During the late spring and early summer of 1861 he had been ordered to remain in Richmond, which had become the South's capital. There, to his discomfiture, he had little to do as Virginia's commander. The Old Dominion's troops, along with those of other Confederate states, had passed officially under President Jefferson Davis' authority. As a sometime soldier himself, Davis craved personal control of the military campaign.

Davis handed Robert an administrative assignment. He must organize the Southern forces for battle. Thus began a year in which Robert found himself mostly obliged to stand in the wings. His doubts in his ability mounted, and he nearly lost hope that he would ever have a meaningful part in trying to save Virginia. As early as July 1861 he had shared his misgivings with Mary, even confessing that "as usual on getting through with a thing, I have broken down a little and had to take to my bed last evening."

His spirits had not lifted when President Davis kept him out of the first Battle of Bull Run at Manassas on 21 July 1861. It was "a glorious victory," Robert assured Mary, but added that he was "mortified at my absence." He urged her not to grieve for those who died. Instead, she should sorrow for those left behind. The fallen soldiers were "at rest." The living "must suffer."

And suffer Robert did, for when Bull Run did not immediately lead the South to overrun the North, an impatient public began to criticize the remote General Lee, believing it was his strategy behind the scenes that hampered the troops. Some of this carping became personal, and rumors in the fall of 1861 were saying that Robert and Mary's marriage had been shattered. An outraged Mary passed these reports to Robert, who advised her to pay "the vile slanderers" no heed. When she insisted that he publish some sort of refutation, he replied: "I am content to take no notice of the slanders you speak of but to let them die out. Everybody is slandered, even the good. Why should I escape?"

What pained Robert more than such rumors was to watch other officers given immediate command of troops while President Davis kept him at a desk pushing paper. "I do not see either advantage or pleasure in my duties," he told Mary. "But I will not complain but do my best." That remained difficult, even when a change of assignment finally came. Between August and November, Robert commanded troops in the mountains of western Virginia, where politics, weather, and poor luck led to frustration and inconclusive results.

Nor was there reason for Lee's spirits to improve in November 1861 when he was ordered to South Carolina to arrange coastal defenses. He remained at this job until March 1862, when he was recalled and given nominal authority over all Confederate military operations. Even so, Robert discovered himself still hamstrung by President Davis' determination to have the final word.

Returning to Richmond in the spring of 1862 brought Robert one deeply felt satisfaction. He was in time to sit at the bedside of a dying distant cousin, William Meade, Episcopal Bishop of Virginia. The venerable priest called the General by his first name and used his last breath to pray that success would come to the Confederacy and to Robert E. Lee.

Even with this supplication, such an outcome seemed for a time yet more unlikely. Robert announced to his family that the Southern people "have not suffered enough." Would a "merciful God," he wondered, somehow "arouse us to a sense of our danger, bless our honest efforts, and drive back our enemies to their homes." This brought Robert to think of Arlington and of his cat, Tom. He sent the good news to daughter Annie that Tom was reported alive. Would not the animal's "precious heart" break if he did not see the family soon? Rallying his spirits for a moment of teasing, Robert suggested a message of encouragement should be sent to Tom under a flag of truce. The General promised to see what could be done about getting word to the cat.

Robert was jesting about Tom in March 1862, just as General George McClellan and his Federal troops began moving into Virginia's Tidewater, having as objective the capture of Richmond. By late May, the Northern forces had overrun Mrs. General Lee's haven at White House, the old Custis farm belonging to Rooney, who was now a Confederate cavalry officer. Briefly, Mary, along with Annie and Mildred, became prisoners. Yankee sentinels were posted around their residence, but a promise of safe passage to Richmond was given to them. Admitting he was worried, Robert tried to be cheerful when he reported the capture to Agnes, who was safe. He told her "all will come right in the end, I know."

It seemed a dwindling hope. Personality conflicts, politics, vacillation in public support for the hostilities, and the emergence of a powerful Northern war machine brought the Confederate cause near to collapse in May 1862. Richmond appeared doomed as Federal troops approached the town from the peninsula to the east. Fearing a disaster was forming, Robert contributed as best he could as an administrator. In theory he had impressive responsibility, but President Davis had delegated little power to him. Davis preferred to keep General Joseph Johnston at the front opposing General McClellan.

Then, on 31 May, Johnston was wounded and Davis became desperate. Even his wife had fled Richmond. He relaxed his grip and gave Lee full authority over the Army of Northern Virginia. Robert sent a note to Mary soon after he took the field. He gave thanks "to our heavenly father for all his mercies. . . . God knows what is best for us." Then General Lee proceeded to lead the Confederate forces, recently so near defeat, to victory in the fearful Seven Days Battles. Along with his own imaginative tactics, Robert had the aid of two talented colleagues, themselves soon to be famous, Generals Stonewall Jackson and Jeb Stuart.

By devising a brilliant repulse of McClellan's army, Robert E. Lee immediately sprang to heroic stature. His deed invigorated the Confederacy. "Pa has taken the field in person," Rooney wrote gleefully to his wife. "We all expect hot work this week." Speaking for many, Rooney said "now that Pa has command, I feel better satisfied." Even Robert seemed encouraged, and hinted that the "God of Battles" just might be marching with the Confederacy. He claimed to "have seen His hand in all the events of the war. Oh, if our people would only recognize it and cease from their vain self boasting and adulation, how strong would be my belief in final success and happiness to our country."

During the year after Lee took actual command, every major military event seemed to favor the Confederate cause. There was the triumph at Second Manassas (or Second Bull Run) in August 1862. Seventeen days later brought a thrilling draw against superior Federal forces at Antietam. Then, on 13 December came the victory at Fredericksburg. After waiting out winter weather, a triumph of sorts emerged from the carnage at Chancellorsville in early May 1863. Unfortunately, at this last engagement the limited success cost Lee his trusted comrade in arms, General Stonewall Jackson, who was mistakenly shot by his own troops.

Despite this loss, which devastated Robert, many observers on both sides now believed that Lee and his Army of Northern Virginia were invincible. Even the cautious Robert was sufficiently encouraged to confide in his family that Virginia's enemies might yet be put to flight. If it proved so, he said the sole reason would be that God had forgiven the sins of the Southern people. For Robert, all events, including battles and his role in them, were disposed by a very personal Heavenly Father.

Only that same religious conviction made it possible for Lee to endure the long agony of defeat which began at Gettysburg in July 1863. The achievement at Chancellorsville had prompted Robert to gamble that an invasion of Pennsylvania would make the Northern populace demand Lincoln's government give up trying to maintain the Union by force. But it seemed that once Lee left Southern soil, his fortunes turned sour. The long engagement at Gettysburg had discouraging news before it began. Lee faced a new Federal commander, General George G. Meade, and a revitalized Northern public sentiment that had responded vigorously to Lincoln's call for volunteers on 15 June.

Fighting at Gettysburg began almost inadvertently, before Lee's troops were in the places he planned for them and thus before he was ready to issue orders for battle. Then he was poorly served by his principal generals, James Longstreet, Richard B. Ewell, Ambrose P. Hill, and others. Perhaps directed too gently by Lee, who believed his subordinates should exercise considerable discretion, these officers committed tactical blunders or were otherwise slow to follow Lee. As a result, at places held by the Federals near Gettysburg—spots bearing such immortal names as Culp's Hill and Cemetery Hill and the advantageous ground called Cemetery Ridge that crossed to another hill known as Little Round Top—the South's losses were to be enormous and unavailing.

Undone to a large extent by his commanders, General Lee was also betrayed by a personal belief which flared into passion during 2–3 July—his conviction that the capacity of his beloved Army of Northern Virginia could win once again in their righteous cause, no matter what the odds. Had they not done so before? But while Lee thus lapsed into emotion, Meade and his leaders acted with unwonted vigor and shrewdness.

The result was a tragedy for the Confederacy, culminating on the afternoon of 3 July when Lee doggedly insisted that Longstreet's men, particularly those of the three brigades under the colorful George E. Pickett, should mount another assault up Cemetery Ridge. Obediently, and with memorable valor in charge after charge, nearly 15,000 Southern men tried to reach the summit and dislodge the Yankees. They were cut down by implacable Federal artillery fire and volleys of musketry. Perhaps half of the men hurled by Lee toward the ridge were slain or wounded. Nearly two-thirds of Pickett's division were slaughtered.

By then, Lee recognized he was defeated. In a moving scene, he went out to meet those troops who could find their way down from the ridge, greeting them with the words: "It is all my fault," and adding, "It is I who have lost this fight." The Battle of Gettysburg is, of course, not so simply summed up. Even today, those who fancy military history show no sign of abandoning the long debate over whom to blame and praise on the bloody ridges and hills at Gettysburg. No one disputes the courage of those from both sides who lived and died in the horror there.

One who still causes perplexity is the Northern commander, General George Meade, who found it difficult to believe he had turned back Lee's forces. Perhaps not wishing to push his luck, Meade allowed rain on the next day, the Fourth of July, to prevent an attack on Lee's retreating army, which was temporarily trapped by the Potomac's flooding. Had Meade seized his advantage, as Lincoln begged him to, many critics believe the war would have ended much sooner.

The Army of Northern Virginia escaped, however, leaving nearly 4000 dead and innumerable men wounded or captured. In November 1863, Abraham Lincoln spoke over these Southern graves and those of nearly as many fallen Federal men. The ghastly place where President Lincoln stood, as well as his words, quickly entered the world's folklore.

The defeat was terrible for Robert, as he bore away memories of his imperfect judgments, of orders that were misunderstood or disobeyed, and of the cost in human suffering. Intensifying these torments was Robert's realization that God might not be marching with the South after all. This awareness led him into an agonizing emotional plight.

It was not enough that he felt he must offer his resignation to Jefferson Davis, who promptly refused it. What Robert could express to no one but members of his family was his suspicion that God had used Gettysburg to punish none other than General Lee himself for enormous personal sins. Taking up this burden, Robert had but one response—God's will be done.

In presenting his resignation to President Davis, Lee said contritely: "No one is more aware than myself of my inability for the duties of my position. I cannot even accomplish what I myself desire. How can I fulfill the expectations of others?" To his wife, however, Robert spoke of how God had chosen otherwise than to sustain the Army of Northern Virginia. All must bow to "His Power." Surely this "great calamity" was sent "to win us from error and selfishness."

Being able to pray that he marched with the Lord usually allowed Robert to sleep after a day of battle. However, nightfall could not silence the moans of the wounded who waited near by for someone's help. The scene ought to make us question how a compassionate person like General Lee, whose faith was in a gospel of love, could order thousands of men into certain death or hideous maiming. Then, at the next moment, this same Lee might be scribbling a letter to his daughters describing how kittens played at his feet.

Some have interpreted Lee's martial fury as another instance where a frustrated and failed personality found release in battle. However, in Robert's case, a more plausible explanation comes with remembering how compulsive he was about duty, particularly when he believed the deed was carried out under Divine authority. General Lee did not presume to face the paradox created when, as he called upon the name of a God whose self-proclaimed essence was love, he had sent men into carnage at places like Gettysburg. He seemed comfortable with a simple explanation—God's ways were inscrutable and best left as such.

Thus would the Confederate leader implore "the great God who rideth in the heavens, to give us strength and courage to do the work He has set before us, and to Him be all the praise!" These prayers continued unabated after Gettysburg, when Robert seemed to know that the cause was lost. Once, when hostilities had finally ceased, he conceded he had foreseen defeat long before anyone else. When asked why he kept silent, Robert said it was a realization which others needed to find for themselves. Watching catastrophe mounting up about him, the General had suppressed most of his anguish within a presence historians have called "the marble man."

No matter what the state of war, Robert rarely allowed his thoughts to be far from that other Divine responsibility, his family. This included more than Mary and their children. Throughout the war, Robert remained mindful of his brothers and sister. Carter, who was too old for military service, kept to his farm on the upper James River in Powhatan County. Smith served in the Confederate navy and sent three sons into the army, including the renowned General Fitzhugh Lee.

Robert's awkward family relationship remained with sister Anne Marshall, whose husband had become "a black Republican," and whose son Louis was an officer in the Federal army. While Anne supported her son and husband, she once sent a message saying she doubted the Federals "can whip Robert." Nephew Louis Marshall served on General John Pope's staff, to Uncle Robert's dismay. "I could forgive [Louis] fighting against us, but not his joining such a miscreant as Pope," Lee admitted to Mary. More than once, Robert spoke of his regret that young Marshall "is in such bad company."

It was possible, of course, for General Lee to speed the careers of his own sons, although he took pains to deflect pressure that they join his staff. Robert confided to Smith Lee that he had worked quietly to have Rooney promoted to brigadier general. "I consider him one of the best cavalry officers." Rooney rode with Jeb Stuart's famed contingent, while Custis, the eldest Lee son, had a general's rank in Richmond, where he was often ill. The youngest son, Rob, left the University of Virginia in 1862 and began a gallant career in the infantry.

On one occasion, Robert encountered Rob in rags. Like so many other Southern soldiers. Rob's main garment was a Yankee coat which he had picked up in battle. That was about all the young man owned. "He did not have a blanket and I had to share mine with him," Robert reported to Mary. "I must try and get him something." The best prospect for Rob, predicted his father, would be to have a wife to "take care of him." That being unlikely at the moment (Rob remained single for many years), Robert scrounged for the son. "I have given him a horse, saddle, and bridle to begin with."

Robert's endorsement of marriage for his sons came from his own love of domesticity. Even though he might carry the demeanor of a great military leader, General Lee remained a paternal figure of manifest tenderness who wished his family near by. After observing that his staff officers "have no fondness for the society of the old General. He is too sombre and heavy for them," Robert told Agnes "I would give them all up if I could have my daughters with me and their mama."

He always begged for mail from home, and not merely for the news it might contain. To Mildred, who spent much of the war at St. Mary's School in Raleigh, North Carolina, he pointed out that "our letters are good representations of our minds. They certainly present a good criterion for judging the character of the individual." This truism makes all the more valuable the cache of Robert's wartime letters to his wife and daughters.

The women in the Lee family were the persons to whom Robert most often wrote, for he viewed his wife and daughters as a special obligation. While he might praise the fortitude of Southern women in an abstract way, Robert rarely saw Mary or their daughters as more than childlike. In part, this came from worry at Mary's crippled state. The dominant theme, therefore, in his letters to his daughters continued to stress their calling in life: "You have a sacred charge, the care of your poor mother." Even after they were well established in spinsterhood, Robert usually referred to his daughters as "our little girls."

Where he often wished aloud that Custis and Rob would find wives, he never spoke of husbands for his daughters, though they were now adults. Instead, Robert continuously reminded these young women of how he and their mother loved and depended upon them. When, early in the war, he heard that "poor little Agnes," (who had passed her twentieth birthday) was facing "an amorous widower [who] had been making sweet eyes at her through his spectacles," Robert sent word that she was "not to distress herself. Her Papa is not going to give her up in that way." Instead, the father wrote to Agnes, who was troubled by facial neuralgia, that he yearned "to kiss you on your poor little face" and "keep away the pain."

So far as we know, Agnes was Robert's only daughter who came close to marriage. In late 1862, she was pursued by her erratic cousin Orton Williams. Though she was attracted to him, she resisted because of his impetuous style. Family legend says that General Lee mistrusted Orton and discouraged the romance. If so, he had good reason. Orton had a madcap military career and was executed as a spy in Tennessee on 9 June 1863, leaving Agnes, according to her relatives, forever subdued. It was an understandable response to the discovery that, at the time of his death, Orton was romancing the wife of another soldier.

Affectionate though General Lee was, the strain of wartime occasionally pushed him to become a bit impatient as a husband and father. He could be irritated when he heard complaints from his family, and he was quick to rebuke any sign of self-indulgence among them. He did not wish his family to be like the rest of the civilian population, whom he charged was always striving after what was most agreeable to personal feelings.

His daughters must perceive, said Robert, "that a life of idleness in times like these is sinful." And when, during the excitement at Chancellorsville, Mary scolded him for not writing, Robert responded with as much bluntness as he ever allowed himself with her: "I see . . . you are relapsing into your old error, supposing that I have a superabundance of time and have only my own pleasure to attend to." Assuring her that he constantly thought of her, Robert implored Mary not to be "always expecting letters from me." He liked to close with the admonition: "Arm yourself with patience and resignation."

One member of the family did not survive the war. Annie died of typhoid fever on 20 October 1862 at age twenty-three. She, along with her mother and sister Agnes, were summering at Jones Springs in North Carolina, not far from the Virginia border. Through Mary's letters, Robert learned that Annie died in a wonderful manner. The stricken daughter's last request was for the hymn entitled "In Extremis," and her final breath had said: " 'I am ready to rise.' "

The report nearly broke Robert's stoic manner. "In the quiet hours of the night, when there is nothing to lighten the full weight of my grief, I feel as if I should be overwhelmed." But he took consolation in realizing that God had mingled mercy with the blow by taking from them "the one best prepared to leave us." Reminding Mary that Annie was spared life's miseries, Robert conceded "I cannot wish her back."

Annie's death represented only one of many domestic calamities that Robert had to shoulder during four years of fighting. His triumphs against McClellan in June and July 1862 had been overshadowed by news of his grandson's death. The little namesake, child of Rooney and Chass, had died of an intestinal disorder, despite grandmother Mary's instructions that the infant should be kept in a "belly band" and ". . . have his stomach rubbed with laudanum." Robert tried to rejoice that the tot was now with the "bright angels." "Oh, what a happy condition."

For Rooney and Chass, the loss was the first of several sorrows. Their plantation, White House, was reduced to ruins by the Federal forces, a catastrophe which brought Rooney, in trying to reassure Chass, to sound much like his father. The destruction of their farm and the death of their son were punishments, Roooney told his wife, "for my many and daily sins." This meant, Rooney said, "that I am the murderer of my boy."

Within a year, Rooney was reduced to writing from captivity. He had been wounded in late spring 1863 and brought to his in-laws' plantation, Hickory Hill, in Hanover County, where Federal troops came upon him. Despite his injury, Rooney was carted off for nine months of imprisonment. Robert tried to get word to his son to be steadfast in prayer. The only refuge was "in Him, the greatness of whose mercy reacheth unto the Heavens." To Chass, Robert urged that she have faith "it will all come right in the end."

But Chass did not live to see her husband's release. Robert kept encouraging her in the summer and fall of 1863, always calling the young wife "you precious child." By year's end, tuberculosis carried her off. Chass was buried in Richmond's Shockoe Cemetery in the Wickham family plot. Beside her were not one but two infant children. Said Robert: "What a glorious thought that she has joined her little cherubs and our angel Annie in Heaven!" Writing to Mary, Robert saw that, "link by link [is] the strong chain broken that binds us to earth, and smooths our passage to another world." He insisted God had taken Chass in order to prepare the family "for a better and brighter world."

The General's preoccupation with a life hereafter came at least in part from his own weakened health. A keen observer of his physical decay, Robert added this to the list of reasons why he should reproach himself. "How great is my remorse at having thrown away my time and abused the opportunities afforded me," Robert told Mary. "Now I am unable to benefit either myself or others, and am receiving in this world the punishment due my sins and follies." As usual, this was quickly followed by the closing exclamation: "But God's will be done!"

His gravest illness was in April 1863, during which Robert admitted the pain in his chest, along his arm, and across his back was dreadful. Nevertheless, he tried to be cheerful, assuring Mary that he had been moved from the tent, where he always insisted on sleeping, to a house. There people in the Fredericksburg area brought him apples, butter, turkey, ham, and an endless array of other things rarely seen in wartime. "So it seems to me I had better remain sick," Robert teased, except he dreaded the many visitors who presented the goodies to him. "You know how pleased I am at the presence of strangers, what a cheerful mood their company produces," he reminded his family. "Imagine then the expression of my face and the merry times I have."

Instead, Robert wished only to have "my little Agnes" as a nurse. She might make him feel less "oppressed." To Agnes, he did his best to be jolly, were she with him, she would soon make him better. "You could have taken all my pills [away] and kept the doctors off me." If she joined him, Agnes must come alone, Robert teased. His "pins" were a bit unsteady, "and the vigorous and violent movements of young women might knock them from under me."

Looking back, today's medical opinion usually concludes that, along with narrowing arteries, the General's immediate disorder must have been acute pericarditis. The disease permanently weakened him. In 1864, Robert admitted to son Custis: "I feel a marked change in my strength since my attack last spring at Fredericksburg, and am less competent for my duty than ever." How particularly discouraging this was, he said, when Grant's arrival in Virginia meant everyone must "put out their strength." Preparing for what would be the South's final stand, the General told Rooney, who was released from captivity in 1864, that "if victorious, we have everything to hope for in the future. If defeated, nothing will be left for us to live for."

Since Mary had finally agreed to settle in one spot, choosing Richmond in 1864, Robert now had an occasional chance to visit at her little rented house in Clay Street. Mary's rheumatic sufferings were such that she could "scarcely move." She lived with Agnes, Mildred, and a squirrel. The creature became a worry to General Lee, who, amid the din of battle, sent orders that the family must get rid of the pet. He was certain it would turn vicious. "Immerse his head under water for five minutes," he admonished Mildred. "It would relieve him and you of infinite trouble." The family resisted the advice, so that the squirrel, named Custis Morgan, was tolerated much longer than Robert wished.

The animal even bit a doctor who was calling on Mary. Robert pointed out how much better it would have been had Mary followed instructions and eaten the squirrel. The nourishment might have rendered medical attention unnecessary, as well as sparing the doctor pain. Surely, Robert argued, the pet could now be turned into soup for wounded soldiers. "It would be most grateful to his feelings to be converted into nutritious aliment for them and devote his life to the good of the country." However, Custis Morgan escaped such a fate by fleeing captivity, probably with Agnes' help.

To Robert's satisfaction, Mary and her daughters began a useful project in Richmond. They joined in knitting socks for the woefully bedraggled Confederate troops. It was a task they carried out with astonishing zeal, shipping stockings in enormous numbers to Robert's personal attention. By the General's orders, they were immediately distributed throughout the army.

Robert rewarded his family's effort by trying to cheer Mary with thoughts of what might lie before them. "I trust there is some place, some quiet, and some comfort in store for us. And that the evening of our lives may be cheerful and happy together." On Mary's birthday, in the swiftly darkening time of October 1864, Robert insisted that "though afflictions have befallen us," God had sent the Lees many fewer hardships than blessings. He begged his wife to trust in the Lord, and even quoted lines from a favorite hymn—". . . be strong and he shall comfort thine heart; and put thy trust in the Lord."

Of course there were still moments when Robert helped his own flagging morale by his pretence of being a ladies' tease. As late as January 1865 he sent messages via his wife urging that several Richmond damsels of his acquaintance visit him. He wanted one and all to know that "when tired of their beaux, they had better come and see me." He promised pictures of himself to those who could not reach Petersburg, a town about twenty miles below Richmond, where the General was directing the Confederacy's last stand.

Lee and his army had been pushed to Petersburg as a consequence of punishing assaults by General U.S. Grant's forces during several weeks of battle above Richmond in late spring of 1864. These engagements had taken a fearful toll on both sides, to which Grant seemed reconciled. In March, he had assumed supreme command of Federal forces and, with rank as lieutenant general, he set out with his Army of the Potomac to pulverize the badly outmanned Army of Northern Virginia. Robert had foreseen what was to come and implored a kinsman to pray for the Confederate forces. Ahead was "a great struggle" and only God's "might to deliver" could "drive its [the South's] enemies before it."

The ensuing fighting was the most brutal of the war. The first encounter, 5–6 May 1864 and called The Wilderness, proved indecisive, thanks to Lee's shrewd maneuvering. Despite heavy losses, Grant pursued Lee to Spotsylvania where, between 8 and 12 May, Lee again skillfully averted defeat, bringing Grant's famous pledge to "fight it out along this line if it takes all summer." Finally, on 3 June at Cold Harbor on Chickahominy Creek, Lee's troops took 12,000 Yankee lives, once more staving off the inevitable.

In a month, Grant had lost more than 60,000 men. While this was nearly twice Lee's casualties, the proportion of human devastation in the dwindling Southern ranks was about the same. The implication was grave, for unlike the Federals with their vast reserve capacity, the Confederacy could not hope to recover from these engagements. It left General Lee dreading the next phase of the war.

Stymied in the Wilderness campaign, Grant chose now to besiege Richmond, intending first to take Petersburg, a transportation center below the capital, thereby separating Richmond from the lower South. Again, Lee and his men managed to forestall the result of this strategy, forcing a siege of nine months to begin at Petersburg in mid-June. Perhaps it was time to pause. The previous seven weeks of conflict had such bruising effect upon Grant's army that it was near exhaustion. But the price Lee paid for this advantage was high. His famed and essential mobility was gone forever and his men were severely wounded.

As the confrontation at Petersburg began, Robert knew the war's close was not far off. He had grown accustomed to commenting after each of the earlier battles that God must be praised "for having sustained us thus far." But now he began often to talk of how the South "must suffer patiently to the end, when all things will be made right."

From the winter of 1864–65, those family letters that managed to survive show Robert speaking almost wistfully of his hopes for what could come from "peace with ourselves and peace with our enemies." Let the reverses suffered by the Confederacy reveal how weak mankind was, Lee urged. Let defeat teach of humanity's dependence upon God. "We must bear all that an ever loving God inflicts upon us, until he is graciously pleased to pardon our sins." Armed with this outlook, the General prepared for the close of hostilities.

~ 20

Final Valor
1865–1870

As the war approached its end, Robert tried to encourage Mary. Admitting that Grant's forces "seem to have everything their own way," he said the Confederacy must trust "a Merciful God, who does not always give the battle to the strong." He offered no prayers for victory, acknowledging that his supplications could only be "that we may not be overwhelmed." Not mentioning how he was outnumbered at Petersburg nearly three to one, Robert merely assured Mary that he would, as always, "do my duty and fight to the last."

With winter turning into the sorrowful spring of 1865, Robert's letters home became the merest notes as he tried desperately at Fort Steadman and Five Forks to repel the Federal power. He placed Mary in the care of brother Smith Lee, who was no longer active in the war, telling them "we can only toil and trust." God could be relied upon to "do all things right." Taking what was left of his army, about 35,000 exhausted hungry men, Robert abandoned Petersburg on 2 April. Forced to allow Richmond to fall, he headed southwest toward Danville, where he thought another show of resistance might be possible.

Grant and his men quickly foiled Lee's last strategy, compelling him to turn for Lynchburg. Along the way, Lee steadily lost troops to weariness and the enemy. On 6 April, a quarter of what remained of the Army of Northern Virginia was captured and much of Lee's pitifully few supplies were destroyed. The next day, after Grant suggested Lee should surrender, the two commanders began an exchange of notes in which Lee showed that he understood his plight: he was virtually surrounded and outnumbered six to one.

Rejecting pleas from his men that they scatter to become guerrilla bands ("We would bring on a state of affairs it would take the country years to recover from," Lee replied), the General made his famous decision: "There is nothing left for me to do but go and see General Grant, and I would rather die a thousand deaths."

In one of the most famous encounters in American history, U.S. Grant and R. E. Lee met on 9 April in the living room of Wilmer McLean's residence in the hamlet of Appomattox Courthouse. The astonished McLean had sought refuge there after a Federal shell had plowed into the dining room of his former home near Manassas. Now he saw the victorious Yankee leader enter somewhat bedraggled, Grant having been unable to change his dusty garments and muddy boots. Paradoxically, the defeated Confederate commander was regally outfitted. Lee had donned his dress uniform and wore a sash and jeweled sword. As the historian James M. McPherson has put it—thus "the son of an Ohio tanner dictated surrender terms to the scion of a First Family of Virginia." It was nearly 4:00 p.m. when it was all over.

The conditions offered to Lee were generous, and the two generals shook hands and exchanged salutes when they departed. Later, Grant wrote how saddened he had felt "at the downfall of a foe who had fought so long and valiantly and had suffered so much for a cause, though that cause was, I believe, one of the worst for which a people ever fought." Meanwhile, Lee rode away from Appomattox Courthouse pondering what he had once ardently believed was a cause uniting God and the Confederate States of America. The contrasting views of the two commanders would survive to divide America for generations beyond 1865.

Later that afternoon, as the concern and dismay of his troops brought him to tears, Lee required time to recover his steady demeanor. There were further visits with Grant, George Meade, and others from both sides of the now completed conflict. The next day, 10 April, Lee signed the final General Order announcing the surrender. Through it, Robert praised the Army of Northern Virginia, assuring his men that they had yielded only to "overwhelming numbers and resources." Praying "that a Merciful God will extend to you His blessing and protection," General Lee concluded: "I bid you all an affectionate farewell."

On 12 April, Robert began the ride back to Richmond, pausing to spend one night with brother Carter Lee at his farm in Powhatan County. Carter's house was small, so Robert insisted upon sleeping one final time in his tent. Then Rooney joined him the following morning, 15 April, and the father and son rode into Richmond, where the Union flag flew over the capitol. Astride Traveller, Robert passed among throngs of citizens turned out to welcome him. He took off his hat repeatedly to acknowledge the tears and cheers that were the public's greeting. Finally, he reached 707 East Franklin Street, where Mary and his daughters awaited him.

Then began the last ordeal for General Lee, as he endured the months and years after surrender. Robert's faith, the core of the man, was now sorely tested by the failure of a cause he believed God had summoned him to lead. While he never intimated he felt forsaken by his Heavenly Father, Robert showed less inclination after the war to pronounce upon Divine intentions. His devout outlook, however, was unchanged, and he prayed steadfastly that God might help "all our afflictions."

When he did speak of the South's defeat, it was usually to remind others of how the war had been a "struggle for States rights and Constitutional Government." To General George W. Jones, Lee allowed himself to say more than customary in a letter of 22 March 1867. "We failed, but in the good providence of God, apparent failure often proves a blessing. I trust it may eventuate so in this instance."

Only to his family could Robert talk of the Confederacy's fall as it affected him personally. He told Mary in autumn 1865: "Life is indeed gliding away and I have nothing of good to show for mine that is past. I pray that I may be spared to accomplish something for the benefit of mankind and the honor of my God." To cousin Markie, Robert was unusually candid. "I am considered now such a monster," he reported to her after he made a trip to Washington in April 1866, "that I hesitate to darken with my shadow the doors of those I love lest I should bring upon them misfortune." As for the "censure" he received from others, Robert said it was "so much lighter than what I inflict upon myself, that it fails in its object."

Troubled by what he felt was the unhealthy state of America's public and political morals after 1865, Robert prescribed a nationwide reading of the Bible. From this "the greatest good would be accomplished." He told Markie in December 1865: "I prefer the Bible to any other book. There is enough in that, to satisfy the most ardent thirst for knowledge, to open the way to true wisdom, and to teach the only road to salvation and eternal happiness." Markie had been seeking without success to have Robert read *Imitation of Christ* by Thomas à Kempis.

The defeated General welcomed civilian life, and occasionally conceded that "[I] find too late that I have wasted the best years of my existence." So long as his dear ones were nearby, he assured brother Smith Lee in 1866: "I should be perfectly content to be with them, where I could make my daily bread, 'the world forgetting, by the world forgot.'" Again and again, Robert expressed the wish to find a quiet farm and there gather his wife and daughters. Always mindful that his worsening health would not allow him long to live, he thought that a bit of land would be the best provision for his family once he was gone.

For a time after Appomattox, the Lees had no idea where they might find refuge and peace. Arlington had been officially lost to the family on 11 January 1864, the cause being unpaid taxes. The federal collectors, of course, had not cared to accept Confederate dollars. Elsewhere, Rooney and Rob faced their own cruel ordeals, trying to rebuild their farms at White House and Romancoke from the wreckage left by the tramp of Northern armies. As for Robert and Mary, their assets were few. The once-commander of the Army of Northern Virginia was not much better off than many of his troops who returned home destitute.

Looking at his plight in May 1865, Robert announced: "We must be resigned to necessity and commit ourselves in adversity to the will of a merciful God as cheerfully as in prosperity. All is done for our good and our faith must continue unshaken." Mary caught the spirit, and asserted that though "our poor unhappy South . . . seems well nigh annihilated," she was certain that "God can raise her from the dust. To Him alone can we look for aid and succor." Robert expressed admiration for his wife, whom he said the war had made "cheerful and uncomplaining, always employed in aiding others."

Of course help for the Lees did come, and from many quarters. There were opportunities of employment for Robert, all of which he rejected as schemes to use his name injudiciously. One act of generosity especially stirred the family. This came from John Stewart, who owned the sizable house which still stands at 707 East Franklin Street in Richmond. This was Mary's last residence in the capital and the place to which Robert returned from Appomatox in April 1865. Stewart implored the Lees to occupy the house as long as they wished. He wanted no rental payment, but if they insisted, he would accept only Confederate money.

Stewart spoke for the South when he wrote to Mrs. Lee: "You do not know how much gratification it has and it will afford me and my whole family—during the remainder of our life, to reflect that we have been brought into contact and to know and appreciate you and all that are dear to you." The Lees declined the offer, realizing there would be little peace for Robert in the fallen Confederate capital. In June, they moved to an area west of town in Powhatan County. There, friends had made available a small farm called Derwent. Ironically, the place was situated on the Lynchburg highway, along which Robert had recently traveled when he returned from the surrender.

At Derwent, Robert wrote to Rooney reminding him of how they must await whatever prosecution the federal government might inflict. He wished there would be no procrastination, for he was impatient to move west with his family "to some humble but quiet abode." Unfortunately, Washington's attitude toward Lee remained ambiguous.

There were rumors in May and June 1865 that a federal grand jury was preparing to indict ex-General Lee for treason. These stories determined Robert to apply on 13 June to President Andrew Johnson for pardon under terms the President had recently announced. In asking for "full restoration of all rights and privileges," Lee was convinced that he, along with the other men paroled after surrendering on General Grant's terms, was due a pardon and not prosecution.

Furthermore, Lee believed that when he himself approached the federal government for pardon, he was dramatizing the importance that all parties adhere to the conditions and spirit of the surrender arrangement—which clearly implied that for parolees there would be no indictments and no trials. Lee consulted Grant before making application to the President, and received the victorious General's full endorsement of the plan. Grant himself wrote to President Johnson urging that Lee be pardoned.

The upshot was inconclusive. There was no indictment of Lee (as there would be of Jefferson Davis), but neither was there a pardon. Increasingly, hatred and retribution dominated the outlook of Congress, led by voices from a so-called Radical Reconstruction faction. The federal government was thus powerless to deal gracefully with one who had commanded rebellious armies, as well as with the South at large.

To worsen matters for Robert, his application for pardon left many of his former soldiers bewildered, hurt, or angry. That their old leader should have thus approached the federal authorities seemed to them an admission of wrong-doing. Lee's last years were darkened not only by the continued uncertainty and controversy over his status, but even more by the new animosities in both North and South fostered by what would be an increasingly harsh treatment of the defeated region by Congress.

During these anxious days, Robert continued to ponder the best place to settle his family. However, his quaint dream of becoming a yeoman farmer never grew beyond an abstraction. Wistfully after 1865, Robert often pictured in his mind the "grass country, where the natural product of the land will do much for my subsistence." He may have been recalling the fertile plains of the Midwest, which he had so admired when he was stationed in Missouri thirty years before.

It was probably just as well that nothing came of these day-dreams, given Robert's enfeebled health and limited experience with agriculture. Instead, his record as superintendent of West Point, along with his belief that education would be vital in reviving the South, led him to accept the presidency of Washington College, then a modest institution for young males situated in the mountain community of Lexington, Virginia. It was the school where Robert's half-brother Henry had briefly enrolled. Admitting to Rooney that he really did not relish the work or the location, Robert said that, for now, the appointment offered a way "I might be of some service to the country and the rising generation."

After pledging to Mary that he would not linger in Lexington "if I find I can accomplish no good," Robert arrived at the college early in the autumn of 1865. He faced not only his work as president but also arranging accommodations for Mary and their daughters. The first assignment, that of getting school under way, he found manageable. But securing a residence for his family proved more difficult. The remainder of 1865 was half comedy, half exasperation, as the great General Lee roamed around Lexington, trying to find lumber, carpenters, and plasterers who could renovate the house provided by Washington College for its president.

Locating workmen and materials was difficult enough. More taxing for Robert, as he lived in a hotel and ate its fare, was the good humor needed while the temporary occupants of the president's house, a family named Madison, took their time about getting out. The Madisons seemed glued in place, and Robert had to keep reminding Mary, back at Derwent, "we shall have to be patient." The only consolation was that Custis Lee had come to teach mathematics in the Virginia Military Institute, also located in Lexington. He took his meals at the hotel with his father.

Finally, on 2 November, in a driving rain, the unfortunate Madisons vacated the presidential residence, and Lee ordered his hired hands into the battle against decay and dirt. Robert did all he could to arrange matters to suit Mary, but he could not gratify her demand that horses be purchased for the daughters to ride. It would be pleasant to keep a stable, Robert acknowledged, but Mary was reminded that "horses do not live on air here, nor do they wait on themselves."

The college president's pay was small, so that the Lees would have barely enough money for existence. Neither they nor the college had any furniture to put in the house. Mary had been obliged to leave nearly everything behind when she fled Arlington in 1861. Consequently, most of the house's contents which greeted Mary when she reached Lexington in early December was arranged by friends. Mildred accompanied her mother, and brother Rob came along to help with the move and to try to recover from malaria.

For a time, neither of the other sisters, Agnes and Mary, was in the new home. Agnes was back in Richmond attending a wedding, while Mary continued her near-perpetual absence from the family circle. Even so, there were more than enough Lees at hand to make Robert feel he was once again surrounded by domesticity. He described to Agnes what was going on around him during a typical Lexington evening: "Custis is promenading the floor, Rob reading the paper, Mildred frocking her dress. Your Mama is up to her eyes in news, and I am crabbed as usual."

Life in the academic village was almost quiet enough to suit Robert. What excitement there was came from such novelties as the campaign to raise money for the struggling Episcopal parish. "You know the Episcopalians are few in number and light in purse," Robert reminded Mildred. As fund-raisers, they must therefore "be resigned to small returns." The Lee women took pleasure in the town's reading club, although Robert attended only once, observing: "As far as I can judge, it is a great institution for the discussion of apples and chestnuts, but is quite innocent of the pleasures of literature."

He found more comfort in the companionship of the family's cats. There was now another Tom, much admired by his master. Always eager to salute man or beast who obeyed the demands of duty, Robert commended Tom for "strict attention to the pursuits of his race." In fact, the pet was also called the Nipper, arising, Robert explained, "from the manner in which he slaughters our enemies, the rats and mice." The rodents were less pesky after a new house was soon built for the presidential family.

None of these familial comforts, however, did much to diminish Robert's wish to leave Lexington as soon as feasible. The impulse was assuredly not because he failed as a college head. Indeed, the General was exemplary as he sought to be patient with student ways. "Ease and pleasure are incompatible with success" was the lesson Lee preached to many young scholars. Nevertheless, he confided to Rooney in 1867 that he planned only one more year at the College, as he dreamed again of having the family on a small farm. He would look for "some spot east of the mountains."

Robert's restlessness came mostly from his worry over owning nothing in Lexington that could support his family when he died. He stressed often that he must prepare a place for his wife and daughters where they could live "after my death." In the same spirit, he tried tightening the bonds he hoped might keep Agnes and Mildred attentive to their mother once he departed. The young women, who were then nearing or past thirty, were addressed diminutively, as of old. Robert called his favorite daughter "my precious little Agnes."

When either Agnes or Mildred managed to escape Lexington for visits, their father trailed them with notes that spoke ruefully of their desertion. He liked to describe his "getting very old and infirm," and to insist that each daughter must "come to her Papa and take care of him."

These sentiments did not include Mary, the eldest female child. Robert's concern for this footloose woman was clearly genuine, but he displayed little of the possessive affection for her that he demonstrated toward the younger daughters. Mary may have recognized this, for she destroyed all her father's letters, many of which must have been models of gentle reproof.

The possibility that Agnes or Mildred might someday marry was a subject their father rarely mentioned cheerfully. To Mildred, who visited Baltimore during much of 1866, Robert admonished: "Experience will teach you, that not withstanding appearances to the contrary, you will never receive such love as is felt for you by your father and mother." The father's motives were doubtless mixed when he urged Mildred: "Do not go out to many parties, pursue your simple tactics and manners, and you will enjoy more pleasure. Plainness and simplicity of dress, early hours, and rational amusements I wish you to practice."

Mildred was advised to avoid novels and other unrealistic treatments of life. Instead, she should read history and "see the world in its true light." Whatever the effect of this grim advice, Mildred soon returned to Lexington and dutifully gave her considerable energies to managing the Lee household. She ruled everyone, her father observed, "and scatters her advice broadcast among the young men of the college."

Then came an alarming development. Robert learned in the fall of 1868 that Mildred was striving to be a successful domestic manager because she believed "a good house is an effective card in the matrimonial telling." Surely, Robert said wistfully, "she is building a castle in the air." The comment was a contrast to those Robert sent to his youngest son, Rob, who was struggling to turn Romancoke into a productive farm. "You must get a nice wife," the father ordered in August 1867. "I do not like you being so lonely. I fear you will fall in love with celibacy."

Lee went on to admonish that Rob choose a mate carefully, "otherwise you had better remain as you are for a time." Then came the General's warning: "An impudent or uncongenial woman is worse than a mink." When Robert heard that Rob was courting Charlotte Haxall, whose parents were close friends of the Lees, he approved heartily and began to help, if that is what one can call his teasing of the young lady about how much competition she had for Rob's attention.

The romance moved slowly, and "Lottie" Haxall did not consent to an engagement with Rob until the summer of 1870. By then, Robert was more certain than ever he had few days left to live. "I already love you as a daughter," he told her, "so I can do nothing more than beg you quickly to become so, for I have but little time to wait."

Fortunately, Robert had been able to attend the wedding of Rooney, who had decided to exchange his place as a widower for one as husband beside Mary Tabb Bolling, a woman from Petersburg who was well known to the Lees. The venerable General claimed he went to the nuptials in late November 1867 much against his best judgment. "I shall be dreadfully in the way." If anyone was underfoot, it was the masses of citizens in Petersburg who gathered for a glimpse of Robert E. Lee.

One of the Lee cousins said that when the train bearing Robert reached the outskirts of Petersburg, it became part of "a triumphal procession." There was a band and an open carriage to haul the hero, every step accompanied by "deafening cheers." The next day, it was claimed that 2000 souls pressed into the church, less to witness the ceremony than to be present with General Lee. Another thousand remained outside craning for sight of him.

This attention did not wholly displease Robert, although he frowned at the elegance of the reception afterwards, observing: "You would have thought we knew nothing of hard times." Even so, he endured the festivity good-humoredly, regaling the guests with amusing tales. This was Robert's means of coping with his awkward sensation when he found himself facing a crowd of strangers. Despite the tactic, his relatives noticed an air of sadness about him.

Among Lee's stories, one was said to have been a favorite with those standing around him. It told of a horseback trip Robert and Agnes had taken the previous summer into the mountains south of Lexington. When evening fell, the only refuge at hand was the cottage of an elderly woman. She refused to take them in, despite Agnes' pleas. Later, upon learning it was General Lee she had turned away, the mortified woman explained that she had a good reason to refuse the strangers. Seeing Robert and his daughter at her door, she had thought "it was an old gentleman with a sprightly young wife, and she had no place that would suit them."

Rooney took his young bride down to White House, where he was slowly restoring the old Custis farm. With a touch of envy Robert saw them go. Their new daughter-in-law, he reported to Mary (who had not attended the wedding), was "in that happy state which causes her to take pleasure in doing what she thinks he [Rooney] prefers." With Robert, it was often the other way around. Each summer, Mary insisted on being taken to one or more of the watering holes among the hills near Lexington and implored Robert to come along. He spent as much time with her as he could, seeing little benefit in the mineral baths.

It was not that Robert particularly disliked the water. He dreaded the press of people encountered on these excursions. Since many were unknown to him, he felt he must treat them with special courtesy. On the other hand, Mary enjoyed the endless talk with friends, relatives, and strangers. She had become the greatest lady in Virginia, and she made the most of it, even in the winter when she could not be taken outside. In those months she toiled at what she made into a sort of cottage industry—sending photos of "the General," as she now loftily called Robert, to all who applied for them. Her husband drew the line at the incessant requests for locks of his hair. To this Mary reluctantly agreed, conceding that he had little enough for himself.

Wherever he appeared, of course, Robert created a sensation. Only the duty of accompanying his wife, with her "shattered constitution," to places of her choosing led him into society. He reminded every relative within earshot of how much he preferred a solitary afternoon ride on his horse Traveller. These were the only times, he said, where he could be alone with his thoughts. Otherwise, he had to be patient with the prattle of people, including a cousin of Mary's who, Robert complained, was always cornering him "with some anxious question on her mind, upon which some weighty, though to me hidden importance depends."

On the other hand, most kinfolk were welcomed by Robert, and on those occasions after 1865 when business carried him to Alexandria, he regretted that the crowds of admirers kept him from quiet chats with his cousins. When there was time to talk, Robert enjoyed reminiscing. He recalled a trip he took as a school boy with his mother to Philadelphia. He found new pleasure in the story that George Washington had married Martha Custis in the modest residence on the White House farm inherited by Rooney, and he deplored how the house had been burned by the Federals. The only newspaper Robert read was from Alexandria, choosing it because it carried him "back to old days."

He took a new interest in the Lee genealogy, depending, as all family members did, upon the statements made by William Lee when he had lived as a merchant in London. This version of the family's origin had been carefully preserved by William's daughter, Portia Hodgson, and Robert drew upon it after 1865 when answering the many requests he received for the story of his ancestry. Always stressing he was a "poor" genealogist, Robert replied as best he could, which meant he innocently added errors to an already cloudy record. He opposed plans to publish a Lee genealogy, calling for the money to "be applied to relieve the poor."

But not all family matters were pleasant. Robert and those around him still grieved over the loss of Arlington and its precious relics. While the place continued under federal control, the Lees hoped it might somehow be retrieved. Eventually, Custis Lee, to whom his grandfather had bequeathed Arlington, received a financial settlement by act of Congress, although Robert and Mary did not live to see this modest gesture. Since then, with its encirclement of graves, Arlington has brooded over the federal capital and particularly the memorial to Abraham Lincoln that sits just across the Potomac. In time, Lincoln's spirit of reconciliation was reborn when Arlington House itself became a national memorial to Robert E. Lee.

To the end of his life, Robert sought doggedly to meet the unfulfilled provisions from the will of his father-in-law Custis. Certain tasks had been completed. The Custis family slaves had been freed in December 1862, meeting one of four major stipulations of the will. Two others were accomplished when Rooney and Rob Lee took possession of the ravaged remains of the farms left to them by their grandfather. But in 1868, Robert fretted that the will's remaining proviso seemed out of reach. This ordered that $30,000 be divided equally among Robert and Mary's daughters, Mary, Agnes, and Mildred. Annie's legacy had reverted to the estate when she died in 1862.

Grandfather Custis had directed that his grand-daughters receive their legacy from the income of the farms given to the grandsons, a prospect which even then seemed remote. Alas, when the boys took over the places, only the bare ground remained, everything having been carried off by the Yankee invasion. Nothing resembling profit from these properties was in sight, making Robert anxious. "My life is very uncertain," he reminded Rooney, and he was impatient to see the daughters paid. After all, he observed, the task was a sacred duty.

Even so, the assignment continued impossible, even after a brighter moment when Robert learned in October 1868 that the remaining bit of Custis realty, Smith Island in the Atlantic, was to be sold at public auction for payment of delinquent taxes. Hoping that if he regained this land, it could be turned over at a profit, Robert directed his sons to try to buy it. There was no competition, and title was returned to the Lees for the minimum price of $10,000, of which the family had scraped together only a thousand in cash. Sympathetic Northampton County officials extended credit for the balance. The heroic effort, however, did nothing to pay the three sisters. A disgusted Robert discovered that, while indeed the island could now be sold, it would yield, at most, $5000 of the $30,000 needed.

The Custis will would likely have been an invincible assignment for its executor in the best of times. Given the circumstances in 1868, Robert had to be reconciled that in this instance he could be forgiven for failing in a duty. And besides, what scant spare time he had was increasingly taken up by a very different family responsibility, one which had been handed to Robert after he was reunited with Carter and Smith Lee.

Since sister Anne Marshall had died in 1864, the trio of brothers was all that remained of Light-Horse Harry and Ann Carter Lee's children.

On his return to Richmond after the surrender at Appomattox, Robert had camped for the first night on Carter's farm. Perhaps during that April evening, Carter may have begun urging that the younger brother must now take an interest in preparing a new edition of their father's memoirs. Carter, it should be remembered, saw himself as a poet and man of letters.

In 1858, he had published a volume entitled *Virginia Georgics,* which included a section on Stratford. Here Carter reported how the youngsters of Thomas and Hannah Lee, including future signers of the Declaration of Independence, had romped "in their childhood's glee." To edify the practical-minded, Carter went on to describe in poetic detail how pigs were fed with offal taken from Stratford's garden.

It seems the Lee family story was rarely out of Carter's mind, making it plausible, once the Civil War ended, that he should call upon Robert to join in one last literary effort on behalf of their forebears. Carter believed that Robert's prominent name would bring distinction (and sales) to a fresh printing of Light-Horse Harry's memoir about the American Revolution which he had written while in debtor's prison.

Furthermore, Carter aimed to incorporate in such a new edition the sermon-like letters his father had sent from the Caribbean islands. These were the epistles Harry had stored in a trunk and which did not reach Carter until many years later. Believing the letters would enhance the book as well as their parent's reputation, Carter successfully stirred Robert's interest in the project by describing how Light-Horse Harry had "raised himself above his sufferings" to pen these epistles. When Carter informed Robert that by these letters their father had hoped to inspire a love of truth, Robert must have heard a special summons to join the editorial project.

While Robert could scarcely remember his father, Carter, who was nine years older, sounded convincing as he recalled the "grandeur" of their father's soul. According to Carter, Light-Horse Harry Lee had been "exalted by the noblest studies," and "sanctified by the holiest affections." Thus, using the care ordinarily reserved for sacred texts, Carter handed to Robert the choicest items from their father's West Indies letters.

Editing Light-Horse Harry's memoirs had not been Robert's first choice as an author. Rather, he wished to write the story of the Civil War in Virginia. "To give a truthful history of the hardships, services, and heroism of the Army of Northern Virginia is now the only tribute to their valorous devotion," he said in July 1865. But the sources were unavailable, for Robert's papers were either lost or scattered.

Consequently, it proved much simpler for him to go along with Carter's plan and bring out a new printing of their father's work. He also agreed when Carter announced that publishing Harry's letters in this new edition of the *Memoirs* would allow these exhortations to become "blest in themselves, and by their beneficial influence a blessing to others."

Several visits with Carter added to Robert's interest in the project and to his amazement that his brother, now sixty-seven, seemed inclined to make up for his late start in marriage by continuing to produce offspring. Reporting to Smith Lee, Robert said in January 1866: "Carter I believe is very well, though I think he has made a mistake in the number of his children. He speaks of his last little daughter as the 'seventh child' and I can only make her out the sixth. Perhaps he is projecting another." Less amusing were Carter's requests for an appointment as professor of history and literature in Washington College. "I do not think it would suit you," Robert finally replied. "The labor is too constant and unceasing."

One of Carter's tasks was to keep Robert assured that a new edition of their father's recollections would be well received. Robert warned his brother that he feared "in the present excited feelings which rage in the country," something with R. E. Lee's name appended would only add to the furor. For this reason, and because he had so many other chores, Robert dallied over his share of work on the edition. The strain of duties as college president were more than enough. Mary reported in May 1867 that, despite Robert's eagerness to complete the edition of Harry Lee's memoirs, he was so steadily busy "he has but little time to bestow upon them."

When the edition was finished in 1868, it suffered from a hasty and uncritical approach, dominated as it was by Carter's adulatory view of Light-Horse Harry. Nor did the work escape error. For example, it pictured all the children of Stratford receiving much wealth from Thomas Lee, news which would have astonished Colonel Phil's brothers and sisters. Another novel claim was that only Harry's love of farming kept him from accepting a command in the French Revolutionary army.

Generally, however, there was little such personal detail in the biographical introduction, for Robert asserted that, as editor, he had omitted from the book many stories about his father because he believed "the mass of readers would only be interested in the main facts." There were a few discerning passages, as when Harry's petulant resignation from the army in 1782 was acknowledged due as much to "care and anxiety of mind" as any disease of the body.

The edition said nothing, of course, about the family's financial disasters, so that Harry's final departure from Stratford was pictured as a selfless move so that life in Alexandria could improve the education of his children. For Carter, the triumph of the book must have been the generous excerpts from Harry Lee's epistles and to read that, as editor, Robert had considered them to be "letters of love and wisdom," imbued with "the sublime doctrine of the immortality of the soul."

While Robert and Carter worked to elevate the memory of their father, their nephew Fitzhugh Lee had the awkward assignment of negotiating with a family who claimed that a forebear had captured an English officer's sabre in the Revolution and then sold it to Harry Lee. The problem apparently was that Harry had never paid for it, and descendants of the seller now demanded the sabre's return.

Fitz Lee along with his parents Smith and Nannie Lee and their other children were favorite visitors in the president's house at Washington College. Smith had married Anna Maria "Nannie" Mason in 1834. The two had become parents seven times. They had the enormous satisfaction of seeing their eldest son, Fitz, rise to a place among the war's finest general officers. Winning many admirers, including his Uncle Robert, Fitz Lee went on to become one of Virginia's most popular governors and then to take an important part in the Spanish-American War. He was the only former Confederate general officer ultimately to earn a similar rank in the U.S. Army.

Smith Lee died in July 1869. Like so many other Southerners, he had entered hard times at the close of the war. His last years were spent struggling to make something productive out of a stubborn old farm in Stafford County. Smith suffered at length from what was considered a liver ailment, but died so suddenly that Robert had no warning, and arrived too late to attend the funeral in Alexandria.

His brother's death made Robert speak of "a sad gap in our family." Losing Smith was " a grievous affliction to me which I must bear as well as I can." He reminded Mary that the event should "prepare us all for the time when we too must part the one from the other, which is now close at hand." And indeed it seemed so. Robert's suffering from heart disease had worsened. By the time Smith died, the frail General's angina pain troubled him even at rest. It ran along his breastbone, across his back, and down his arms. He could not walk with comfort the short distance from his residence to his office in the college chapel.

His condition brought Robert to tell Markie Williams: "My interest in time and its concerns is daily fading away and I try to keep my eyes and thoughts fixed on those eternal shores to which I am fast hastening." Urged by family and friends, he consulted many doctors, but he had no confidence in their encouraging talk. The science of cardiology was in its infancy, so that most doctors diagnosed Lee's condition as an "adhesion of the lungs and pleura" and assured him that his heart was sound.

Actually, Robert's heart was starving, for the arteries that fed it must have been virtually blocked. A century later, sufferers in Robert's condition could renew life through the surgical procedure called a coronary bypass. But for Robert, there was no hope, and he realized it. Nevertheless, he was a co-operative patient, even obeying the doctors in March of 1870 when they insisted he travel south to seek the comfort of an earlier spring season. Tolerantly, Robert remarked to Mildred: "I know they [doctors] do not know anything and yet I have often had to do what I was told without benefit to myself, and I shall have to do it again."

Taking Agnes with him and escorted by one of his former aides, Robert set out in March for Savannah. He consoled himself that the junket would at last allow him to visit the grave of daughter Annie in North Carolina. "I wish to see how calmly she sleeps away from us all," Robert told Rooney. He visualized "her dear hands folded over her heart as if in mute prayer, while her pure spirit is traversing the land of the Blessed." Annie's burial spot was seen, and Robert also paid his respects, this for the second time, at Light-Horse Harry's grave on Cumberland Island. But there were few such quiet moments along the journey.

General Lee's excursion has become a legend. He was loudly cheered, wept over, and universally greeted by throngs everywhere. There was in Lee's noble presence apparently such consolation for the multitudes as to help them bear knowing the War for Southern Independence had failed. Wherever the train passed or stopped, crowds were standing at any hour and even in heavy spring downpours. They chanted "Lee, Lee, Lee," as the hero was carried past. The result was little recuperation for the ill man, and Robert often expressed regret that he had left home.

He took no consolation when physicians in Georgia endorsed the diagnosis that his affliction was "adhesion of the parts and not from any injury from the lungs and heart." Why, then, Robert wondered, did the pain sometimes keep him awake. He grew more eager to be back in Virginia.

In early May he returned, arriving in Norfolk for what proved the most moving event of his journey. When his hosts suggested that the General attend Sabbath services, Robert found the route he walked from the house to the church was lined by a silent multitude. Most of the spectators stood reverently and weeping as their hero painfully trudged to worship and then returned, where the crowds waited to see him again. Each man along the way removed his hat as Robert passed.

There was less rest than anticipated when Robert was back in Lexington. Instead of being left alone according to his wish, he was hustled once again into travel, this time for more medical consultations in Baltimore. As Robert reported to his family, the summer heat nearly finished him. His pain was so great he could not visit his sister-in-law Nannie, Smith's widow. Then, when he was once again at home, he learned he must depart for the mineral springs, where some advisers believed his "rheumatic attack" would be helped.

Robert bore it all patiently, counting the days until fall when he expected to be left in peace. He wrote one of his last letters from Hot Springs on 22 August 1870 to his nephew, Edward Lee Childe. Dismayed by the outbreak of the Franco-Prussian War, Robert said he did not foresee that arbitration would replace force in international controversy. "We are not yet ready for such an elevated art and must butcher and slaughter each other I fear for years to come."

In the late afternoon of 28 September, soon after returning to Lexington, Robert slowly walked through a drizzle to a vestry meeting at the Episcopal Church, located not far from his residence. Then the General managed to get back to the house for supper. He seated himself at the table and undertook to say a prayer, but he could not speak. He had been silenced when one of the clogged arteries to his brain apparently ceased to function. Death did not come immediately. Robert lingered, bedfast, until the morning of 12 October. His family, Virginians everywhere, and all the South stood watch.

Many took it as a sign when the region endured an endless rain storm, which halted only as Robert died and his body was carried to lie in state at the college chapel. A cadet from the Military Institute came over to pay his respects to the famous man he had often seen around town. He found the corpse difficult to recognize. "He looked to be reduced to half his original size, and desperately thin." It was hard to believe that the General was only sixty-three.

Robert's death left Carter Lee as the last to survive. He was now seventy-two and drifting into senility. Many of Robert's garments were taken to Carter for his use, causing the old man to burst into tears. The clothes were not needed, for Carter died early in 1871. Mary worried that his many children were now "rather helpless." Of herself, Mary wrote in the last entry to her journal, dated 6 December 1870: "I am left to pursue my weary pilgrimage alone."

However, Mary reminded herself that Robert had provided something very special for his family. "What a name and inheritance he has left his children." One of these offspring, daughter Mildred, who carried on as manager of the Lee household, grew indignant over the picture of her father chosen for display around the mournful South. Why, she wondered, must everyone use the photo taken late in life when he was ill?

"I can't bear Papa in those horrid black clothes," Mildred complained. "He was a soldier from first to last, and should wear the dress of a soldier." Nor was the face of illness fair to him, she insisted. Then, saying more about her beloved "Pa's" character than she may have realized, Mildred pronounced what can stand as Robert E. Lee's most searching benediction: "He kept his suffering locked up in his great heart and it did not show in his face."

EPILOGUE

At the Chapel

A Lee crypt was prepared on the ground floor of the chapel at Washington College. Robert's remains, and eventually those of his family, were interred there. An effigy of General Robert E. Lee was placed at the front of the chapel sanctuary. The sculptor, Edward Valentine, depicted a recumbent figure in full uniform, ready at any moment to rise and take command.

The college was promptly renamed Washington and Lee University, and Robert's son Custis was appointed his father's successor as president. Then, for a time, life in Lexington went on much as usual for Robert's survivors as they continued to use the presidential residence on the campus. Mary, the Widow Lee, lived for three more years, writing innumerable letters eulogizing her husband and his impressive manner of dying. In her last months, she was able to do a bit of visiting, even at Arlington, that "dear old home." She found it "so changed," and was perplexed that heaven "seems to smile on the desecration."

In October 1873, Agnes succumbed to the tuberculosis which had plagued her life, and soon thereafter, her mother died. Both were buried beside Robert in the chapel crypt. Custis continued as college president until 1897, dutifully cared for by Mildred. When they retired, the brother and sister went to live at Ravensworth, that familiar estate not far from Arlington. The property had been bequeathed by Aunt Maria Fitzhugh to Rooney who, with his family, had settled there.

Rooney died in 1891 during his third term as a congressman. Mildred lived until 1904, while Custis went on until 1913 and Rob until 1914. All were buried alongside their parents. In 1918, the nomadic sister Mary was the last of Robert's children to be entombed in the crypt. Earlier, the remains of Light-Horse Harry and Ann Carter Lee had been brought from Cumberland Island and Ravensworth and reinterred in Lexington.

By the time the family was thus united in death, Robert E. Lee had been enshrined as a national hero. Over the years, thousands of visitors have come to the Lee crypt to honor the Confederacy's great general and his family. Yet this popular regard was slow to gather. For an interval after 1870, Robert's repute was nurtured mostly by reverent veterans of the Confederate army. Some of Lee's associates published memoirs of the hero, although ultimately the best of these would be written by the General's son Rob.

Unfortunately, there was a bit of unseemly quarreling among the faithful as factions in Virginia competed to monopolize the choice of a memorial. Consequently, it was from France that some of the loftiest praise for Lee was first heard. In Paris, the late hero's nephew Edward Lee Childe published a volume which predicted that "in our age [where] there is a want of *character*," Robert E. Lee's "great soul" would soothe and fortify mankind's conscience. Childe asserted that never had there been "a nobler soldier, gentleman, and Christian."

While this refrain would soon be taken up by numerous books and articles, in Childe's time it seemed that as soon as faithful kinsmen and soldiers had vanished, the General, like other controversial Lees, would be mostly forgotten. But then, after awkward delays in raising funds and deciding upon a location, Virginia's memorial to Robert E. Lee was erected. In 1890 a splendid equestrian figure of him was dedicated at a circle dominating Monument Avenue in Richmond. There, he and Traveller were made to face south toward the region where, if in any locale, Robert's fame might be expected to linger.

Soon, there was much more than provincial fame. An international appreciation of Lee arose, due in large measure to the 1905 visit in Richmond of the admired man of letters, Henry James. An American who lived in England, James had stopped in Virginia's capital while touring the country for observations which he later published as *The American Scene*. He found the city to have "the invalid gentleness of a patient who has been freely bled." That would have remained James' impression, except he happened to see the Lee monument before leaving town.

James was delighted by Lee's statue, calling it a "precious pearl of ocean washed up on a rude bare strand." He said it drew a "strange eloquence" from its isolated location. According to James, the Lee figure had "a kind of melancholy nobleness," as it "looks off into desolate space." All around it was the city of Richmond which, James asserted, displayed "the irony of fate."

Viewing Lee's likeness, towering above all that Henry James considered so depressing in Richmond, the author had a brilliant insight. Lee's posture, Henry James said, suggested "a quite sublime effort to ignore, to sit, as it were, superior and indifferent . . . so that the vast association of the futile for the moment drops away from it." Years before James wrote, those who saw Robert on his solitary rides near Lexington might have reached a similar conclusion.

It required another Yankee visitor in Virginia to complete the elevation of Lee's repute. The occasion was an observance of the Centennial of Robert's birth, a memorable event taking place on 19 January 1907 in the chapel at Washington and Lee University. As the orator for the day, the college faculty and its president passed over several surviving Confederate figures to choose a New Englander who had fought against Lee's army across much of Virginia.

They picked Charles Francis Adams II, great-grandson of John Adams. At first glance, it might seem a dubious selection. Not only had Charles Adams served courageously in the federal army, but his regiment of black troops had been the first to occupy Richmond after the capital had been abandoned by Lee. Furthermore, Charles' father, Charles Francis Adams I, stood in stature next to Abraham Lincoln among the civilians who had worked to override the secession of Virginia and her sister states.

Despite these apparent demerits, Charles Adams offered much that the College believed recommended him as the best orator for the Lee birthday celebration. As a prominent public speaker, Adams had pioneered in praising Lee. During an address of 1901 in which he condemned the Boer War going on in South Africa, Adams recalled how, in 1865, America had been spared much similar devastation when General Lee did not follow a stubborn Jefferson Davis' desperate last order to begin guerrilla warfare. Adams then concluded his speech by asserting it was time "to set forth the debt of gratitude this reunited country of ours—Union and Confederate, North and South—owes to Robert E. Lee of Virginia."

In 1902, Adams enlarged his Lee tribute when he spoke to the University of Chicago's chapter of the Phi Beta Kappa Society. His theme was Lee's courageous loyalty to Virginia in 1861. Adams claimed that the issues before the nation at that time were much more complex than many persons could appreciate. According to Adams, Lee's decision to remain with Virginia displayed "all that goes to make up the loftiest type of character." Like George Washington in 1776, Robert E. Lee stood with his native province in 1861. Both of these great men, said Adams, had allowed conscience to guide them.

Expressions like these made Charles Adams seem to officials of

Washington and Lee University as a speaker who would be divinely inspired about General Lee. Adams' enlightened outlook, along with the
credentials of his own great family name and his brave military service,
made him appear the perfect orator for the Lee Centennial. Hastening
to invite Adams to make the address, the president of Washington and
Lee assured him that his appearance would make the occasion "a notable
one in the history of the country." Joseph Bryan, president of the Virginia Historical Society, sent the speaker advance thanks, predicting that
Adams would be known as "the discoverer of the true General Lee."

Charles Adams arrived in Lexington carrying an address seventy pages
in length. Under a cloudy sky and punctually at 11:00 a.m., the platform
guests marched into a chapel filled with veterans of the Civil War. First,
the audience sang Robert's favorite hymn, "How Firm a Foundation,"
and then heard it announced that there was "no more splendid spectacle
in human history" than the celebration under way. After an effusive
introduction, Adams arose to speak and (as Charles noted later in his
diary) the mountain mists began to lift.

His oration lasted one hour and a quarter, with sunlight bursting
into the room just as he reached his warmest tribute to Lee. It was strength
of character, Adams said, that carried Lee nobly through agonizing decisions in 1861 and 1865. This sublime behavior was possible, the speaker
contended, only because of Lee's untarnished life, because of his devotion to his family, and because of his deep religious faith.

Adams then depicted how desperately twentieth-century America
needed a person like Robert E. Lee as its leader. According to the orator, Lee was one of those rare persons who had the wind's power, while
ordinary individuals were like grass, bending with the breeze. In this
spirit the oration continued, so that before he sat down Charles Adams
had seemed to picture Lee as human perfection, a glorious example for
America.

After the speech was concluded and another hymn sung, the congregation burst into such applause as to astonish Adams. Then Confederate
veterans rushed up to shake his hand, bringing him to admit privately
how gratifying it was to be among "so many good people—so simple,
straightforward, and genuine." It made their "absolute adoration" for
Robert E. Lee a profound inspiration, Adams noticed. Two days later,
Adams left Lexington, accompanied to the railroad station by the entire
student body. He stood on the train's rear platform waving as the young
men, who, "shouting and cheering," swarmed after the car. How "decid-
edly agreeable" it all was, Charles confided to his diary.

There was to be even more satisfaction for the orator. The Centennial address had been widely circulated, so that letters of commendation

from around the nation soon reached Adams at his country estate near Lincoln, Massachusetts. Some correspondents claimed that, thanks to Adams, there now was a "re-born Union," while others spoke of a restoration of friendship between "Puritan and Cavalier."

Mary Lee, Robert's daughter, announced that all her friends were calling Charles Adams the greatest man in America for having brought the entire nation reverently and humbly before her father. Indeed, it was an astonishing feat. An old warrior himself, Adams had converted a Confederate general into civilization's hope by arguing that Lee's gentle, loving, selfless virtues must somehow recapture America.

While Adams' demand that the nation emulate Lee's qualities apparently was asking too much, his decree that Lee be admired drew an awesome response. Since that call went forth on 19 January 1907, the American public habitually approaches R. E. Lee in a spirit verging upon reverence—as in the case of the puzzled youngster who is said to have come home from Sunday School to ask a parent whether the story of General Lee was found in the Old Testament or in the New.

Many years ago, an explanation for this phenomenon was attempted by Lee's greatest biographer, Douglas Southall Freeman. After a lifetime of pondering the Civil War, Freeman concluded the ordeal was "an adventure that mercifully ended in failure, though it gave us a blessed history of valor for the enrichment of all American souls." Particularly for Lee, Freeman asserted the war became "a drama of ill-fortune nobly borne, and in that way a triumph of character over catastrophe."

The story of the Lees between 1640 and 1870 seems at times to be little more than a succession of catastrophes challenging the family's character. More often than not, their responses became triumphs of a sort. Like Robert E. Lee, Alice Lee Shippen and Hannah Lee Corbin transcended their plights through spiritual inspiration. Their grandfather, Richard Lee the Scholar, took similar consolation when he was buffeted by Bacon's rebels and then by disease. The Revolutionary brothers—Arthur, William, Frank, and Richard Henry—relied upon fraternal commiseration to sustain them as their political viewpoint fell before adversaries.

Clearly, it was the fate of many Lees, perhaps the most notable of them, to stand alone, estranged from their times. In this they were much like the Adams family. One difference was that of temperament. The Adamses could be detached and deeply rational. The Lees were passionate and eager for involvement. How ironical, then, that it was left for Charles Adams to advise that American civilization build its future in the spirit of General Robert E. Lee.

Yet with all of this bountiful regard for Robert Lee, few of his admirers have detected that special quality setting him apart from other members of his clan—and from most of us. It came from a quiet achievement which, more than his military attainments, should command our admiration and affection. Unlike the biblical figure of Job, Robert did not quarrel when God seemed to forsake him. Instead, he quietly accepted defeat and despair, while trusting Heaven to make all things work eventually for good. By patiently serving and hoping, Robert E. Lee gave America its greatest lesson in valor.

Acknowledgments and Sources

By the time an author gets to this point in writing a book, the task should be light-hearted. Usually, it has been so for me. This essay, however, begins on a note of regret. With the end of my writing about the Lee family, I close some associations that have become more than just helpful. I shall miss seeing these new friends. My indebtedness for assistance and encouragement is as broad as the subject.

My largest obligation speaks in the dedication of this book. The courage to begin came from Mary Tyler McLenahan (then Mrs. Leslie Cheek, Jr.). She knew the hazard of such an undertaking, having watched her father, Douglas Southall Freeman, write a masterful biography in four volumes of Robert E. Lee. After inspiring me to write about the Lee family, Mrs. McLenahan then introduced me to her colleagues on the Board of Directors of the Robert E. Lee Memorial Association, the foundation that maintains Stratford Hall Plantation and the Jessie Ball duPont Library, located at Stratford. In 1986, that organization established fellowship support for me, while encouraging other foundations to aid in the cause.

Therefore, I am deeply grateful to the Board of Directors of the R. E. Lee Memorial Association. Their backing and confidence in my work have been essential and humbling. I am also thankful to the Councillors of the Lee Associations who provided a timely grant for my aid. Now it remains to hope that no one will be disappointed in what their support has wrought, for I alone am responsible for this interpretation of the Lee family.

Two additional foundations gave financial assistance. Without their help I would not have been free to put other work aside and concentrate upon the Lees. One of these is the Jessie Ball duPont Religious, Charitable, and Educational Fund. The second is the Clisby Charitable Trust, formerly the Flagler Foundation. I offer my thanks to the officers of these two organizations.

Visits to Stratford brought me a sense of the place that abounds with Lee memories. I worked happily among the Association's collection of manuscripts, always made welcome and offered all the help I could use. I appreciate the kindness shown by John F. Wall, executive director of the Robert E. Lee Memorial Association, Thomas E. Bass III, emeritus director, and the Association's staff. I thank particularly Elizabeth M. Laurent, formerly curator and associate director, Barbara H. Jones, the Association's secretary, and Judy Hynson, assistant curator.

For a variety of reasons I am obliged to C. Vaughan Stanley, librarian and historian for the duPont Library at Stratford. I shall not soon forget the expedition he guided into the Northern Neck as we searched for ancient Lee burying grounds. Owing to him, we found them.

This book would still be under way were it not for the aid I received from Jeanne A. Calhoun, research scholar at the duPont Library. I have benefited from my conversations with her about the Lees of Stratford and have drawn heavily from her scholarship and insight. I found much of value in her unpublished essay on Thomas Lee. Several times she brought a manuscript or other source to my attention that I might otherwise have missed, and she cheerfully ran errands for me at Stratford when I could not readily do so. Jeanne Calhoun represents the historical profession at its best.

Stratford is by no means the only place where I have been met with much kindness. There is space here to mention only the most extraordinary obligations. To Mr. and Mrs. R. Carter Wellford who preside over Sabine Hall, another great house in the Northern Neck, I offer my thanks for their encouragement—especially on that afternoon when Carter led me through green pastures to find the grave of Francis Lightfoot Lee. The master of Sabine Hall obviously inherited the kinder side of his awesome forebear, Robert "King" Carter.

Among the present-day descendants of Richard Lee and Anne Constable, the family's founders in America, Nora Lee Antrim gave me freely of her library and has never failed to supply me with her special variety of good cheer. I cherish my friendship with General Lee's granddaughter, Mary Custis Lee deButts. For their kindness, I thank Marga Lee Mahoney, Catherine Lee Davis, and Fitzhugh Lee III.

I'm widely obligated to many fellow biographers and historians. My conversations with Emory Thomas of the University of Georgia have saved me more than one misstep. His one-volume biography of Robert E. Lee, when published, should fill an important need in an admirable way. Richard W. Slatten, prince among Virginia genealogists, has been a sure-footed guide through several uncertainties. It was he who brought my attention to the recent discovery of Richard Lee I's parents.

Much gratitude goes to Graham Hood, vice president and Carlisle H. Humilsine Curator of the Colonial Williamsburg Foundation, who helped me so generously from his unrivaled knowledge of portraits and painters in Virginia and England during the seventeenth and eighteenth centuries. I also thank Virginius C. Hall, Jr., associate director of the Virginia Historical Society, for his counsel as I chose illustrations, and for much other assistance. I'm greatly obligated to Howson W. Cole, senior librarian of the Virginia Historical Society for his patient advice when I was fretting about the location and extent of Lee family manuscripts. My good friend and neighbor, Lauren A. Woods, M.D., enlightened me about the medical complaints expressed by some of the Lees.

The Lee manuscripts are widely scattered, but the major collections can be found in five depositories. I have already mentioned that there are valuable resources in the duPont Library at Stratford Plantation. The largest aggregation of Lee papers, however, is held by the Virginia Historical Society, whose research staff has been never-failing in its helpfulness. In addition to Virginius Hall and Howson Cole, I must thank Frances Pollard, Robert Strohm, Waverly K. Winfree, and Linda Leazer.

The manuscript department in the University of Virginia Library has wonderful collections bearing upon the Lee family. I'm grateful to Edmund Berkeley, Jr., the curator of manuscripts and archivist of the University for his encouragement and help. I owe a similar debt to James H. Hutson, chief of the Manuscript Division of the Library of Congress, for his guidance as I used that Division's invaluable Lee, Shippen, and Collins papers.

Other important collections are to be found in the Virginia State Library and Archives, and in the libraries of Washington and Lee University, Duke University, the Colonial Williamsburg Foundation, the Massachusetts Historical Society, and the City of Alexandria, Virginia. The staffs of these institutions have my gratitude.

Celeste Walker, one of the editors of the Adams Papers at the Massachusetts Historical Society helped me locate Lee material in the Adams collection and to track down Carter Lee's record at Harvard. She has aided me often in the past and always it is a pleasure to thank her. Another special obligation is the one I owe our son Jeff Nagel. Variously an artist, curator, and art historian, he has given me his excellent advice concerning illustrations for this book, and particularly in preparing the map.

Four persons to whom I am deeply indebted are at Oxford University Press. Sheldon Meyer, senior vice president for the editorial division, has guided all of my books published by Oxford, which means that our friendship and collaboration extend beyond three decades. What I owe him for his wisdom and kindness through those years is more than I can express here. Nor can I adequately thank Leona Capeless, whose renowned talent and patience as an editor did not flinch before the challenge of my manuscript. Working with her has been rewarding and pleasant. I'm also very grateful to two other valued friends at Oxford, Marjorie Mueller and Joellyn Ausanka.

Fortunate indeed am I to know Richard and Eleanor Hankins. Not only have they been keenly interested in my work, but they have allowed me to use as the frontispiece for this book the portrait of General Lee which Dick's relative Eugene A. Poole painted from life in December 1865. I am deeply grateful to Mr. and Mrs. Hankins for allowing this portrait for the first time to be admired by the public.

While my wife Joan Peterson Nagel contributed much more than spouses usually do to my previous books, this one made even heavier demands, so that Joan's presence in these pages is everywhere. Again and again, I had to impose upon her talents as a librarian, a genealogist, and an intelligent reader. It was she who prepared the genealogical chart for the book's endpapers. And in sharing my endless ruminations about the Lees, Joan exemplified what the word "helpmate" means.

Despite all the aid I've received in writing this book, errors may remain in it. If so, the blame for them rests entirely with me.

Now, some comments about the sources for the Lee family story. As I have said, the important manuscript collections repose in various locations. The duPont Library at Stratford has a share of the surviving volumes of William Lee's letterbooks, and has gathered copies of Philip Ludwell Lee letters. It has a fragment of Colonel Phil's letterbook, as well as a copy of the remarkable exchange of letters between Henry Lee IV and Dr. James Mayo. There is also a Lee family collection containing a miscellany of letters. Some by Mrs. Robert E. Lee are particularly important, as are others in the E. J. Lee Collection and the Laird Collection. More generally, Stratford's library has materials concerning the history of Westmoreland County and the Northern Neck.

Most of the sources for this book were drawn from the manuscript collections of the Virginia Historical Society in Richmond. The Society's card catalogue has many trays devoted to Lee family material, most of it in seventeen Lee collections, of which the Lee family papers is the largest. Other major groups include the Arthur Lee papers; the George

Bolling Lee papers, which have many Custis family items; the Richard Bland Lee papers; the Henry Lee III (Light-Horse Harry) papers; the Henry Lee IV papers; and last, but by no means least, several vast collections of Robert E. Lee papers, both official and private. The Society has the larger share of William Lee letterbooks. Recently, it was given Agnes Lee's girlhood journal.

Additionally, the Society possesses many collections parts of which bear significantly upon the Lee family. The Peckatone Papers offer the only means of recapturing Hannah Lee Corbin, but they also contain useful documents relating to Henry Lee IV. The Talcott Papers have important Robert E. Lee materials. The Ludwell Papers are useful for the Green Spring story. Another collection features Elizabeth Collins Lee holograph material as well as typescript copies of letters from the library of the National Society of Colonial Dames of America. The George Harrison Sanford King Papers are now at the Virginia Historical Society, bringing the life's work of a distinguished genealogist and local historian. Included are valuable insights about the Lee family, their relatives, and their friends.

The Society's reading room is the place to study rare editions of published works by the Lees, of which the memoirs of Light-Horse Harry, along with the edition by Robert E. Lee, are especially important. Not to be overlooked is Henry Lee's attack on Thomas Jefferson and his apotheosis of Napoleon. A volume of Charles Carter Lee's poetry is also available.

In Charlottesville, the University of Virginia library has rich holdings of Lee family material. First, however, I should applaud the library's publication in 1966 on microfilm of *The Lee Family Papers, 1742–1795,* edited by Paul P. Hoffman. The set comes with a useful guide which explains how in eight reels the edition draws together Lee papers, most of which were once possessed by Richard Henry Lee II. He chose to allocate these among Harvard University, the American Philosophical Society, and the University of Virginia. Besides bringing these together, the edition has a few items scattered among the Historical Society of Pennsylvania, Yale University, Minnesota Historical Society, and the Library of Congress. As filmed, this extraordinary collection contains most of the manuscripts that survive from Thomas Lee, Thomas Ludwell Lee, Richard Henry Lee, Francis Lightfoot Lee, William Lee, and Arthur Lee.

Many unfilmed collections are at the University of Virginia, several of which are indispensable for writing about the Lee family. To be prized among these is the Jessie M. Fraser Papers, containing the results of a career devoted to research about Arthur Lee. Contents of the following collections comprise a splendid variety of Lee material: F. W. Gilmer

Papers; P. R. Fendall Collection; E. J. Lee Papers; Stuart Family Papers; Coles Collection; McGregor Collection; Cocke Family Papers; and the Elizabeth Collins Lee Papers. The University of course has several collections under the general designation of Lee family correspondence.

From the University of Virginia, the path leads to the Manuscript Division of the Library of Congress with its Richard Bland Lee Papers, Shippen Family Papers, and the Stephen Collins Papers, all vital in the story of the Lee family. Fortunately, the voluminous Shippen papers are available on fifteen reels of microfilm. The Division also has a variety of scattered Lee items.

The Massachusetts Historical Society in Boston owns a small number of Lee documents, and a huge quantity of Adams family material wherein a number of Lee letters are found. Also present, of course, are the helpful diaries of John and John Quincy Adams, as well as epistles from the Adamses to members of the Lee clan. All of these can be consulted on the microfilm edition of the Adams Papers or, in some cases, in the letter-press edition of the Adams Papers being published by Harvard University Press.

Back in Virginia, the State Library and Archives has on microfilm the Charles Carter Lee papers, a collection essential to following the career of Henry Lee IV, Ann McCarty Lee, and Carter Lee. (The originals are deposited in the Manuscript Division of the University of Virginia library.) The State Library and Archives also has an important and varied assortment of Lee family letters, including the letterbooks of William Hodgson, husband of Portia Lee. The archives and library of Washington and Lee University in Lexington have helpful items concerning General and Mrs. R. E. Lee. Finally, a trip to the library of the Colonial Williamsburg Foundation in Williamsburg is sure to be both rewarding and pleasant. Its collection has material of value for the eighteenth-century phase of the Lee family's career.

Some of the Lee family manuscripts have been printed, but these usually are handicapped by many deletions. Largely of antiquarian interest are Richard Henry Lee II's *Memoir of the Life of Richard Henry Lee* (Philadelphia, 1825), 2 vols.; and *Life of Arthur Lee, L.L.D.* (Boston, 1829), 2 vols. Quite another matter is the charming genealogical study by Edmund Jennings Lee (ed.), *Lee of Virginia* (Philadelphia, 1895). While it is out of date and incomplete, it contains copies of wills and many other documents otherwise difficult or impossible to find.

James Curtis Ballagh edited in two volumes *The Letters of Richard Henry Lee* (New York, 1911). While useful, his work omits much. An even more guarded approach must be made to Worthington C. Ford (ed.), *Letters of William Lee* (Brooklyn, 1891), 3 vols. Helpful, but no substitute for reading the original diary is Ethel Armes (ed.), *Nancy Shippen, Her Journal Book* (Philadelphia, 1935). Fortunately, the highest professional care went into Clifford Dowdey and Louis Manarin (eds.), *The Wartime Papers of R. E. Lee* (Boston, 1961), although letters have been omitted which the editors deemed duplications.

A charming and helpful work is Mary Custis Lee deButts (ed.), *Growing Up in the 1850's. The Journal of Agnes Lee* (Chapel Hill, 1984). Many of Robert E. Lee's most revealing letters are printed in Avery Craven (ed.), *"To Markie"* (Cambridge, Mass., 1934). Two intimate views of R. E. Lee from family members are: Robert E. Lee [Jr.], *Recollections and Letters of General Robert E. Lee* (New York, 1905); and Edward Lee Childe, *The Life and Campaigns of General Lee* (London, 1875, translated from the French by George Litting). Some of Robert E. Lee's letters not found elsewhere are cautiously included by William Jones, *Life and Letters of Robert Edward Lee* (New York and Washington, 1906).

Other valuable printed manuscripts include that priceless glimpse of eighteenth-century life in the Northern Neck, Hunter D. Farish (ed.), *The Journal of Philip Vickers Fithian* (Williamsburg, 1943). Several of the few letters surviving about Richard Lee II are in Richard Beale Davis (ed.), *William Fitzhugh and His Chesapeake World, 1676–1701* (Chapel Hill, 1963). Alice Lee's husband Dr. William Shippen appears in George W. Corner (ed.), *The Autobiography of Benjamin Rush* (Philadelphia and Princeton, 1948). A contemporary opinion of Colonel Phil is in "Narrative of George [Daniel] Fisher," *William and Mary Quarterly*, Series One, XVII (October 1908–January 1909), 100–39, 147–76. Charles C. Jones, *Reminiscences of the Last Days, Death and Burial of General Henry Lee* (Albany, 1870), offers a description of Light-Horse Harry's final hours.

The books written by family members begin with Henry Lee, *Memoirs of the War in the Southern Department of the United States* (Philadelphia, 1812), 2 vols. Among the later versions the most relevant is Henry Lee, *Memoirs of the War in the Southern Department of the United States . . . A New Edition, with Revisions, and a Biography of the Author by Robert E. Lee* (New York, 1869). There are two editions of Henry Lee IV's diatribe against Jefferson, of which the most useful is the second: Charles Carter Lee (ed.), H. Lee, *Observations on the Writings of Thomas Jefferson, with Particular Reference to the Attack They Contain on the Memory of the Late General Henry Lee* (Philadelphia, 1839). The first edition was published in 1831. The other volume by the unfortunate Major Lee is H. Lee, *The Life of the Emperor Napoleon* (New York, 1835), Volume One. Also worth consulting is Charles Carter Lee, *Virginia Georgics* (Richmond, 1858), a collection of Carter's poetry.

Two publications essential to the final exaltation of Robert E. Lee are: Henry James, *The American Scene* (1907) (Bloomington, 1968)—a fine edition prepared by Leon Edel; and Charles Francis Adams, *Lee's Centennial* (Boston and New York, 1907).

Following are the secondary works which benefited me most. The listing is, of course, culled from an enormous historical and biographical literature that deals with the Lees and their times. Two biographies of the family were written over fifty years ago, but remain useful. The best is Burton J. Hendrick, *The Lees of Virginia* (Boston, 1935). Still valuable is Ethel Armes, *Stratford Hall, the Great House of the Lees* (Richmond, 1936). For my purposes, the most interesting general account is Cazenove Gardner Lee, Jr., *Lee Chronicle* (New York, 1957), edited by Dorothy Mills Parker. A helpful assembly of information and photographs is in Eleanor Lee Templeman, *Virginia Homes of the Lees* (Arlington, 1973, 1985).

For background about Westmoreland County, see David W. Eaton, *Historical Atlas of Westmoreland County, Virginia* (Richmond, 1942), and Walter B. Norris, Jr., *Westmoreland County Virginia* (Montross, Va., 1983). Fortunately, there is now an excellent history of seventeenth- and eighteenth-century Virginia: Warren M. Billings, John E. Selby, and Thad W. Tate, *Colonial Virginia, A History* (White Plains, N.Y., 1986).

More detailed background and interpretation of the colonial era is in T. H. Breen, *Tobacco Culture: The Mentality of the Great Planters on the Eve of Revolution* (Princeton, 1985); Richard Beale Davis, *Literature and Society in Early Virginia, 1608–1840* (Baton Rouge, 1979); Thad W. Tate and David L. Ammerman, *The Chesapeake in the Seventeenth Century* (Chapel Hill, 1979); and Darrett B. Rutman and Anita H. Rutman, *A Place in Time, Middlesex County, Virginia 1650–1750* (New York, 1984).

The best general analysis of affairs in the Northern Neck during the first half of the eighteenth century remains Douglas S. Freeman, *George Washington, A Biography:* Volume One, *Young Washington* (New York, 1948).

There are few secondary accounts of the early Lees. The most important is William Thorndale, "The Parents of Colonel Richard Lee of Virginia," *National Genealogical Society Quarterly* 76 (December 1988), 253–67. Some value remains in Ludwell Lee Montague, "Richard Lee the Emigrant, 1613?–1664," *The Virginia Magazine of History and Biography* 62 (January 1954), 3–49. The only commentary on Richard Lee II is a chapter in Louis B. Wright, *The First Gentlemen of Virginia* (San Marino, Calif., 1940). A helpful treatment touching on the Maryland Lees is Jacob M. Price, "One Family's Empire: The Russell-Lee-Clark Connection in Maryland, Britain, and India, 1707–1857," *Maryland Historical Magazine* 72 (Summer 1977), 165–225.

Comparatively more writing has been done on the Lees of the Revolutionary era. As the best background for that time, I strongly recommend Robert Middlekauff, *The Glorious Cause: The American Revolution, 1763–1789* (New York, 1982). The details about how Virginia fared in that crisis are well presented in John E. Selby, *The Revolution in Virginia, 1775–1783* (Williamsburg, 1988). The Lees' ties with the Adams family unfold in Paul C. Nagel, *Descent from Glory: Four Generations of the John Adams Family* (New York, 1983). The Widow Corbin is remembered in Louise B. Dawe and Sandra G. Treadway, "Hannah Lee Corbin, the Forgotten Lee," *Virginia Cavalcade* 29 (Autumn, 1979), 70–77.

Though woefully brief, the best biography of Richard Henry Lee is a chapter in Pauline Maier, *The Old Revolutionaries* (New York, 1980). Another account is John Carter Matthews, *Richard Henry Lee* (Williamsburg, 1978). This slender volume is part of a notable series commemorating the bicentennial of the American Revolution in Virginia, which also includes Alonzo T. Dill, *Francis Lightfoot Lee, the Incomparable Signer* (Williamsburg, 1977); A. R. Riggs, *The Nine Lives of Arthur Lee, Virginia Patriot* (Williamsburg, 1976); and Alonzo T. Dill, *William Lee, Militia Diplomat* (Williamsburg, 1976).

The only major recent biography of a Stratford son is Louis W. Potts, *Arthur Lee, a Virtuous Revolutionary* (Baton Rouge 1981). Some valuable insights about William Lee are in Archibald B. Shepperson, *John Paradise and Lucy Ludwell of London and Williamsburg* (Richmond, 1942). A bit unreliable is Randolph S. Klein, *Portrait of an Early American Family: The Shippens of Pennsylvania Across Five Generations* (Philadelphia, 1975).

There are interesting if rather hostile glimpses of Richard Henry and his early political troubles in David J. Mays, *Edmund Pendleton, 1721–1803, a Biography* (Cambridge, Mass., 1952), 2 vols. Of importance is Joseph Albert Ernst, "The Robinson Scandal Redivivus: Money, Debts, and Politics in Revolutionary Virginia," *Virginia Magazine of History and Biography* 77 (April 1969), 146–73. An invaluable explanation of Lee skirmishes in the Continental Congress can be found in Jack N. Rakove, *The Beginnings of National Politics* (New York, 1979). The most helpful biography of a famous troublemaker for the Lees is Esmond Wright, *Franklin of Philadelphia* (Cambridge, Mass., 1986). Richard Henry Lee's role in the ratification controversy is ably discussed in Robert H. Webking, "Melancton Smith and the *Letters from the Federal Farmer*," *William and Mary Quarterly* 44 (July 1987), 510–28.

For material about the Livingston clan, see Clare Brandt, *An American Aristocracy; The Livingstons* (Garden City, 1986). There are bits about Dr. William Shippen, Jr., in Carl Binger, *Revolutionary Doctor, Benjamin*

Rush (1746–1813) (New York, 1966) and Whitfield J. Bell, Jr., *The Colonial Physician* (New York, 1975).

The best study recently written about a Lee is Charles Royster, *Light-Horse Harry Lee and the Legacy of the American Revolution* (New York, 1981). This is an admirable work, although the Harry Lee I found is less worthy of sympathy than the figure Royster uncovers. A workmanlike if overly sympathetic account is Thomas E. Templin, "Henry 'Light-Horse Harry' Lee: A Biography," unpublished doctoral dissertation, University of Kentucky, 1975. A useful discussion of Richard Bland Lee and his wife Elizabeth Collins is in Robert S. Gamble, *Sully, the Biography of a House* (Chantilly, Va., 1973).

The finest introduction to the era in which Robert E. Lee became famous is James M. McPherson, *Battle Cry of Freedom: The Civil War Era* (New York, 1988). A matchless achievement in the field of biograpy is Douglas S. Freeman, *R. E. Lee, a Biography* (New York, 1934), 4 vols. Freeman's masterpiece should be read principally as fine literature and a gripping account of the Civil War's embrace of General Lee. Its interpretation of Lee's personality is shaped by Freeman's adoration of his subject.

After consulting Freeman about R. E. Lee, readers should turn to Thomas L. Connelly, *The Marble Man: Robert E. Lee and His Image in American Society* (Baton Rouge, 1978), and to Charles B. Flood, *Lee, the Last Years* (Boston, 1981). An earlier biography still worthwhile is Margaret Sanborn, *Robert E. Lee, a Portrait* (Philadelphia and New York, 1966), 2 vols. A helpful comparison of two clashing careers is Nancy S. Anderson and Dwight Anderson, *The Generals: Ulysses S. Grant and Robert E. Lee* (New york, 1988). A well-written briefer account of the General is Alf J. Mapp, Jr., *Frock Coats and Epaulets* (New York, 1963, 1987).

For a larger discussion of Charles Francis Adams and the Lee centennial celebration at Washington and Lee University in 1907, see Paul C. Nagel, "Reconstruction, Adams Style," *The Journal of Southern History* 52 (February, 1986), 3–18.

Anyone who develops an interest in the Lee family's history and genealogy will find it both enjoyable and profitable to read the annual reports of the Society of the Lees of Virginia. These bulletins, as they have accumulated over the years, can be found in the library of the Virginia Historical Society and elsewhere in the state. The Lee Society has existed in one form or another for over a century and has a national membership of nearly eight hundred proven descendants. It meets each year in order to visit locations important in the Lee family saga and to receive the latest word on matters genealogical, biographical, and historical. Through the Society's efforts, and particularly those of Eleanor Lee Templeman, its historian, the Commonwealth of Virginia recently established Leesylvania State Park at the lovely place on the Potomac where, nearly 250 years ago, Henry Lee and Lucy Grymes began a new line of the Lee family.

Index